Communications in Computer and Information Science 1893

Rationale

The CCIS series is devoted to the publication of proceedings of computer science conferences. Its aim is to efficiently disseminate original research results in informatics in printed and electronic form. While the focus is on publication of peer-reviewed full papers presenting mature work, inclusion of reviewed short papers reporting on work in progress is welcome, too. Besides globally relevant meetings with internationally representative program committees guaranteeing a strict peer-reviewing and paper selection process, conferences run by societies or of high regional or national relevance are also considered for publication.

Topics

The topical scope of CCIS spans the entire spectrum of informatics ranging from foundational topics in the theory of computing to information and communications science and technology and a broad variety of interdisciplinary application fields.

Information for Volume Editors and Authors

Publication in CCIS is free of charge. No royalties are paid, however, we offer registered conference participants temporary free access to the online version of the conference proceedings on SpringerLink (http://link.springer.com) by means of an http referrer from the conference website and/or a number of complimentary printed copies, as specified in the official acceptance email of the event.

CCIS proceedings can be published in time for distribution at conferences or as postproceedings, and delivered in the form of printed books and/or electronically as USBs and/or e-content licenses for accessing proceedings at SpringerLink. Furthermore, CCIS proceedings are included in the CCIS electronic book series hosted in the SpringerLink digital library at http://link.springer.com/bookseries/7899. Conferences publishing in CCIS are allowed to use Online Conference Service (OCS) for managing the whole proceedings lifecycle (from submission and reviewing to preparing for publication) free of charge.

Publication process

The language of publication is exclusively English. Authors publishing in CCIS have to sign the Springer CCIS copyright transfer form, however, they are free to use their material published in CCIS for substantially changed, more elaborate subsequent publications elsewhere. For the preparation of the camera-ready papers/files, authors have to strictly adhere to the Springer CCIS Authors' Instructions and are strongly encouraged to use the CCIS LaTeX style files or templates.

Abstracting/Indexing

CCIS is abstracted/indexed in DBLP, Google Scholar, EI-Compendex, Mathematical Reviews, SCImago, Scopus. CCIS volumes are also submitted for the inclusion in ISI Proceedings.

How to start

.To start the evaluation of your proposal for inclusion in the CCIS series, please send an e-mail to ccis@springer.com.

Ranjeet Singh Tomar · Shekhar Verma ·
Brijesh Kumar Chaurasia · Vrijendra Singh ·
Jemal H. Abawajy · Shyam Akashe ·
Pao-Ann Hsiung · Ramjee Prasad
Editors

Communication, Networks and Computing

Third International Conference, CNC 2022
Gwalior, India, December 8–10, 2022
Proceedings, Part I

 Springer

Editors
Ranjeet Singh Tomar ⓘD
ITM University
Gwalior, India

Brijeshar Kumar Chaurasia ⓘD
IIIT Lucknow
Lucknow, India

Jemal H. Abawajy
Deakin University
Burwood, VIC, Australia

Pao-Ann Hsiung
National Chung Cheng University
Chiayi, Taiwan

Shekhar Verma ⓘD
IIIT-Allahabad
Allahabad, Uttar Pradesh, India

Vrijendra Singh
IIIT-Allahabad
Allahabad, India

Shyam Akashe ⓘD
ITM University
Gwalior, Madhya Pradesh, India

Ramjee Prasad
Aarhus University
Herning, Denmark

ISSN 1865-0929   ISSN 1865-0937 (electronic)
Communications in Computer and Information Science
ISBN 978-3-031-43139-5   ISBN 978-3-031-43140-1 (eBook)
https://doi.org/10.1007/978-3-031-43140-1

This Springer imprint is published by the registered company Springer Nature Switzerland AG
The registered company address is: Gewerbestrasse 11, 6330 Cham, Switzerland

Paper in this product is recyclable.

Preface

The book focuses on communication, networks, and computing to simplify the real-time problems occurring in different domains of communication, networks, and computing. Presently, research is entering a new era of convergence of these domains wherein the established models and techniques are being challenged. New ideas are being proposed and established ideas are being retested. Evaluating the performance of emerging smart technologies, however, poses a huge challenge.

The book includes high-quality papers presented at the 3rd International Conference on Communication, Networks and Computing (CNC 2022), organized by ITM University Gwalior, India. Offering significant insights into this domain for academics and industry alike, we hope the book will inspire more researchers to work in the field of next-generation networks for communication systems. The theme of the conference was "Next-Generation Digital Technology Innovations for Society". This theme covered the exciting new areas of wired and wireless communication systems, high-dimensional data representation and processing, networks and information security, computing techniques for efficient networks design, vehicular technology and applications and electronic circuits for communication systems that promise to make the world a better place to live in.

ITM University Gwalior, India, is a multidisciplinary university with an international reputation for the quality of its research and teaching across the academic spectrum. The university has received more than 40 awards and has been ranked in the top category by a number of governmental and other agencies. The university is ranked 32nd in management and 58th in engineering in 2016 by the National Institutional Ranking Framework, Ministry of HRD, Government of India. The university is approved by the regulatory bodies required to run courses in engineering, management, pharmacy, commerce, agriculture, architecture, computer applications, teacher education, art and design, physical education, sciences, law, India and South Asia studies, journalism, nursing etc. It is at the forefront of learning, teaching and research and the leader in different fields. It seeks to sustain and enhance its excellence as an institution of higher learning through outstanding teaching and the world-class societies it serves.

The ITM School of Engineering and Technology is one of the flagship and leading schools of central and north India. The school is unique in that it tries to assimilate cutting-edge ideas in engineering and technology through a variety of projects in association with industry. In addition, prominent industries directly contribute to the knowledge and skill sets of students through various augmentation programs customized for students of ITM University. A mix of lectures, tutorials, laboratory studies, seminars and projects are used to groom the conceptual and analytical abilities of students. For the first time in India, ITM University Gwalior has taken the initiative to introduce activity-based continuous assessment (ABCA) and project-based learning (PBL) in order to increase the employability of students.

This conference was successful in facilitating academics, researchers and industry professionals to deliberate upon the latest issues, challenges and advancements in communication, networks and computing. In total, 152 papers were submitted for six tracks. After a thorough review process, 52 papers were selected for oral presentation during the conference. All these selected papers were presented at the conference and only those best 52 papers are published in the book.

This conference proceedings volume will prove beneficial for academics, researchers and professionals from industry as it contains valuable information and knowledge on the recent developments.

June 2023

Ranjeet Singh Tomar
Shekhar Verma
Brijesh Kumar Chaurasia
Vrijendra Singh
Jemal H. Abawajy
Shyam Akashe
Pao-Ann Hsiung
Ramjee Prasad

Organization

Chief Patron

Ramashankar Singh (Founder Chancellor)	ITM University Gwalior, India
Ruchi Singh Chauhan (Chancellor)	ITM University Gwalior, India

Patrons

Kanupriya Singh Rathore (Chairperson)	ITM (SLS) Baroda University, India
Ravindra Singh Rathore (Managing Director)	ITM (SLS) Baroda University, India
Daulat Singh Chauhan (Pro Chancellor)	ITM University Gwalior, India
Sher Singh Bhakar (Vice-chancellor)	ITM University Gwalior, India
Santosh K. Narayankhedkar (Pro Vice-chancellor)	ITM University Gwalior, India
Omveer Singh (Registrar)	ITM University Gwalior, India

General Chairs

Shekhar Verma	IIIT Allahabad, India
Ranjeet Singh Tomar	ITM University Gwalior, India
Ramjee Prasad	Aarhus University, Denmark

Program Chairs

Pao Ann Hsiung	National Chung Cheng University, Taiwan
Vijay K. Bhargava	University of British Columbia, Canada
Brijesh Kumar Chaurasia	IIIT Lucknow, India

Technical Committee Chairs

Jemal Abawajy   Deakin University, Australia
Vrijendra Singh   IIIT Allahabad, India
Shyam Akashe   ITM University Gwalior, India

Publications Chairs

Sanjay Jain   ITM University Gwalior, India
Sadhana Mishra   ITM University Gwalior, India

Publicity Chairs

Pallavi Khatri   ITM University Gwalior, India
Shashikant Gupta   ITM University Gwalior, India

Workshop/Tutorial Chairs

Rishi Soni   ITM University Gwalior, India
Arun Kumar Yadav   ITM University Gwalior, India

Hospitality Chairs

Mukesh Kumar Pandey   ITM University Gwalior, India
Keshav Kansana   ITM University Gwalior, India
Manish Sharma   ITM University Gwalior, India

Local Organizing Committee

Geetanjali Surange   ITM University Gwalior, India
Shailendra Singh Ojha   ITM University Gwalior, India
Ashish Garg   ITM University Gwalior, India
Bhupendra Dhakad   ITM University Gwalior, India
Abhishek Saxena   ITM University Gwalior, India
Abhishek Tripathi   ITM University Gwalior, India
Upendra Bhushan   ITM University Gwalior, India

Organizing Secretariat

Mayank Sharma   ITM University Gwalior, India

Contents – Part I

Contents – Part II

Computing Techniques for Efficient Networks Design

Vehicular Technology and Applications

Wired and Wireless Communication Systems

An Analytic Assessment of Medical Applications of the Internet of Things (IoT) During Covid-19 and Possible Future Pandemics

Rakesh Kumar[1], Sampurna Panda[2]([✉]), Mini Anil[1], Anshul G.[3], and Ambali Pancholi[1]

[1] School of Nursing Sciences, ITM University, Gwalior, Gwalior, India
[2] School of Engineering and Technology, ITM University, Gwalior, Gwalior, India
sampurna.ee@itmuniversity.ac.in
[3] School of Medical and Paramedical Sciences, ITM University, Gwalior, Gwalior, India

Abstract. The term "Internet of Things" (IoT) is used to describe a system in which interconnected electronic devices can automatically collect, transmit, and store data. Health care delivery, including illness prevention, diagnosis, treatment, and monitoring of patients both in and out of the hospital, stands to benefit greatly from the IoT. In response to the unprecedented spread of COVID-19, governments around the world are taking action to expand people's access to modern medical care. It is crucial for health systems to be aware of how current and future IoT technologies may help them provide safe and effective care. An review of current Internet of Things (IoT) healthcare technology, how IoT devices are improving health service delivery, and how IoT technology may modify and disrupt global healthcare over the next decade are the goals of this perspective paper. We delve deeper into the potential of IoT-based healthcare by theorizing about how it could improve people's access to public health prevention programs and how it could reshape our current system of secondary and tertiary care to be more preventative, continuous, and coordinated. Finally, this paper will discuss some of the potential issues that Internet of Things-based healthcare creates, such as trust and acceptance, privacy and security, interoperability, standardization and compensation, data storage, control, and ownership, and barriers to market adoption from healthcare professionals and patients alike. Accelerators of IoT in modern healthcare include policy support, cybersecurity-focused standards, cautious strategic planning, and transparent policies within healthcare organizations. Connected medical devices have the potential to greatly improve population health and system efficiency.

Keywords: Internet of Things · Covid-19 · Pandemics · Smart Phone · Wearables · Drones

1 Introduction

These days, the area is swarmed by high-quality Mechanism. Every facet of modern life is rife with new inventions and innovations that affect humans. Until men learn to innovate, they will never be able to achieve the kind of high-quality of life that will bring

R. S. Tomar et al. (Eds.): CNC 2022, CCIS 1893, pp. 3–16, 2023.
https://doi.org/10.1007/978-3-031-43140-1_2

them true happiness. Concurrently, we have become increasingly reliant on machines, and this has opened the door for technologists to develop and explore new ways to improve our quality of life [1]. Our justifications, frameworks, and philosophies are all being updated to improve that aspect of the experience. However, due to the world's expanding population, doctors and medical assistants are unable to provide the best possible care for their patients. The Internet of Things (IoT) allows everyday objects to connect to the web and exchange data with one another and with humans.

Sensing, machine learning, real-time analysis, and embedded systems are just a few examples of how the Internet of Things (IoT) idea has developed. It's all about "smart hospitals" and other tech that can be managed via the Internet, whether wired or wirelessly. Data can be captured and shared between smart devices in everyday life to complete the work at hand. Smart cities, automobiles, electronics, entertainment systems, residences, and even connected healthcare are all benefiting from the Internet of Things. Sensors, medical equipment, AI, diagnostic tools, and state-of-the-art imaging systems are at the heart of IoT applications in healthcare. In both established businesses and emerging social systems, these tools boost output and quality of life. The Internet of Things (IoT) automates data flow over the Internet by connecting all computational, mechanical, and digital devices without requiring human intervention. The use of this technology to track medical conditions has skyrocketed during the current COVID-19 Pandemic [2, 3]. Many people nowadays perish because they lack access to accurate and timely health information. Through the use of sensors, this technology is able to provide timely notifications about potential health problems. Care for patients with COVID-19 is aided by the fact that all patient data is maintained on the cloud. This technology can monitor a person's routine and send warnings if any potential health issues arise.

In order to carry out a procedure successfully in the medical area, it is crucial to have access to the appropriate tools. The Internet of Things is very capable of performing successful surgeries and analyzing post-operative progress. During the current COVID-19 Pandemic, the use of IoT has contributed to enhanced patient care. IoT's real-time monitoring has saved countless lives by detecting potentially deadly conditions including diabetes, heart failure, asthma attacks, high blood pressure, and more. Through the use of a smartphone, health data collected by connected smart medical equipment can be easily transmitted to a doctor [4]. Oxygen, blood pressure, weight, glucose levels, etc. are also measured and recorded by these devices.

2 Reasons Why This Research is Necessary

During the COVID-19 Pandemic, the Internet of Things (IoT) swiftly assumes the major responsibility of developing a dependable digital information system within the medical community. When trying to gain a better understanding of the technologies already in use, their benefits, and the critical applications that call for them, one runs across a number of challenges. With its vast resources and innovative information, it will be able to aid in solving a wide range of issues that may arise during the COVID-19 Pandemic [5].

2.1 Integrating IoT in the Health Care Industry

Sensing and capturing data about a patient's health or sickness with the help of sensors is essential (Fig. 1).

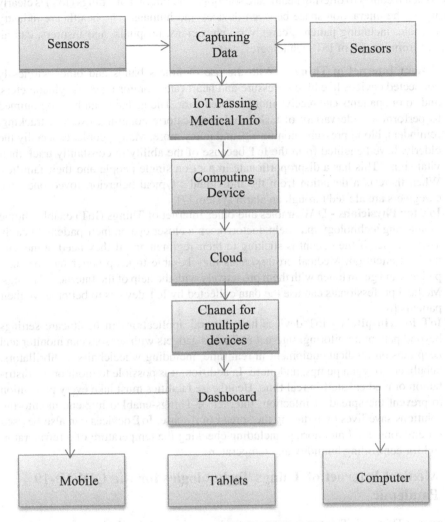

Fig. 1. Integrating IoT in the Health Care Industry

In this scenario, all physical items are networked and monitored in real time by connected gadgets. As needed, relevant medical data is delivered to the appropriate clinicians.

IoT-enabled gadgets have made remote monitoring possible in healthcare, which has the potential to improve both patient outcomes and physician efficiency. Patient participation and satisfaction have increased as a result of the streamlined and quick nature of contacts with healthcare professionals. In addition to reducing hospital stays and preventing unnecessary readmissions, remote patient monitoring also has other benefits. As a result of reducing costs and increasing treatment efficacy, connected devices also have a significant impact on the healthcare industry's bottom line [6].

When it comes to offering healthcare solutions, the Internet of Things (IoT) is clearly changing the interaction space between devices and humans. The healthcare industry as a whole, including patients, caregivers, physicians, hospitals, and insurers, can all benefit from the use of IoT technologies.

a) **Patient Internet of Things** - With the use of fitness bands and other wirelessly connected devices like blood pressure and heart rate monitoring cuffs, glucometers, and so on, patients can receive more tailored care. The gadgets can be programmed to perform a wide variety of tasks, including calorie counting, exercise tracking, reminders, blood pressure monitoring, and many more. Many people, especially the elderly, have benefited from the IoT because of the ability to constantly track their vital signs. This has a disproportionate impact on single people and their families. When there is a deviation from the individual's typical behavior, loved ones and caregivers are alerted through an alarm system [7].

b) **IoT for Physicians** - D Wearables and other Internet of Things (IoT) enabled home monitoring technology may help doctors keep a closer eye on their patients' health. They can see if the patient is sticking to their regimen and if they need immediate medical attention. Medical professionals may be able to keep better tabs on their patients and get in touch with them proactively with the help of the Internet of Things. Medical professionals can use the data collected by IoT devices to better serve their patients [8].

c) **IoT for Hospitals** - IoT devices have several applications in healthcare settings beyond patient monitoring. Internet of Things gadgets with sensors can monitor and keep tabs on medical equipment in real time, including wheelchairs, defibrillators, nebulizers, oxygen pumps, and more. In addition, it is possible to monitor the distribution of medical staff in real time. Healthcare facilities must take every precaution to prevent the spread of infection. Internet of Things-enabled hygiene monitoring solutions save lives by reducing the spread of disease. IoT devices can also be used for environmental monitoring, including checking the temperature of a refrigerator, and for controlling humidity and temperature.

3 Medical Internet of Things Technologies for the COVID-19 Pandemic

Internet of Things (IoT) interconnects medical equipment and gadgets to construct adaptive information networks for COVID-19 patients. In order to increase output, quality, and insight into future diseases, a new interdisciplinary strategy is required. By monitoring for shifts in critical patient data, IoT devices can help identify important insights.

IoT technologies have a significant impact on high-quality medical devices, which helps provide a tailored response during the COVID-19 Pandemic. Data may be collected, stored, and analyzed digitally with the help of these instruments. All patient records are now digitized, allowing doctors instantaneous access and transmission of life-saving data over the internet in the event of an emergency [9].

a) Wearables

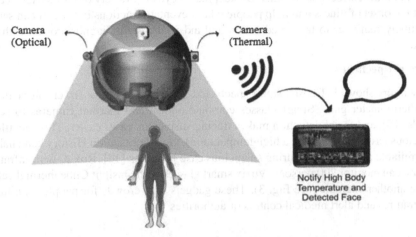

Fig. 2. Smart helmet using thermal and optical cameras [10]

Wearable smart helmets as displayed in Fig. 2 equipped with a thermal camera have been shown to be safer than an infrared thermometer gun during the COVID-19 pandemic, as they result in fewer direct human interactions [10]. This gadget uses the smart helmet's thermal camera to pinpoint the wearer's exact location and capture an image of their face using an optical camera whenever abnormal heat is detected. As shown in Fig. 2, they are then transmitted to the designated mobile device, accompanied by an alarm, allowing a health officer to identify the infected individual and take appropriate action [11]. In addition, the smart helmet can be integrated with Google Location History to track the suspect's movements after they've been spotted [12]. Countries like China, the United Arab Emirates, and Italy have begun using this wearable device to monitor crowds from a distance of just 2 m away from pedestrians [13]. The results of this model are interesting. For instance, the KC N901 smart helmet made in China can detect abnormally high core body temperatures with a 96-percent degree of accuracy.

Throughout the course of the COVID-19 epidemic, the Internet of Things (IOT) can also be used to aid the medical community. It's the most time- and labour-saving method of keeping tabs on everyone's whereabouts, leading to shorter lines overall. New conveniences are introduced to enhance the lives of those who are ill. Instruments including blood-gas analyzers, thermometers, smart beds, glucose meters, ultrasonography, and X-ray equipment have allowed for significant advances in in-patient treatment. The Internet of Things has the potential to supplement or even replace a biological function or system. In the event of a widespread COVID-19 pandemic, its implementation could prove useful for a variety of medical applications, including but not limited to: connected imaging; clinical procedures; drug delivery; patient monitoring; laboratory tests; and medication management. The Internet of Things has opened the door for improved medical care. During the 2009 COVID-19 Pandemic, it might be utilized to construct a centralized information system in a hospital, where all activities are digitally preserved,

8   R. Kumar et al.

and other Data analytics could be employed to help uncover answers [14]. In the event of an emergency, this state-of-the-art technology makes it simple to keep tabs on a patient's vitals and draw correct conclusions. By keeping an eye on a variety of biometrics, it can detect the onset of illness and help people take preventative actions in time. It can serve as a timely reminder to take medication and aid in the early diagnosis of an asthma attack.

b) Smart Spectacles

Below figure shows IoT-based smart spectacles. Smart glasses have fewer interactions than thermometer guns. Smart glasses combine optical and thermal cameras to scan crowds [15], and facial detection makes tracing suspicious cases easier. This identifies suspicious cases (person with a high temperature). Google Location History can enable more reliable actions by capturing suspicious case locations [16]. Rokid, with infrared sensors, can monitor 200 persons. Vuzix smart glasses with Onsight Cube thermal camera are another example (see Fig. 3). These gadgets scan crowds for people with high temperatures and alert medical centres or authorities.

Fig. 3. Temperature-taking smart glasses [19]

c) Thermal Imaging Drone

Finding infected people in large groups is essential for early COVID-19 discovery and control. Finding infected people and areas during a pandemic can also be done with the help of unmanned aerial vehicles and Internet of Things-based drones. Drones eliminate the need for humans to physically move and access remote areas. Figure 5 shows a thermal imaging drone meant to capture crowd temperatures for early diagnosis. This drone paired with VR can recognize people with high temperatures (fevers). This gadget requires fewer human interactions and less time than thermometer guns [14]. A Canadian business developed the Pandemic Drone program [19] as displayed in Fig. 4 for remote monitoring and identifying illness by capturing temperature, respiratory symptoms including heart rate, and sneezing or coughing.

d) Disinfectant Drone

A disinfectant drone as shown in Fig. 5 can sanitize and disinfect areas during a quarantine [17]. Drones reduce virus contamination and protect healthcare workers. DJI's drone can disinfect 100 m per hour. Spain has used this type of drone to disinfect.

Fig. 4. Thermal imaging drone [20]

e) Quarantine Robots

Quarantine robots are autonomous. They may disinfect hazardous hospital facilities, convey patients' treatments, and check their respiratory signs with minimal or no human interactions as displayed in Figure 5. These will reduce healthcare personnel' risk of infection when patients are segregated [18]. Xenex's disinfection robot can remove viruses and germs.

Figure 6 shows how Xenex uses UV lamps to destroy viruses. Danish UVD robots disinfect hospitals with powerful UV light, which breaks virus DNA.

f) Smartphone Applications

Cost-effectiveness, efficient monitoring, proper treatment, fewer mistakes, and outstanding diagnoses are just some of the primary benefits of the increasing usage of IoT in healthcare. We'll talk about how certain smartphone apps were made in direct reaction to the difficulties of reopening after the outbreak.

1. Aarogya Setu

To help spread information about this virus and find ways to combat it, users can use an app called Aarogya Setu on their cell phones. The goal of developing Aarogya Setu was to facilitate more open lines of communication between patients and medical professionals. The app will ask the user questions about their recent travels and whether or not they have noticed any symptoms of COVID-19. Aarogya Setu analyzes user input data together with monitoring information to notify users if they have had contact with someone who is already or becomes a proven case [19].

Fig. 5. Disinfectant Drone

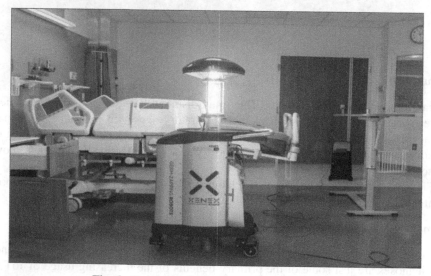

Fig. 6. Xenex disinfecting autonomous robots [20]

2. Trace Together

Singapore released a program called Trace Together to collect information from people who were in close proximity to one another by using an encrypted ID. Until a close contact identification is made, the collected data will not be used. Information such as the length of the visit and the social distance between the two parties will be saved for 21 days to facilitate future contact discovery [20].

3. Hamagen

Israel is the home of the company responsible for this contact-finding software. Hamagen employs GPS tracking to determine if its user has recently been in physical proximity to a COVID-19 carrier. To protect users' privacy, this software will not transmit their information outside of the user's smartphone [21].

4. Coalition

Coalition is a secure contact tracing solution built on the blockchain and the Internet of Things. Each user is given a unique ID within the app, and when a new case is discovered, those users closest to it are alerted [22].

5. Be Aware Bahrain

In Bahrain, the Be Aware Bahrain app has been launched as a contact tracing tool to warn the public if they have come into contact with a confirmed case of COVID-19 or are about to enter a contaminated region. Additionally, this app is useful for the next stage of this pandemic because it tracks where self-isolated cases are for 14 days and permits users to exit quarantine regions for testing appointments [23].

6. eRouska

This program records and logs when two users are in close proximity to one another. When a user's COVID-19 test comes back positive, eRouska will send out an alert to the community so they can take preventative measures [24].

Literature review in a tabular format has been presented in Table 1 listing various IoT applications in hospital and medical industry.

Table 1. Various Internet of Things technologies for use in healthcare during the COVID-19 pandemic

Sl No	Technologies	Description	References
1	Big data	a) To collect, store, and analyse the COVID-19 patient's data, Big Data appears to be one of the best methods available today b) Traditional medical data storage relied on expensive hard copies of records c) Digital data storage is strength of large data	[17, 19, 20]
2	Cloud computing	a) It utilizes the capabilities of the computer system to provide data storage on demand and data description via the Internet b) In times of emergency, information about patients infected with COVID-19 is rapidly shared c) The best way to aid doctors and surgeons is to share the confidential information they've accumulated over the years d) Besides improving data quality, it also decreases storage costs	[22, 24–26]

(continued)

Table 1. (*continued*)

Sl No	Technologies	Description	References
3	Sensing tech	a) Smart sensors are excellent at conveying information across electronic networks and producing trustworthy outcomes in the medical field b) All aspects of a patient's health are constantly monitored and managed c) Check the COVID-19 patient's vitals, infusion pump, glucose level, and infusion rate with ease d) Useful for learning about one's current health, faulty bone, and the surrounding biological tissue	[26, 26, 28]
4	Software	a) Medical professionals now have access to specialized software that helps them better care for their patients by recording and organizing information about their diagnoses, treatments, and outcomes b) Allows for more effective two-way communication between patients and clinicians c) A patient's medical records can be safely stored in the COVID-19 database, where sensitive information and diseases can be quickly located and controlled	[28, 31, 32]
5	Artificial intelligence	a) With a controlled setting, AI aids in data performance, evaluation, validation, prediction, and analysis b) Offer superior abilities to foresee and manage viral outbreaks c) It is with this technology that doctors and surgeons are able to perform their jobs with greater ease, precision, and efficacy d) It tracks the COVID-19 patient's pain levels while their dosage is adjusted	[33–35]
6	Actuators	a) When a system has to take action in the world, it does so using a device called an actuator b) Accuracy maintenance and parameter regulation are two primary actuator uses in the medical field	[36, 37]

4 Critical Analysis

Therefore, the potential of the Internet of Things may be summarized as a rapidly developing field of study in the healthcare sector. These shifts present an excellent opportunity for healthcare systems to improve disease prevention, precise diagnosis, effective treatment, and patient monitoring outside of the hospital. The Internet of Things (IoT) will either augment or replace conventional means of delivering health care as more services are bolstered by technology, allowing health systems to provide more flexible forms of treatment. If the Internet of Things (IoT) is to be effective in healthcare, there must be a clear and strong code of practice for managing data, privacy, confidentiality, and cyber-security in the supply and utilization of IoT devices. Internet of Things (IoT) technology, the healthcare system, and the individuals who use IoT all have significant knowledge gaps [39].

Standards for Internet of Things (IoT) devices and their compatibility with national and international healthcare networks should be the subject of future study. It is important to evaluate blockchain storage against centralized cloud-based solutions when thinking about IoT-enabled healthcare delivery. From the viewpoint of the healthcare system, it is necessary to have clinical guidelines on digital health prescriptions and strong policies on how primary and secondary care services supplied through IoT should be reimbursed. In conclusion, more study is required to learn how patients and doctors view IoT and how well they understand how to use it to enhance health care delivery and the patient experience. While this opinion is based on a summary of some information rather than a thorough systematic evaluation of all literature, we believe that a stronger emphasis on these areas for future study will go far toward encouraging more people to use IoT, which can lower costs and promote patient-centered care.

5   Future Prospects

Through the use of IOT, hospitals of the future will be able to monitor a patient's health in real time or very close to it. The ultimate purpose of this method is to digitally record all the specific data required to finally resolve the ongoing problems associated with treating patients with COVID-19. New technologies will be required of healthcare practitioners. The Internet of Things (IoT) is cutting-edge, ever-evolving technology that has multiple applications in the delivery of individualized medical care by enabling a more efficient method of assessing vital information, data, and testing. In the future, medical inventory and supply chain management may be used to ensure that essential medications and equipment are never out of stock. As a result, intelligent IoT gadgets must be able to function independently. Cloud-based technologies, including storage in both private and public clouds, are anticipated to be utilized to expedite the processes of disease identification and subsequent follow-up. In order to implement Medical 4.0 and provide cutting-edge medical care, a complete overhaul of the healthcare system's informational foundations is required.

6   Conclusion

The Internet of Things allows for significant advancements in fields as diverse as chronic disease management, emergency care, patient-care, fitness, blood pressure monitoring, health check system, measurement & control system, heart rate checking system, and hearing aids (IoT). It can boost the level of customization available to medical providers and provide reliable real-time monitoring of COVID-19 patients. COVID-19 patients now have the option of keeping their medical records digitally, which may be accessed from a variety of databases thanks to Internet of Things-enabled devices. This kind of technology can help us cut down on paper records. Making a well-informed decision improves its efficiency and reliability. During the COVID-19 Pandemic, this technology can be used to increase the intelligence and efficiency of medical equipment and networks. Therefore, the patient's quality of life can improve thanks to the increased access to timely information and broader channels of expression made possible by these innovations. This breakthrough will be used to prevent future COVID-19 pandemics and enhance current patient treatment.

References

1. Raj, A., Gupta, M., Panda, S.: Design simulation and performance assessment of yield and loss forecasting for 100 KWp grid connected solar PV system. In: 2016 2nd International Conference on Next Generation Computing Technologies (NGCT), pp. 528–533. IEEE (2016)
2. Panda, S., Gupta, M., Malvi, C.S.: Modified MPPT algorithms for various step size and switching frequency using MATLAB/SIMULINK. Solid State Technol. **63**(5), 8863–8872 (2020)
3. Panda, S., et al.: A review on advanced cooling techniques for photovoltaic panel. Mater. Today: Proc. **62**, 6799–6803 (2022)
4. Panda, S., Gupta, M., Malvi, C.S., Panda, B.: Effect of depositions on PV panel with proposal of a self cleaning system. In: 2021 IEEE 2nd International Conference on Applied Electromagnetics, Signal Processing, & Communication (AESPC), pp. 1–6. IEEE (2021)
5. Panda, S., Dhaka, R.K., Panda, B., Pradhan, A., Jena, C., Nanda, L.: A review on application of machine learning in solar energy & photovoltaic generation prediction. In: 2022 International Conference on Electronics and Renewable Systems (ICEARS), pp. 1180–1184. IEEE (2022)
6. Panda, S., Gupta, M., Malvi, C.S.: Comparative study of photo voltaic panel cooling methods for efficiency enhancement. In: Tomar, R.S., et al. (eds.) CNC 2020. Communications in Computer and Information Science, vol. 1502, pp. 291–300. Springer, Singapore (2020). https://doi.org/10.1007/978-981-16-8896-6_23
7. Panda, S., Guptaa, M., Malvib, C.S.: Advances in perturb and observe based MPPT algorithm. In: WEENTECH Proceedings in Energy, pp. 21–27 (2020)
8. Panda, S., Dhaka, R.K.: Application of artificial intelligence in medical imaging. In; Machine Learning and Deep Learning Techniques for Medical Science, pp. 195–202. CRC Press (2022)
9. Panda, S., Panda, B., Jena, C., Nanda, L., Pradhan, A.: Investigating the similarities and differences between front and back surface cooling for PV panels. Mater. Today: Proc. **74**, 358–363 (2022)
10. Hoogwijk, M., Faaij, A., van den Broek, R., Berndes, G., Gielen, D., Turkenburg, W.: Exploration of the ranges of the global potential of biomass for energy. Biomass Bioenergy **25**, 119e33 (2003)
11. Ejupi, A., Menon, C.: Detection of talking in respiratory signals: a feasibility study using machine learning and wearable textile-based sensors. Sensors. **18**(8), 2474 (2018)
12. Klang, E.: Deep learning and medical imaging. J. Thorac. Dis. **10**(3), 1325 (2018)
13. Nakata, N.: Recent technical development of artificial intelligence for diagnostic medical imaging. Jpn. J. Radiol. **37**(2), 103–108 (2019). https://doi.org/10.1007/s11604-018-0804-6
14. Hafizović, L., Čaušević, A., Deumić, A., Bećirović, L.S., Pokvić, L.G., Badnjević, A.: The use of artificial intelligence in diagnostic medical imaging: systematic literature review. In: 2021 IEEE 21st International Conference on Bioinformatics and Bioengineering (BIBE), pp. 1–6. IEEE (2021)

15. Lin, M., et al.: Artificial intelligence in tumorsubregion analysis based on medical imaging: a review. J. Appl. Clin. Med. Phys. **22**(7), 10–26 (2021)
16. Cook, T.S.: The importance of imaging informatics and informaticists in the implementation of AI. Acad. Radiol. **27**(1), 113–116 (2020)
17. Shaikh, F., et al.: Artificial intelligence-based clinical decision support systems using advanced medical imaging and radiomics. Curr. Probl. Diagnostic Radiol. **50**(2), 262–267 (2021)
18. Dellepiane, S., Serpico, S.B., Venzano, L., Vernazza, G.: Structural analysis in medical imaging. In: Proceedings of the 7th European Conference on Electrotechnics (EUROCON 86) (1987)
19. Oikonomou, E.K., Siddique, M., Antoniades, C.: Artificial intelligence in medical imaging: a radiomic guide to precision phenotyping of cardiovascular disease. Cardiovas. Res. **116**(13), 2040–2054 (2020)
20. Larrazabal, A.J., Nieto, N., Peterson, V., Milone, D.H., Ferrante, E.: Gender imbalance in medical imaging datasets produces biased classifiers for computer-aided diagnosis. Proc. Natl. Acad. Sci. **117**(23), 12592–12594 (2020)
21. Tanenbaum, L.N.: Artificial intelligence and medical imaging: image acquisition and reconstruction. Appl. Radiol. **49**(3), 34–36 (2020)
22. Li, X., Pan, D., Zhu, D.: Defending against adversarial attacks on medical imaging AI system, classification or detection? In: 2021 IEEE 18th International Symposium on Biomedical Imaging (ISBI), pp. 1677–1681. IEEE (2021)
23. Santosh, K.C., Antani, S., Guru, D.S., Dey, N. (eds.): Medical Imaging: Artificial Intelligence, Image Recognition, and Machine Learning Techniques. CRC Press, Boca Raton (2019)
24. Kim, M., et al.: Deep learning in medical imaging. Neurospine **16**(4), 657 (2019)
25. Group, SFR-IA, and French Radiology Community. Artificial intelligence and medical imaging 2018: French radiology community white paper. Diagnostic Intervent. Imaging **99**(11), 727–742 (2018)
26. Suri, J.S., et al.: COVID-19 pathways for brain and heart injury in comorbidity patients: a role of medical imaging and artificial intelligence-based COVID severity classification: a review. Comput. Biol. Med. **124**, 103960 (2020)
27. Chakraborty, S., Chatterjee, S., Ashour, A.S., Mali, K., Dey, N.: Intelligent computing in medical imaging: a study. In: Advancements in Applied Metaheuristic Computing, pp. 143–163. IGI global (2018)
28. Lee, L.I.T., Kanthasamy, S., Ayyalaraju, R.S., Ganatra, R.: The current state of artificial intelligence in medical imaging and nuclear medicine. BJR | Open **1**, 20190037 (2019)
29. Mulryan, P., et al.: An evaluation of information online on artificial intelligence in medical imaging. Insights Imaging **13**(1), 1–11 (2022)
30. Langlotz, C.P., et al.: A roadmap for foundational research on artificial intelligence in medical imaging: from the 2018 NIH/RSNA/ACR/the academy workshop. Radiology **291**(3), 781–791 (2019)
31. Ahmad, H.M., Khan, M.J., Yousaf, A., Ghuffar, S., Khurshid, K.: Deep learning: a breakthrough in medical imaging. Curr. Med. Imaging **16**(8), 946–956 (2020)
32. Born, J., et al.: On the role of artificial intelligence in medical imaging of COVID-19. Patterns **2**(6), 100269 (2021)
33. Oren, O., Gersh, B.J., Bhatt, D.L.: Artificial intelligence in medical imaging: switching from radiographic pathological data to clinically meaningful endpoints. Lancet Digit. Health **2**(9), e486–e488 (2020)
34. Avanzo, M., et al.: Artificial intelligence applications in medical imaging: a review of the medical physics research in Italy. PhysicaMedica **83**, 221–241 (2021)
35. Zhou, L.-Q., et al.: Artificial intelligence in medical imaging of the liver. World J. Gastroenterol. **25**(6), 672 (2019)

36. Mavrogiorgou, A., Kiourtis, A., Perakis, K., Pitsios, S., Kyriazis, D.: IoT in healthcare: achieving interoperability of high-quality data acquired by IoT medical devices. Sensors **19**(9), 1978 (2019)

37. Wood, D., Apthorpe, N., Feamster, N.: Cleartext data transmissions in consumer IoT medical devices. In: Proceedings of the 2017 Workshop on Internet of Things Security and Privacy, pp. 7–12 (2017)

38. Sabban, A.: Small new wearable antennas for IOT, medical and sport applications. In: 2019 13th European Conference on Antennas and Propagation (EuCAP), pp. 1–5. IEEE (2019)

39. Lu, D., Liu, T.: The application of IOT in medical system. In: 2011 IEEE International Symposium on IT in Medicine and Education 2011, vol. 1, pp. 272–275. IEEE (2011)

Analysis and Comparison of Posture Detection Using Deep Learning Algorithm

Shivani Singhai[1]([✉]), Pratima Gautam[1], Jitendra Singh Kushwah[2], and Sanjeev Kumar Gupta[1]

[1] Rabindranath Tagore University, Bhopal, MP, India
shivanisinghai5@gmail.com, pratima.gautam@aisectuniversity.ac.in
[2] Institute of Technology and Management, Gwalior, MP, India
jitendra.singhkushwah@itmgoi.in

Abstract. Human posture detection is the latest topic in the research field and lots of research has been done on this topic. For research, posture detection can be used in many situations, like yoga, health care, medical care, self-learning concepts etc. Deep learning plays a wide role in our everyday life, such as digital assistance, voice-enabled TV remotes, credit card fraud detection and emerging technologies, like self-car-driving use the concept of deep learning. The paper reviews the literature of deep learning algorithm for posture recognition. We describe the algorithms and literature of deep learning that were most widely used for posture detection and did a comparative analysis based on parameters that were used in literature.

Keywords: Deep Learning · Artificial Intelligence · Posture Detection

1 Introduction

Around the globe, the World Health Organization (WHO) predicts that by2025, there would 1.2 billion people aged 60 and older, and by 2050, it expects that there would be 2 billion [1]. The aging of the population is a global phenomenon and with rising health care costs and a continually aging population, geriatric health monitoring has grown increasingly vital in modern life. Seniors frequently suffering from Cognitive and physical disabilities necessitate the need for assistance with daily life, which is typically provided by human caregivers in most cases. The recognition of human activities is a well-known problem in computer vision that has been described as having several hurdles over the years. This is a consequence of the challenges in determining crucial points and the location of the human body from sensor data. There are several applications for activity recognition from biometrics and video surveillance to assisted living and sports arbitration. It is necessary to monitor and recognize their actions to assess and anticipate an individual's health condition. The identification of human actions is an area with enormous potential. Posture recognition is a technique that analyzes and recognizes the posture of a person and has garnered great interest in the domain of computer vision. Posture is the organization of the body structure that from the movement of a person

R. S. Tomar et al. (Eds.): CNC 2022, CCIS 1893, pp. 17–27, 2023.
https://doi.org/10.1007/978-3-031-43140-1_3

[2]. Figure 1 demonstrated Ensemble deep models using the preprocessed images with different Convolutional Neural Network (CNN) models.

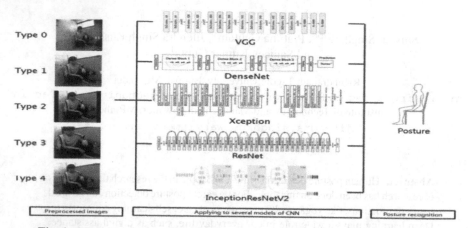

Fig. 1. Ensemble deep models using the preprocessed images with different CNN

Studies of posture, including recognition, estimation, and other related activities, have been the subject of research. There have been several investigations into posture estimation using deep learning [3].

2 Used Terminology

2.1 Neural Network-Based Motion Posture

A neural network indicated that, unless the conditions or environmental components around them vary dramatically, the usual picture follows a conventional pattern as a consequence of the physical activations of the image [4]. Physical activity patterns must be observed and analyzed for every photograph, which can help to prevent the occurrence of unusual behavioral changes in a person. The image has a significant number each picture is made up of many pixels' connections between various aspects of the image, and each picture is made up of nerve-like protrusions. Identifying the diverse images and developing a pattern from them is one of the issues in posture identification posed by the neural network. The image was sorted into several categories using neural networks that included background image and blur image classifications with the use of an Application-Specific Integrated Circuit (ASIC). The neural network classification technique must be used to address the nonlinear issue because it complies with the requirements of multi-layer systems [5].

Neural networks were developed independently of one another. Because each neuron's output comprises a deep neural network that integrates the outcomes of human categorization in its output, the outcomes of each features are computed independently of the others [16].

2.2 Deep Learning

Deep learning is subfield of machine learning that is drives many artificial intelligent services and applications that improves performing analytical, automation and physical tasks with human intervention. Many sources of knowledge such as, neuroscience and game theory, and many of model of mimic (basic structure of human nervous system) gives the model of deep learning. We can see many everyday products and services, such as digital assistance, voice- enabled TV remotes, credit card fraud detection and emerging technologies, like self-car- driving use the concept of deep learning. Deep earning model [6] includes a neural network with three or more layers in their structure. Figure 2, shows the layers of deep neural networks.

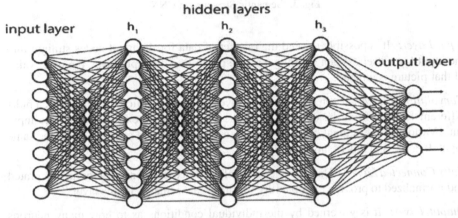

Fig. 2. Deep Neural Network

Many hidden layers are encompassed between input and output layer in deep learning neural network. The lower layer and the high layer of the model process the 'how' and 'why' respectively.

2.3 Convolutional Neural Network (CNN)

CNNs are neural networks that consist of one or more convolutional layers and are primarily used for image processing, separation, classifications, and other auto-correlated data analysis. CNN's [6, 7] are a kind of deep neural network that is most.

Frequently used to evaluate visual information. Convolution is the term used to describe the process of moving a filter over an input signal. It can do classification and regression on large amounts of high-dimensional raw data without the need for feature engineering before understanding the capabilities of each feature (Ashok and Varma 2020). The structure of the CNN is shown in Fig. 3.

As shown in Fig. 3, the fundamental components of CNN design may be separated in to five categories. The following section provide a full explanation of each components.

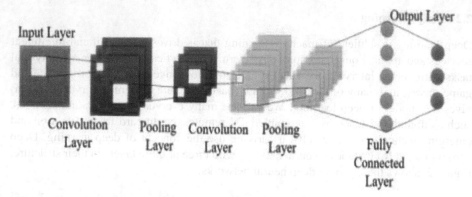

Fig. 3. Semantic Structure of CNN

Input Layer: It is possible to send the raw set of data for the input nodes straight into the input layer itself. When entering a single photo into the input layer, the pixel value of that picture is utilized.

Convolutional Layer: Each convolutional layer has a convolutional kernel, which pulls different features from the data based on the characteristics extracted from the input data. Various convolutional kernels are used to extract different attributes from the same input data set, and this is shown in Fig. 3.

Fully Connected Layer: The characteristics of the preceding convolutions are integrated and normalized to provide a probability for different scenarios in this layer.

Output Layer: It is governed by the individual conditions as to how many neurons should be present in this layer.

2.4   Recurrent Neural Networks (RNNs)

Recurrent neural networks (RNNs) are multi-layered network which form a directed cycle and stored information in the form of nodes. It is an artificial neural networks (ANNs) [8] whose connection between nodes make a loop. Figure 4 shows the RNNs model, includes one input layer three hidden layer and one output layer.

Input Layer: Layer of the RNNs model takes the input and processes and passes it to the next hidden layer (middle layer).

Hidden Layer: the middle layer can consist of multiple hidden layers. Each hidden layer has its own functions, weights and biases [9, 10]. The main and most features of RNNs is hidden layers that have memory to store information.

Output Layer: Output layer connected with the middle layer and generates the output.

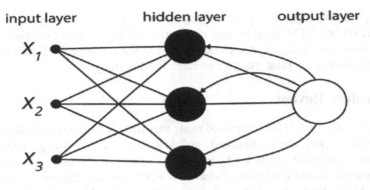

Fig. 4. Recurrent Neural Networks (RNNs)

2.5 Long Short-Term Memory (LSTM)

Long short- Term Memory (LSTM) is a kind of RNNs Model and the handled the long-term dependencies problems where RNNs fail. RNNs stored information for short term while LSTM stored it for long term. Figure 5 shows the visualization of the LSTM Network [7].

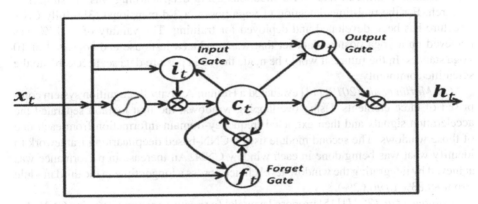

Fig. 5. Visualization of Long Short-Term Memory Network

Figure 5, shows the architecture of LSTM network, LSTM networks block which comprises with three logistic sigmoid gates. Gates within the model determined the part of information which be needed by then exit cell or to be discarded.

The output of these gates is usually the range of "0–1". Zero shows "rejected all" while one shows "included all".

3 Material and Method

In order to complete this study, articles were collected from following databases: Google Scholar, Research Gate, Science Direct, PubMed, and Online Library. The collection of articles was done using the following keywords: deep learning, yoga posture recognition using deep learning algorithm, posture recognition using CNN or a deep learning algorithm or RNN or LSTM, hand posture recognition, sitting posture detection. Articles that were written in English were included this study and available for download in full-text pdf. We have study prior five-year research for this study.

4 Literature Review

Kulikajevas et al., (2021) [12] discussed many real-life applications including assisted living, healthcare, physical training, and rehabilitation relied on human posture recognition to gather kinematic data of the body. Deep learning and computer vision advancements might substantially aid in the endeavor. It was the goal of the study to provide an improved MobileNetV2-based Deep Recurrent Hierarchical Network (DRHN) model that eliminated the occlusion issue associated with posture identification. It was possible to obtain 91.47% accuracy in the detection of sitting position the images are shown at the speed of approximately 10 Frames Per Second (FPS).

Jain et al., (2021) [13] suggested for yoga position recognition, existing strategies developed classifiers using handmade features that were calculated from data collected in a controlled setting. Existing yoga position identification algorithms were limited since these strategies typically failed in complicated real-world circumstances. Yoga stance identification in difficult real-world situations using deep learning was the subject of research. For the real-time detection of yoga poses, a 3-dimensional (3D) fully CNN structure has been developed and deployed for training. The validity of 91.15% was achieved on a yoga posture data set that was produced in-house and consisted of 10 yoga stances. In the future, it would be made the yoga posture data set accessible to the scientific community.

Gil-Martín et al., (2019) [14] evaluated a Human Activity Recognition system comprised of three elements. Using overlapping windows, the first method separated the acceleration signals and then extracted frequency-domain information from each one of those windows. The second module used a CNN-based deep learning framework to identify what was being done in each window CNN. An increase in performance was achieved by integrating the window-level choice across a longer time in the third module (from 89.83% to 96.62%).

Naigong et al. (2021) [15] proposed a model for posture recognition using CNN, this method is recognized the human joint point and validate using the Willow data sets. The data set include seven pose categories: title to the 'Interacting with a computer', 'Photographing', 'Playing Music', 'Riding Bike', 'Riding Horse', 'Running', and 'Walking'. As a result, accuracy of experiment gives 1% higher than when images were expanded from original and the accuracy is also higher than of their model using Willow data set compare with previous research.

Jianbo Liu et al., (2020) [16] proposed a novel framework for 3D CNN- based skeleton- based posture detection. To examine the skeleton posture detection, this work creates writing posture data set with 113.400 samples of 30 people with 15 different postures to test the usefulness of the method. Extensive tests on MSRA body pose dataset, proposed writing posture dataset, and public MSRA hand gesture dataset show that 3D PostureNet performs noticeably better on both skeleton- based human posture and hand posture detection task.

Limin Qi et al., (2021) [17] presented a comparison study with previous five research work. For this experiment, they select human motion image with 32 frame sub block, 46 frame sub block, and 60 frame sub block sequences. When they applied their proposed human motion posture detection using deep reinforcement algorithm, find that the number of sub blocks is less than the other five human motion posture detection algorithms.

Vivek Anand Thoutam et al., (2022) [18] They proposed a deep learning-based incorrect yoga posture detection model. With this approach, users can choose the practice pose they want to employ and upload videos of themselves doing it. The user pose is transmitted to train models that produce the aberrant angles between the user pose and the actual pose that were discovered. Afterwards, the system gives the user advice on how to fix the yoga stance by identifying its flaws. The proposed method was compared with previous research and give 0.9958 accuracy while requiring less computational complexity.

R. SantoshKumar et al., (2019) [19] developed FDCNN model. This model predicts the emotions of human body on sequence of frames. They work on five different datasets: like, angry, happy, sad, fear, and untrustworthy. I order to extract saliency information at different scales, this model represents deep convolutional features. This model's performance is superior to that of the base models.

Table 1 is a summarization of the previous review that was based on the topic covered and studied.

Table 1. Summary of the Related Review of Posture Detection using Deep Learning Algorithm

Survey, Review and References	Main Focus
Three- Dimensional CNN-inspired Deep Learning architecture for Yoga Pose Recognition in the real world (Shrajal Jain et al., 2020)	Proposed a 3D CNN for yoga posture recognition
Human Activity Recognition Based on Deep Learning Techniques (Manuel Gil-Martín et. al., 2019)	Evaluated a Human Activity Recognition system comprised of three elements
Human Body Posture Recognition Algorithm using Still Images (Naigong Yu and Jian lv, 2020)	Focused on human joint point recognition on Willow datasets using CNN algorithm
3D Posture: A Unified framework for skeleton- based posture recognition (Liu, Wang et. al. 2020)	Focused on develop a framework that recognized a skeleton based posture with WPD using 113,400 samples of 30 subjects
Human Motion Posture Detection Algorithm using Deep Reinforcement Learning (Limin Qi, Yong Han 2021)	Compared with literature and show the better effectiveness of deep learning reinforcement method

(continued)

Table 1. (*continued*)

Survey, Review and References	Main Focus
Detection of Sitting Posture using Hierarchical image composition ad deep learning (Kulikajewas et al. 2021)	Proposed a method to detect spine posture detection while sitting
Yoga Pose Estimation and Feedback Generation Using Deep Learning (Vivek Anand Thoutam et al. 2022)	Develop a model that detect incorrect yoga pose
Deep Learning Approach for Emotion Recognition from Human Body movements with Feedforward Deep Covolution Neural Networks (R. SanthoshKumar et. al., 2019)	Focused on Human Body Emotion recognition using FDCNN model

WPD: Writing Posture Detection

5 Comparative Study

A study based on the intelligent model for posture recognition during exercise offers a prediction model to determine the data analytics. Comparative analysis [11] of studies is performed to identify the performance of classifiers by assessing their accuracy. Comparison among classifiers such as the Proposed CNN- Model, Multistage CNN Architecture, Artificial Neural Network, 3DCNN, Deep Neural Network, and DRHN Based on MobileNetV2, neural networks are performed to gain accuracy. Author Lui et. al., (2020) utilize the 3DCNN model, and author Liang et al. (2020) utilize the Deep Neural Network Classifier, which shows the highest and lowest accuracy among all classifiers. 3 DCNN has a minimum accuracy rate of 97.77%. Table 2 depicts a comparative analysis of the accuracy of different classifiers. The comparison and the analysis were based on the topics covered and studied. Figure 6 depicts the bar graph of comparison of prior research This figure analyzes the accuracy of deep learning algorithms which have been used in previous research work.

Table 2. Systematic Analysis and Comparison of Posture Detection using Deep Learning Algorithm Based on Prior Research

Paper	Feature	Device	Image Type	Method	Accuracy (%)
Wang et al., 2020	n/a	Smartphone	Acceleration Data	Proposed CNN-Model	92
Zang, Yan and Li, 2018	3D Body Skeleton	RGB Camera	RGB-Images	Multistage CNN Architecture	94.9

(*continued*)

Table 2. (*continued*)

Paper	Feature	Device	Image Type	Method	Accuracy (%)
Kal et al., 2018	n/a	Wirelessly (WI-Fi) Acquiring	Sensor Data	Artificial Neural Network	97.58
Liu et al., 2020	Gaussian Voxel Feature	RGB Camera	RGB images	3DCNN	97.77
Liang and Hu, 2020	Coordinate threshold of joint points	KinectV1	RGB image	Deep Neural Network	91
Kalikajewas et al., 2021	Spine posture	RGBD Camera	RGB – D	DRHN based on MobileNetV2 Neural Network	91.47
SanthoshKumar and Kalaiselvi Geetha, 2019	–	–	RGB	FDCNN	95.4

n/a: data is not available.

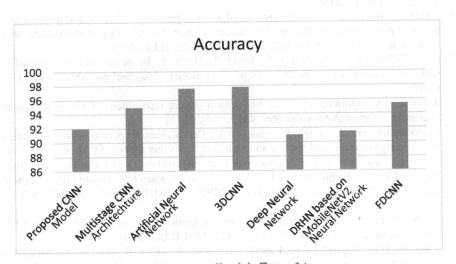

Fig. 6. Comparison Graph in Term of Accuracy

6 Conclusion

This paper is examined deep learning algorithm for posture recognition and analyze, result and methods. In addition, we have discussed about features that extract from methods. In this paper, we draw a table that show a systemic comparison and analysis of different technique of deep learning algorithm for posture detection.

We have analyzed and conclude that deep learning algorithm offer a very good result with high accuracy and also conclude that among them Three Dimension Conventional Neural Network algorithm offers the highest accuracy.

Posture detection is a hot topic in current research and has been extensively research in recent year. Following the analysis of the articles included in this study. It can be concluded that deep learning algorithm gives high accuracy of posture recognition in the field of yoga, human health care etc. Comparative bar graph shows the high accuracy of literature.

References

1. Liu, Z., Song, Y., Shang, Y., Wang, J.: Posture recognition algorithm for the elderly based on BP neural networks. In: The 27th Chinese Control and Decision Conference (2015CCDC), pp.1446–1449. IEEE (2015)
2. Nasri, N., Orts-Escolano, S., Cazorla, M.: A semg-controlled 3D game for rehabilitation the rapies: real-time time hand gesture recognition using deep learning techniques. Sensors 20(22), 6451–6459 (2020)
3. Zhang, C., Wang, Y., Guo, J., Zhang, H.: Digital recognition based on neural network and FPGA implementation. In: 2017 9th International Conference on Intelligent Human-Machine Systems and Cybernetics (IHMSC), vol. 1, pp. 280–283. IEEE (2017)
4. Ma, S., Zhang, X., Jia, C., Zhao, Z., Wang, S., Wang, S.: Image and video compression with neural networks: a review. IEEE Trans. Circuits Syst. Video Technol. 30(6), 1683–1698 (2019)
5. Rautaray, S.S., Agrawal, A.: Vision-based hand gesture recognition for human computer interaction: a survey. Artif. Intell. Rev. 43(1), 1–54 (2015)
6. Kushwah, J.S., Jain, D., Singh, P., Pandey, A.K., Das, S., Vats, P.: A comprehensive system for detecting profound tiredness for automobile drivers using a CNN. In: Shaw, R.N., Das, S., Piuri, V., Bianchini, M. (eds.) Advanced Computing and Intelligent Technologies. Lecture Notes in Electrical Engineering, vol. 914, pp. 407–415. Springer, Singapore (2022). https://doi.org/10.1007/978-981-19-2980-9_33 Print ISBN: 978-981-19-2979-3, Online ISBN: 978-981-19-2980-9
7. Wu, Y., Zheng, B., Zhao, Y.: Dynamic gesture recognition based on LSTM-CNN. In: 2018 Chinese Automation Congress (CAC), pp. 2446–2450. IEEE (2018)
8. Nagendra, H.R., Nagarathna, R., Rajesh, S.K., Amit, S., Telles, S., Hankey, A.: Niyantrita Madhumeha Bharata 2017, methodology for a nationwide diabetes prevalence estimate: part1. Int. J. Yoga 12(3), 179 (2019)
9. Kushwah, J.S., et al.: Comparative study of regressor and classifier with decision tree using modern tools. In: First International Conference on Design and Materials (ICDM)-2021 of "Materials Today: Proceedings", vol. 56, Part 6, pp. 3571–3576 (2022). ISSN 2214-7853
10. Vidyarthi, A., et al.: Wireless Communications and Mobile Computing, pp. 1–11. Wiley-Hindawi (2022).https://doi.org/10.1155/2022/1191492. Article ID 1191492

11. Kushwah, J.S., et al.: Analysis and visualization of proxy caching using LRU, AVL tree and BST with supervised machine learning. In: 1st International Conference on Computations in Materials and Applied Engineering–2020 of "Materials Today: Proceedings (2020). https://doi.org/10.1016/j.matpr.2021.06.224. ISSN 2214-7853

12. Kulikajevas, A., Maskeliunas, R., Damaševičius, R.: Detection of sitting posture using hierarchical image composition and deep learning. PeerJ Comput. Sci. **7**, e442 (2021). https://doi.org/10.7717/peerj-cs.442

13. Jain, S., et al.: Three-dimensional CNN-inspired deep learning architecture for Yoga pose recognition in the real-world environment. Neural Comput. Appl. **33** (2021). https://doi.org/10.1007/s00521-020-05405-5

14. Gil-Martín, M., et al.: Human activity recognition based on deep learning techniques. In: 6th International Electronic Conference on Sensors and Applications, vol. 42, no. 1, p. 15 (2019). https://doi.org/10.3390/ecsa-6-06539

15. Yu, N., Lv, J.: Human body posture recognition algorithm using still images. In: The 3rd Asian Conference on Artificial Intelligence Technology (ACAIT 2019), vol. 2020, no. 13, pp. 322–325 (2020). https://doi.org/10.1049/joe.2019.1146. eISSN 2051-3305

16. Liu, J., et al.: 3D PostureNet: a unified framework for skelton-based posture recognition, vol. 140, pp. 143–149 (2020). https://doi.org/10.1016/j.patrec.2020.09.029

17. Qi, L., Ha, Y.: Human motion posture detection algorithm using deep reinforcement learning. Mob. Inf. Syst. **2021**, 1–10 (2021). https://doi.org/10.1155/2021/4023861. Article ID 4023861

18. Thoutam, V., Shrivastava, A., et al.: Yoga pose estiamtion and feedback generation using deep learning. Hindawi, Computational Intelligence and Neuroscience, vol. 2022, pp. 1–12 (2022). https://doi.org/10.1155/2022/4311350. Article ID 4311350

19. Santhoshkumar, R., Kalaiselvi Geetha, M.: Deep learning approach for emotion recognition from human body movemets with feedforward deep convolution neural network. In: International Conference on Pervasive Computing Advances and Applications - PerCAA 2019, vol. 152, pp. 158–165 (2019)

20. Ali, M.A., Hussain, A.J., Sadiaq, A.T.: Human body posture recognition approaches: a review. ARO-Sci. J. Koya Univ. **X**(1), 75–84 (2022)

Design and Analysis of 16 Channel WDM-OFC System with Minimum BER for 5G Applications

Bhupendra Dhakad[✉], S. K. Narayankhedkar, Ranjeet Singh Tomar, Shyam Akashe, Shailendra Singh Ojha, and Sadhana Mishra

Department of Electronics and Communication Engineering, ITM University Gwalior, Gwalior, Madhya Pradesh, India
{bhupendradhakad.ece,sknarayankhedkar,ranjeetsingh,shyam.akashe, shailendraojha.ec,sadhanamishra.ec}@itmuniversity.ac.in

Abstract. Day by day the number of internet users are increases, requires large bandwidth and maximum bit rate with less bit error rate (BER) for the applications of IoT and 5G. Optical communication with wavelength division multiplexing technique can full fill the today's demand of users with low BER. WDM is a bidirectional data transmission technique enabled multiple users to simultaneously data transmission through a single channel. In this paper we have design the WDM based optical communication network which provide high data rates with low BER and also identified the parameters which affect the BER.

Keywords: WDM · BER · OPM · EDFA · OFC

1 Introduction

WDM, multiplex number of different wave length of optical signals and transmit through optical fiber towards the receiver. OFC consist transmitter circuit (Includes M-Z modulator, NRZ generator, bit generator, WDM) channel (Optical fiber) and receiver (DMUX, PIN diode, Filter, BER and Q factor analyzer, Regenerator).WDM device is used at transmitter side to multiplexed users data, optical fiber is used as a channel and WDM De-MUX is used at the receiver end to separate out or splits the multiplexed signals of users [1, 2] (Figs. 1 and 2).

Transmitter circuit is the combination of devices given below.

Pseudo-Random Bit Sequence Generator: Generates binary bits in random way. NRZ-Pulse Generator: Generation of Non return to zero pulse. The positive and negative voltage is defined for one and zero. NRZ pulse does not include any rest condition like RZ pulse. NRZ pulse have grater energy then the RZ pulse. CW laser: Generates continuous Electromagnetic waveform. M-Z modulator: it is used for controlling the optical wave amplitude. Wavelength-division multiplexer: Use to multiplexed user optical data and data is transmitted through optical cable. it enables bidirectional communication. Optical fiber: It is plastic or silica made flexible and transparent fiber cable. Optical power meter (OPM): OPM measures the amplitude of optical wave and provide the data in term

R. S. Tomar et al. (Eds.): CNC 2022, CCIS 1893, pp. 28–39, 2023.
https://doi.org/10.1007/978-3-031-43140-1_4

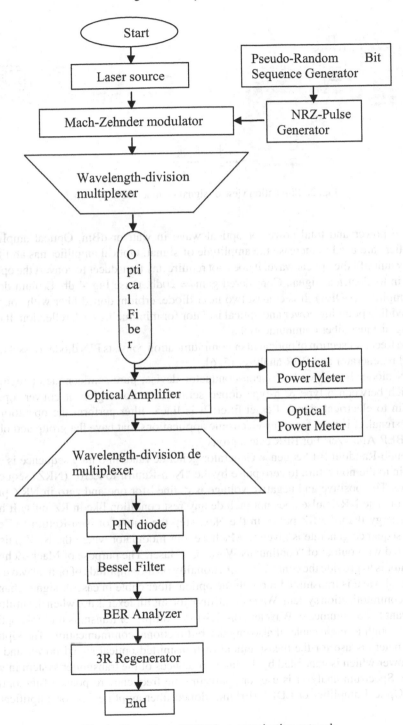

Fig. 1. Flow Chat of WDM communication network

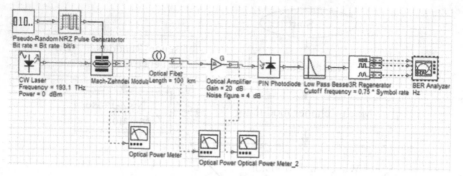

Fig. 2. Simulation view of signal channel OFC System

of noise power and total power of optical wave in watt or dBm, Optical amplifier: Amplifiers are used to increase the amplitude of signal. Optical amplifier has ability to directly amplify the optical wave. It does not require any transducer to convert the optical signal in to electrical signal. Considered gain = 20db, noise Fig. 4 db. Erbium-doped fiber amplifier (EDFA): It is consist two laser diode, erbium doped fiber with couplers for providing pumping power and optical isolator for minimizing back reflection. It used for long distance fiber communication.

The Receiver section of optical fiber communication consists PIN diode, Bessel filter, Optical regenerator and BER analyzer [5, 6].

PIN diode: It is three layer semi-conductor devise, pure semiconductor region is sandwich between p-type & n-type doped semi conductor region. it convert optical signal in to electrical signal. Bessel filter: It is linear filter perform the operation on analog signal. It is used for many electronic applications that have flat group and phase delay. BER Analyzer: For BER calculations.

Pseudo-Random Bit Sequence Generator generate random binary sequence is converted in to the non return to zero pulse by the "Non-Return-to-Zero" (NRZ) sequence generate. The positive and negative voltage is defined for one and zero in NRZ pulse generator. The NRZ pulse does not include any rest condition like in RZ pulse.It have grater energy then the RZ pulse. In the Next step the output of Non-Return-to-Zero" (NRZ) sequence generate is given to Mach Zender modulator where the NRZ pulse is modulated with output of "continuous Wave" CW laser. The purpose of Mach-Zehnder modulator is to provide the controlling functionality on the amplitude of optical wave and the optical wave is transmitted through the optical fiber cable in case of signal channel optical communication system. Wavelength division multiplexer is use when the multiple users want to communicate. Wavelength-division multiplexer transmits multiple optical waves through a single cable. It also enables bidirectional communication. The Optical power meters is use for the measurement of transmitted optical signal power and the noise power which is generated by the internal devices of the transmitter system in watt or dBm. Spectrum analyzer is use for analyzing the frequency response of the optical signal. Optical amplifier or EDFA (Erbium-doped fiber amplifier) is for amplification purpose of the optical signal. EDFA consist two laser diode, erbium doped fiber with di chroic fiber couplers for providing pumping power and optical isolator for minimizing back reflection. It used for long distance fiber communication. WDM Demultiplexer is use use in case of multiple user share the common optical fiber cable. In the continuous with the next step the amplified optical wave is given to the PIN photodiode. PIN photo diode. It is use to convert the optical signal in to electrical signal. In the next low pass Bessel is use for removing the unwanted signal and noise. Then for the re-amplification purpose 3-R regenerator is used and the bit error rate in the output is calculated by the BER analyzer.

1.1 Two Channel WDM Communication System

In 2 channel WDM communication network the 2 users can transmit data simultaneously by using 2*1 WDM multiplexer and 1*2 WDM de-multiplexer (Figs. 3, 5, 6 and 7).

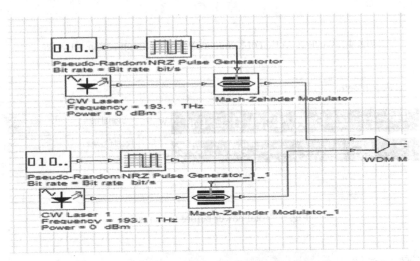

Fig. 3. Transmitter circuit of 2 channel WDM communication network

The following observations are taken by using optical power meter.

[1] Total power before the transmission is 484.406E-6 W or −3.148 dBm and after the transmission is 4.844E-6 W or −23.147 dBM. it reduce due to the optical fiber cable attenuation which is 0.2 db per KM.

[2] The noise power before or after the transmission is same which is 0 W or − 100.00 dBm because there is no noise before the transmission and the optical fiber is ideal that is why it does not introduced any noise but in practical case optical fiber added some noise due to bending and joints.

[3] The optical amplifier have gain 20 db or noise figure is 4 so total power after theamplifier is 900.508E-6 W or −0.455 dBm and it introduce noise and the noise power is after the amplifier is 396.058E-6 W or −4.022 dBm.

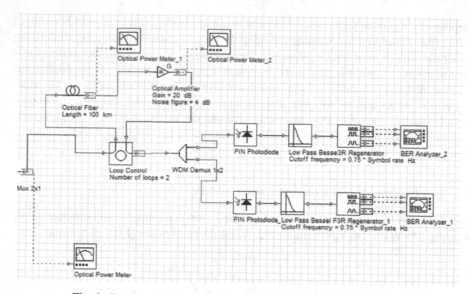

Fig. 4. Receiver section of 2 channel WDM communication network

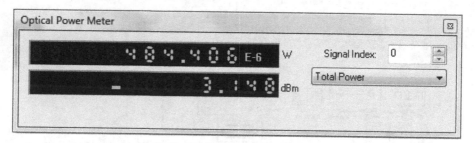

Fig. 5. Total power before transmission

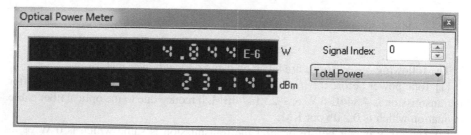

Fig. 6. Total power after transmission

[4] Minimum BER is 0.0307485. It can be reduce up to zero by selecting the optimal values of parameter.

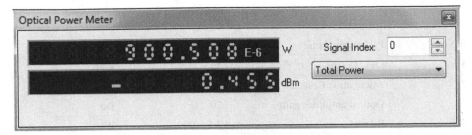

Fig. 7. Total power after amplifier

1.2 16 CHANNEL WDM-OFC SYSTEM fOR ZERO Minimum BER

In 16 channel WDM-OFC Network the 16 users can transmit data simultaneously by using 16*1 WDM multiplexer and 1*16 WDM de-multiplexer (Fig. 8 and Table 1).

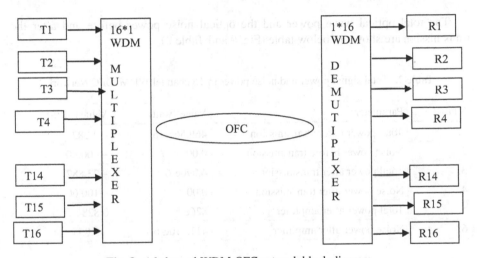

Fig. 8. 16 channel WDM-OFC network block diagram

Table 1. Optimal values of Parameters of 16 channel WDM-OFC network

S.No	Parameter Name	Values	Units
1.	OFC Length	103	KM
2.	Attenuation Constant	0.2	db/KM
3.	Optical amplifier gain	20	Db
4.	Bit rate	2.5e+009	Bit/s
5.	Time window	51.2e-009	S
6.	Sampling rate	160e+009	Hz
7.	Guard bit	0	
8.	Symbol – rate	2.5e+009	Symbols/s
9.	Number of samples	8192	

The total optical wave power and the optical noise power before and after the transmission are shown in below table (Fig. 9 and Table 2).

Table 2. Total signal power and noise power in 16 channel WDM-OFC Network

S.No	Parameter	Value (watt)	Value (dBm)
1.	Total power before transmission	469.566e-6	−3.282
2.	Noise power before transmission	0.00	−100.00
3.	Total power after transmission	4.090e-6	−23.882
4.	Noise power after transmission	0.00	−100.00
5.	Total power after amplifier	826e-6	0.828
6.	Noise power after amplifier	411.610e-6	−3.855

Above figure shows the eye diagram of 16 channel WDM network gives the information about the BER and Q factor by considering the simulated parameter shown in Table 3.

Effect of Bit Rate: (Except bit rate other parameter are same specified in above table).
    If bit rate is 2.5e + 009 then zero bit error rate can be achieve up to 103 km.
    By decreasing the bit rate the zero bit error rate can be achieve comparatively large length of optical fiber.

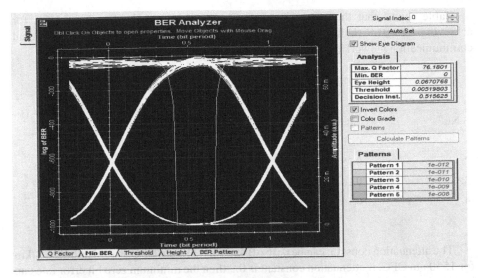

Fig. 9. 16 channel WDM-OFC network simulation result and eye diagram

Table 3. Effect of bit rate on the length of OFC for achieving zero BER

S.No	Bit rate	Optical fiber length in km
1.	2.5e+9	103
2.	2.0e+9	108
3.	1.5e+9	110
4.	1.0e+9	113

2 Minimum Bit Error Rate for Bend Optical Fiber

Attenuation is a loss of optical power due to absorption, scattering, bending, and some other loss mechanisms as the light wave travels through optical fiber. The attenuation constant of bend optical fiber is highly depends on bending angle.

$$\alpha = 2n_0 k \left(\theta_c^2 - \theta^2 \right) \exp \left[\left(-\frac{2}{3} n_0 kR \right) \left[\theta_c^2 - \theta^2 - \left(\frac{2\alpha}{R} \right) \right]^{\frac{3}{2}} \right] \quad (1)$$

where α is attenuation constant, n_0 is refractive index of optical fiber core, R is radius of optical fiber curvature, a is radius of optical fiber core, k is denoted wave number [7–9].

$$K = 2\pi / \lambda \quad (2)$$

θ is bending angle, θ_c is critical angle.

$$\theta_C = \left[1 - \left(\frac{n_1}{n_0} \right)^2 \right]^{\frac{1}{2}} \quad (3)$$

Table shows that the effect of attenuation constant on the length of OFC for achieving zero BER (Other parameter are same, specified in 16 channel WDM optical communication network) (Table 4).

Table 4. Effect of attenuation constant

S.No	Attenuation constant	OFC length (KM)
1.	0.20	103
2.	0.18	111
3.	0.16	118
4.	0.14	125

The attenuation constant can be 0.36 dB/km for 1310 nm OFC as well as 0.22 dB/km for 1550 nm OFC. if attenuation constant is 0.2 then the minimum zero bit error rate can be achieve up to 103 km length of optical fiber by decreasing the attenuation constant of optical fiber the zero BER can be achieve comparatively long length of optical fiber. The total attenuation constant α between two arbitrary points X and Y of OFC is

$$\alpha(dB) = 10\log_{10}(P_X/P_Y). \tag{4}$$

where P_X is the power at point X. P_Y is the power at point Y. Point X is closer to the optical source and point Y is at destination and l is distance between point X and Y

$$P_y = P_x e^{-\alpha l} \quad \ldots\ldots \quad \text{Beer's equation} \tag{5}$$

Power at the source $= P_x$ dB then power at the ending point of optical fiber

$$Py\ (dB) = Px\ (dB) - \alpha l(dB) \tag{6}$$

where α is attenuation constant

The total attenuation constant of optical fiber is depends on length of fiber.

Case1. Considering length of optical fiber is l_1 and attenuation constant α_1 then received power at the ending point of optical fiber is

$$P_{y1} = P_x - \alpha_1 l_1 \tag{7}$$

Case2. Considering length of optical fiber is l_2 and attenuation constant α_2 then received power at the ending point of optical fiber is

$$P_{y2} = P_x - \alpha_2 l_2 \tag{8}$$

From Eq. (7) & (8)

$$P_{y2} = P_{y1} + \alpha_1 l_1 - \alpha_2 l_2 \tag{9}$$

BER is inversely proportional to the SNR so for achieving Zero minimum BER, required a particular amount of received power at the end of OFC. The power after the optical amplifier is the sum of power at the ending point of OFC and noise power introduced by the optical amplifier.

Considering the AWG noise (mean value = 0) in digital communication. Probability distribution function of AWG is given as

$$f(x) = \frac{1}{\sigma\sqrt{2\pi}} e^{\frac{-x^2}{2\sigma}} \tag{10}$$

the probability of bit error in digital communication is given by

$$P_e = Q\{\gamma^2/4\}^{1/2} \tag{11}$$

where γ^2 is signal to noise ratio, f_b is bit rate

$$BER = f_b * P_e \tag{12}$$

Effect of Attenuation Constant on BER and Total Signal Power at both the end of Optical Fiber: Below figure conclude that by increasing attenuation constant BER is also increase proportionally at all the receivers. This is happen because when we increase the value of attenuation constant of optical fiber then the transmitted signal power decreases due to that signal to noise ratio degraded and it causes the reduction in BER. There is no effect of attenuation constant on total signal power at starting edge of optical fiber because the attenuation constant is related to optical fiber and we are observing total power at starting edge of cable. The total power at ending edge of cable is continuously degraded this can be seen in below figure (Figs. 10 and 11).

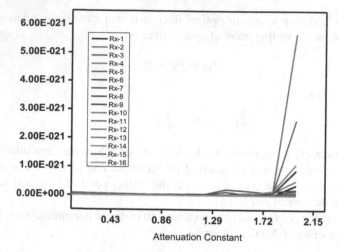

Fig. 10. Attenuation constant Vs BER

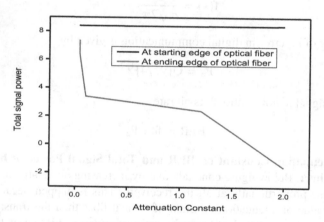

Fig. 11. Attenuation constant Vs Total power

3   Conclusion

BER is inversely proportional to wave length spacing among the users. Bit error rate is increases by increasing the length of optical fiber length. By increasing the length of EDFA amplifier the zero BER can be achieved for large distance and by reducing the Attenuation constant, the zero BER can be achieved for longer length of optical fiber.

References

1. Dhakad, B., Ojha, S.S., Sharma, M.: WDM communication network with zero bit error rate. In: Tomar, R.S., et al. (eds.) Communication, Networks and Computing. CNC 2020. CCIS, vol. 1502, pp. 18–28. Springer, Singapore (2021). https://doi.org/10.1007/978-981-16-8896-6_2

2. Babu, P., Singh, M.K., Pal, S.: Optimization of a single-channel optical communication system and an 8-channel WDM system using EDFA. In: Rakesh, P.K., Sharma, A.K., Singh, I. (eds.) Advances in Engineering Design. LNME, pp. 453–464. Springer, Singapore (2021). https://doi.org/10.1007/978-981-33-4018-3_42

3. Sekh, M.A., Rahim, M., Begam, A.: Design of EDFA based 16 channel WDM system using counter directional high pump power. J. Opt. Commun. (2021)

4. Kaur, P., Bhatia, K.S., Kaur, H.: Performance analysis of 16 channel WDM system with 4 OADM. J. Opt. Commun. 36(2), 169–173 (2015)

5. Ivaniga, T., Ovseník, L.U., Turán, J.: The four-channel WDM system using semiconductor optical amplifier. In: 26th Conference Radioelektronika 2016, April 19–20 2016, Koice, Slovak Republic 978-1-5090-1674-7/16/ IEEE (2016)

6. Maharjan, R., Lavrinovica, I., Supe, A., Porins, J.: Minimization of FWM effect in nonlinear optical fiber using variable channel spacing technique. In: 2016 Advances in Wireless and Optical Communications (RTUWO) (2016)

7. Shanker, R., Srivastava, P., Bhattacharya, M.: Performance analysis of 16-Channel 80-Gbps optical fiber communication system. In: 2016 International Conference on Computational Techniques in Information and Communication Technologies (ICCTICT) (2016)

8. Lian, Y., et al.: Ultralow bending-loss trench-assisted single-mode optical fibers. IEEE Photonics Technol. Lett. 29(3) (2017)

9. Chen, T., Xie, Z., Li, Z.H., Zhou, Y.M., Guo, H.Y.: Study on the monotonicity of bending loss of polymer optical fiber. J. Lightwave Technol. 33(10) (2015)

Classification Techniques in Remote Sensing: A Review

Nishtha Parashar[✉]

Department of CEA, GLA University, Mathura, UP, India
nishtha2909@gmail.com

Abstract. In order to find building supplies and offer precise geographic data, remote sensing is mostly utilized to study potential dam, bridge, and pipeline locations. Images taken by satellites and drones are used in image remote sensing analysis to study the Earth's surface. Any classification method's primary goal is to give semantic labels to photos that have been collected. Using these labels, the images may then be sorted in a semantic order. In many areas of remote-sensing, image retrieval and video analysis, the semantic layout of images is used. Early approaches to remote sensing picture analysis were built on the extraction and representation of low- and mid-level features. By utilizing feature optimization and machine learning algorithms, these systems have demonstrated good performance. Small-scale image datasets were utilized in these previous methods. Deep learning models are now being used more frequently for remote sensing picture analysis. The employment of multiple hybrid deep learning algorithms has demonstrated significantly better outcomes than the previous models. A thorough analysis of historical patterns is provided in this review paper, utilizing conventional machine learning principles. For the purpose of remote sensing visual analysis, a list of publicly accessible image benchmarks is also provided.

Keywords: Remote Sensing · Image Classification · Machine Learning · Deep Neural Network · Image Dataset

1 Introduction

Applications for deep learning and computer vision include action recognition, image identification in industries, image identification in medical field, image categorization, and remote-sensing [1–4]. In the discipline of civil engineering, there are various uses for satellite image analysis, including mapping of mineral availability, agriculture and in geology. Satellite images are thought to be the primary source for obtaining geographic information [5]. Data obtained from satellite sources is massive and growing at an exponential rate; in order to manage these big scale of data, effective approaches for data extraction are required. These images taken from satellite can be organized in semantic order by image categorization. The process of categorizing satellite photos involves several stages and starts with the extraction of features from the images [6]. Designing a system for the classification of desired images is the first stage in the step-by-step process of image classification. The photos are then pre-processed, which

R. S. Tomar et al. (Eds.): CNC 2022, CCIS 1893, pp. 40–50, 2023.
https://doi.org/10.1007/978-3-031-43140-1_5

includes scaling, image enhancement, image clustering, and other processes. In the third stage, those photos' desired regions are picked out, and preliminary clusters are created. Following the application of the algorithm to the images to achieve the required categorization, which is often referred to as postprocessing, corrective actions are taken. The accuracy of this classification will be evaluated in the final stage.

Classification of images for remote sensing involves the process of assigning a set of predefined categories to the pixels or objects of an image. This process can be used to identify and monitor changes in land use, vegetation, water bodies, and other features of the Earth's surface over time. Here are some general steps for image classification in remote sensing:

  i. Image preprocessing: This involves correcting for distortions and removing noise from the raw image data. Preprocessing steps may include geometric correction, radiometric calibration, and atmospheric correction.
 ii. Feature extraction: This involves identifying relevant features in the image that can be used to distinguish between different categories. Examples of features may include texture, color, shape, and spectral characteristics.
iii. Training data selection: This involves selecting a representative set of training data for each category. These training data are used to train a classification algorithm to recognize the features that distinguish each category.
 iv. Classification algorithm selection: There are several types of classification algorithms, including supervised, unsupervised, and hybrid methods. Supervised methods require labeled training data, while unsupervised methods do not. Hybrid methods combine both supervised and unsupervised techniques.
  v. Classification: This involves applying the chosen algorithm to the image data to assign each pixel or object to a specific category.
 vi. Post-classification analysis: This involves evaluating the accuracy of the classification results and refining the classification as needed. Post-classification analysis may include error matrix analysis, accuracy assessment, and visual inspection of the classified image.

In summary, classification of images for remote sensing involves a series of steps that include preprocessing, feature extraction, training data selection, algorithm selection, classification, and post-classification analysis. The choice of algorithm and the quality of training data are critical factors that determine the accuracy of the classification results. However, there are several classification techniques that can be used for remote sensing, depending on the type of data and the classification task at hand. Here are some commonly used classification techniques for remote sensing. Maximum Likelihood Classification: This is a supervised classification technique that is based on statistical models of the spectral signature of each class. The technique assumes that the data in each class follows a normal distribution and calculates the probability of each pixel belonging to each class based on its spectral characteristics. Support Vector Machine Classification: This is a supervised classification technique that is based on the principle of maximum margin classification. The technique finds the hyperplane that best separates the data into different classes, based on their spectral characteristics. It is particularly useful for classification problems with a large number of features. Random Forest Classification: This is a supervised classification technique that uses an ensemble of decision trees to classify the data. The technique is based on the idea that combining the predictions of multiple decision trees can lead to better classification accuracy. K-means Clustering: This is an unsupervised classification technique that groups pixels with similar spectral characteristics into clusters. The technique does not require any prior knowledge of the classes and can be useful for identifying patterns and structures in the data. Object-based Classification: This is a classification technique that groups pixels into objects based on their spectral and spatial characteristics. The technique can provide more accurate classification results than pixel-based methods, especially for complex landscapes. Deep Learning Classification: This is a recent development in classification techniques that uses deep neural networks to learn complex patterns and features from the data. Deep learning techniques have shown promising results in remote sensing classification tasks, especially for tasks that require large amounts of labeled data. In summary, the choice of classification technique for remote sensing depends on the type of data and the classification task at hand. Supervised methods such as Maximum Likelihood and Support Vector Machine Classification are useful when prior knowledge of the classes is available, while unsupervised methods such as K-means clustering can be useful for identifying patterns in the data. Object-based classification and deep learning techniques are recent developments that have shown promising results in remote sensing classification.

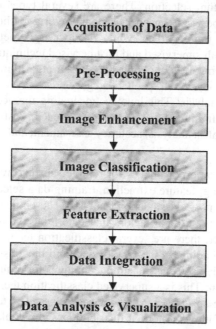

Fig. 1. Steps for Processing Remotely Sensed Data

Figure 1 specifies the general steps that are required for processing remotely sensed data. Moreover, the current study has mainly concentrated on scene-based classification [7, 8], one of the three primary categories of distant image classifications that are primarily pixel, object and scene-based. There is no need to categorize distant images based on pixels, and the study direction has shifted to image classification based on objects. Semantics or scene units are referred to as "items of remotely sensed images" [9, 10]. Processing an image's visual elements has been a time-consuming, computationally expensive activity that has needed a lot of work and resources over the past two decades. Supervised and unsupervised approach is considered as one of the most prominent techniques for the implementation of classification techniques for remote sensing. Using these approaches numerous satellite photos can be arrange in sequential order for the classification of images.

Furthermore, in terms of supervised and unsupervised algorithms, supervised classification involves training a classifier using a set of labeled training data, where each pixel or image segment is assigned a class label based on ground truth information. The classifier learns to recognize patterns in the training data and then applies those patterns to classify new, unlabeled data. Commonly used supervised classification techniques include maximum likelihood, support vector machines, and decision trees. Unsupervised classification, on the other hand, involves clustering pixels or image segments based on their spectral similarity without prior knowledge of the classes present in the scene. The analyst then assigns class labels to each cluster based on their spectral characteristics and spatial context. Commonly used unsupervised classification techniques include k-means clustering, hierarchical clustering, and ISODATA.

Each approach has its own advantages and disadvantages. Supervised classification is typically more accurate and produces more reliable results, especially when the training data is carefully selected, and the classifier is well-tuned. However, it requires a significant amount of labeled training data and can be time-consuming and costly to create. Unsupervised classification, on the other hand, is faster and more automated, but it may not produce as accurate results as supervised classification, especially if the classes are not well separated spectrally.

Ultimately, the choice of classification approach depends on the specific needs of the analysis, including the available data, the level of accuracy required, and the available resources. We may distinguish between supervised and unsupervised learning using the following simple terms: While unsupervised learning algorithms are trained utilizing unlabeled data, supervised learning algorithms do so. Methods like K-means clustering, and Principal component analysis (PCA) were later presented in the situation of unsupervised learning. These methods have the advantage of being able to automatically pick up on the features. But when there are larger datasets, these unsupervised learning strategies fall short [11]. These remote images can now be certainly identified by initializing weights in training layers thanks to advancements in deep learning based approaches and parallel computing [12]. This will allow for more accurate scene prediction in later deep learning layers.

2 Recent Trends in Remote Sensing for Classification of Images

Remote sensing refers to the use of satellite or airborne sensors to acquire information about the Earth's surface from a distance. One of the main applications of remote sensing is image classification, which involves assigning a set of predefined categories to the pixels of an image. Here are some recent trends in remote sensing for image classification. Deep Learning: Deep learning algorithms, such as convolutional neural networks (CNNs), have shown excellent performance in remote sensing image classification. These methods can automatically learn a hierarchy of features from the input data, allowing for accurate and efficient classification. Multi-sensor fusion: Combining data from multiple sensors can provide more comprehensive and accurate information about the Earth's surface. Recent research has focused on developing methods to fuse data from different sensors, such as optical and radar sensors, to improve classification accuracy. Transfer learning: Transfer learning involves training a deep learning model on a large dataset, and then fine-tuning the model on a smaller dataset for a specific task. This approach has shown promising results in remote sensing image classification, where there may be limited labeled data available for a specific region or application. Object-based classification: Object-based classification involves grouping pixels into meaningful objects, such as buildings or vegetation, and classifying these objects based on their attributes. This approach has shown better accuracy than pixel-based classification methods for certain applications, such as urban land cover classification. Cloud computing: Cloud computing platforms, such as Google Earth Engine, provide access to large amounts of satellite imagery and processing power, allowing for efficient analysis of remote sensing data. These platforms also provide tools for machine learning and data visualization, making it easier for researchers to develop and test image classification algorithms.

Computer science's field of machine learning (ML) combines supervised and unsupervised learning methods [13–16]. It addresses both classification and regression issues [17]. In machine learning, a comprehensive dataset is created that takes the majority of system factors into account. When theoretical knowledge is insufficient to forecast some information, machine learning is helpful [18, 19]. It has a wide range of uses, including issues with land use and cover [20], disaster relief, climate change, and many more [21]. AI is divided into machine learning (ML) and AI [22].

Convolutional neural networks can be in handy in a variety of multimedia applications where automatic image classification is required. In this study, feature-extraction was carried out using different models including Alex-Net, VGG-19 and ResNet-50. The experiments were conducted on separate datasets including SAT-4, SAT-6, and UCMD. Photos for SAT-4 and SAT-6 were taken from the NAIP dataset, which contains over 3 lakh scene images from across the globe. While the labels for the SAT-4 and SAT-6 datasets are grounds, buildings, roads, water, and so on, the given dataset uses photos that were taken from the USGS, a sizable dataset. It contains 20 classes. For SAT datasets, the training and testing ratio is chosen to be 80:20 and 70:30, respectively [23, 24].

Figure 2 demonstrates how the spatial resolution of photographs has dramatically enhanced as a result of better research [25]. There is no need to categorize distant images based on pixels, and the study direction has shifted to image classification based on objects.

Overall, these recent trends in remote sensing for image classification have led to significant improvements in accuracy and efficiency, making it easier to monitor and understand changes in the Earth's surface over time.

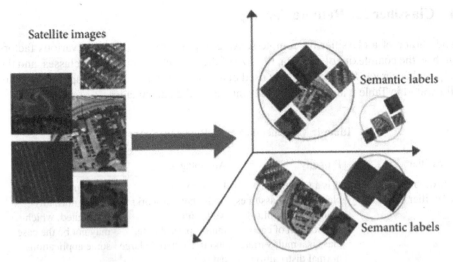

Fig. 2. Image Classification in Remote Sensing Field

3 Selection for Remotely Sensed Data

The selection of remotely sensed data depends on the specific application and research question being addressed. However, some general considerations for selecting remotely sensed data include:

Spatial resolution: The spatial resolution of the sensor determines the level of detail that can be observed in the data. Higher spatial resolution sensors can capture more detailed features but may have a smaller coverage area. Lower spatial resolution sensors may have a larger coverage area but may not be able to capture as much detail. Spectral resolution: The spectral resolution of the sensor determines the number of spectral bands that are available. More spectral bands can provide more information about the physical properties of the observed objects. Temporal resolution: The temporal resolution of the sensor refers to how frequently the sensor acquires data over a given area. Sensors with high temporal resolution can provide information about changes over time, such as vegetation growth or land use change. Availability and cost: The availability and cost of the data may also be important considerations. Some sensors may be freely available, while others may require a purchase or subscription. Data format and compatibility: The data format and compatibility with existing software and tools should also be considered to ensure that the data can be used effectively in the analysis.

Accuracy and precision: The accuracy and precision of the data should be considered when selecting the data for a specific application. The accuracy of the data depends on the calibration of the sensor, while the precision depends on the signal-to-noise ratio and other factors. Data processing and analysis requirements: The data processing and analysis requirements should also be considered when selecting the data. Some sensors may require more extensive processing to derive useful information, while others may be easier to use out of the box.

4   Classifier for Remote Sensing

The choice of a classifier for remote sensing applications depends on various factors such as the complexity of the data, the size of the dataset, the number of classes, and the required accuracy. Some commonly used classifiers for remote sensing applications are illustrated in Table 1 along with the advantages and disadvantages.

Table 1. Classifier details for Remotely Sense Data

Classifier	Property	Advantages	Disadvantages
Maximum Likelihood Classifier (MLC)	It is a parametric classifier that assumes that the probability distribution of each class is a multivariate normal distribution	It is easy to implement, it works well with multi-spectral data, and it can handle large datasets	It assumes that the data is normally distributed, which may not be the case in some applications
Support Vector Machines (SVM)	SVM is a non-parametric classifier that separates the data into different classes using a hyperplane	It can handle non-linear data, it is robust to outliers, and it can handle high-dimensional data	It can be computationally expensive and may require tuning of the parameters
Random Forest Classifier (RFC)	RFC is an ensemble classifier that consists of multiple decision trees	It can handle non-linear data, it is robust to outliers, and it can handle high-dimensional data	It can be sensitive to noise and may overfit the data if the number of trees is too high
Artificial Neural Networks (ANN)	ANN is a non-linear classifier that consists of multiple layers of interconnected neurons	The advantages of ANN are that it can handle complex data, it can learn from the data, and it can handle high-dimensional data	However, ANN can be computationally expensive, and it may require tuning of the parameters

To summarize, the choice of a classifier for remote sensing applications depends on the specific requirements of the application. Some factors to consider when choosing a classifier include the complexity of the data, the size of the dataset, the number of classes, and the required accuracy. Each classifier has its advantages and disadvantages, and the best approach is to test different classifiers and choose the one that performs the best for a particular application.

5   Datasets

Following is a description of various remote sensing datasets that are publicly available including total number of images, total number of classes, image size and year (Table 2).

Table 2. Publicly Available Remote Sensing Datasets

Dataset	Total Images	Total Classes	Image Size	Year
WHU-RS19	1005	19	600*600	2012
NWPU VHR-10 dataset	800	10	VHR	2014
RSSCN7	2800	7	400*400	2015
Brazilian coffee scene	2876	2	64 * 64	2015
SAT4	500000	4	28*28	2015
SAT6	405000	6	28*28	2015
SIRI-WHU	2400	12	200×200	2016
OPTIMAL	1860	31	256×256	2018
DIOR and DIOR-R datasets	23,463	20	VHR	2020

6 Performance Evaluation Criteria

In the literature, there are numerous methods for assessing the effectiveness of classification [24]. The type of classification we'll execute and the kind of outcomes needed will alone determine the performance measure we use. The range of classification technique has a significant impact on the performance metric choice as well. The performance metrics used to evaluate the classification's correctness are listed below: True positive (TP): the proportion of accurately classified photos True Negative (TN): the proportion of mislabeled photographs False positive (FP): labelling an image with a class it doesn't belong in False negative (FN): failing to classify an image when it clearly belongs in that category.

The following are a few of the ways to gauge the effectiveness of content-based picture retrieval. Precision value is used to measure the proportion of pertinent output to all output images. Average precision refers to the average answer to all pertinent queries. Mean-average-precision is referred to as the average of all the pertinent questions' means. Recall/sensitivity is the metric that measures the proportion of pertinent output to all input and output queries. The harmonic-mean between precision and accuracy is known as the F-measure. The ratio of accurately labelled negative-images to all negatively-labelled-images is known as the negative predictive value.

Specificity is measured by the proportion of correctly classified negative photos to all negative-images. Accuracy is the percentage of all outcomes that have been correctly or incorrectly labelled to the total number of labels that have been applied. Overall accuracy is calculated as the ratio of all correctly classified photos to all previously existing images where overall accuracy, total accurate cells, and sum of all non-diagonal entries in confusion-matrix.

Mean square error metric is the most widely used to gauge error. It calculates the square difference between the goal and the result that the model predicts as the average. Where N represents the most recent iterations, the true value, and the value anticipated by the model [25]. The mean absolute error, or MAE, is used when attempting to calculate the average between the actual value and the anticipated value. The metric's mathematical representation is shown below. Where N represents the most recent iterations, the true value, and the value anticipated by the model. Root-mean-square error is simple to calculate and provides a more accurate indication of how better the model is working. Simply take the square-root of the square difference between the projected value and the goal value. That is commonly used to evaluate the performance of remote sensing data for binary classification problems. In this context, the binary classification problem involves classifying a pixel or a set of pixels as either belonging to a target class or not. The AUROC evaluates the accuracy of the classification results and provides a quantitative measure of the performance of the classification algorithm. Area under the receiver operating characteristic curve (AUROC), also known as AUC-ROC score/curves, is a very interesting statistic and is represented mathematically as (xiv). True positive rate (TPR) and false positive rate (FPR) are used for calculating AUROC.

7 Conclusion and Future Direction

Many real-time applications, including Earth monitoring, urban planning, water resource engineering, supplying building specifications, and agricultural planning, use remote sensing picture processing. The research community engaged in remote sensing applications is still grappling with the open research question of image processing and categorization. Multimedia items, such as videos and digital photos, are multiplying exponentially in both quantity and size as a result of recent advances in imaging technology. The automatic categorization of photographs is an open research challenge for the community of computer vision researchers due to the rise in the volume of digital images. In recent years, several study models have been put forth, but there is more research to be done before machines can perceive what humans do. The research communal investigating image analysis in remote sensing field is looking into potential research trajectories that can close this gap as a result. In the past, low-level feature extraction and mid-level feature representation have been the foundation for remote sensing image analysis methods. On small-scale picture benchmarks with few training and testing examples, these methods performed well. The performance of the learning model can be improved by the usage of discriminating feature interpretation with multi-scaling features. While the current period requires assigning many labels to a single image based on contents, these approaches can only primarily assign single labels to photos. Building a significant-scale image standard that can be used to train a complicated deep network is one of the key prerequisites for a deep learning model. One of the key prerequisites and an active research topic in this field is the development of a large-scale image benchmark comprising all conceivable kinds of remote sensing images. Most contemporary deep learning research models primarily use fine-tuning and data augmentation strategies to improve learning. Another potential study area is the development of deep learning models that require less computations and can be applied to hardware with limited processing power. In the realm of remote sensing image categorization, the application of few-shot/zero-shot learning algorithms can be investigated.

References

1. Shi, C., Zhang, X., Sun, J., Wang, L.: Remote sensing scene image classification based on self-compensating convolution neural network. Remote Sens. **14**(3), 545 (2022)
2. Karimi Jafarbigloo, S., Danyali, H.: Nuclear atypia grading in breast cancer histopathological images based on CNN feature extraction and LSTM classification. CAAI Trans. Intell. Technol. **6**(4), 426–439 (2021)
3. Zhang, X., Wang, G.: Stud pose detection based on photometric stereo and lightweight yolov4. J. Artif. Intell. Technol. **2**(1), 32–37 (2022)
4. Shabbir, A., Rasheed, A., Rasheed, H., et al.: Detection of glaucoma using retinal fundus images: a comprehensive review. Math. Biosci. Eng. **18**(3), 2033–2076 (2021)
5. Zhang, W., Du, P., Fu, P., et al.: Attention-aware dynamic self-aggregation network for satellite image time series classification. IEEE Trans. Geosci. Remote Sens. **60**, 1–17 (2022)
6. Hamid, N., Abdul Hamid, J.R.: Multi level image segmentation for urban land cover classifications. In: IOP Conference Series: Earth and Environmental Science, vol. 767, no. 1, Article ID 012024 (2021)
7. Li, K., Wan, G., Cheng, G., Meng, L.,Han, J.: Object detection in optical remote sensing images: a survey and a new benchmark. ISPRS J. Photogramm. Remote Sens. **159**, 296–307 (2020)
8. Asif, M., Bin Ahmad, M., Mushtaq, S., Masood, K., Mahmood, T., Ali Nagra, A.: Long multi-digit number recognition from images empowered by deep convolutional neural networks. Comput. J. **117**, 4 (2021)
9. Wang, Q., Liu, S., Chanussot, J., Li, X.: Scene classification with recurrent attention of VHR remote sensing images. IEEE Trans. Geosci. Remote Sens. **57**(2), 1155–1167 (2019)
10. Li, S., Song, W., Fang, L., Chen, Y., Ghamisi, P., Benediktsson, J.A.: Deep learning for hyperspectral image classification: an overview. IEEE Trans. Geosci. Remote Sens. **57**(9), 6690–6709 (2019)
11. Elkholy, M.M., Mostafa, M.S., Ebeid, H.M., Tolba, M.: Unsupervised hyperspectral band selection with deep autoencoder unmixing. Int. J. Image Data Fusion **13**(3), 244–261 (2021)
12. Vali, A., Comai, S., Matteucci, M.: Deep learning for land use and land cover classification based on hyperspectral and multispectral earth observation data: a review. Remote Sens. **12**(15), 2495 (2020)
13. Govind, M., Pandeyand Dr, S.K.: A Comparative Study on Supervised and Unsupervised Techniques of Land Use and Land Cover Classification (2022)
14. De Luca, G.: A survey of NISQ era hybrid quantum classical machine learning research. J. Artif. Intell. Technol. **2**(1), 9–15 (2022)
15. Alyas Khan, M., Ali, M., Shah, M., et al.: Machine learning-based detection and classification of walnut fungi diseases. Intell. Autom. Soft Comput. **30**(3), 771–785 (2021)
16. Nasiri, V., Darvishsefat, A.A., Arefi, H., Griess, V.C., Sadeghi, S.M.M., Borz, S.A.: Modeling forest canopy cover: a synergistic use of sentinel 2, aerial photogrammetry data, and machine learning. Remote Sens. **14**(6), 1453 (2022)
17. Cabrera, D., Cabrera, L., Cabrera, E.: Perspectives organize information in mind and nature: empirical findings of point-view perspective (p) in cognitive and material complexity. Systems **10**(3), 52 (2022)
18. Ali, N., Bajwa, K.B., Sablatnig, R., et al.: A novel image retrieval based on visual words integration of sift and surf. PLoS One **11**(6), Article ID 0157428 (2016)
19. Wang, M., Wander, M., Mueller, S., Martin, N., Dunn, J.B.: Evaluation of survey and remote sensing data products used to estimate land use change in the United States: evolving issues and emerging opportunities. Environ. Sci. Policy **129**, 68–78 (2022)

20. Jacobsen, R., Bernabel, C.A., Hobbs, M., Oishi, N., Puig-Hall, M. and Zirbel, S.: Machine learning: paving the way for more efficient disaster relief. In: AIAA SCITECH 2022 Forum, p. 0397 (2022)

21. Zheng, Z., Du, S., Taubenböck, H., Zhang, X.: Remote sensing techniques in the investigation of aeolian sand dunes: a review of recent advances. Remote Sens. Environ. **271**, Article ID 112913 (2022)

22. Shabbir, A., Ali, N., Ahmed, J., et al.: Satellite and scene image classification based on transfer learning and fine tuning of resnet50. Math. Probl. Eng. **2021**, Article ID 5843816, 1–18 (2021)

23. Kadhim, M.A., Abed, M.H.: Convolutional neural network for satellite image classification. In: Huk, M., Maleszka, M., Szczerbicki, E. (eds.) Intelligent Information and Database Systems: Recent Developments. ACIIDS 2019. SCI, vol. 830, pp. 165–178. Springer, Cham (2020). https://doi.org/10.1007/978-3-030-14132-5_13

24. Deepan, P., Sudha, L.R.: Scene classification of remotely sensed images using ensembled machine learning models. In: Gopi, E.S. (eds.) Machine Learning, Deep Learning and Computational Intelligence for Wireless Communication. LNEE, vol. 749, pp. 535–550. Springer, Singapore (2021). https://doi.org/10.1007/978-981-16-0289-4_39

25. Mehmood, M., Shahzad, A., Zafar, B., Shabbir, A., Ali, N.: Remote sensing image classification: a comprehensive review and applications. Math. Probl. Eng. **2022** (2022). https://doi.org/10.1155/2022/5880959

Analysis of Probability of Detection in Relay Assisted WBAN

Hafsa Rafiqi[1], Sindhu Hak Gupta[1]([✉]), and Jitendra Singh Jadon[2]([✉])

[1] Department of Electronics and Communication Engineering, Amity School of Engineering and Technology, Amity University, Sector-125, Noida 201303, India
Shak@amity.edu
[2] Department of Artificial Intelligence, Amity School of Engineering and Technology, Amity University, Sector-125, Noida 201303, India
jsjadon@amity.edu

Abstract. This paper examines the working of a Cognitive Radio based Wireless Body Area Network (WBAN) based on Probability of Detection (P_D) as a performance metric. The variation in values of Probability of Detection (P_D) with variable factors such as Dynamic Threshold, Noise uncertainty & sampling time (N_S) for zero relay & multi relay system respectively has been conducted using MATLAB.

Keywords: Cognitive radio · Wireless Body Area Network · Relay based communication · Probability of detection · Dynamic threshold · Noise uncertainty

1 Introduction

The fast-evolving notion of Internet of Things (IoT) has brought upon a phenomenal progression in human way of living. It is a thought of connecting "things" such as sensors, watch, mobile, vehicle etc. with internet for the process of collecting, analysing & then distribution of data among themselves or with internet [1]. Some prominent applications of IoT are in the fields of agriculture, home automation, military, healthcare, environment monitoring, smart grid, navigation, logistics & many more [2]. One of the leading IoT based architecture in healthcare application is WBAN [3].

It is a communication mesh network among all wearable or implanted sensor nodes existent in a human body [4]. These sensor nodes consistently monitor & collect the specified personal health information of a patient. After data collection, the sink node then performs data aggregation. On the basis of patient's acquired medical status a pertinent diagnosis is provided by the medical staff [5]. In [6], authors have discussed the growth of IoT technology in healthcare sector with some of its future scope. They have presented an IoT based prototype model using Zigbee as its communication standard. Results show better energy efficiency & network stability when compared with similar studies. Another IoT based remote healthcare monitoring system has been presented, studied as well as compared in detail by authors of [7]. It is evident that WBAN has

R. S. Tomar et al. (Eds.): CNC 2022, CCIS 1893, pp. 51–65, 2023.
https://doi.org/10.1007/978-3-031-43140-1_6

empowered the realm of remote heath monitoring, assisted living & cost-effective smart medication a reality [8]. Just as there are many advantageous points of WBAN, they are not without drawbacks. Some challenging issue that WBAN faces are quality of service, security, mobile network topology, power consumption, reliable signal transmission, interferences & spectrum availability [9–11]. Several literatures have addressed these challenges proposing a suitable solution. In [12], authors have proposed a cooperative energy harvesting based routing protocol that deals the issue of energy efficiency and network lifespan of WBAN. Similarly, authors of [13] have taken into account the issue of security & power consumption in WBAN putting forward an anonymous mutual authentication & key agreement scheme. Amidst all these problems current work strives to tackle spectrum scarcity issue for WBAN devices.

The inauguration of Cognitive Radio (CR) technology as a potential solution was a game changer in communication systems all over the world. This technology empowers a CR user or also called as secondary user (SU) with the ability to detect the spectrum usage information of a primary user (PU). PU are the licensed users having higher priority over the designated spectrum, whereas the SU are the unlicensed users having lower priority of spectrum access [14]. SU are only able to reuse the target spectrum opportunistically in absence of a PU [15]. This whole CR cycle as described in Fig. 1 is done in 4 stages: i.) Spectrum sensing based on the sensed Radio spectrum environment. ii.) Spectrum analysis with decision whether the spectrum is available for SU or not. iii.) Spectrum mobility which is defined as the dynamic change of operating radio frequency by CR. iv.) After spectrum decision is made the remaining step is the spectrum sharing process [15, 16].

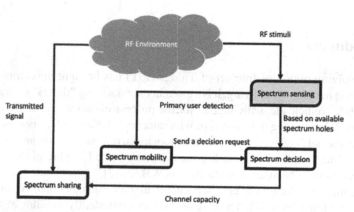

Fig. 1. Cognitive Radio cycle [15, 16].

Owing to its growing influence and need, spectrum sensing techniques are classified into different types such as cyclostationary based, energy detection based, matched filter based, eigen value based, primary receiver-based detection, covariance based, distributed & centralized based sensing etc. [17–19]. The computational simplicity & cost effectiveness of energy detection-based spectrum sensing (EDSS) has garnered its high experimentation & exploration [20]. However, in low SNR conditions EDSS encounters

Noise uncertainty issues, affecting the detection robustness. Even if detection is performed over larger duration spectrum detection remains unreliable [21, 22]. This susceptibility of EDSS in presence of noise uncertainty as stated in [23] can be addressed using dynamic threshold selection. Authors of [24] have proposed an approach for optimal threshold selection in low SNR environment. This approach provides better throughput than traditional constant detection rate selection. Similarly, authors of [25] have presented a certain relation between Dynamic threshold with Noise uncertainty factor in low SNR conditions.

Use of relay nodes in a communication model significantly boosts the entire capability of a system. There are various literatures incorporating relays in WBAN systems such as authors of [26] have maximized the system reliability & efficiency by proposing a three-stage cooperation of relays in WBAN. They have also presented an analytical expression of Energy efficiency (EE) & Packet error rate (PER). Authors of [27] have used decode & forward relaying with maximum ratio combining at receiver end of a WBAN and have investigated its performance in cooperative communication. They have also compared it with direct communication, concluding that cooperation-based communication is superior. In [28] authors have designed two master nodes based on cognitive cooperative communication in a WBAN model. This model pursues the heavy traffic issue as well as provides better transmission quality relative to direct communication.

Based on studied literature, this paper attempts to study the effect of multiple relays on probability of detection (P_D) for wearable WBAN users operating in Industrial Scientific & Medical band (ISM) (unlicensed) i.e., 2.4 GHz. The contribution of the paper is:

1. Implementation of EDSS on WBAN devices working in Wireless medical telemetry service (420–450 MHz) frequency band as primary network based on CM3A channel model.
2. Change in value of Probability of detection (P_D) as a result of Dynamic Threshold, Noise uncertainty & sampling time (N_S) for zero relay & multi relay WBAN.

The remainder paper is structured as follows: Sect. 2 outlines a brief description of Wireless Body Area Network. Section 3 gives an overview of energy detection-based spectrum sensing approach in proposed system model. The performance analysis parameters are explained in Sect. 4. Simulation results and discussion are presented in Sect. 5, followed by the conclusion in Sect. 6.

2 Wireless Body Area Network

It may be described as a network mesh of miniature size, low power, light weight sensor nodes attached outside or placed inside a human body for 24/7 supervision of a person's biological signals such as electrocardiogram (ECG), blood pressure, glucose level, temperature, heart beat etc. [29]. One can say that WBAN has unearthed advanced level of human body monitoring system. Hence it has been acknowledged & employed in medical as well as several non-medical applications. Spectrum regulators adopted the Fixed Spectrum Access policy (FSA) to allot a fixed frequency band to dedicated users known as licensed users & the equivalent spectrum as licensed spectrum [15]. The unauthorised users are called as unlicensed users. Like any other technology WBAN also operates in a given spectrum resource. Summary of operating frequency bands (licensed and unlicenced) allocated for WBAN is mentioned Table 1 given below.

Table 1. WBAN operating spectrum.

Operating band	Frequency range
Human body communications (HBC)	5–50 MHz [30, 31]
Medical implant communication service spectrum (MICS)	402–405 MHz [30, 31]
Medical device radio communications	401–406,413–419,426 -432,438–444,451–457 MHz [30]
Wireless medical telemetry service (WMTS)	420–450 MHz [32] 608–614,1395–1400, 1427–1432 MHz [30, 31]
Industrial, scientific and medical (ISM)	2360–2500 MHz [30, 31]
Ultra-wideband (UWB)	3.1–10.6 GHz [30, 31]

The 2.4 GHz ISM band is the only unlicensed band which also incorporates WBAN devices. Some of the WBAN licensed spectrum are MICS & WMTS band. This reveals the issue of static spectrum as a resource when subjected to competition with different technologies working in unlicensed spectrum. Therefore, an Energy detection spectrum sensing (EDSS) approach in WBAN model with its effect on relays is presented in next section.

3 System Model and Spectrum Sensing Approach

This paper proposes a EDSS based WBAN communication model having multi relay system. The primary network assumed is WBAN communication operating in licensed WMTS spectrum. Whereas sensing is performed by WBAN wearables accommodating 2.4 GHz ISM band. A general architecture of CR enabled WBAN model implementing EDSS is depicted in Fig. 2.

In EDSS, the PUs signal $S(n)$ is detected based upon the energy level, $Y(n)$, measured by the energy (ED) detector over defined sampling time (N_S) with the help of a predefine threshold value (γ). The ED postulates two testing binary hypothesis determining the present state or absent state of PU as given in [14] & given as:

$$
\begin{aligned}
H_0 &: Y(n) = W(n) && : \text{PU absent} \\
H_1 &: Y(n) = S(n) + W(n) && : \text{PU present}
\end{aligned}
\tag{1}
$$

Here, $W(n)$ is additive white Gaussian noise having zero mean present in the network.

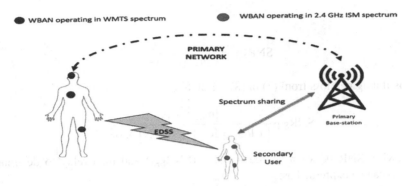

Fig. 2. EDSS based WBAN architecture.

3.1 PUs SNR Calculation

As stated earlier, in EDSS PUs SNR plays a key role in determining the present state of a PU by CR. Hence PUs SNR calculation in proposed multi-relay based WBAN model employing two relays has been discussed in detail. Figure 3 shows the diagrammatic view of considered primary WBAN model. It can be discerned from Fig. 3 that the considered model supports both relay & non-relay-based communication. It comprises of four components that is a source node (S), two relay nodes (R1 & R2) & destination node (D). Both the non-relay & relay assisted WBAN model communicate wirelessly. To imitate this wireless nature of communication channel, a suitable pathloss model is inevitable.

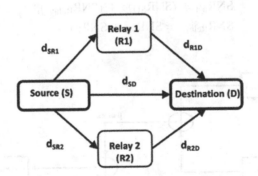

Fig. 3. Uplink non-relay & relay based WBAN model.

For on-body WBAN devices operating in WMTS spectrum a CM3A pathloss model for nodes at distance d having a & b as coefficients of liner fitting & N is normally distributed variable with standard deviation σ_N as stated in [33] is given as:

$$PL_{S,D}(dB) = a \; \log_{10}(d) + b + N \tag{2}$$

SNR between any node S & D having unit channel gain (h_{SD}), transmission power (p_t), path loss between them as $PL_{S,D}$ and noise variance σ^2 based on [33] is expressed as:

$$SNR_{S,D} = \frac{|h_{S,D}| \times p_t}{PL_{S,D} \times \sigma^2} \tag{3}$$

Substituting pathloss from (7) in (8) we obtain:

$$SNR_{S,D} \frac{|h_{S,D}| \times p_t}{[a \ \log_{10}(d_{S,D}) + b + N] \times \sigma^2} \tag{4}$$

Likewise, SNR between source to relay (SNR_{SRi}) and then relay to destination (SNR_{RiD}) can be expressed as:

$$SNR_{S,Ri} = \frac{|h_{S,Ri}| \times p_t}{[a \ \log_{10}(d_{S,Ri}) + b + N] \times \sigma^2} \tag{5}$$

$$SNR_{Ri,D} = \frac{|h_{Ri,D}| \times p_t}{[a \ \log_{10}(d_{Ri,D}) + b + N] \times \sigma^2} \tag{6}$$

3.2 SNR Combining Diversity

The central thought of cooperative communication is to improve the altogether system potential. This is done by the induction of SNR combining diversity exercised at destination end. The mathematical expression as well as its diagrammatic representation is given in Eq. (7) & Fig. 4 respectively

$$SNR_{net} = (SNR_{SD})\alpha + (SNR_{Relays})\beta$$
$$SNR_{Relays} = SNR_{R1} + SNR_{R2} \tag{7}$$

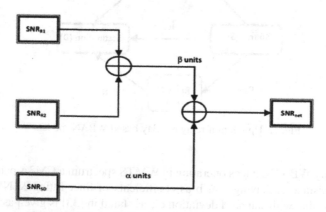

Fig. 4. SNR combining diversity at receiver (gateway).

SNR_{Ri} denotes the SNR computed with the help of 'i' number of relays & SNR_{net} is the total SNR we obtain after applying SNR combining diversity for 'i = 1, 2' relays.

The proposed diversity combines the SNR calculated by cumulative relays & SNR with direct communication i.e., without relays in % ratio of 5:95. This process significantly increases the PUs SNR in relay assisted WBAN communication. This gives rise to high SNR scenario for relay aided WBAN model. EDSS in high SNR network will always give high value to probability of detection even if there are lesser devices operating. To overcome this problem, SNR threshold term is proposed.

3.3 SNR Threshold

SNR threshold (SNR_{th}) is defined as that value to SNR below which concentration of PUs is comparatively less. This term clears the incorrect detection of high density of PUs due to original high SNR value. It defines two states as given in following expression:

$$SNR_{th} \leq SNR_{Com} : \text{ less number of PU present}$$
$$SNR_{th} > SNR_{Com} : \text{ more number of PU present} \qquad (8)$$

Regardless, in both the conditions correct detection is solely dependent upon the value of probability of detection. Computed SNR (SNR_{Com}) for without relay (W0R), with one relay (W1R) & with two relays (W2R) is calculated and then its average is designated value of SNR_{th} in considered WBAN model. For calculation of probability of detection in different scenarios based on SNR threshold concept the SNR terms are substituted with a relative SNR i.e. ($SNR_{Com} - SNR_{th}$).

4 Performance Analysis Parameters

This section lists the parameters used in performance analysis of EDSS WBAN model.

4.1 Probability of Detection (P_D)

It is the principal analysis criterion involved in estimation of spectrum environment of a primary network. It represents the correctly predicted state of a PU in target spectrum [34]. Their mathematically expression as stated in [35, 36] is expressed as:

$$P_D = Q \left\{ \frac{\gamma - (P + \sigma_n^2)}{\sqrt{2(P + \sigma_n^2)^2 / N_S}} \right\} \qquad (9)$$

where the average signal power is denoted as P, σ_n^2 is the noise variance and Q(.) is the Gaussian complementary distribution function. The predefined threshold is expressed as γ with sampling time as N_S.

4.2 Noise Uncertainty (ρ)

Noise uncertainty factor determines the influence of noise in the operating system and is denoted as ρ. Its assumed value is always greater than unity. Induction of Noise uncertainty influences the noise variance σ_n^2 in the system such that it lies within c σ_n^2/ρ, $\rho\sigma_n^2$. Time interval. In EDSS this factor greatly effects the spectrum detection performance. Its mathematical expressed in terms of Probability of false alarm (P_{FA}), replacement of SNR term with relative SNR ($SNR_{Com} - SNR_{th}$) & Probability of detection P_D as given in [35] is:

$$P_D = Q\left\{ \frac{\rho Q^{-1}(P_{FA}) - \left[(SNR_{Com} - SNR_{Th}) - \left(\rho - \frac{1}{\rho}\right)\right]\left(\sqrt{N_S/2}\right)}{\left(\frac{1}{\rho} + (SNR_{Com} - SNR_{Th})\right)} \right\} \quad (10)$$

4.3 Dynamic Threshold (ρ')

Noise uncertainty factor, whenever included in a system greatly impacts the spectrum detection process. Thus, for better spectrum sensing the concept of Dynamic threshold was introduced. It is represented as ρ' with value always greater than unity. It also influences and change the system threshold value such that it lies within time interval $\gamma \in [\gamma/\rho', \rho'\gamma]$. . In a similar its mathematical expressed in terms of Probability of false alarm (P_{FA}), replacement of SNR term with relative SNR ($SNR_{Com} - SNR_{th}$) & Probability of detection P_D in [35, 36] is:

$$P_D = Q\left\{ \frac{\rho Q^{-1}(P_{FA}) - \left[\rho'^2(SNR_{Com} - SNR_{Th}) + \left(\rho'^2 - 1\right)\right]\left(\sqrt{N_S/2}\right)}{\rho'^2(1 + (SNR_{Com} - SNR_{Th}))} \right\} \quad (11)$$

4.4 Sampling Time (N_S)

It is defined as the total sensing duration in which spectrum sensing in performed. For the last scenario, effect of probability of detection for various combinational pair of both Noise uncertainty & Dynamic threshold is considered. Here, value of threshold and noise variance lie between $[\gamma/\rho', \rho'\gamma]$ & $[\sigma_n^2/\rho, \rho\sigma_n^2]$ respectively. Its mathematical expression as given in [36] is:

$$P_D = Q\left\{ \frac{\rho Q^{-1}(P_{FA}) - \left[\rho'(SNR_{Com} - SNR_{Th}) + (\rho'/\rho - \rho/\rho')\right]\left(\sqrt{N_S/2}\right)}{\rho'^2(1/ + (SNR_{Com} - SNR_{Th}))} \right\} \quad (12)$$

MATLAB analysis of P_D for multi relay WBAN system w.r.t Noise uncertainty, Dynamic threshold & sampling time is simulated and talked about in next section.

Table 3. Value of fixed parameters.

Parameters	Values
Transmitted signal power (P_T)	25 μw
Coefficient for linear fitting (a & b)	9.2 & 3.38
Noise variance (σ^2)	–201 dB
Normally distributed variable with standard deviation σ_N (N)	4.40
Frequency band	WMTS (420–450 MHz)
Channel model	CM3A
Probability of false alarm (P_{FA})	0.5

5 Simulation Results and Discussion

This section gives forth a comprehensive MATLAB analysis of spectrum detection for multi relay WBAN system based on the derived formulations with respect to different parameters such as Noise uncertainty, Dynamic threshold & Sampling time (N_S). Fixed values assumed of different parameters in considered WBAN system is stated in following Table 3:

In this paper spectrum sensing in different scenarios has been studied and stated as follows:

5.1 Noise Uncertainty

Current work tries to analyze effect of Noise uncertainty factor in multi relay WBAN system on probability of detection (P_D). Table 4 depicts the numerical results obtained through Eq. (10), when P_D calculated for Noise uncertainty at changing values i.e., 1.01 to 1.06 and its graphical representation is shown in Fig. 5.

Table 4. P_D versus Noise uncertainty variation for multi relays at sampling time (N_S) = 200.

Noise uncertainty factor (ρ)	Probability of detection (P_D) at N_S = 200		
	W2R	W1R	W0R
1.01	1.0000	0.8960	0.5231
1.02	1.0000	0.8795	0.4839
1.03	1.0000	0.8612	0.4448
1.04	1.0000	0.8412	0.4062
1.05	1.0000	0.8193	0.3686
1.06	1.0000	0.7957	0.3321

The graph clearly shows that increase in Noise uncertainty factor deteriorates spectrum detection in considered WBAN system. If we see in terms of relays, it can be said that good number of relays have a constructive effect on probability of detection. It can be confirmed from the graph that probability of detection vs Noise uncertainty with 2 relay (W2R) system performs the best followed by 1 relay (W1R) and then without relay (W0R) at $N_S = 200$ & $P_{FA} = 0.5$. For fixed number of samples $N_S = 200$ and increasing value of Noise uncertainty $\rho = 1.01$ to 1.06 the detection probability from W0R to W1R and then from W1R to W2R system increases to approximately 49.9% & 18% respectively. This simply implies that spectrum detection at lower values of Noise uncertainty factor with higher number of relay assistance is optimal.

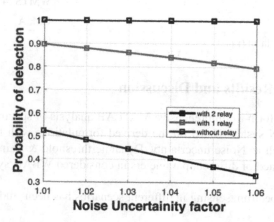

Fig. 5. P_D versus Noise uncertainty variation for multi relays at sampling time $(N_S) = 200$.

5.2 Dynamic Threshold

Table 5 depicts the numerical results obtained through Eq. (11), when P_D calculated for different values of Dynamic threshold from 1 to 1.05 and its graphical representation is shown in Fig. 6.

Table 5. P_D versus Dynamic threshold variation for multi relays at sampling time $(N_S) = 200$.

Dynamic threshold factor (ρ')	Probability of detection (P_D) at $N_S = 200$		
	W2R	W1R	W0R
1.01	1.0000	0.9439	0.6804
1.02	1.0000	0.9662	0.7705
1.03	1.0000	0.9767	0.8222
1.04	1.0000	0.9843	0.8662
1.05	1.0000	0.9898	0.9025
1.06	1.0000	0.9935	0.9311

From the graph it can be stated that there is a positive response of Dynamic threshold factor against probability of detection. Similarly, with increasing relay assistance the spectrum detection reaches maximum value of 1. Here also the probability of detection with 2 relay (W2R) system outshines others followed by 1 relay (W1R) and then without relay (W0R) at $N_S = 200$ & $P_{FA} = 0.5$. For fixed number of samples $N_S = 200$ and increasing value of Dynamic threshold $\rho' = 1$ to 1.05 the detection probability from W0R to W1R and then from W1R to W2R system increases to approximately 18.82% & 2.51% respectively. This indicates that higher value of Dynamic threshold combined with a greater number of relays provides peak value of probability of detection.

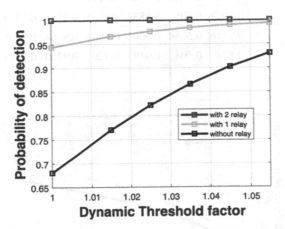

Fig. 6. P_D versus Dynamic threshold variation for multi relays at sampling time $(N_S) = 200$.

5.3 Sampling Time (N_S)

Table 6 depicts the numerical results obtained through Eq. (12), when P_D calculated at a different values of sampling time (N_S) of 10, 20, 50, 90, 110 & 170 in proximity of both dynamic threshold & noise uncertainty.

Its MATLAB simulated plot for without relay (W0R) & with 1 relay (W1R) is presented in Fig. 7 & Fig. 8 respectively. Both the plots show that sensing for a more sampling time (N_S) gives better value of probability of detection. For in depth analysis, four different combinations of Noise uncertainty & Dynamic threshold are taken. Out of all $\rho = 1.001$, $\rho' = 1.035$ pair performs the best and $\rho = 1.05$, $\rho' = 1.025$ pair gives an unacceptable performance in both W0R & W1R scenarios. In 1 relay system (W1R) for $\rho = 1.05$, $\rho' = 1.015$ pair to $\rho = 1.011$, $\rho' = 1.035$ pair there is approximate increase of 13.4% in spectrum detection performance.

Similarly, when calculated for without relay system (W0R) for $\rho = 1.05$, $\rho' = 1.015$ pair to $\rho = 1.011$, $\rho' = 1.035$ pair there is approximate increase of 40.03% in spectrum detection performance. It may be said that high value of dynamic threshold with low value of Noise uncertainty factor form the best combination among all. For fixed pair of values $\rho = 1.02$, $\rho' = 1.03$ from without relay to with 1 relay, spectrum detection

Table 6. P_D versus N_S in presence of Dynamic threshold & Noise uncertainty

Number of Samples (N_S)	Probability of detection (P_D)							
	$\rho = 1.05, \rho' = 1.025$		$\rho = 1.02, \rho' = 1.03$		$\rho = 1.001, \rho' = 1.035$		$\rho = 1.001, \rho' = 1.015$	
	W1R	W0R	W1R	W0R	W1R	W0R	W1R	W0R
10	0.6094	0.5019	0.6544	0.5588	0.6772	0.5883	0.6450	0.5492
20	0.6528	0.5027	0.7129	0.5829	0.7422	0.6239	0.7005	0.5694
50	0.7328	0.5043	0.8128	0.6297	0.8481	0.6912	0.7972	0.6089
90	0.7977	0.5058	0.8834	0.6715	0.9161	0.7485	0.8677	0.6447
110	0.8216	0.5064	0.9062	0.6882	0.9364	0.7705	0.8913	0.6591
170	0.8740	0.508	0.9493	0.7291	0.9710	0.8213	0.9374	0.6949

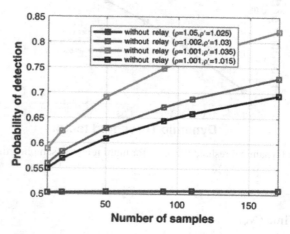

Fig. 7. P_D versus N_S in presence of Dynamic threshold & Noise uncertainty (W0R system).

increases by 26.98%. This highly shows that relay assisted system increases the spectrum detection even in presence of high noise uncertainty factor.

6 Conclusion

Current work scrutinizes the operation of EDSS in WBAN communication model. The effect of relays on resultant value of probability of detection (P_D) in closeness with Noise uncertainty, Dynamic threshold and Sampling time (N_S) is investigated and studied. The simulated results states that probability of detection vs Noise uncertainty with 2 relay (W2R) system performs the best followed by 1 relay (W1R) and then without relay (W0R) at $N_S = 200$ & $P_{FA} = 0.5$. For fixed number of samples $N_S = 200$ and increasing value of Noise uncertainty $\rho = 1.01$ to 1.06 the detection probability from W0R to W1R and then from W1R to W2R system increases to approximately 49.9% & 18%

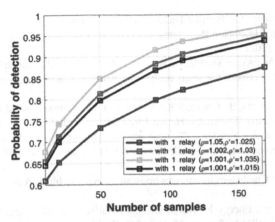

Fig. 8. P_D versus N_S in presence of Dynamic threshold & Noise uncertainty (W1R system).

respectively. In presence of Dynamic threshold, for fixed number of samples $N_S = 200$ and increasing value of Dynamic threshold $\rho' = 1$ to 1.05 the detection probability from W0R to W1R and then from W1R to W2R system increases to approximately 18.82% & 2.51% respectively. Similarly, in 1 relay system (W1R) for $\rho = 1.05$, $\rho' = 1.025$ pair to $\rho = 1.001$, $\rho' = 1.035$ pair there is approximate increase of 13.4% in spectrum detection performance. When calculated for without relay system (W0R) for $\rho = 1.05$, $\rho' = 1.025$ pair to $\rho = 1.001$, $\rho' = 1.035$ pair there is approximate increase of 40.03% in spectrum detection performance. For fixed pair of values $\rho = 1.02$, $\rho' = 1.03$ from without relay to with 1 relay, spectrum detection increases by 26.98%. These results infer that multi relays have a productive role in improving the spectrum performance. Dynamic Threshold & sampling time (N_S) significantly refines the spectrum sensing performance whereas Noise uncertainty factor impairs proper spectrum sensing process.

References

1. Reggio, G., Leotta, M., Cerioli, M., Spalazzese, R., Alkhabbas, F.: What are IoT systems for real? An experts' survey on software engineering aspects. Internet Things **12**, 100313 (2020)
2. Nižetić, S., Šolić, P., González-de, D.L.D.I., Patrono, L.: Internet of Things (IoT): opportunities, issues and challenges towards a smart and sustainable future. J. Clean. Prod. **274**, 122877 (2020)
3. Poongodi, T., Rathee, A., Indrakumari, R., Suresh, P.: IoT sensing capabilities: sensor deployment and node discovery, wearable sensors, wireless body area network (WBAN), data acquisition. In: Peng, SL., Pal, S., Huang, L. (eds.) Principles of Internet of Things (IoT) Ecosystem: Insight Paradigm. Intelligent Systems Reference Library, vol. 174, pp. 127–151. Springer, Cham (2020). https://doi.org/10.1007/978-3-030-33596-0_5
4. Wang, J., et al.: A logistic mapping-based encryption scheme for wireless body area networks. Futur. Gener. Comput. Syst. **110**, 57–67 (2020)
5. Arfaoui, A., Boudia, O.R.M., Kribeche, A., Senouci, S.M., Hamdi, M.: Context-aware access control and anonymous authentication in WBAN. Comput. Secur. **88**, 101496 (2020)
6. Akkaş, M.A., Sokullu, R., Cetin, H.E.: Healthcare and patient monitoring using IoT. Internet Things **11**, 100173 (2020)

7. Roy, S., Chowdhury, C.: Remote health monitoring protocols for IoT-enabled healthcare infrastructure. In: Healthcare Paradigms in the Internet of Things Ecosystem, pp. 163–188. Academic Press (2021)

8. Ahad, A., Tahir, M., Aman Sheikh, M., Ahmed, K.I., Mughees, A., Numani, A.: Technologies trend towards 5G network for smart health-care using IoT: a review. Sensors **20**(14), 4047 (2020)

9. Chakraborty, C., Gupta, B., Ghosh, S.K.: A review on telemedicine-based WBAN framework for patient monitoring. Telemed. e-Health **19**(8), 619–626 (2020)

10. Taleb, H., Nasser, A., Andrieux, G., Charara, N., Motta Cruz, E.: Wireless technologies, medical applications and future challenges in WBAN: a survey. Wirel. Netw. **27**(8), 5271–5295 (2021)

11. Asam, M., et al.: Challenges in wireless body area network. Int. J. Adv. Comput. Sci. Appl. **10**(11) (2019)

12. Khan, M.D., et al.: Energy harvested and cooperative enabled efficient routing protocol (EHCRP) for IoT-WBAN. Sensors **20**(21), 6267 (2020)

13. Xu, Z., Xu, C., Chen, H., Yang, F.: A lightweight anonymous mutual authentication and key agreement scheme for WBAN. Concurr. Comput. Pract. Exp. **31**(14), e5295 (2019)

14. Nadeem, A., Khan, M., Han, K.: Non-cooperative spectrum sensing in context of primary user detection: a review. IETE Tech. Rev. **34**(2), 188–200 (2017)

15. Motta, M.: A survey on data and decision fusion strategies on spectrum sensing in cognitive radio networks. Int. J. Adv. Res. Comput. Commun. Eng. **3**(07), 7510–7518 (2014)

16. Sharma, V., Joshi, S.: A Literature review on spectrum sensing in cognitive radio applications. In: Second International Conference on Intelligent Computing and Control Systems (ICICCS), pp. 883–893 (2018)

17. Arjoune, Y., Kaabouch, N.: A comprehensive survey on spectrum sensing in cognitive radio networks: recent advances, new challenges, and future research directions. Sensors **19**(1), 126 (2019)

18. Ramani, V., Sharma, S.K.: Cognitive radios: a survey on spectrum sensing, security and spectrum handoff. China Commun. **14**(11), 185–208 (2017)

19. Kakalou, I., Papadopoulou, D., Xifilidis, T., Psannis, K.E., Siakavara, K., Ishibashi, Y.: A survey on spectrum sensing algorithms for cognitive radio networks. In: 2018 7th International Conference on Modern Circuits and Systems Technologies (MOCAST), pp. 1–4. IEEE (2018)

20. Syed, T.S., Safdar, G.A.: History-assisted energy-efficient spectrum sensing for infrastructure-based cognitive radio networks. IEEE Trans. Veh. Technol. **66**(3), 2462–2473 (2016)

21. Tandra, R., Sahai, A.: SNR walls for signal detection. IEEE J. Sel. Top. Signal Process. **2**(1), 4–17 (2008)

22. Yao, J., Jin, M., Guo, Q., Li, Y., Xi, J.: Effective energy detection for IoT systems against noise uncertainty at low SNR. IEEE Internet Things J. **6**(4), 6165–6176 (2018)

23. Lorincz, J., Ramljak, I., Begušić, D.: A review of the noise uncertainty impact on energy detection with different OFDM system designs. Comput. Commun. **148**, 185–207 (2019)

24. Kumar, A., Thakur, P., Pandit, S., Singh, G.: Analysis of optimal threshold selection for spectrum sensing in a cognitive radio network: an energy detection approach. Wirel. Netw. **25**(7), 3917–3931 (2019)

25. Mahendru, G., Shukla, A.K.: Effect of dynamic threshold on sensing duration for robust detection in cognitive radio systems for low SNR scenarios. In: 2017 3rd International Conference on Advances in Computing, Communication & Automation (ICACCA) (Fall), pp. 1–5. IEEE (2017)

26. Yousaf, S., Javaid, N., Khan, Z.A., Qasim, U., Imran, M., Iftikhar, M.: Incremental relay based cooperative communication in wireless body area networks. Procedia Comput. Sci. **52**, 552–559 (2015)

27. Paul, P.M., Babu, A.V.: Performance evaluation of cooperative communication in WBANs with maximal ratio combining. In: 2015 International Conference on Computing and Network Communications (CoCoNet), pp. 627–632. IEEE (2015)

28. Alkhayyat, A., Sadkhan, S.B., Abbasi, Q.H.: Multiple traffics support in wireless body area network over cognitive cooperative communication. In: 2019 2nd International Conference on Electrical, Communication, Computer, Power and Control Engineering (ICECCPCE), pp. 199–203. IEEE (2019)

29. Ayed, S., Chaari, L., Fares, A.: A survey on trust management for WBAN: investigations and future directions. Sensors **20**(21), 6041 (2020)

30. Sodagari, S., Bozorgchami, B., Aghvami, H.: Technologies and challenges for cognitive radio enabled medical wireless body area networks. IEEE Access **6**, 29567–29586 (2018)

31. Hasan, K., Biswas, K., Ahmed, K., Nafi, N.S., Islam, M.S.: A comprehensive review of wireless body area network. J. Netw. Comput. Appl. **143**, 178–198 (2019)

32. Gupta, S.H., Devarajan, N.: Performance exploration of on-body WBAN using CM3A-IEEE 802.15. 6 channel model. J. Ambient Intell. Humaniz. Comput. 1–12 (2020)

33. Kaushik, M., Gupta, S.H., Balyan, V.: An approach to optimize performance of CM3A cooperative WBAN operating in UWB. Sustain. Comput. Inform. Syst. **30**, 100523 (2021)

34. Akyildiz, I.F., Lo, B.F., Balakrishnan, R.: Cooperative spectrum sensing in cognitive radio networks: a survey. Phys. Commun. **4**(1), 40–62 (2011)

35. Mahendru, G., Shukla, A., Banerjee, P.: A novel mathematical model for energy detection based spectrum sensing in cognitive radio networks. Wirel. Pers. Commun. **110**(3), 1237–1249 (2020)

36. KKorumilli, C., Gadde, C., Hemalatha, I.: Performance analysis of energy detection algorithm in cognitive radio. Int. J. Eng. Res. Appl. **2**(4), 1004–1009 (2012)

Methodologies to Classify Faults in Power Transmission Lines

V. Rajesh Kumar[1]([✉]), P. Aruna Jeyanthy[2], R. Kesavamoorthy[3], and K. Mahesh[1]

[1] Sir M. Visvesvaraya Institute of Technology, Bengaluru, India
vsr2787@gmail.com, drmaheshk_eee@sirmvit.edu
[2] Kalasalingam Academy of Research and Education, Krishnankoil, Virudhunagar, India
p.arunajeyanthy@klu.edu.in
[3] CMR Institute of Technology, Bengaluru, India
kesavamoorthy.r@cmrit.ac.in

Abstract. The vast array of electrical power systems and its applications necessitates the development of appropriate fault classifications algorithms in an electrical power transmission lines in order to improve the efficiency of the system and avert catastrophic damage. A wide variety of methods are proposed in the technical literature for this goal. This survey paper examines different methodologies used to classify faults in an electrical power transmission lines as and summaries its key approach.

Keywords: fault analysis · fault identification · fault detection · SVM · GSM · Pilot Scheme

1 Introduction

Safeguarding electric power lines requires the utmost responsibility of protecting transmission lines from potential faults. The recognition of anomalous signals that signify defects in a power transmission system is achieved through the use of protective relaying. In a transmission line, swift and accurate fault classification is crucial for efficient protective relaying, thereby ensuring uninterrupted power supply. Engineers are becoming more interested in soft computing techniques as a result of recent technical advancements. Previously, numerous scholars presented various fault categorization systems. The issue is that when a new user begins their investigation in this field, he or she may be confused about which method to apply to classify the type of the error. Because so many researchers have previously devised several ways, each of which has its own set of pros and cons. So, by selecting papers from reputable publications, this review article will provide a clear overview of all the existing fault classification algorithms. The simulation process can be carried out using a variety of software.

1.1 Background

Transporting power a power grid begins with power transmission, which involves fundamental components such as transformers, switches, towers, relays, power lines, and

R. S. Tomar et al. (Eds.): CNC 2022, CCIS 1893, pp. 66–77, 2023.
https://doi.org/10.1007/978-3-031-43140-1_7

reclosers, as shown in Fig. 1. This system is vulnerable to several challenges that includes power loss that converts to thermal energy (I2R), where I represent current, and R represents resistance. The skin effect is another challenge that leads to increased resistance. If not human, these contribute to transmission element faults.

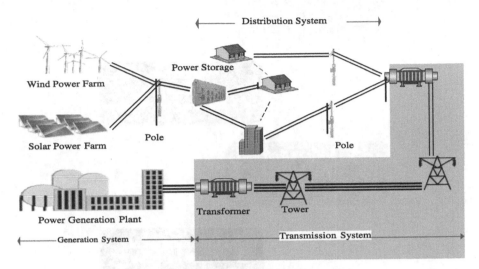

Fig. 1. A schematic of a transmission system.

A recent review [1] in this field presented various techniques but the review was lacking a clear taxonomy. To address this issue, researchers employed fault-analysis methods to classify previous works. Other surveys categorized the works differently, based on their computational intelligence features.

1.2 Review Methodology

Figure 2 depicts a flowchart that provides a clear and concise visual representation of the different constituents of our approach. Although the subsequent sections contain detailed descriptions of each component, this flowchart presents our review approach as a cohesive whole.

The following is a breakdown of how this article was put together. First, Sect. 1 provides the classification of faults and monitoring. Section 3 focuses on the fault analysis techniques followed by Sect. 4 that reviews the methods used for fault identification with a summary at the end. The concluding remarks of the paper is presented in Sect. 5.

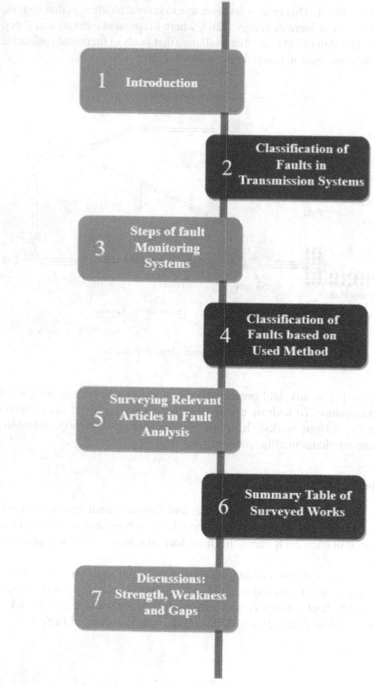

Fig. 2. The Route Flow of our Review Approach.

2 Fault Classification and Monitoring

Figure 3 shows that transmission power systems can encounter various types of faults, classified as transient and intransient. Transient faults are typically difficult to locate and may not be visible to power technicians. These faults can cause temporary power outages that are restored once the fault clears. Examples of transient faults include tree branches or animals contacting power lines, lightning strikes, and storm-related phase clashing. In contrast, intransient faults are permanent [2].

Open-circuit faults can produce very high which can cause voltage instability and may even develop into short-circuit faults, posing a danger to humans and animals.

Short-circuit faults cause unpredictable events such as severe weather conditions, animals, supply/demand unbalancing, and aging. Compared to open-circuit faults, short-circuit faults can cause more severe damage and require prompt attention from power technicians to ensure public safety and system stability.

Transmission power systems are vulnerable to faults that can be classified as transient or intransient, with the former being difficult to locate and the latter being permanent until fixed by power engineers. Intransient faults can be open-circuit or short-circuit faults. Open-circuit faults can be classified into phase or ground faults.

Resiliency and self-healing processes are crucial to maintaining the reliability of power grids. Sensors can be deployed to enable legacy power grids to assess parameters such as active current, voltage, phasors, etc., and act proactively to prevent faults. Furthermore, the power in a transmission line can flow in either direction according to the load at the two ends, and hence the information from the endpoints of transmission lines is necessary to develop a holistic picture of the state of a transmission system.

To address this limitation, researchers have proposed various fault localization techniques that leverage advanced technologies such as data analytics, machine learning, and artificial intelligence. These techniques use sensor data to estimate the location of the fault and identify the affected components, thus expediting the repair process and minimizing power outage time.

One common approach is the use of phasor measurement units (PMUs) that measure the current, voltage, and phase angle at different locations within the transmission system. These measurements are then used to estimate the fault location and type.

Another approach is the use of artificial neural networks (ANNs) that can learn the normal behavior of the power system and detect anomalies, including faults. Furthermore, researchers have proposed the use of big data analytics to process the vast amounts of sensor data generated by modern power grids. This approach can provide a comprehensive view of the power system and detect faults before they cause significant damage.

In summary, fault localization in transmission power systems is critical for maintaining the system's resilience and reducing outage time. Advanced techniques such as PMUs, ANNs, and big data analytics can significantly improve fault localization accuracy and speed up the repair process, ultimately improving the overall reliability of the power grid.

Recent research has combined the wavelet transform with other tools such as entropy-based methods to accurately and quickly identify the characteristics with sufficient

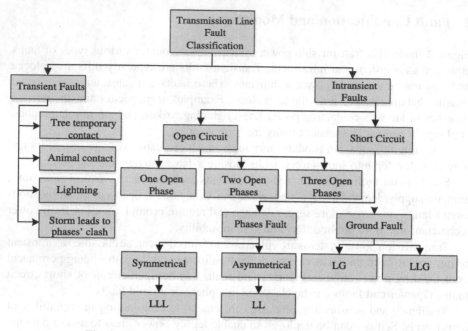

Fig. 3. Classification of faults in overhead transmission lines.

noise tolerance. Fault-monitoring systems have three primary objectives: detection, identification or classification, and localization, as illustrated in Fig. 4.

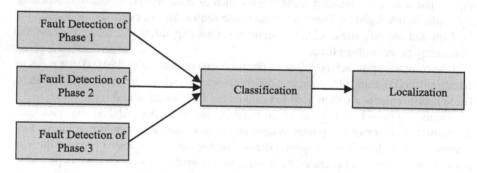

Fig. 4. Steps in fault-monitoring systems.

Fault detection involves identifying instability in the transmission system. Second step is classifying and identifying the fault type. Monitoring all transmission lines enables better identification of fault types. The final step is fault localization, which involves locating the fault precisely.

3 Fault Analysis Techniques

This article presents a new method for classifying fault analysis techniques based on their tasks, such as detection, identification, and localization, and the methods employed. Figure 5 illustrates the classification of fault analysis techniques according to the methods they use. The techniques can be categorized into conventional or modern approaches for analyzing faults.

If a fault is cleared after breaker reclosing, it is temporary, while a permanent fault needs to be repaired to restore power service. Despite being fast and reliable, Distance relays are not sufficiently accurate in localizing faults. To address this limitation, other techniques are necessary to identify and classify faults.

Wavelet-based techniques are effective in analyzing transient power faults, especially for fault detection and localization [3, 4]. Maximum wavelet coefficients (WCs) can be used to improve fault detection and location accuracy.

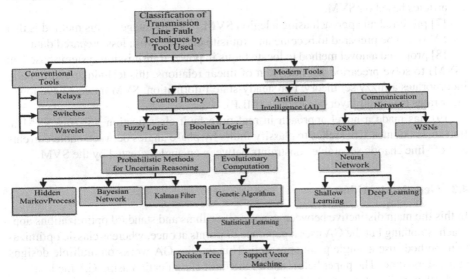

Fig. 5. Classification of fault analysis techniques.

In [5], an equation was developed using only the wavelet readings. Fault localization was achieved by dividing the circuit into two parts: before and during the fault. Each part provided an equation for the current and voltage.

4   Review on Fault Classification Methods

Feature extraction is a crucial step in analyzing faults in power grids, as it enables the correct setup of most fault analysis methods. AI-based systems depend on the mined features. Clustering techniques can then use these extracted features to divide the power grid and identify the fault place [6]. The significance and application of this topic are broad and diverse, as emphasized multiple times in the text.

4.1   (SVM) Support Vector Machine

Support Vector Machine is a unique approach to learn about (Pattern recognition functions) separately to classify the tasks or to perform functioning estimation in regression issues (SVM). It's a statistical learning theory-based computer learning technique. In this approach the input vectors are unsystematically mapped onto a topological feature space. It is used to solve a variety of classification issues. The following are the explanations for articles based on SVM.

[7] preferred an approach using a legion SVM. The advantage in this method is that the SVM can be prepared to become an exquisite classifier with less prepared data.

[8] proposed a novel method to locate faults in power transmission systems based on (SVM) to solve precariousness division of linear relations, this technique additionally incorporates a fuzzy set theory. For steady-state information, SVM models have lower error rates than multilayer perceptions (MLP).

[9] has made a novel approach in real time fault classification utilizing SVM in transmission lines. This relies to classify faults by phase angles between cable currents and off-line chaotic separable constraints between an angles created by the SVM.

4.2   Genetic Algorithm

In this the main distinctive between genetic algorithms and standard optimizations approach is nothing but the GA uses a populace of points at once, whereas classic optimization methods use a single point approach. This implies GA works on multiple designs at the same time. The paper below shows the fault classification using GA method.

[10] introduced a new methodology based on genetic algorithm neural network (GANN).

4.3   DWT-ELM Approach

In a series indemnify transmission framework, the method gives an accurate hybrid strategy for fault classification. Fusion of Discrete-Wavelet-Transform (DWT) and Extreme-Learning-Machine (ELM) is utilized to classify the fault. The suggested fault classifier is compared and has been found that this type of classifier has higher accuracy as well as it takes a less duration to learn than any other [11].

4.4 FPGA Method

The use of Field Programmable Gate Array (FPGA) in the branch of electric power systems is increasing due to new advancements in the FPGA leading edge technology mostly in the hardware and software. And due to the reduction in cost. [12] provided a fault analysis in electric transmission lines by FPGA method.

4.5 GSM Method

[13] created a massive GSM approach that can be used to improve the reliability of previously built special protection systems during network outages. Here, a significant GSM is used to send information from one network to another and also to identify any changes in transmission parameters to secure the entire transmission and distribution process.

4.6 PMU Method

[14] proposed a PMU-based protection mechanism. It demonstrated an adaptive transmission system protection strategy based on synchronised phasor readings. The protection scheme for the phasor measuring unit (PMU). To reach the whole line protection, this technique used synchronised phasor quantity to construct a multi-functional protecting relays.

4.7 Decision Tree Based Method

This is certainly the ultimate advanced approach to split the sample information into a set of decision protocols. Tree classification are also called as decision tree which is used to solve classification problems. The below publications shows the decision tree method process aids to classify the faults.

A decision tree method created by [15] is used in the power transmission system to classify faults.

4.8 Motley-Information Measurements

[16] developed a unique method to classify fault based on motley-information measurements of fault ephemeral, as well as information entropy and complexity measurements. This approach can be used with a variety of transitory components.

4.9 Fast Estimation Method Using Phasor Components

[17] suggested a new approach for identifying problematic phases in transmission systems. This proposed approach was based on phase current readings and quick phasor component estimating in a limited information window. The key collection technique makes use of the relationships between current magnitudes for various fault loops. By the use of neutral and phase currents, this approach can distinguish between grounded and ungrounded faults.

4.10 PCA Method

[18] suggested a novel fault classification approach. This research depends on phase currents in the initial 1/4th of a cycle in a consolidated system that utilizes the symmetrical components method and principal component investigation to deliver unrivaled discoveries (PCA). This algorithm has the advantage of being able to be utilised at either extremity of a transmission lines and eliminating the exigency for data communication devices.

4.11 Pilot Method

[19] proposed a new method of classification for faults based on reactive power in both usual and fault conditions. The indication of reactive power estimated by one relay should be connected in a pilot technique. This technique does not require any kind of setup. To specify a threshold for any parameter, the relay is not required.

4.12 FACI Method

[20] introduced a new approach that practically addresses the transmission line phases. The classification and detection technique is created using a collection of faults by simulation of a real data set, and it is evaluated using the model parameters.

5 Summary of the Fault Analysis Techniques

Table 1 provides a summary of fault analysis techniques, including whether they use one or two transmission line terminals to achieve their objective. While modern techniques like ANN and ML are increasingly being used, they may not always be effective in detecting all transient events. For instance, voltage drops due to generator malfunctions or overloading often affect all three phases equally, making it difficult for ANN to detect abnormal voltage and current differences between phases. This highlights the need for further feature engineering to account for such events.

The use of sensors is crucial for data acquisition in modern technologies, but cybersecurity is a major concern for grid operators. Cyber attackers can manipulate voltage and current readings to appear normal, leading to false negatives or positives. During normal loading, sensor readings are usually balanced. Techniques based on time difference of travelling signals for fault localization often suffer from accuracy issues due to time measurement inaccuracies.

The following table shows the comparison of fault classification techniques.

Table 1. Comparison of Fault Classification Techniques.

No	Name of the Approach	Reference Number	Techniques Used	Simulation Tools Used
1	Support vector machines	Malathi and Marimuthu (2008); Wang and Zhao (2009); Youssef (2009); Tripathi et al. (2011); Singh et al. (2011)	SVM classifier, wavelet	MATLAB SVM toolbox, EMTP, MATLAB/SIMULINK, ATP
2	Genetic algorithm	Song (1997); Upendar et al. (2008)	GA, NN	EMTP, MATLAB
3	DWT-ELM approach	Ray et al. (2012)	DWT, ELM	MATLAB/SIMULINK
4	Theory and FPGA- based implementation	Valsan and Shanti Swamp (2009)	Field-programmable gate array (FPGA)	Real time windows target toolbox of MATLAB
5	GSM technique	Sujatha and Vijay Kumar (2011)	Global system for mobile communication (GSM)	Embedded based hardware design
6	PMU-based protection scheme	Jiang et al. (2002, 2003); Rahideh et al (2013)	Phasor measurement unit	EMTP/ATP
7	Decision tree based method	Mahanty and Dutta Gupta (2004); Shahrtash and Jamehbozorg (2008); Jamehbozorg and Shahrtash (2010)	Discrete Fourier transform	EMTDC/PSC AD
8	Multi-information measurements	Ling et al. (2009)	Multi-information measurements	MATLAB
9	Fast estimation of phasor components	Saha et al. (2010a,b)	Zero-component current phasors	ATP-EMTP
10	PCA based framework	Alsafasfeh et al. (2010)	Principal component analysis	PSCAD
11	Pilot scheme	Mahamedi (2011)	Pilot scheme	MATLAB
12	Functional analysis and computational intelligence	De Souza Gomes et al (2013)	Pilot scheme	MATLAB
13	Euclidean distance based function	Prasad and Prasad (2014)	DWT	MATLAB/SIMULINK
14	Pattern recognition approach	Srinivasa Rao and Baddu Naik (2013)	Multi resolution analysis	MATLAB/SIMULINK

6   Conclusion

Several new fault classification methods, as well as their key characteristics, were incorporated in this paper. All of these approaches have unique characteristics, and research is still ongoing to reduce the operation time of relays at high speeds. As a result, new algorithms based on sophisticated optimization approaches and flexible alternating current transmission strategies are more computationally effective and suitable for real-time applications are required.

Acknowledgement. We would like to express our sincere gratitude to our colleges, Sir M. Visvesvaraya Institute of Technology, Bangalore, Kalasalingam Academy of Research and Education, Krishnankoil, CMR Institute of Technology, Bengaluru, who provided valuable support and assistance throughout the development of this paper. Their contributions were invaluable in shaping our ideas and improving the quality of our work. We also thank the experts in the field who generously shared their knowledge and experience with us during the course of this study. Their insights and feedback were instrumental in guiding our research and ensuring its relevance and accuracy. Finally, we extend our thanks to our families and loved ones for their unwavering support and encouragement, which helped us to persevere in the face of challenges and complete this work to the best of our abilities.

References

1. Liao, Y.: Generalized fault-location methods for overhead electric distribution systems Trans. Power Deliv. **26**, 53–64 (2011)
2. Abass, A.Z., Pavlyuchenko, D.A., Hussain, Z.S.: Survey about impact voltage instability and transient stability for a power system with an integrated solar combined cycle plant in iraq by using ETAP. J. Robot. Control (JRC) **2**, 134–139 (2021)
3. Yang, Z., Zhong, H., Xia, Q., Kang, C.: Optimal transmission switching with short-circuit current limitation constraints. IEEE Trans. Power Syst. **31**, 1278–1288 (2016)
4. Medeiros, R.P., Costa, F.B., Silva, K.M., Popov, M., de Chavez Muro, J.J., Lima Junior, J.R.A.: Clarke-wavelet-based time-domain power transformer differential protection. IEEE Trans. Power Deliv. **37**, 317–328 (2021)
5. Takagi, T., Yamakoshi, Y., Yamaura, M., Kondow, R., Matsushima, T.: Development of a new type fault locator using the one-terminal voltage and current data. IEEE Trans. Power Appar. Syst. **101**, 2892–2898 (1982)
6. Hassani, H., Razavi-Far, R., Saif, M.: Fault location in smart grids through multicriteria analysis of group decision support systems. IEEE Trans. Ind. Inform. **16**, 7318–7327 (2020)
7. Malathi, V., Marimuthu, N.S.: Multi-class support vector machine approach for fault classification in power transmission. In: IEEE Conference Publications, pp. 67–71 (2008)
8. Jia, Z.: Power transmission line fault classification using support vector machines". Master's theses, p. 104 (2012)
9. Rongjie, W., Haifeng, Z.: Application of SVM in fault diagnosis of power electronics rectifier. In: 7th World Congress on Intelligent Control and Automation. Chongqing, China (2008)
10. Song, Y.H.: Genetic algorithm based neural networks applied to fault classification for EHV transmission lines with a UPFC. In: IET Conference Publications, pp. 278–281 (1997)
11. Ray, P., Panigrahi, B.K., Senroy, N.: Extreme learning machine based fault classification in a series compensated transmission line. In: IEEE Conference Publications, pp. 1–6 (2012)
12. Karim, E., Memon, T., Hussain, I.: FPGA based on-line fault diagnostic of induction motors using electrical signature analysis. Int. J. Inf. Technol. **11**, 165–169 (2018). https://doi.org/10.1007/s41870-018-0238-5
13. Okokpujie, K., Elizabeth, A., Robert, O., John, S.: Monitoring and fault detection system for power transmission using GSM technology (2017)
14. Jiang, J.-A., Chen, C.-S., Liu, C.-W.: A new protection scheme for fault detection, direction discrimination, classification, and location in transmission lines. IEEE Trans. Power Deliv. **18**(1), 34–42 (2003)
15. Jamehbozorg, A., Shahrtash, S.M.: A decision-tree-based method for fault classification in single-circuit transmission lines. IEEE Trans. Power Delivery **25**(4), 2190–2196 (2010). https://doi.org/10.1109/TPWRD.2010.2053222

16. Ling, F., He, Z., Bo, Z.: Novel approach to fault classification in EHV transmission line based on multi-information measurements of fault transient. In: IEEE Conference Publications, pp. 1–4 (2009)

17. Chen, C., Liu, C., Jiang, J.: A new adaptive PMU based protection scheme for transposed/untransposed parallel transmission lines. IEEE Trans. Power Del. **17**(2), 395–404 (2002)

18. Alsafasfeh, Q., Abdel-Qader, I., Harb, A.: Symmetrical pattern and PCA based framework for fault detection and classification in power systems. In: IEEE Conference Publications, pp. 1–6 (2010)

19. Vasilic, S., Kezunovic, M.: Fuzzy art neural network algorithm for classifying the power system faults. IEEE Trans. Power Del. **20**(2), 1306–1314 (2005)

20. de Souza Gomes, A., Costa, M.A., de Faria, T.G.A., Caminhas, W.M.: Detection and classification of faults in power transmission lines using functional analysis and computational intelligence. IEEE Trans. Power Deliv. **28**(3), 1402–1413 (2013)

Recent Copy Move Forgery Detection Techniques: A Review

Nishtha Parashar[✉]

Department of CEA, GLA University, Mathura, Uttar Pradesh, India
nishtha2909@gmail.com

Abstract. Due to the advent of photo editing softwares and tools the manipulation of digital images can be performed at an ease. As a result, maintaining the authenticity and trustworthiness of digital images has become a challenging task. Thus, copy-move forgery detection (CMFD) has become one of the key domains in the current research field for the authentication of digital images. Copy-move forgery is the way of duplicating one area in an image over another in the same image. In this paper recent state of arts have been surveyed in the field of CMFD. Also, comparative evaluation of various approaches has been performed to analyze the strength and limitation when comparing one approach with another.

Keywords: Image Forgery · Copy-Move · Image Tampering · Copy-Move Forgery Detection

1 Introduction

Due to the readiness of various image editing tools and software's the attempt of manipulating digital images has become a known problem globally throughout the world on vast scale since early 90's [3]. The digital images can be very easily used due to the advancements in tools and technology and has become a matter of concern as it can be used to degrade the authenticity of the original image [1, 17, 18]. In the current era the genuineness of the digital images plays a very important role as it can be used in many sections of societies especially as evidence in a medical record of a person, in a court of law or in newsletters. Thus, digital image forgery detection plays a crucial role in image forensics [2]. Figure 1. Shows the detailed taxonomy of the fields of image forgery detection. Image-forgery detection can be categorized into two main categories namely active and passive methods. When any prior information is required about the image then it comes under active approach comprising of digital signature and digital watermarking techniques and when no prior information is required then it is referred to as passive approach. Tampering and source-device comes under this approach. However, active approach is not useful in handling the images from unknown source.

The principal objective line of this paper is to present several facets of digital image forgery detection techniques precisely focusing on copy-move forgery identification that are introduced in past by the scholars. Also, a comparative assessment of recent cutting-edge methods is provided along with the advantages and limitations that will assist the scholars in choosing the appropriate methodology to be adapted in this area of research.

© The Author(s), under exclusive license to Springer Nature Switzerland AG 2023
R. S. Tomar et al. (Eds.): CNC 2022, CCIS 1893, pp. 78–87, 2023.
https://doi.org/10.1007/978-3-031-43140-1_8

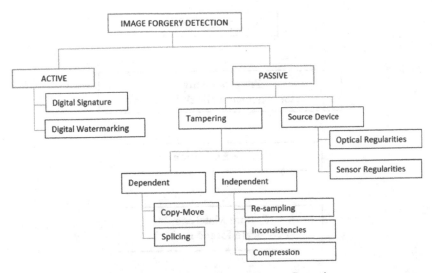

Fig. 1. Classification of Image Forgery Detection

2 Copy-Move Forgery Detection

Copy-move forgery detection is a passive approve in which one or more regions are duplicated in the same image. Hiding of an object in an image like in steganography or focusing on a particular object of interest in an image are few of the motivations for such type of forgery detection. The task of manipulating image can be performed with ease and in a very effective manner with copy-move forgery approach as both the source and target regions are as of the similar image. Figure 2. Shows an illustration of the same.

Fig. 2. (a) Original Image (b) Forged Image

Thus, to detect the forged locality from the original image a generalized workflow is followed by various copy-move forgery detection practices/methods which is represented in Fig. 3.

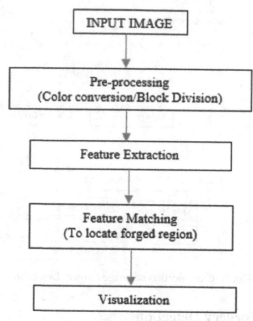

Fig. 3. CMFD Process

As, copy-move forgery is a type of digital image tampering where a part of an image is copied and pasted into another part of the same image to create a forgery. Detecting copy-move forgery is an important task in digital image forensics. Some common techniques for copy-move forgery detection are listed as follows.

i. **Block matching:** This technique involves dividing the image into small blocks and comparing the blocks to find any identical blocks in different parts of the image. This can indicate the presence of copy-move forgery [3]. Some common block matching techniques for copy-move forgery detection are as follows. Exhaustive search: In this technique, all possible block pairs are compared to find matching blocks. This is a time-consuming process and is generally not practical for large images. Fast Fourier Transform (FFT)-based method: This technique involves applying FFT to the image and comparing the Fourier coefficients to detect identical blocks. This is a computationally efficient method, but it may not be as accurate as exhaustive search. Locality Sensitive Hashing (LSH): LSH is a method for indexing high-dimensional data in a way that enables efficient similarity search. LSH can be applied to block matching by hashing blocks into buckets based on their content, and then comparing blocks only within the same bucket. This can significantly reduce the number of block comparisons needed and improve the efficiency of the algorithm. Singular Value Decomposition (SVD)-based method: This technique involves applying SVD to the image and analyzing the singular values to identify any blocks that have been copied and moved. This method is particularly effective for detecting partial copy-move forgeries, where only a part of a block has been copied and moved. Harris Corner-based method: This technique involves detecting Harris corners in the image and comparing the blocks around the corners to identify any copied blocks. This method is particularly effective for detecting copy-move forgeries in textured regions of the image. It's important to note that block matching techniques have some limitations, including their sensitivity to image compression and noise. Additionally, these techniques may not be effective for detecting copy-move forgeries that involve significant modifications to the copied blocks, such as changes in brightness, contrast, or color. A combination of different techniques may be used to achieve better results in detecting copy-move forgeries.

ii. **Keypoint-based methods:** These techniques extract keypoints or feature points from the image and compare them to find matching keypoints in different parts of the image. Keypoints can include corners, edges, and blobs [18]. Keypoint-based methods are generally more robust to image modifications such as resizing and rotation. Some common keypoint-based techniques for copy-move forgery detection are as follows. Scale-Invariant Feature Transform (SIFT): SIFT is a popular method for detecting and describing local features in images. SIFT-based techniques involve extracting SIFT features from the image and comparing them to find matching features in different parts of the image. SIFT is particularly effective for detecting copy-move forgeries that involve scaling or rotation. Speeded-Up Robust Features (SURF): SURF is a faster and more robust version of SIFT. SURF-based techniques involve extracting SURF features from the image and comparing them to find matching features in different parts of the image. Features from Accelerated Segment Test (FAST): FAST is a method for detecting corners in images. FAST-based techniques involve detecting FAST corners in the image and comparing the blocks around the corners to identify any copied blocks. This method is particularly effective for detecting copy-move forgeries in textured regions of the image. Binary Robust Independent Elementary Features (BRIEF): BRIEF is a binary descriptor that can be used to describe local features in images. BRIEF-based techniques involve extracting BRIEF features from the image and comparing them to find matching features in different parts of the image. Oriented FAST and Rotated BRIEF (ORB): ORB is a combination of the FAST corner detector and the BRIEF descriptor. ORB-based techniques involve detecting ORB features from the image and comparing them to find matching features in different parts of the image. It's important to note that keypoint-based techniques can be sensitive to changes in lighting conditions and may not be as effective in detecting copy-move forgeries in regions of the image with low texture. A combination of different techniques may be used to achieve better results in detecting copy-move forgeries.

iii. **DCT-based methods:** Discrete Cosine Transform (DCT) is a popular method for analyzing image content. DCT-based techniques involve applying DCT to the image and analyzing the resulting coefficients to detect any inconsistencies that may indicate copy-move forgery [3]. Some common DCT-based techniques for copy-move forgery detection are as follows. DCT-based block matching: This technique involves dividing the image into small blocks and applying DCT to each block. The DCT coefficients are then compared to identify any identical blocks in different parts of the image. This technique is particularly effective for detecting copy-move forgeries in images that have been compressed or resized. DCT-based feature extraction: This technique involves extracting features from the DCT coefficients to identify any copied and moved blocks. One such feature is the histogram of DCT coefficients, which represents the distribution of DCT coefficients within a block. The histograms of the suspected copied and moved blocks are compared to identify any similarities. Another feature is the DCT energy, which represents the total energy of the DCT coefficients within a block. The energy of the suspected copied and moved blocks is compared to identify any similarities. DCT-based singular value decomposition (SVD): This technique involves applying SVD to the DCT coefficients and analyzing the singular values to identify any copied and moved blocks. The singular values represent the amount of energy in each block, and any similarity in the singular values of the suspected copied and moved blocks indicates a potential forgery. DCT-based clustering: This technique involves clustering the DCT coefficients of the image to identify any copied and moved blocks. The DCT coefficients are clustered based on their similarity, and any clusters that contain blocks from different parts of the image indicate a potential forgery. It's important to note that DCT-based techniques are sensitive to image compression and may not be effective in detecting copy-move forgeries that involve significant modifications to the copied blocks, such as changes in brightness, contrast, or color. A combination of different techniques may be used to achieve better results in detecting copy-move forgeries.

iv. **SIFT-based methods:** Scale-Invariant Feature Transform (SIFT) is a technique for detecting and describing local features in images. SIFT-based methods involve extracting SIFT features from the image and comparing them to find matching features in different parts of the image [7]. Some common SIFT-based techniques for copy-move forgery detection are as follows. SIFT-based block matching: This technique involves dividing the image into small blocks and extracting SIFT features from each block. The SIFT features are then compared to identify any identical blocks in different parts of the image. This technique is particularly effective for detecting copy-move forgeries that involve scaling or rotation. SIFT-based feature extraction: This technique involves extracting SIFT features from the image and analyzing them to identify any copied and moved blocks. One such feature is the SIFT descriptor, which describes the local appearance of an image region based on the distribution of gradients within the region. The SIFT descriptors of the suspected copied and moved blocks are compared to identify any similarities. SIFT-based clustering: This technique involves clustering the SIFT features of the image to identify any copied and moved blocks. The SIFT features are clustered based on their similarity, and any clusters that contain features from different parts of the image indicate a potential forgery. SIFT-based geometric verification: This technique involves using SIFT features to estimate the transformation between the copied and moved blocks. The SIFT features are matched between the suspected copied and moved blocks, and the transformation is estimated based on the matched features. The estimated transformation is then used to align the copied and moved blocks, and any residual differences between the blocks indicate a potential forgery. It's important to note that SIFT-based techniques can be computationally expensive and may not be effective in detecting copy-move forgeries in regions of the image with low texture. A combination of different techniques may be used to achieve better results in detecting copy-move forgeries.

v. **SURF-based methods:** Speeded-Up Robust Features (SURF) is a faster and more robust version of SIFT. SURF-based methods involve extracting SURF features from the image and comparing them to find matching features in different parts of the image. Some common SURF-based techniques for copy-move forgery detection are as follows. SURF-based block matching: This technique is similar to the SIFT-based block matching technique and involves dividing the image into small blocks and extracting SURF features from each block. The SURF features are then compared to identify any identical blocks in different parts of the image. This technique is particularly effective for detecting copy-move forgeries that involve scaling or rotation. SURF-based feature extraction: This technique is similar to the SIFT-based feature extraction technique and involves extracting SURF features from the image and analyzing them to identify any copied and moved blocks. The SURF descriptors of the suspected copied and moved blocks are compared to identify any similarities. SURF-based clustering: This technique is similar to the SIFT-based clustering technique and involves clustering the SURF features of the image to identify any copied and moved blocks. The SURF features are clustered based on their similarity, and any clusters that contain features from different parts of the image indicate a potential forgery. SURF-based geometric verification: This technique is similar to the SIFT-based geometric verification technique and involves using SURF features to estimate the transformation between the copied and moved blocks. The SURF features are matched between the suspected copied and moved blocks, and the transformation is estimated based on the matched features. The estimated transformation is then used to align the copied and moved blocks, and any residual differences between the blocks indicate a potential forgery. It's important to note that SURF-based techniques can also be computationally expensive and may not be effective in detecting copy-move forgeries in regions of the image with low texture. A combination of different techniques may be used to achieve better results in detecting copy-move forgeries.

vi. **Deep learning-based methods:** Deep learning techniques have shown promising results in copy-move forgery detection. Convolutional Neural Networks (CNNs) can be trained to detect copy-move forgery by analyzing image patches and learning to distinguish between genuine and manipulated patches [15]. Some common deep learning-based techniques for copy-move forgery detection are as follows. Convolutional Neural Networks (CNNs): CNNs are a popular type of deep learning algorithm that have been used for copy-move forgery detection. The basic idea is to train a CNN to classify image patches as genuine or tampered. CNN is trained on a large dataset of genuine and tampered images, and once trained, it can be used to classify new image patches as either genuine or tampered. Siamese Networks: Siamese networks are another type of deep learning algorithm that have been used for copy-move forgery detection. The basic idea is to train a Siamese network to compare two image patches and determine whether they are the same or different. The Siamese network is trained on a large dataset of genuine and tampered image pairs, and once trained, it can be used to compare new image patches and determine whether they are the same or different. Generative Adversarial Networks (GANs): GANs are a type of deep learning algorithm that have been used for copy-move forgery detection. The basic idea is to train a GAN to generate realistic images that are similar to the original image, but with the tampered regions replaced with genuine regions. The GAN is trained on a large dataset of genuine and tampered images, and once trained, it can be used to generate new images that have the tampered regions replaced with genuine regions. Attention-based Networks: Attention-based networks are another type of deep learning algorithm that have been used for copy-move forgery detection. The basic idea is to train an attention-based network to focus on the important regions of the image, while ignoring the less important regions. The attention-based network is trained on a large dataset of genuine and tampered images, and once trained, it can be used to highlight the regions of the image that are likely to be tampered. It's important to note that deep learning-based techniques require a large amount of labeled data for training and can be computationally expensive. However, they have shown promising results in detecting copy-move forgeries, especially in cases where traditional techniques may not be effective.

It is worth noting that each technique has its own strengths and weaknesses, and a combination of techniques may be used to achieve better results. Additionally, these techniques are not foolproof and may not detect all instances of copy-move forgery, especially if the forgery is well-executed.

3 Related Work

There are several practices that have been developed by several researchers for detecting copy-move image forgery.

H Liyang Yu et al in [4] has proposed a 2-stage feature detection technique for enhancing the matched regions by using MROGH and HH descriptors. In [5] a novel hybrid approach is proposed by E. Ardizzone et al. in which the triangles are compared in place of blocks or single points in a given image. This approach was found robust against geometric transformations. In [7] B. Yang et al. proposed a modified SIFT-based detector which helps in evenly interspersing the key-points across the image for improved results. In [8] the concept of bounding rectangle is presented by K. M Hosny et al. that covers the detected object in the given image. The procedure is much quicker as contrasted to the previous cutting-edge methods and is also robust alongside various outbreaks including rotation, scaling, jpeg-compression, and Gaussian-noise. In [9] a new approach based on SIFT features is presented by M.A. Basset et al. for identifying multiple forged regions in a single image, also 2-level clustering feature is incorporated in the same. In [10] Osamah M et al. improved the matching results using CMFD pipeline and k-means clustering approach. Also, using LSH based matching the processing time is reduced. In [11], fractional quaternion cosin-transfrms (FrQCT) are introduced by B. Chen et al. to simplify the conservative fractional cosin-transfrms (FrCT) to quaternion signal processing. In [12] SIFT and LIOP are used by Cong Lin et al. for combining the features and then transitive matching is applied to enhance the results. In [13] the concept of pyramid model and Zernike moments is proposed by J. Ouyang et al. Also, RANSAC algorithm is applied resulting in improved results on arbitrary rotation angle. In [14] adaptive key-point filtering and iterative region merging is introduced by J.L. Zhong et al. for CMFD resulting in high precision rate. In [15] Dense-InceptionNet is proposed by J.L. Zhong et al. which provided best performance against many attacks. In

[16] pixel based CMFD method is introduced by A. Parveen et al. which uses k-means algorithm for block clustering and features are matched using radix sort resulting in efficient detection of forged regions from digital images.

4 Comparative Assessment

Table 1 provides the relative assessment of the previous methodologies along with its advantages and limitations.

Table 1. Comparative Assessment of Existing CMFD Approaches

Method Used	Advantages	Limitations
MROGH Descriptor and HH Descriptor [4]	-Robust against jpeg compression and rotation. -Can resist modest degree of additive noise, combined effects and scaling.	-Performance decreases as these attacks become stronger.
Hybrid Approach using Delaunay Triangularization [5]	-The major novelty is that the objects are depicted as a mesh of triangles. -High precision rate in identifying the tampered region. -This approach is two-order of magnitude quicker than block-based approach. -Less false positive rates.	-Performance degrades in complex scenes -Cannot be applied if there is no point of interest in the image.
Modified SIFT-based Descriptor [7]	-Sufficient number of key-points can be identified. -Invariance to mirror transformation and rotation is enhanced.	-Not verified on areas in images with non-affine transformations.
PCET moments and morphological operators [8]	-As the copied objects are enclosed in bounding box thus computation time is required only for the objects that are segmented. -Technique is robust to various attacks like Gausian-noise, jpeg-compresion, rotation and scaling.	-Tested on small data set.
2-Levels of clustering strategy [9]	-Efficient in detecting the existence of several copy move forgeries in a single scene.	-Efficiency needs to be enhanced in terms of time taken. -Image undergoes blurring or Gaussian noise.
Enhanced CMFD pipeline via k-means clustering [10]	-Accuracy and speed both are enhanced due to the use of k-means clustering.	-No reduction in processing time.
Adaptive key-point Filtering and iterative region merging [14]	-Detected regions are filled more precisely by combining the super pixels and suspected regions. -Improved performance under post processing operations.	-Adaptive key point filtering can further be applied to improve the precision.
Pixel-based CMFD using DCT [16]	-This technique detects forged regions twice the speed when the size of overlapped blocks gets increased.	-Forged regions are not identified in certain set of images.

5 Datasets

Due to the interminable developments running in image scientific exploration a necessity of standard datasets is constantly at hand. A compilation of both true and false images is offered in it which will facilitate in obtaining further summarized outcomes for various practices. A thorough description of a few publicly accessible datasets is presented in Table 2. Which will assist the investigators to determine which dataset to decide for a given CMFD approach.

Table 2. Publicly Available Datasets

Name of Dataset	Image Size	Total Images	Description
MICC-F2000 [4, 9, 15]	2048 × 1536 pixels	2000	original images: 1300 tampered images: 700
NISL-FIM [6]	400 × 300 to 4000 × 3000 pixels	878	original images: 439 tampered images: 439
MICC-F220 [9, 15, 18]	722 × 480 to 800 × 600 pixels	220	original images: 110 tampered images: 110
MICC-F8 [9]	2048 × 1536 pixels	8	tampered images: 8 with realistic multiple cloning
CMH [10, 14, 15]	845 × 634 to 1296 × 972 pixels	108	108 realistic cloning images in PNG format
CoMoFoD [10]	512 × 512 to 3000 × 2000 pixels	200	Manipulation performed using 25 distinctive patterns of tampering
GRIP [11]	768 × 1024 or 1024 × 768 pixels	80	original images: 80
FAU [11]	3000 × 2000	48	48 high-resolution source images
IMD [12]	300 × 2300	1488	Contain images in patches of 100
COVERAGE [15]	400 × 436	200	100 base images and 100 forged images
SUN [15]	Images resized to have max 120,000 pixels and compressed with 72 JPEG quality	108,754	397 groups and 108,754 base images

6 Conclusion

Copy-move forgery detection is a prevalent line of work in recent past. It is the process of identifying regions in a digital image that have been duplicated and pasted in the same image or a different image to create a fake or manipulated image. This type of forgery is a common technique used to deceive people by manipulating images for malicious purposes, such as propaganda, fake news, or to create false evidence. In this survey, an overview of existing various copy-move forgery detection techniques that have been introduced by previous scholars have been analyzed in this paper. The comparative assessment of present-day state of arts in the field of copy-move forgery detection has been performed specifically; the strength and limitations of the existing practices are summarized in the process of CMFD including a detailed list of publicly available datasets.

References

1. Jun-Wen, W., Guang-Jie, L., Zhan, Z., Yue-Wei, D.: Fast and robust forensics for image region duplication forgery. Acta Automtica Sinica **35**(12), 1488–1495 (2009)
2. Hany, F.: Image forgery detection. IEEE Sig. Process. Mag. **26**(2), 16–25 (2009)
3. Judith, R., Wiem, T., Jean-Luc, D.: Digital image forensics: a booklet for beginners. Multimedia Tool Appl. **51**(1), 133–162 (2011)
4. Yu, L., Han, Q., Niu, X.: Feature point-based copy-move forgery detection: covering the non-textured areas. Multimedia Tool Appl. **75**(2), 1159–1176 (2014)
5. Edoardo, A., Alessandro, B., Giuseppe, M.: Copy-move forgery detection by matching triangles of keypoints. IEEE Trans. Inf. Forensic Secur. **10**(10), 2084–2094 (2015)
6. Warif, N.B.A., Wahab, A.W.A., et al.: Copy-move forgery detection: survey, challenges and future directions. J. Netw. Comput. Appl. **75**, 259–278 (2016)
7. Bin, Y., Xingming, S., Hoglei, G., Zhihua, X., Xianyi, C.: A copy-move forgery detection method based on CMFD-SIFT. Multimedia Tool Appl. **77**(7), 837–855 (2017)
8. Khalid, H., Hanaa, H., Nabil, L.: Copy-move forgery detection of duplicated objects using accurate PCET moments and morphological operators. Imaging Sci. J. **66**(6), 330–345 (2018)
9. Abdel, B., Manogaran, G., Fakhry, A.E., El-Henawy, I.: 2-Levels of clustering strategy to detect and locate copy-move forgery in digital images. Multimedia Tool Appl. **79**(3), 5419–5437 (2018)
10. Osamah, A., BeeEe, K.: Enhanced block-based copy-move forgery detection using k-means clustering. Multidimension. Syst. Sig. Process. **30**, 1671–1695 (2018)
11. Beijing, C., Ming, Y., Qingtang, S., Leida, L.: Fractional quaternion cosine transform and its application in color image copy-move forgery detection. Multimedia Tool Appl. **78**, 8057–8073 (2018)
12. Cong, L., et al.: Copy-move forgery detection using combined features and transitive matching. Multimedia Tool Appl. **78**, 30081–30096 (2018)
13. Junlin, O., Yizhi, L., Miao, L.: Robust copy-move forgery detection method using pyramid model and Zernike moments. Multimedia Tool Appl. **78**, 10207–10225 (2018)
14. Jun-Liu, Z., Chi-Man, P.: Copy-move forgery detection using adaptive keypoint filtering and iterative region merging. Multimedia Tool Appl. **78**, 26313–26339 (2019)
15. Jun-Liu, Z., Chi-Man, P.: An end-to-end dense-InceptioNet for image copy-move forgery detection. IEEE Trans. Inf. Forensic Secur. **15**, 2134–2146 (2019)
16. Azra, P., Zishan, H.K., Syed, N.A.: Block-based copy–move image forgery detection using DCT. Iran J. Comput. Sci. **2**, 89–99 (2019)
17. Songpon, T., Tetsutro, U.: Copy-move forgery detection: a state-of-art technical review and analysis. IEEE Access **7**, 40550–40568 (2019)
18. Sunita, K., Kishna, A.N.: Efficient keypoint based copy move forgery detection method using hybrid feature extraction. In: International Conference on Innovative Mechanisms for Industry Application, pp. 670–675 (2020)

A Robust Graphical Authentication System for the Shoulder Surfing Attack

Shailja Varshney[1,2,3]($\boxtimes$), Sonam Kumari[1,2,3], Anannya Agarwal[1,2,3], and Prashant Pal[1,2,3]

[1] Department of Computer Science and Engineering, ITS Engineering College, Greater Noida, India
shailja.varshney@gmail.com
[2] Department of Computer Science and Engineering, Rajkumar Goel Institute of Technology, Ghaziabad, India
[3] Department of Computer Science and Engineering, Birla Institute of Technology, Mesra, India

Abstract. The technique of determining whether a user is legitimate or not is known as authentication. It needs a secret field (password) that only the actual user knows. Every security system is created in such a way that it must include at least one authentication technique to safeguard an individual's identity. There are numerous authentication methods available today, but each method has its own advantages and drawbacks that allow attackers to carry out various exploits including dictionary attacks and shoulder surfing attacks, among others. With some tweaking, graphic password authentication may have fewer drawbacks. A modified version of the graphical password technique is employed in this paper. The user is assigned a three-digit unique number in this that must be kept private. Each digit has a unique value that is determined by a set of computations and algorithms. This makes it difficult for the attacker to decrypt the password and makes it possible to prevent numerous cyber attacks like dictionary attacks and shoulder surfing attacks.

Keywords: Authentication · Graphical Password · Decrypt

1 Introduction

Humans are in the topmost height among all the species in the world. This is so as people can engage their brains and comprehend things more effectively. Technology is currently experiencing a boom. More data security is a result of the technology's quick advancement [1, 2]. To safeguard personal information, a variety of password authentication techniques are used, such as graphic or text-based passwords. Password authentication works by comparing a username to its corresponding password; if the two match, the authentication is considered successful. The password or PIN based authentication methods are more likely to have dangers concerning various cyber threats like dictionary attack.

© The Author(s), under exclusive license to Springer Nature Switzerland AG 2023
R. S. Tomar et al. (Eds.): CNC 2022, CCIS 1893, pp. 88–100, 2023.
https://doi.org/10.1007/978-3-031-43140-1_9

The text-graphic password entry system [3, 12], which combines text and graphical based passwords, is one of the solutions that have been developed to date to strengthen the weaknesses of password or PIN based authentication. We humans have a huge impact of pictures on our mind, so a hybrid password [4] authentication technique based on shape and text is being developed to get over the weaknesses of text- and graphic-based passwords.

Now that someone sitting next to you can see your pattern, graphical passwords are also prone to shoulder surfing attacks. Our method is based on graphic-based passwords with certain modifications, such as the requirement that the user select a three-digit number that is confidential and has its own meaning thanks to specific algorithms.

2 Background

We knows three types of Authentication methods:

- Token-based authentication
- Knowledge-based authentication
- Biometric-based authentication

Token Based Authentication Systems used Bank card, ATM card, Smart card etc. for verification. Sometimes token based authentication system combined with knowledge based password.

Biometric based Authentication systems used fingerprint, iris scan, face recognition etc. these system has some drawback like unreliability due to Hardware devices. Biometric based Authentication system are more secure than others.

Knowledge-based authentication methods are also divided in two sub methods:

- Text password based Authentication System
- Graphical password based Authentication System

3 Proposed Scheme

Our technique is based on a hybrid authentication system that employs both text-based and graphical-based passwords. Here, the textual password is used to compare it to the username to determine whether the user has been authenticated or not, while the graphical password uses some techniques to secure or authenticate the textual password.

Registration Phase

The user's email address, username, password, and a three-digit secret number must all be entered during the registration phase. Now, this three-digit secret code should be super secretive, and the user can only select it once, during the registration procedure. Figure 1 depicts the actual layout of the registration form.

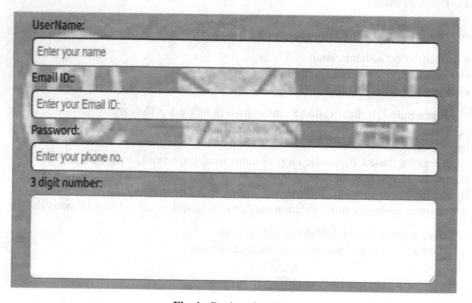

Fig. 1. Registration Page

A. Login Phase

The user must reenter their username and password during the login process in order to be authenticated. In this case, the username will remain the same, but the password will change with each entry. The algorithm we are employing here makes this possible and the 2D matrix which will contain 3 rows for the 3-digit numbers having 0–9 numbers in it. The 1st row is for the 1st number, second row is for the 2nd number and the 3rd row is for the 3rd row.

0	2	9	1	7	4	6	3	8	5
2	7	5	3	9	4	8	1	6	0
3	9	0	8	1	6	5	2	4	7

This matrix also contains a 9 × 10 grid having the characters along with their block numbers in the form of 2D array.

Now suppose the user has entered the username as ANKUSH and having the **password** as **@An%kusH*#**. He chooses 356 s as a 3-digit secretnumber. Figure 2 shows the matrix related to the 3-digit number.

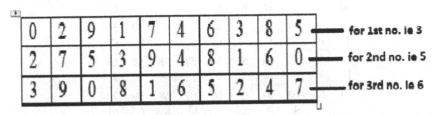

Fig. 2. Matrix Example

To update a password that has the same meaning as the actual password i.e. **@An%kusH*#**, use the algorithm below.

4 Algorithm Used

Three requirements, which are repeated after every three characters of the password, are the foundation of our method. Here, 'i' denotes the position of the elements of new password which we are representing as an array.

0	1	2	3	4	5	6	7	8	9

1. **If i%3 == 0** then raw = raw + arr[1][3] and actual block = block no. + arr[1][3] % 100, Here 3 denotes the 1st number and 1 denotes the 1st row.
2. **If i%3 == 1** then column = column + arr[2][5] and actual block = block no. + 10 * arr[1][3] % 100, Here 5 denotes the 2nd number and 2 denotes the 2nd row.
3. **If i%3 == 2** then raw = raw − arr[3][6] and actual block = block no. − arr[1][3] % 100, Here 6 denotes the 3rd number and 3 denotes the 3rd row.

01	02	03	04	05	06	07	08	09	10
A	v	!	@	R	#	Z	s	0	J
11	12	13	14	15	16	17	18	19	20
5	B	w	S	%	T	t	K	^	=
21	22	23	24	25	26	27	28	29	30
1	+	C	G	(	u	L	*	&	F
31	32	33	34	35	36	37	38	39	40
M	)	a	D	h	6	-	{	\	C
41	42	43	44	45	46	47	48	49	50
}	n	Y	B	E	i	X	]	l	O
51	52	53	54	55	56	57	58	59	60
[	<	o	N	3	2	j	>	?	$
61	62	63	64	65	66	67	68	69	70
,	z	4	P	_	d	G	k	/	M
71	72	73	74	75	76	77	78	79	80
	P	y	V	q	W	e	H	l	7
81	82	83	84	85	86	87	88	89	90
Q	:	;	X	U	r	9	f	I	8
91	92	93	94	95	96	97	98	99	100
L	M	4	7	!	l	o	q	e	a

NO. is 356

Now according to the algorithm 1st row is for the 1st number now we have 3 as our 1st number and in 1st row in 3rd place, we have **1**.

CASE 1: So, i = 0
Now 0%3 == 0 i.e., 1st element

Therefore, actual block = (04 + 1) % 100 = 05. So, we will write **R** in place of @.

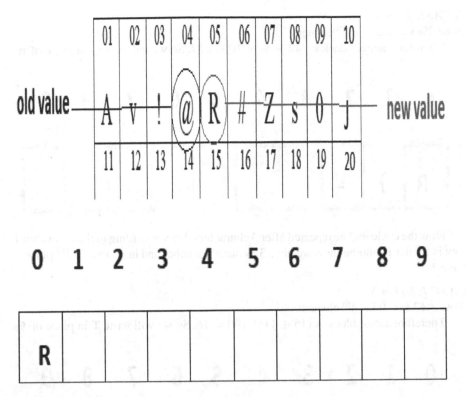

2nd row is for the 2nd number now we have 5 as our 2nd number and in 2nd row in 5th place we have **4**.

CASE 2: So, i = 1
Now 1%3 = = 1 i.e., 2nd element
    Therefore, actual block = (01 + 10 * 4) % 100 = 41. So we will write} in place of **A**.

3rd row is for the 3rd number now we have 6 as our 3rd number and in 3rd row in 6th place we have

5. _CASE 3_: So, $i = 2$
Now $2\%3 == 2$ i.e., 3rd element
   Therefore, actual block $= (42 - 5) \% 100 = 37$. So we will write - in place of **n**.

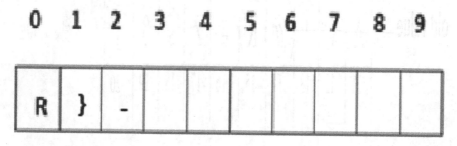

Now the cycle will be repeated after 3 characters. Now according to the algorithm 1st row is for the 1st number now we have 3 as our 1st number and in 1st row in 3rd place we have **1**.

CASE 1: So $i = 3$
Now $3\%3 == 0$ i.e. 4th element
   Therefore actual block $= (15 + 1) \% 100 = 16$. So we will write **T** in place of **%**

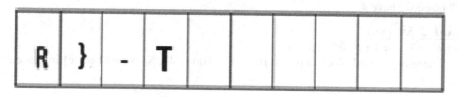

2nd row is for the 2nd number now we have 5 as our 2nd number and in 2nd row in 5th place we have **4**.

CASE 2: So $i = 4$
Now $4\%3 == 1$ i.e. 5th element
   Therefore actual block $= (68 + 10 * 4) \% 100 = 08$. So we will write **s** in place of **k**.

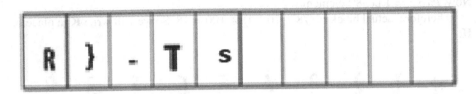

3rd row is for the 3rd number now we have 6 as our 3rd number and in 3rd row in 6th place we have **5**.

CASE 3: So i = 5

Now 5%3 == 2 i.e. 6th element

Therefore actual block = (26 − 5) % 100 = 21. So we will write **1** in place of **u**.

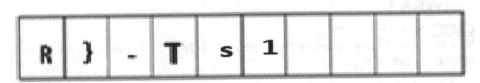

Now the cycle will be repeated after 3 characters. Now according to the algorithm 1st row is for the 1st number now we have 3 as our 1st number and in 1st row in 3rd place we have **1**.

CASE 1: So i = 6

Now 6%3 == 0 i.e. 7th element

Therefore actual block = (08 + 1) % 100 = 09. So we will write **0** in place of **s**.

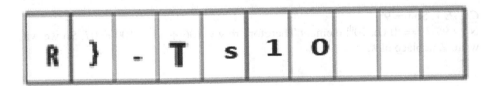

96   S. Varshney et al.

2nd row is for the 2nd number now we have 5 as our 2nd number and in 2nd row in 5th place we have **4**.

CASE 2: So i $= 7$
Now 7%3 $== 1$ i.e. 8th element
    Therefore, actual block $= (78 + 10 * 4) \% 100 = 18$. So we will write **K** in place of **H**.

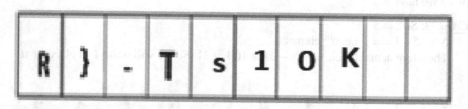

3rd row is for the 3rd number now we have 6 as our3^{rd} number and in 3rd row in 6th place we have **5**.

CASE 3: So i $= 8$
Now 8%3 $== 2$ i.e. 9th element Therefore row $= (28 - 5) \% 100 = 23$. So we will write **C** in place of *****.

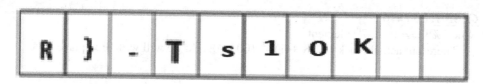

    Now the cycle will be repeated after 3 characters. Now according to the algorithm 1st row is for the 1st number now we have 3 as our 1st number and in 1st row in 3rd place we have **1**.

CASE 1: So i $= 9$
Now 9%3 $== 0$ i.e. 10th element Therefore row $= (06 + 1) \% 100 = 07$. So we will write **Z** in place of **#**.

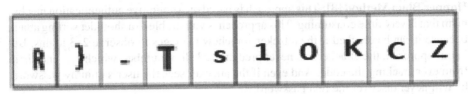

Now the new password will be **"R}-Ts10KCZ"** which has the same meaning as **@An%kusH*#** Both the matrix and the grid will be shuffled after every login so it is impossible for the attacker to guess the real password.

5 Password Space

Calculating the password space will allow us to determine how strong our password is against a brute force attack. The formula for the password space is $PS = A^N$ Where PS defines password space. A defines the number of total characters i.e. 89, N defines the length of the password In our system we defined N as $4 < N < 13$ If we calculate the password space for $N = 8$ then it is $PS = 2.1 * 10^{14}$.

6 Comparison

Cued Click Point (CCP) [5]: In this system the user must click five points on five distinct photos to create a pattern. The user must re draw the pattern by clicking on the same pixel locations during the login process.

The fundamental drawback of this approach is that shoulder surfing attacks can still be successfully launched against it. In contrast, our system doesn't employ any pattern methods; instead, it employs a security algorithm that uses dummy passwords and is protected against the shoulder surfing attack.

Graphical System Using ASCII Values [6]: In this system, a graphical password is used in which user can select any size 2D matrix and create a pattern on it. This system to add up all the ASCII values corresponds to the characters in the pattern.

However, the disadvantage is that anyone sitting nearby might observe your pattern, making you vulnerable to shoulder surfing attacks. Contrarily, our method does not employ ASCII values or any other pattern; rather, it will just need a secret three-digit number selected by the user during the registration process, after which our algorithm will function and it will be difficult for the attacker to obtain the user's credentials. The shoulder surfing attack is thus repelled.

Graphical Arrangement of Rows and Columns Using Specific Scale [7]: In this system, the user must define the row and column as well as scale them. The biggest disadvantage of it is that anyone sitting close to you can see your row and column scaling, leaving you vulnerable to shoulder surfing attacks. However, since users might forget the scaling, our solution doesn't require a row and column structure. Instead, users only need to remember a three-digit number and a simple algorithm that will defend against all types of attacks.

Hopper Blum Method [8]: This approach is based on a cognitive authentication mechanism that is very time consuming. This approach is vulnerable to a shoulder surfing attack because it can be cracked if the attacker somehow manages to observe 2–3 logins. But in our approach, the attacker can never predict the 3-digit number, which prevents them from ever cracking the code. And even if the attacker sees the user's dummy password, he will never discover the real password.

7   Comparison Based on Password Space

Our system provides a better way or it provides the advantages over many previously used password authentication schemes:

a. As our system has large password space i.e.10^{14} so it has minimize the risk of brute force attack to a very good extent.
b. Our system uses a very simple algorithm which is understandable by most of the users.
c. Our system does not require any complex calculations so anyone can understand it.
d. Our System is providing high security against many attacks like brute force attack, shoulder surfing attack and dictionary attack.

8   Result

Our approach is essentially a modified version of the graphical password approach. Here, we've utilized a dummy password scheme that requires the user to register using a confidential 3-digit number. And based on this three-digit number, we created an algorithm that creates unique dummy passwords for each login by the user. The original password is the same as this dummy password.

The main benefit of this strategy is that even if the user notices our dummy password, he will never be able to figure out the real password because the next time he logged in using the same dummy password, he would receive the message that his password was incorrect because the matrix and grid would be shuffled after each login and the values would change to reflect our three-digit number.

Because of this, we have reduced or even eliminated several forms of attacks, including dictionary attacks [11], brute force attacks [10], and shoulder surfing attacks [9]. Therefore, we may conclude that our strategy offers excellent resistance to significant attacks like shoulder surfing attack.

9   Conclusion

In this paper we have proposed a scheme that is based on graphical user authentication technique and secure from shoulder surfing attack, brute force attack, and dictionary attack. This scheme is a combination of knowledge-based authentication and graphic based matrices. The security analysis proves that this scheme effectively resists shoulder surfing attack because there is some cryptography-based algorithm applied that is based on some random digits that is changed their position in matrix at the time of each and every login. This feature enhances security without sacrificing the usability aspect. This authentication scheme can be used in public places, ATMs, access-control, etc.

References

1. The Economic Times. The EconomicTimes, October 2021. https://economictimes.indiatimes.com/definition/authentication
2. Geeks for geeks, April 2020. https://www.geeksforgeeks.org/graphical-password-authentication/
3. Johnson Durai, A.R., Vinayan, V.: A novel crave-char based password entry system resistant to shoulder-surfing. Int. J. Comput. Algorithm 3(3), 954–958 (2014). Joseph's College of Arts and Science (Autonomous), Cuddalore, 273–276
4. Zheng, Z., Liu, X., Yin, L., Liu, Z.: A Hybrid Password Authentication Scheme based on shape and text. J. Comput. 5, 765–772 (2010)
5. Bhand, A., Desale, V., Shirke, S., Shirke, S.P.: Enhancement of password authentication system using graphical images. In: International Conference on Information Processing (ICIP), pp. 217–219, December 2015 (2015)
6. Gupta, D.: A new approach of authentication in graphical systems using ASCII submission of values. In: 2017 13th International Wireless Communications and Mobile Computing Conference (IWCMC), pp. 1362–1369 (2017)
7. Istyaq, S., Umar, M.S.: Novel hybrid authentication by graphical arrangement of rows and columns using specific scale. Int. J. Comput. Math. Sci. 6(7), 2347–8527 (2017)
8. Joy, J.P., Jyothis, T.S.: Secure authentication. In: 2016 Online International Conference on Green Engineering and Technologies (IC-GET), pp. 1–3 (2016)
9. Wikipedia, the free encyclopedia. Wikipedia, the free encyclopedia. https://en.wikipedia.org/wiki/Shoulder_surfing_(computer_security)
10. Fatima, R., Siddiqui, N., Sarosh Umar, M., Khan, M.H.: A novel text-based user authentication scheme using pseudo-dynamic password. In: Fong, S., Akashe, S., Mahalle, P. (eds.) Information and Communication Technology for Competitive Strategies. LNNS, vol. 40, pp. 177–186. Springer, Singapore (2019). https://doi.org/10.1007/978-981-13-0586-3_18
11. Varshney, S., Umar, M.S., Nazir, A.: A secure shoulder surfing resistant hybrid graphical user authentication scheme. In: Cybernetics, Cognition and Machine Learning Applications. AIS, pp 79–87. Springer, Singapore (2019). https://doi.org/10.1007/978-981-15-1632-0_9
12. Varshney, S.: A secure shoulder surfing resistant user password authentication scheme. In: International Conference on Communication, Networks and Computing. Springer, Singapore (2020)
13. Varshney, S., Kumarl, L.: A secure authentication system for blind users. J. Appl. Sci. Comput. 1–9 (2018). UGC Approved Journal
14. Dhamija, R., Perrig, A.: Déjà Vu: a user study using images for authentication. In: 9th USENIX Security Symposium (2000)
15. Brostoff, S., Sasse, M.: Are passfaces more usable than passwords? A field trial investigation. In: McDonald, S., Waern, Y., Cockton, G. (eds.) People and Computers XIV—Usability or Else!, pp. 405–424. Springer, London (2000). https://doi.org/10.1007/978-1-4471-0515-2_27
16. Zheng, Z., Liu, X., Yin, L., Liu, Z.: A stroke-based textual password authentication scheme. In: First International Workshop on Education Technology and Computer Science, May 2009. IEEE (2009)

17. Lashkari, A.H., Abdul Manaf, A., Masrom, M., Daud, S.M.: Security evaluation for graphical password. In: Cherifi, H., Zain, J.M., El-Qawasmeh, E. (eds.) DICTAP 2011, Part I, CCIS, vol. 166, pp. 431–444. Springer, Heidelberg (2011). https://doi.org/10.1007/978-3-642-21984-9_37
18. Sobradoand, L., Birget, J.-C.: Graphical passwords. Department of Computer Science, Rutgers University, An Electronic Bulletin for Undergraduate Research, vol. 4 (2002)
19. Wiedenbeck, S., Waters, J., Sobrado, L., Birget, J.C.: Design and evaluation of a shoulder-surfing resistant graphical password scheme. In: Proceedings of Advanced Visual Interface (AVI 2006), May, pp. 23–26 (2006)
20. Forget, A.: A world with many authentication schemes. A Thesis at Carleton University, November 2012 (2012)

Networks and Information Security

Implications of Forensic Investigation in Dark Web

Ngaira Mandela[(✉)], Amir Aboubakar Shaker Mahmoud, and Animesh Agrawal

National Forensic Sciences University, Gandhinagar, India
ngairamandela@gmail.com

Abstract. The dark web has become a critical area of concern for law enforcement agencies and cybersecurity experts due to its association with illegal activities such as drug trafficking, money laundering, and cybercrime. Dark web forensics involves the collection, analysis, and preservation of digital evidence from the dark web, which presents several challenges such as anonymity, encryption, and the use of cryptocurrencies. This paper presents a comprehensive review of the current state of research on dark web forensics, with an emphasis on the methods, tools, and challenges associated with this field. The continuous improvement of darknet forensics technology has important practical significance for law enforcement agencies to combat darknet crimes.

Keywords: Tor · dark web · deep web · Dark Web Forensics · Digital Forensics · Cybercrime · Cryptocurrencies · Anonymity

1 Introduction

The dark web market is home to a wide variety of illegal and criminal activities, including the sale of sensitive personal information, firearms, drugs, and even films depicting terrorist attacks, to name just a few. One can find a wealth of resources on the dark web, but to access them, one needs a specialized browser such as Tor. The Tor browser was developed to protect users' privacy and anonymity. Although utilizing Tor to access the dark web helps users keep their private information hidden, it also contributes to an increase in the amount of criminal activity that occurs online. Cybercriminals gain access to the dark web through the Onion Router browser. This allows them to post and trade information on the dark web. The anonymity and privacy protection offered by the onion router browser are two of the reasons for its widespread adoption. Due to this privacy protection mode, network investigators have experienced great difficulty. The abundance of sales of personally identifiable information (PII), terrorist activities, hire murderers, buying and selling of drugs, weapons, and child pornography on the dark web presents a significant challenge for law enforcement agencies that deal with cyber security. Because of this, it is necessary to develop forensic methods exclusive to the dark web. Previous research has focused on identifying and monitoring dark web traffic, studying the identities of dark web users, and even examining the forensic usage traces of dark web browsers like Tor browsers. These are all essential aspects of the dark web anonymity network.

R. S. Tomar et al. (Eds.): CNC 2022, CCIS 1893, pp. 103–115, 2023.
https://doi.org/10.1007/978-3-031-43140-1_10

2 Literature Review

Tor's (in) a famous new method of anonymous networking has attracted the attention of the cyber security sector, which has mostly resulted in studies on the de-anonymization of users from a network perspective. On the other hand, the Tor Project aims to protect the user from both network and local risks. Anti-forensics techniques offer features and design choices intended to hide network activities and stop browsing session data from being stored on disk.

Numerous researchers have investigated the dark web and how it affects forensic investigation. Muir et al. (2019) performed a forensic audit of the Tor Browser bundle. They performed a forensic study of the software and its interactions with the host OS to determine how well the Tor Browser protected the user from such an opponent. They performed live forensics on the RAM, static forensics on the VM snapshot, and the analysis on the NTUSER.DAT. The result shows that when all three of these data streams from the same system are analyzed, different, yet nevertheless pertinent, corroborative, or complementary evidence. The live forensic showed that while the browser is open, Tor can be ascribed to four processes; the bundled obfs4 proxy's usage can be identified, and one Firefox process remains after the user ends their internet session. The authors discovered through static forensics that it is impossible to stop Tor from writing to the disk and enable secure deletion of the browser. A forensic investigator could demonstrate, based on the findings above, that: Tor is still being used even after a user has tried to uninstall the browser; the time and date of the most recent execution, information on the pages seen during a browsing session, The Tor network was used instead of Firefox, and the language of the nation where the server used to leave it is located.

A book regarding research on the dark web was written by Akhgar et al. in 2021. They created case studies of several instances in which the dark web was used for harmful purposes. Hansa, formerly regarded as the third-biggest Dark Web market in the world and the largest Dark Web market in Europe, was used as an example in the first case study on the dark web markets. The Dutch authorities could identify the corporation talking with other organizations using a Tor-protected server after conducting a network forensic analysis using wiretaps. The investigation revealed that the company's entire information flowed through a Tor-protected server. Updating, maintenance, and bitcoin addresses are some of the data. The investigative agencies could locate the drug traffickers connected to the groups after carefully observing the network traffic for a considerable time. Additionally, they were able to identify every Hansa organization service provider. The Wall Street market was another case study in the book. Wall Street users utilized robust VPNs to conceal their identities. Law enforcement authorities' forensic examination, though, recovered the artefacts. For instance, the first user was discovered when the service provider connection dropped, and the IP address was revealed. On the other side, the metadata that revealed the IP address led to the capture of the second user. A forensic investigator can learn from these two case studies that VPNs contain flaws that can be exploited to gather artifacts.

Moronwi (2021) performed Tor browser forensics on the windows operating system. He described how Tor changes the path an internet user's traffic takes through a series of arbitrary internet relays. Elliptic curve encryption is impenetrable by brute force and is used first to layer the data and the destination IP address. The information is subsequently transmitted using a virtual circuit with several nodes. The following location on the system where the TOR browser is installed is crucial: >\Data\Tor - two files are found here providing important information, including State and Torre. While the Torre file contains the location from which the Tor Browser was launched with the drive letter, the state file includes the application's most recent execution date (Figs. 1 and 2).

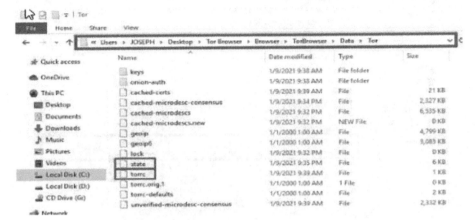

Fig. 1. Tor browser most recent execution.

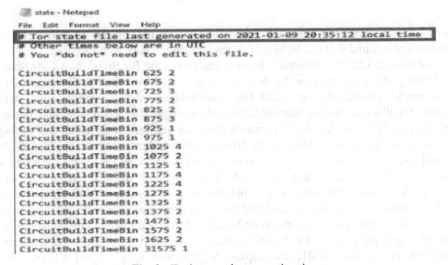

Fig. 2. Tor browser last execution time.

Prefetch contains crucial data like the first and last execution dates, the last eight execution dates, the number of executions, the install data, the execution path, and the browser version that an analyst can get from them (Fig. 3).

While the user is using private browsing, >pagefile contains information about HTTP. Tor takes advantage of Mozilla Firefox's private browsing function. This

Fig. 3. Tor browser execution path in prefetch file.

work helps forensic investigators to understand the virtual directories where crucial information is found that can be helpful when performing dark web forensics.

Jadoon et al. (2019) conducted a forensic analysis of the Tor Browser: A Case Study for Privacy and Anonymity on the Web. A forensics analysis of the Tor browser using Windows 8.1 is provided in the article. They searched the hard disk, memory, and system registry for all traces the Tor browser leaves behind on the user's computer both during and after use. They looked for information about the configuration, using, and surfing of Tor. According to the results, the Tor browser leaves a significant number of artifacts behind, especially in system memory. Three registry keys are added by the Tor browser during installation, according to the registry's investigation. All of these keys are still there in the registry after removal, proving that the program did not entirely delete all registry artifacts. They also noticed that these keys are placed in different sequences under different circumstances, including Install and Run and Install Only. The opening and closing of the browser left behind artifacts on the hard drive. They examined the hard disk on both the VDMK and snapshot VDMK files using magnet Axiom. After closing the Tor browser, no traces of the browser could be discovered in the OS VMDK file. The list of artifacts they found in the converted snapshot VMDK file is shown in the picture below. If a researcher wishes to learn whether a user downloaded the Tor browser and started using it right away, these scenarios will be helpful (Fig. 4).

Keller (2016) performed a forensic investigation study on the Tor browser. In his research, he demonstrated how malicious actors use Tor; APT. APTs are strong cyber-criminals who access darknet marketplaces using the Tor browser to distribute stolen

Instance	Open Tor browser		Closed Tor browser	
	OS Vmdk File	Converted Snapshot Vmdk File	OS Vmdk File	Converted Snapshot Vmdk File
Browsing	• No artifacts	• No artifacts found	• No artifacts	• No artifacts found
Pictures	-	• Only Tor browser icon was present in recovered pictures	-	• No artifacts found
		• No picture and videos were present from browsing activities		
Downloads	-	All downloads were present	-	• No artifacts found
		• Downloaded pictures		
		• Downloaded torrent files(.torrent files)		
Operating system	-	• Only location of firefox.exe was present	-	• Only location of firefox.exe was present
		• No other artifacts of Tor browser were present		• No other artifacts of Tor browser were present
Registry artifacts	-	• Two registry keys 1 and 2 were present and third key was missing	-	• Two registry keys key 1 and key 2 were present and third key was missing

Fig. 4. Tor Usage.

info. APTs use three main techniques to steal data: infiltration, persistence, and exfiltration. APTs can affect both persons and organizations in the public and private sectors. They are extremely smart threats that gather information about their targets to maximize their success. APTs can sell, exchange, or leak stolen data using the Tor browser.

Hawkins (2016) performed research under the ocean of the internet called the deep web, which comprises the dark web and the dark net. In his study, he identified what is found in the ocean of the internet. He explained that two types of Deep Web usage could be distinguished into Legal activity and illegal action. The illicit material uses Silk Road, the Hidden Wiki, and Dark Web Hidden Services. Although Silk Road was shut down, it was one of the most frequently visited websites when it was active. Tor is the most popular method for connecting to the Deep Web. As a result, a forensic investigator needs to be able to identify Tor traffic on your network. In a packet capture, Tor traffic will appear to be typical HTTPS communication. However, suppose an investigator examines the certificates used in Tor traffic. In that case, they will notice that the issuer and subject ID are using domain names that are randomly generated, indicating that these certificates are dubious, as shown in the figure below (Fig. 5).

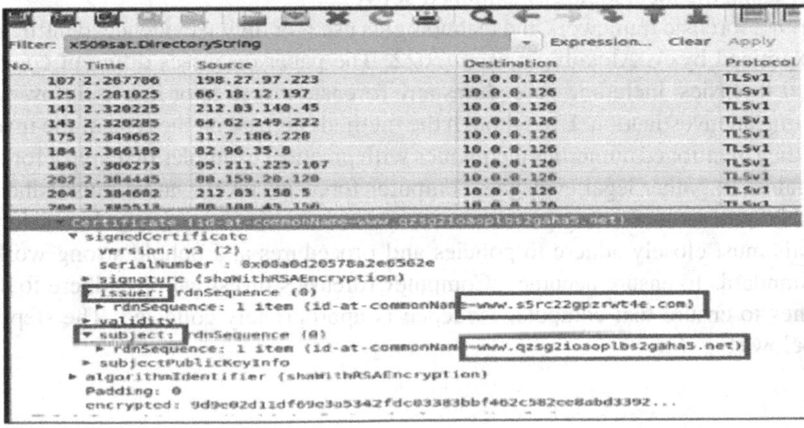

Fig. 5. ID issued.

The implication of this research to forensic investigation is that it helps a forensic investigator to understand where to locate information on the deep web. It is critical to realize that everything is not harmful. The Deep Web has many benefits, including browsing the internet privately. The future of the internet depends on our ability to comprehend the Deep Web and its capabilities.

Forensic analysis was used by Arshad et al. (2021) to analyse the Tor Browser Artifacts on Windows 10. The goal of the study was to identify the anti-forensic properties of the Tor browser. The reader can replicate this research using the detailed instructions for installing the Tor Browser and the provided forensic techniques. The Tor Browser must, among other things, "fight against both network and local forensic attackers," according to Arshad et al. For instance, "the browser MUST NOT write to the disk any information created from or that discloses browsing behavior". This allegation that nothing had been written to disk while carving and recovering cookies, histories, and caches from Firefox's artifacts was corroborated by the discovery. The author tried utilizing MZHistoryView, MZCacheView, and MZCookieView, tools from Nirsoft, but he was unable to get the programs to read the relevant DLLs. That was the only on-disk artifact found when a VM snapshot was taken while the user was connected to Tor, browsing, and bookmarked google.com. On Google.com, the visited location was saved in the locations.sqlite database. Even if it is simply kept in the Tor installation directory, the browser history kept on disk implies a security/usability compromise. Tor Opsec gives a full list of steps for suitable Operational Security (OPSEC) when using Tor to handle this issue as well as others. If the user wishes to use Tor and preserve the highest level of anonymity, they are necessary. The Tor project's goal of leaving a minimal carbon footprint on disk after creating the system and user hives, prefetch file, and Mozilla on-disk files is supported by the filesystem analysis that was previously discussed. Several artifacts from the memory analysis indicated to links between the Tor Browser's installation location and the browser's internet addresses. In summary, dozens of points to artifacts are provided to let other investigators locate and use the Tor Browser using the methodology mentioned above.

Darknet forensic framework and technologies used for digital evidence identification were examined by A. Alotaibi, et al. in 2022. The paper discusses different concepts in digital forensics, including procedures any forensic investigator has to follow when conducting an investigation. Even though the methods depend on the type of the investigation, they mentioned numerous techniques with practical examples that help a forensic investigator. To gather legal evidence, computer forensics investigators must adhere to established protocols. The top priority in computer forensics is accuracy. Forensic professionals must closely adhere to policies and procedures and uphold strong working ethics standards to ensure accuracy. Computer forensics investigations adhere to strict guidelines to ensure that computer evidence is appropriately collected. The steps are listed below (Fig. 6):

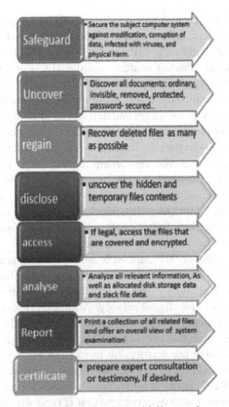

Fig. 6. Forensic investigation guidelines and procedure

The overall goal of the paper was to investigate the notion of digital evidence detection techniques that can serve as a starting point for navigating a crime scene on a dark web. Once the directories are located through digital evidence, this can lessen the amount of work required to investigate the crime.

Understanding the dark web and how it may help with an investigation is the subject of a blog post by Ashburn (2021). Special software is needed to access the dark web. Each dark web version has its dataset, encryption services, and threats. Most darknet users utilize Tor. It provides layers of encryption (thus the onion analogy) to anonymize intelligence workers' communications. By routing client traffic through many nodes, the origin of files and sites can be concealed, making them harder to trace. Multi-layered encryption protects users and service providers. Many websites have onion URLs. As with any browser, activity and hacking concerns can be tracked. Tor's major weakness is between the exit node and the destination site. This unencrypted area exposes users. ZeroNet is a 2015 peer-to-peer web hosting solution that doesn't use IP addresses or domains. Sites aren't hosted by a conventional service and are only accessible by a public key. It makes sites free to build, share, and shut down. You can visit ZeroNet with a browser and a background application. It can be used online and offline. The content is shared via BitTorrent, which distributes bits of data to multiple peers. By spreading the information among numerous hosts, it's difficult to find or remove all site material. After downloading, peers can reshare and disseminate. ZeroNet isn't anonymous. I2P, released in 2003, is another network. I2P encrypts user communication, unlike the previous two websites and file-sharing sources. Unlike Tor, it encrypts peer-to-peer. I2P employs a browser and background app. It creates one-way peer tunnels for untraceable communication. After 10 min, each client becomes a tunneling node. "Garlic routing" describes the system. One-way messages and delivery instructions are encrypted. 2000's Freenet is another decentralized peer-to-peer network. "Opennet" connects to any user, but "darknet" only connects to friends. Backend web application access requires a key. Initially used by dissidents to escape censorship regulations, cybercriminals now use it to unload stolen and malicious content. The closest nodes in the open net route traffic efficiently. Only trusted people know your node's IP address in the darknet. Darknet's security outweighs its inconvenience. This mechanism keeps data when the publisher disconnects. The blog post gives forensic investigators information about the software used on the dark web and how to extract evidence.

The entirety of what users of the dark web should know was covered in a blog post by Goswami et al. (2022). They outlined how easy it is to become a victim of identity thieves and hackers after a victim's money or sensitive personal information and how the internet is a terrifying place for digital privacy. Additionally, exercising caution when accessing the internet is crucial, notably if the user is signing in from a new computer or device or is utilizing an unreliable connection. The dark web is a fantastic resource for finding private information or purchasing, but users must exercise caution. When using the internet at home or work, they recommended that consumers practice good digital hygiene and utilize a VPN. Using a VPN, which stands for virtual private network, users can access and transfer data over content that is typically forbidden or limited by their internet service provider (ISP). Using a computer or mobile device linked to the VPN server, one can securely and privately access the internet. They won't be able to communicate with anyone or do anything the ISP can see. A forensic investigation can comprehend the various methods that dark web users use to conceal their identities.

Leng et al. 2021, proposes a dark web forensics framework that entails the analysis of all the evidence related to digital forensics that includes the network, memory, bitcoin and disk forensics. The research identified reliable evidence in their analysis that can be essential during the forensic investigation of Tor browser usage.

In his research on darknet forensics from 2017, Rathod (2017) divided the field into two categories: bitcoin forensics and forensics related to Tor. TOR browser forensics: There are four ways to extract evidence related to the TOR browser. The first type of memory forensics is RAM forensics, regarded as volatile. The Belkasoft RAM capturer can record RAM dumps, and the Hex dump can read RAM dumps in hexadecimal format. RAM forensics aims to gather information about the file kinds and websites visited. Second, registry forensics can be performed using Regshot, and the extracted evidence reveals details about the installation of TOR and the most recent access date. Third, network forensics can be performed using Wireshark and network miner, and the collected evidence gives details about web traffic. Lastly, Database: Locations the TOR browser's database can be found at the Tor Browser Browser TorBrowser Data Browser profile. To view the contents of the database, use the default and database viewer. On the other hand, it is possible to do Bitcoin Transaction Forensics by obtaining forensic artifacts from a user's PC with a Bitcoin wallet application installed. Internet Evidence Finder can recover Bitcoin artifacts. The summary is as shown in the table below (Tables 1, 2 and Fig. 7).

Table 1. Dark web forensics tools and techniques

Techniques	Forensic Tools used	Goal
RAM forensic evidence	• Belkasoft RAM • FTK imager • HXD • Volatility	The Tor browser saves the contents in the RAM while running hence the investigation of the RAM obtains the websites visited, files downloaded and the documents
Registry forensics	• Regshot tool	Regshot tool is used to find the registry changes during the running of the Tor browser on the device
Network forensics	• Wireshark • miner network	Perform traffic analysis to gather the web traffic evidence
Database forensics	• sql lite tool	The Tor Browser creates a folder and database on the system and hence the data base can be analyzed to identify the websites visited and the content accessed in the dark web
Bitcoin wallet	• Internet Evidence Finder	For extracting the bitcoin information from Bitcoin wallet that is downloaded on the device of the client

Table 2. Summary of Existing work.

Author	Advantages of the paper	Notes
(Leng et al. 2021)	The paper proposes a dark web forensics framework that entails the analysis of all the evidence related to digital forensics	The proposed framework only tested on windows 10 operating system
(Jadoon et al. 2019)	The author performed Tor browser forensics on Windows 8.1 the author performed forensics on the memory, hard disk, and registry	Network forensics was not performed, it was identified that the access to the dark web was not done

(continued)

Table 2. (*continued*)

Author	Advantages of the paper	Notes
(Muir et al. 2019)	The paper proposes to use both live forensics and static forensics to identify all the traces related to Tor browser usage	Wallet forensics was not done
(Arshad et al. 2021)	The paper analyzes the tor browser artifacts in windows and android operating system	The proposed methodology should be tested on Linux and Mac operating systems
(Chetry and Sharma 2021)	The paper discusses the dark web as a challenge to forensic investigators and how the memory can be used to identify the evidence from end devices	The evidence acquisition is incomplete only memory forensics exploited as source of evidence
(Sandvik 2013)	The paper tests 3 scenarios where the user does not have the administrative privileges or doesn't know how to delete the tor browser, the image was taken and analyzed and only the traces left behind by Tor browser were considered	Only disk forensics performed
(Darcie et al. 2014)	The paper sets p 4 different virtual scenarios and analyzed the network forensic statistics, memory, registry and virtual analysis	The paper focusses on network traffic only
(Al-Khaleel et al. 2014)	The paper discusses the forensic investigation of the Tor browser traces left behind. Memory forensics artifacts were explored	Limited usage of Tor browser and only considered memory forensics
(Warren 2017)	The paper presents the TOR browser evidence based on three snapshots that include the file system artifacts, memory, hives and prefetch file	Bitcoin forensics not covered and also network forensics
(Huang et al. 2018)	The paper analysis the different cybercrimes and compares the different browsers	Only database, cookies and memory considered

(*continued*)

Table 2. (*continued*)

Author	Advantages of the paper	Notes
(Dayalamurthy 2013)	The paper discusses memory forensics related to TOR browser and proposes a memory forensics Framework	No experimentation was done
(Kulm 2020)	The paper performs a forensic analysis of the tor browser artifacts on the disk on windows and mac operating systems. The paper proposes the framework to be used in investigating Tor browser evidence	Only the disk forensics was done
(Rathod 2017)	The paper proposes that dark web forensics should combine memory forensics, network forensics, registry forensics, cryptocurrency forensics and disk forensics	No experimentation was done

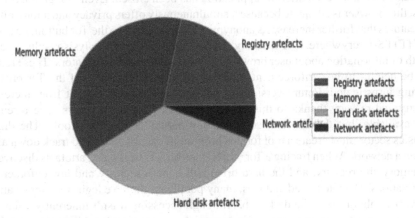

Fig. 7. Graphical representation of artefacts covered in each research.

3 Challenges Facing Dark Web Forensics

The encryption method and anonymity of the dark web present the biggest challenge to forensic investigators regarding its regulation. Since the dark web is an entirely anonymous environment, it is challenging to gather enough evidence to fight cybercrime and find those who use it for illegal purposes. Since there is no accepted definition of cyber terrorism, it is much more challenging for intelligence agencies to determine the appropriate jurisdiction for the crime. Cyberspace poses a variety of risks, and the majority of them are interconnected. Users and services on the dark web are anonymous, making it harder to investigate their activities. On the dark web, it is impossible to determine the location of any computer or person, making it extremely difficult for law enforcement agencies to take action when necessary because they cannot determine which jurisdiction has jurisdiction over a particular situation.

Is there a reliable way to track dark web users back to their actual locations? This is the issue that many forensic investigators and law enforcement agencies are attempting to answer. The application of advanced analytics to the communications and information forensic investigators locate on the dark web is one approach that some have taken to overcome these issues. Although computers may not be able to be tracked or attributed, users frequently and unintentionally reveal information about the people with whom they connect and how they do so.

4 Conclusion

The two main obstacles to freedom of expression are censorship and surveillance. As more websites migrate to the onion domain to overcome these obstacles, it is anticipated that the Tor browser will soon rank among the top five online browsers. Although this browser offers some privacy, it doesn't provide as much as what can be seen from the findings above, particularly the memory analysis results, which show that it leaves a lot of artefacts in memory even after the application has been closed. Even though it has these flaws, this browser is adequate because it simultaneously offers privacy and anonymity. It has features that further increase its anonymity and privacy, like the Tor button, no script, and HTTPS-Everywhere. The memory, registry and hard disk analysis results reveal a wealth of information about user browsing habits to forensic investigators. These results may be helpful to law enforcement agencies in cases when a user of the Tor browser is being investigated. Future versions of the Tor browser will benefit from increased security and privacy thanks to this information. All popular browsers have forensics tools available, but the Tor browser lacks any particular forensics tools. The digital forensics sector must create a tool for this browser. It cannot be easy to track down a Tor user on a network. When tracing a Tor user's steps back is necessary, artefacts discovered in memory, the registry, and the hard drive will benefit security and law enforcement organizations. Despite the advantages, many people might have legitimate reservations and worries about using the dark web. Although accessing it isn't inherently unlawful, it is advisable to take precautions against any risks or potential legal hazards, especially when entering parts of the dark web where criminal behavior is being carried out. Since law enforcement frequently monitors dark web marketplaces or forums, it might be challenging to distinguish between criminal actors and legitimate investigators. Having a plan will help you avoid implications or attribution. Before acquiring information or entering a criminal forum, write down your strategy. Keep thorough records of all actions taken when using the dark web and establish "rules of engagement" for use on any sites where criminal conduct occurs. The Security of investigators' equipment is another risk. Even while the dark web aims to offer some anonymity, there are still risks of downloading harmful content or being identified. Using a secure cyber-service product is the safest method of gaining access.

References

Akhgar, B., et al.: Dark web investigation. Security Informatics and Law Enforcement (2021, Preprint). https://doi.org/10.1007/978-3-030-55343-2

Al-Khaleel, A., Bani-Salameh, D., Al-Saleh, M.I.: On the memory artifacts of the tor browser bundle. In: The International Conference on Computing Technology and Information Management (ICCTIM), p. 41. Society of Digital Information and Wireless Communication (2014)

Alotaibi, M., et al.: Computer forensics: dark net forensic framework and tools used for digital evidence detection. Int. J. Commun. Netw. Inf. Secur. (IJCNIS) **11**(3), 424–431 (2022). https://doi.org/10.17762/ijcnis.v11i3.4407

Arshad, M.R., Hussain, M., Tahir, H., Qadir, S., Memon, F.I.A., Javed, Y.: Forensic analysis of tor browser on Windows 10 and Android 10 operating systems. IEEE Access **9**, 141273–141294 (2021)

Ashburn, M.: Understanding the dark web and how IT can aid your investigation, authentic8 (2021). https://www.authentic8.com/blog/understanding-dark-web-and-how-it-can-aid-your-investigation. Accessed 3 Oct 2022

Chetry, A., Sharma, U.: Dark web Activity on Tor—Investigation challenges and retrieval of memory artifacts. In: Gupta, D., Khanna, A., Bhattacharyya, S., Hassanien, A.E., Anand, S., Jaiswal, A. (eds.) International Conference on Innovative Computing and Communications. AISC, vol. 1165, pp. 953–964. Springer, Singapore (2021). https://doi.org/10.1007/978-981-15-5113-0_80

Darcie, W., Boggs, R.J., Sammons, J., Fenger, T.: Online anonymity: forensic analysis of the tor browser bundle. Forensic Science International (2014)

Dayalamurthy, D.: Forensic memory dump analysis and recovery of the artefacts of using tor bundle browser–the need (2013)

Goswami, G., Pandit, D., Patel, A.: Dark web intelligence: everything that you need to know: India (2022). https://heritagecyberworld.com. https://heritagecyberworld.com/blog-dark-web-intelligence-everything-that-you-need-to-know. Accessed 3 Oct 2022

Hawkins, B.: Under the ocean of the Internet-the deep web. SANS Institute InfoSec Reading Room, pp. 1–19 (2016)

Huang, M.J.C., Wan, Y.L., Chiang, C.P., Wang, S.J.: Tor browser forensics in exploring invisible evidence. In: 2018 IEEE International Conference on Systems, Man, and Cybernetics (SMC), pp. 3909–3914. IEEE (2018)

Jadoon, A.K., Iqbal, W., Amjad, M.F., Afzal, H., Bangash, Y.A.: Forensic analysis of Tor browser: a case study for privacy and anonymity on the web. Forensic Sci. Int. **299**, 59–73 (2019)

Keller, K.: The Tor browser: a forensic investigation study. Doctoral dissertation, Utica College (2016)

Kulm, A.: A Framework for Identifying Host-based Artifacts in Dark Web Investigations (2020)

Leng, T., Yu, A.: A framework of darknet forensics. In: 2021 3rd International Conference on Advanced Information Science and System (AISS 2021), pp. 1–6 (2021)

Moronwi, J.: Digital investigator, Digital Investigator (2021). https://digitalinvestigator.blogspot.com/. Accessed 2 Oct 2022

Muir, M., Leimich, P., Buchanan, W.J.: A forensic audit of the Tor Browser Bundle. Digit. Invest. **29**, 118–128 (2019). https://doi.org/10.1016/j.diin.2019.03.009

Rathod, D.: (PDF) darknet forensics - Researchgate, Darknet Forensics (2017). https://www.researchgate.net/publication/321698383_Darknet_Forensics. Accessed 3 Oct 2022

Sandvik, R.A.: Forensic analysis of the tor browser bundle on OS X, Linux, and windows. Technical report, pp. 1–13 (2013)

Warren, A.: Tor browser artifacts in Windows 10. SANS Institute InfoSec Read, Room (2017)

Review on Analyzing and Detecting Crimes

Amir Aboubakr Shaker(✉), Ngaira Mandela, and Animesh Kumar Agrawal

National Forensic Sciences University, Gandhinagar, India
amirlyphd@gmail.com

Abstract. Crime is a term that means a disastrous act for the entire humanity and an obstacle to communities' safety and life. With the increasing use of technology in solving crimes, computer Scientists in addition to Analysts have begun working with law enforcement organizations to improve the speed of investigating crimes. Crime intelligence analysis helps to discover patterns of crimes and criminal behavior that may help in the discovery of where and why crimes are likely to occur, but this data should be authentic and obtained from real-world sources or online resources such as social media, news websites or any other resources. Thus, efficient data analysis techniques can be used for this purpose. This review paper will examine in detail some of the current literature on analyzing and detecting crimes to help in proposing new methods to extract information from real-world crime data to develop an intellectual framework for analyzing and detecting crimes which can be of significant help to support the judicial agencies and law enforcement specialists for detecting and preventing crimes.

Keywords: Crimes analysis · machine learning · social network analysis · news analysis · law enforcement

1 Introduction

Crime rates are on the rise every day according to many studies, crime is defined as an act committed in violation of the law that prohibits it and for which punishment is imposed [1], with the development of modern technologies that allow criminals to carry out their crimes easily, crime prediction results cannot be guaranteed as accurate as they should be, but machine learning techniques can be used which have the capability to extract information from large data and enables computers to learn from previous experiences [2], which makes it suitable for analysis of crime data that can be collected from diverse sources which are help in identifying the future nature of crimes patterns, and criminal activities [3].

The key obstacle to any research is how to create a tool that is more effective at identifying crime patterns [1], intelligent crime analysis and the discovery of patterns of crimes and offenders help to reduce crime to a low level to ensure security in crime-prone areas, thus, there is a need to propose an efficient framework for analyzing and detecting crimes using machine learning techniques and crimes data that is collected from various and important resources to support law enforcement agencies during putting appropriate strategies to reduce crimes.

R. S. Tomar et al. (Eds.): CNC 2022, CCIS 1893, pp. 116–127, 2023.
https://doi.org/10.1007/978-3-031-43140-1_11

2 Past Studies

Several studies have been carried out that are pertinent to the analysis and detection of crimes using machine learning to determine the various aspects that make a significant contribution towards the incidence of crime and its influence on our societies. Crime analysis and detection using machine learning techniques has been a hot topic for research. Some of the pertinent studies that have been done that are connected to this topic are summarized in this section.

In this work [2], Datasets were gathered from the Vancouver data catalog. For this research, two categories of datasets were used: crime and neighborhood, while the crime data (crime set) was acquired from the VPD (around 31624 per year, about the type of crime committed and the time and location of the offense) since 2003, neighborhood set contained twenty-two local areas also used for drawing maps. For crime prediction purposes, this paper examined ML tools (decision tree and KNN) using Vancouver crime dataset for 15 years. The accuracy was (39%: 44%). Although this model achieved low accuracy, it provides an initiatory framework for further studies.

In this paper [3], the author referred to the importance of data mining techniques to discover hidden and valuable information from unstructured data. Using Bayes theorem, numerous news articles were used to train and build a system to predict areas that have crime-sensitive in India and display it, these crimes are related to arson, robbery, vandalism, sex abuse, murder, burglary, etc. This data was stored using Mongo DB. Also, Apriori algorithm and factors/attributes of a place were used to extract frequent crime patterns. For testing purposes, this study used some data to test the model and the result was achieved (more than 90% accuracy) using the Bayes theorem.

In this study [4], the ML algorithm (K-means) was applied to analyze the crime data between (2016 and 2017) in Chicago city. This dataset is available on the Kaggle website, also python libraries were used for pre-processing the crime data. For analysis purposes, crime attributes were divided into types (Robbery, Offense, Theft, Sexual Crime, Kidnapping), time, location of the crime (Street, Residence, Apartment, Public), and arrests made. This experiment found that robberies were at their supremacy, Overall, this method of analysis proved to the crimes have been analyzed efficiently using k-means.

Mahajan [5] referred that almost the Indian population's mindset and their life are available digitally because of using social media. By identifying five Indian regions from the Nation Crime Records Bureau (NCRB) that were selected based on the rate of crime, this study attempted to discover relations between the Crime pattern and geo-tagged tweets in India using Data Mining and Python (pip package manager). Crime Data were acquired (around 20 days in Dec 2019/over 30,000 tweets from 512 users) from several sources (NCRB, online news). Crime types were divided into (violence against women and children, suicide, cybercrime, etc.). The results illustrated a relationship between the predicted crime patterns (from Tweets) and actual reported crime, and the performance of this approach was 84.74% using sentiment analysis (BiLSTM) and neural networks). The authors showed that the limitations of this work were the unavailability of Twitter geotagged tweets because of user privacy. And google maps will be used to make this research more effective to improve this work in the future.

McClendon [6] mentioned that machine learning plays a significant role in detecting crime, so WEKA was used to carry out a comparison between the crime pattern in the Crime Dataset provided by the repository of California-Irvine University and real crime statistics for Mississippi (Was collected by FBI / 2013), this data included features such as the population, the number of violent crimes committed, population distribution by age, and the rate of crimes (per 100K persons), and this study mentioned that the number of populations was around three million. For analysis purposes, the algorithms (Decision Stump, Linear Regression, Additive Regression) were implemented. After using the training sets for the three methods, the linear regression often outperformed the other two.

This study [7] summarized the different techniques used to analyze present crimes to use in predicting future crimes. Tools were used to predict crime such as artificial neural networks, k-means, decision trees, and deep learning. Mudgal mentioned that There is a significant need for techniques that can be working in real-time (in the present) to detect crime at high speed and accuracy, so, The Proposed system that can be working in real-time to predict crimes by tracking people's actions, it was implemented using Kalman filter and Gaussian Mixture Model, this system used the videos that obtained from the CCTV cameras where are in the smart places and cities that use to monitor and report if some suspicious activity like hitting, robbery, etc. is occurring, this system analyzes these videos to extracts the used features for the analysis process. The experimental result of the proposed system (hybrid approach) showed acceptable results and it can be used for tracking human actions and action recognition.

This work [8] used time series algorithms to analyze the Chicago crime data that were tracked by the Chicago Police Department's Bureau of Records (CLEAR system) which includes about eight lakhs of crimes. This crime occurred from January 1, 2017, to May 27, 2020. Time series (ARIMA) were used to make predictions of five crimes (theft, assault, criminal damage, battery, and deceptive practice), the ARIMA technique is helpful for analyzing longitudinal data with a correlation among neighboring observations. The accuracy of the proposed Arima algorithm was 91.4%. The results showed that most of the crimes occurred in the duration of May to August. The Future enhancement of this study is to apply ML for more accuracy.

This study [9] mentioned that criminals use social media for different activities such as planning and execution of criminal acts, in addition to the intention expression is a useful tool supporting investigators to analyze suspicious social network posts. This work proposed a framework that explores computational ontologies and machine learning tools. to identify suspicious posts and analyze them, the author employed the ontology of criminal expressions to describe crime concepts and correlates them with criminal slang idioms. Using learned models from previous postings, automatically the criminal intention in any article is classified. The framework was evaluated using a case study with tweets (more than eight million tweets). The results showed the framework achieved the purpose of this study. The authors mentioned that the future work will include additional concepts such as regionalism and other languages, will apply other ML techniques such as deep learning, and will use a larger ML training dataset, and visualization techniques.

In this paper [10], a crime analytics platform with Interactive visualization features was developed, which processes newsfeed data analysis between 1st January 2017 to 1st January 2018 for several types of crimes. To help criminologists to determine the relationships between attributes of crime, the analytics steps were as; The RSS feeds are classified based on their relevancy, such as Crime location, crime types, etc., and are transformed into an XML format. The pre-processing steps help in cleaning all data and extracting the key features. The data is then classified using the feature set. For analytic purposes, the research method used Kernel Density Estimation (KDE) and several mathematical methods. Crime hotspots and Cartographic of different geographic areas of India and Bangalore were the output of this work for determining crime patterns better, also, the change in criminal activity and the relationships between commercial places and crime types have been calculated. With high accuracy, the model can predict all cases using the KDE algorithm and some Crime keywords Such as (Drunkenness, Arson, Burglary, Fraud, Gambling, etc.).

The authors [11] suggested a method for Crime analysis to help security agencies using k-means, which created two crime clusters that have the same crime features. Also, Google maps were utilized for visualization purposes, on the other hand, Using the KNN algorithm Criminal identification was analyzed. This work used two tools, Java language and WEKA to analyze data during the period of 2000–2012 (5,038 cases/35 attributes.) with an accuracy of 93.62 and 93.99%. In the future, this study mentioned that it will enhance accuracy, data privacy, and other security features also it will collaborate with Investigating agencies in India.

This research [12] proposed using four features of crime detection as crime probability, hotspots, time zones, and performing vulnerability analysis to increase the accuracy of the used ML algorithms. Two datasets were used to implement the proposed methodology, while four attributes were presented from the first dataset (Los Angeles), there were six attributes from the second dataset (San Francisco). This study applied evaluation techniques that were accuracy, precision, and recall. The results produced successful results (accuracy of 97.5%) using Naïve Bayes (NB) after using four ML algorithms (NB, SVM, random forest, K nearest neighbor).

This paper [13] provides a solution to protect internet users from threats of terrorism by creating a system to define good and bad Kurdish websites using NB and K-Nearest Neighbor algorithms. The proposed approach included four steps; for the data collection step, the dataset was obtained from some Kurdish websites, this data consisted of two thousand documents that were divided into two categories ("Good" or "Bad"), these documents were passed through a pre-processing stage that is divided into three steps; these are Tokenization (the decomposition of the texts into separate words), Normalization(the process of unifying the written texts), and stemming (e.g. remove suffixes and prefixes of words to get the original root), the result showed that the NB algorithm achieved a higher precision than K-Nearest Neighbors. Finally, the proposed work can be modified and used for another purpose such as examining fraud documents.

This work [14] aimed to realize the cybercrime that occurs in social media to help the police in preventing cybercrime. Python Libraries like (Matplotlib, Pandas, Seaborn, Ggplot, and Plotly) were used for the analysis and understanding of the data. For analysis purposes, cybercrime data, which consisted of 574 cases from the Statistics Canada agency in addition to attributes such as (types of cybercrime, years, age, education, and family background) were analyzed from the year 2014 to 2018. The result of this analysis showed that poverty and a low level of education are causing of increase in cybercrimes. in addition, the ages between twenty and twenty-five may perform more crimes. So, these results would assist the police to understand and solve cybercrime.

In this study [15] Data mining as an analysis data technique was employed in this paper to reveal undetected relationships among this data. This work focused on analyzing SMS text spam (Short Message Service) based on two software (RapidMiner and Weka), and data consisting of 5,572 instances (4,825 ham messages and 747 as spam) was gotten from Machine Learning Repository (UCI). Two processes were accomplished with different machine learning algorithms; Classification of spam using Supervised ML such as (SVM, NB, and KNN) was a process of messages differentiation between spam, on the other hand, clustering using Unsupervised ML Algorithms such as (K-Means, Cobweb. And Hierarchical) was a process of partitioning messages into groups according their similar features. This experiment proved that for spam classification, SVM was the most suitable algorithm and for spam clustering, K-Means was the best algorithm.

According to [16], one of the crucial areas of research for law enforcement agencies all around the world is crime analysis using data from social media platforms like news websites, Twitter, Facebook, etc. So, the researcher proposed a novel approach based on data mining techniques and R language to analyze the news feeds to predict spatial, temporal and the probability of any crime will occur (they determined sixteen types of crime) in which area in India and Bangalore using the coordinates of the crimes regions, this work used news feeds (27782 News related to crime) from 2017 Jan to 2018 Jan, the results have shown that the proposed approach showed acceptable results.

This study [17] proposes a suitable tool based on ML techniques to classify cyber-crimes. NB was used as a classification algorithm and the clustering purpose k-means was used, on the other hand, the TFIDF was used for feature extraction purposes. The data has been utilized from various sources such as Kaggle and CERT-In (two thousand instances) and the eight crime features such as location, offender, incident, victim, age, etc., that happened in India from 2012 to 2017, also, this data was divided into 70% for training and 30% for validation. The current work focuses on only the classification and clustering of cybercrime patterns but as the future scope, this work can be enhanced by using deep learning tools. The results proved that the proposed framework is efficient in the classification and clustering of cybercrime (Table 1).

Table 1. Summary of the Literature Survey.

RefNo	Purpose of study	Dataset used/Country	Used Method/Algorithm	Results	Weaknesses/Notes
[2]	Crime Analysis Through ML	31624 per year/2003/VPD of Vancouver	KNN, boosted decision tree	39%: 44%	Although the accuracy was low, it offers a foundation for future studies
[3]	Using DM for analyse and predict crimes	RSS feeds, social media, blogs	Bayes theorem/Apriori algorithm/Mongo DB	The accuracy was 90%	This work will be more accurate if it considers specific state or region. Also, the crime time
[4]	Using K-Means for analyzing crime data	crime data from 2012 to 2017/Chicago	k-means clustering technique/Jupyter Notebook in Python	The analysis process has represented the crimes through graphs, the k-means clustering technique proves to be feasible and is crimes have been analyzed efficiently	This study should use more than one algorithm for example deep learning, Decision tree, etc. to achieve high accuracy
[5]	Using sentiment analysis, this study attempted to discover relations between the Crime pattern and geo-tagged tweets in India	five regions of India/(NCRB)/2nd Dec. 2019 to 22nd Dec. 2019 (over 30,000 tweets from 512 users)	DM/Python/(BiLSTM)	84.74% using sentiment analysis, and the results illustrated a correlation between Tweets and reported crime	Authors showed that the limitation of this work was the privacy and unavailability of Twitter geotagged tweets
[6]	Using ML to Analyzing Crime	FBI dataset/2013	ML, WEKA, data mining, Decision Stump, Additive Regression, Linear Regression	Linear regression was the more efficient	This study noted that the study's focus did not include learning crime trends, profiling criminals, or crime hotspots
[7]	Theoretical and empirical analysis of crime data	Videos that obtained from the CCTV cameras	DM, hybrid approach, association rules, ANN, k-means, DT, and DL	This work showed acceptable results and it can be used for tracking human actions and action recognition	This model relies on only one source of data (CCTV)

(continued)

Table 1. (*continued*)

RefNo	Purpose of study	Dataset used/Country	Used Method/Algorithm	Results	Weaknesses/Notes
[8]	Using Arima Model for Crime Analysis & Prediction	Chicago's Police / 2017 to 2020	time series algorithms, Arima Model	The accuracy (91.4%)	This work needs to apply machine learning and optimization algorithms will be applied for more accuracy
[9]	A Case Study on Twitter for Identifying Criminal Acts' Intentions	8,835,290 tweets	ANN /SVM/Random Forest	The research showed the advantages of identifying users' intentions in written criminal tweets	this study can be utilized additional concepts such as regionalism and other languages, will apply other ML tools such as DL, and use a larger training dataset, and visualization tools
[10]	Using KDE, geospatial crime analysis for the Indian context can determine crime density	News feed data from January 2017 to January 2018/India, Bangalore	Excel/Kernel Density Estimation	Predicting crime using spatial and temporal information and textual analysis	This study should use more than one algorithm for example deep learning, Decision tree, etc. to achieve high accuracy
[11]	Using DM for criminal identification and crime detection in India	2000/2012 (5,038 cases)/India	k-means clustering/KNN/Java and WEKA/Google map/	The accuracy almost 93.62%	this study mentioned that it will enhance accuracy, data privacy, and other security features
[12]	Approach to Crime Detection using ML and Big Data	4 attributes (Los Angeles dataset) & 6 attributes (San Fran-cisco dataset)	NB, kNN, SVM, random forest	Naïve Bayes achieved successful result (accuracy of 97.5%)	This study focused on only two standard datasets; it can be utilized any additional resources such as online websites
[13]	Using A Systematic Web Mining for Forecasting Terrorism	some Kurdish websites (2000 documents)	NB, kNN	Naïve Bayes achieved better result compared with K-Nearest Neighbors	This study used only Naive Bayes, kNN, didn't focus on spatial and temporal information
[14]	Cybercrime analysis on Social Media websites	574 cases from the Statistics Canada agency/2014 to 2018	Python Libraries/Jupyter	The results indicated that poor and the people aged between 20 and 25 committed more crimes	the samples and factors were limited. Also, this project can be expanded using AI techniques

(*continued*)

Table 1. (*continued*)

RefNo	Purpose of study	Dataset used/Country	Used Method/Algorithm	Results	Weaknesses/Notes
[15]	A Study of Different Text Spam Classification and Clustering Algorithms	5,572 instances	NB, SVM, KNN/K-Means, Cobweb. And Hierarchical/Weka, RapidMiner	SVM was a suitable classifier for spam & K-Means was suitable for clustering	this simulation can be carried out for different and advanced algorithms such as the employment of an Artificial Immune System (AIS)
[16]	Using Newsfeed for Crime analysis in Indian Context	India and the Bangalore (2017 2018) & (27782 cases)	/RSS/R Language/KDE and ARIMA	The proposed approach showed acceptable results	The performance of the algorithm with hotspots has not been fully examined, according to this paper
[17]	Using ML to classify cybercrime crimes	2000 cases from Kaggle and CERT-In/(2012–2017)	NB/k-means/ TFIDF techniques	The results proved that the proposed framework is efficient in the classification and clustering of cybercrime	this work can be enhanced by using deep learning tools

3   Challenges and Proposed Solutions

From the previously discussed related work, predicting future crime patterns or trends includes tracking changes in the crime rate from one year to the next, thus there are many challenges such as the vast amount of crime data that needs to collect, stored, and handled, and determining various methods and structures used to record this data, in addition to, the problem of identifying techniques that can accurately analyze this data because the available data is incomplete and inconsistent, thus the analysis procedure becomes more difficult as a result. On the other hand, there is some limitations in obtaining crime data from law enforcement agencies such as the complexity of the issues and privacy, also in some cases, the criminal investigation takes a long time to provide crime data.

The author in [18] asserts after reviewing many studies that the dataset affects the accuracy of crime prediction. When a large dataset is utilized, model training is achieving acceptable accuracy, but when a small dataset is used, model training is inaccurate. Additionally, the method of training affects prediction accuracy. If the model has had extensive training, the accuracy will be higher; however, if the model has not received extensive training, the accuracy will be lower.

To overcome these problems, ML algorithms such as (K-means, ANN, SVM, Random Forest, Naïve Bayes, decision tree, Linear regression, deep learning, etc.) are important tools to be used in the analysis of real data for crime prediction, which are obtained from social media, news websites, and other resources [19], the mentioned algorithms in past studies section are summarized in Fig. 1. In addition to tools such as (Python, WEKA, RapidMiner, etc.) are represented efficient environment for use in this purpose.

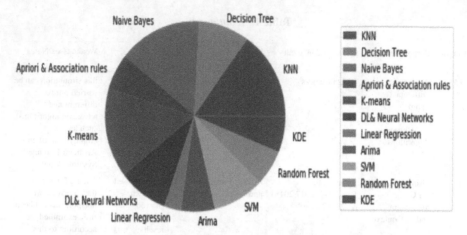

Fig. 1. Summary of the mentioned algorithms in the Past Studies section.

Besides that, utilizing hybrid approaches in predicting crimes, which combines many prediction algorithms and different recourses, helps in obtaining the most accurate information and outcomes, an example is shown in Fig. 2.

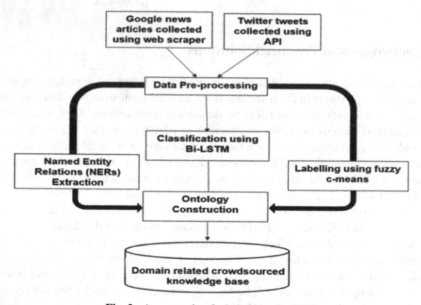

Fig. 2. An example of a hybrid method [19]

Also, it's possible that a single model won't be enough to describe all the characteristics of the crime, thus, in this study [20] proposed another example of a hybrid model is shown in Fig. 2, which is used to predict crimes rate in the US depending on economic aspects (Fig. 3).

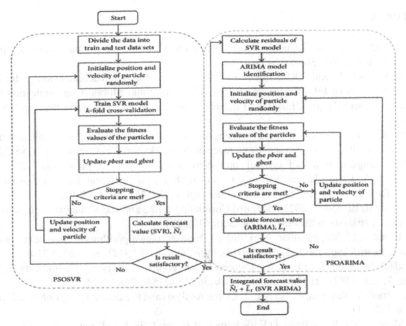

Fig. 3. Example of a hybrid method [20].

Generally, there is a need to propose an intelligent framework for analyzing and detecting crimes more efficiently using machine learning techniques, to overcome the shortcomings of present approaches and get better results and performance.

4   Conclusion

Crime can take place at any time and in any area [21], so analyzing and detecting crimes is the prime concern of this paper. Most researchers and law enforcement agencies are focused on creating a tool or systems for analyzing and detecting crimes, these tools are based on the enormous collection of real-world crime data whether that was obtained from law enforcement managements or online resources, or any other resources. So many authors have proposed several techniques and methods that depend on ML algorithms as has been brought out in the background section. After the survey of some used technologies has been done in this paper for this purpose, there should be a more intelligent method supported with an Interactive platform to extract and analyze the real-world crime data from various resources such as social networks, newsfeeds, and any other resources using machine learning techniques, which can be of significant help to support the judicial agencies and law enforcement specialists for detecting and decrease or preventing crimes.

Acknowledgments. The authors would like to thank Egyptian and Indian governments for their valuable support, also many thanks to Egyptian Ministry of Justice and National Forensic Sciences University (India) for helping us to complete this work successfully.

References

1. Patel, H.M., Patel, R.: Enhance algorithm to predict a crime using data mining. J. Emerg. Technol. Innov. Res. **5**(04) (2017)
2. Kim, S., Joshi, P., Kalsi, P.S., Taheri, P.: Crime analysis through machine learning. In: 2018 IEEE 9th Annual Information Technology, Electronics and Mobile Communication Conference, IEMCON 2018. Institute of Electrical and Electronics Engineers Inc., pp 415–420 (2019)
3. Sathyadevan. S., Devan, M.S., Surya Gangadharan, S.: Crime analysis and prediction using data mining. In: 1st International Conference on Networks and Soft Computing, ICNSC 2014 - Proceedings. Institute of Electrical and Electronics Engineers Inc., pp 406–412 (2014)
4. Saleh, M.A.: Crime data analysis in python using K-means clustering. Int. J. Res. Appl. Sci. Eng. Tech. **7**(4), 151–155 (2019). https://doi.org/10.22214/ijraset.2019.4027
5. Mahajan R, of VM-IJ, 2021 undefined Correlating crime and social media: using semantic sentiment analysis. pdfs.semanticscholar.org 12:2021
6. McClendon, L., Meghanathan, N.: Using machine learning algorithms to analyze crime data. Mach. Learn. Appl. Int. J. **2**, 1–12 (2015). https://doi.org/10.5121/mlaij.2015.2101
7. Mudgal, M., Punj, D., Pillai, A.: Theoretical and empirical analysis of crime data. J. Web Eng. **7**, 113–128 (2021). https://doi.org/10.13052/jwe1540-9589.2016
8. Vijayarani, S., Suganya, E., Navya, C.: Crime Analysis and Prediction Using Enhanced Arima Model (2021)
9. de Mendonça, R.R., de Brito, D.F., de Franco, R.F., dos Reis, J.C., Bonacin, R.: A framework for detecting intentions of criminal acts in social media: a case study on twitter. Information (Switzerland) **11**, 154 (2020). https://doi.org/10.3390/info11030154
10. Prathap, B.R., Ramesha, K.: Geospatial crime analysis to determine crime density using kernel density estimation for the Indian context. J. Comput. Theor. Nanosci. **17**, 74–86 (2020). https://doi.org/10.1166/jctn.2020.8632
11. Tayal, D.K., Jain, A., Arora, S., Agarwal, S., Gupta, T., Tyagi, N.: Crime detection and criminal identification in India using data mining techniques. AI Soc. **30**, 117–127 (2015). https://doi.org/10.1007/s00146-014-0539-6
12. Palanivinayagam, A., Gopal, S.S., Bhattacharya, S., Anumbe, N., Ibeke, E., Biamba, C.: An optimized machine learning and big data approach to crime detection. Wirel. Commun. Mob. Comput. **2021**, 1–10 (2021). https://doi.org/10.1155/2021/5291528
13. Rashid, T.A., Rashad, D.D., Gaznai, H.M., Shamsaldin, A.S.: A systematic web mining based approach for forecasting terrorism. In: Mohamed Ali, M.S., Wahid, H., Mohd Subha, N.A., Sahlan, S., Md. Yunus, M.A., Wahap, A.R. (eds.) AsiaSim 2017. CCIS, vol. 752, pp. 284–295. Springer, Singapore (2017). https://doi.org/10.1007/978-981-10-6502-6_25
14. Almansoori, A., Alshamsi, M., Abdallah, S., Salloum, S.A.: Analysis of cybercrime on social media platforms and its challenges. In: Hassanien, A.E., et al. (eds.) AICV 2021. AISC, vol. 1377, pp. 615–625. Springer, Cham (2021). https://doi.org/10.1007/978-3-030-76346-6_54
15. Zainal, K., et al.: An Analysis of Various Algorithms For Text Spam Classification and Clustering Using RapidMiner and Weka (2015)
16. Boppuru, P.R., Ramesha, K.: Geo-spatial crime analysis using newsfeed data in indian context. Int. J. Web-Based Learn. Teach. Technol. **14**, 49–64 (2019). https://doi.org/10.4018/IJWLTT.2019100103
17. Ch, R., Gadekallu, T.R., Abidi, M.H., Al-Ahmari, A.: Computational system to classify cyber crime offenses using machine learning. Sustainability **12**(10), 4087 (2020). https://doi.org/10.3390/su12104087
18. Shamsuddin, N.H.M., Ali, N.A., Alwee, R.: An overview on crime prediction methods. In *2017 6th ICT International Student Project Conference (ICT-ISPC)*, pp. 1–5. IEEE (2017)

19. Deepak, G., Rooban, S., Santhanavijayan, A.: A knowledge centric hybridized approach for crime classification incorporating deep bi-LSTM neural network. Multimedia Tools Appl. **80**(18), 28061–28085 (2021)

20. Alwee, R., Shamsuddin, S.M., Sallehuddin, R.: Hybrid support vector regression and autoregressive integrated moving average models improved by particle swarm optimization for property crime rates forecasting with economic indicators. Sci. World J. **2013** (2013)

21. Kaur, N.: Data mining techniques used in crime analysis:-a review. Int. Res. J. Eng. Technol. (IRJET) **3**(08), 1981–1984 (2016)

Prevention and Detection of Poisoning Attacks in Medical-Based Machine Learning Web Applications

T. Sheela$^{(\boxtimes)}$, C. K. Gnana Padmesh, and V. Lokesh

Department of Information Technology, Sri Sai Ram Engineering College, Chennai, India
hod.it@sairam.edu.in, {gnanapadmesh.ck,lokeshlokss7}@ieee.org

Abstract. Machine Learning concepts and processes are widely used in all the fields for automated, accurate, and immediate decisions. But, hackers have vigorous motives to change the outcomes of the models and applications generated by algorithms and techniques of machine learning. The project revolves around the detection and prevention of poisoning attacks on the medical models of machine learning by either an Anomaly detection method or cryptographically based authentication and provenance. Anomaly detection is an application of cybersecurity where an anomaly detector is built. It identifies the rare occurrence of any unfamiliar data from the model and prevents the models from poisoning attacks. The web application holds cryptographic authentication and provenance through a secure socket layer and by some framework methods, through which the poisoning attacks can be detected and prevented. On this basis, our projects prevent hacks from occurring in the field of medicine.

Keywords: Poisoning data · Anomaly Detector · Poisoning attacks · Cryptographic authentication

1 Introduction

Machine learning methods and techniques, and Web applications have turned familiar and their use cases have expanded due to their rising popularity. Machine learning technologies are very beneficial for massive development in versatile sectors, but they also have significant weaknesses. One such major vulnerability is poisoning attacks on the models of machine learning. One of the most relevant emerging threats and recent risks to machine learning is Poisoning attacks.

A poisoning attack happens when an attacker or hacker injects malicious or undesirable data into the machine learning model's training pool. Poisoning attacks target the model through either Machine Learning's availability or its wholeness. Since many applications rely on unreliable data gathered in the wild, attackers can inject malicious data that can specifically affect how the system operates. Anomaly detection is a notion or a concept that is a part of machine learning and data mining that seeks out the observations, data points, etc., that differ from the typical behavior of the dataset.

R. S. Tomar et al. (Eds.): CNC 2022, CCIS 1893, pp. 128–139, 2023.
https://doi.org/10.1007/978-3-031-43140-1_12

1.1 Objective and Motivation of this Project

The ultimate motivation of this research work is to build a website to integrate the anomaly detector with that. Nowadays hackers directly access and attack the datasets and web apps of many models. In which medical-based i.e., patients' information and records stored in a hospital dataset are being hacked and it is being modified by them which leads to the storage of false information. To stop and detect those cyberattacks, our project is built up.

2 Review of Literature

In [1], the authors conducted a comprehensive analysis of poisoning attacks and their defenses for machine learning models based on linear regression. To prevent these attacks, they suggested a new theoretically-grounded optimization framework. They designed a new principled robust defense strategy based on principles that are extremely resistant to all poisoning attempts. They evaluated their protection strategies and algorithms on various datasets from the medical, loan evaluation, and real estate industries. They then used a case study health application to illustrate the practical effects of poisoning attacks.

In [2], the authors presented a unique approach that identifies the poisoning data and prevents online and often retrained machine learning applications by exploiting the context information regarding the origin and modification of data points in the training set. They proposed a defense methodology that uses data provenance such as including the data origin, what happens to it, and where it moves to prevent poisoning attacks. Two different iterations of the approach have been presented. One is for only a small portion of data sets that may be trusted, while the other is for all data sets.

In [3], the authors illustrated a data poisoning attack on machine learning models' categorization approach. They also proposed a protection methodology that makes machine learning models more resistant to poisoning attacks. They employed MNIST, a popular data set based on character detection, in their investigation to undertake data poisoning assaults. By utilizing a generative model like Auto Encoder, they were able to construct classification models for the poisoned MNIST dataset that was more trustworthy.

In [4], the authors proposed a defense mechanism with the principle of an outlier-detection-based scheme, which is used to lessen the impact of the poisoning attacks in Machine learning web apps and can identify the points which are against the linear classifiers. Here they have used MNIST Dataset for testing and they also stated that performing this outlier detection will be very challenging in high-dimensional datasets. Table 1 shows the summarization of research works along with the comparative study of the first four papers.

In [5], The authors analyzed the robustness of online anomaly detection with a limited horizon against poisoning attacks. For testing it, the authors have used the Optimal Greedy Attack algorithm. Their experimental evaluation showed that online anomaly detectors are insecure for high-dimensional network data attacks.

In [6], the authors prescribed that on preventing Data Poisoning attacks in both online learning and machine learning they have developed their algorithm known as the Attackers' algorithm with optimization problems. They also inferred the rate of attacks through visual representation using a graph,

In [7], the authors described the process of creating and mimicking a model and it is used to duplicate the behavior of the target model. Augmenting the training data and mimicking model construction is done by Generative Adversarial Networks (GANs). In comparing the outcome results of both models, the author explicitly recognizes and showcases the poisoned data from the cleaned data set.

In [8], the authors highlighted the importance of studying backdoor poisoning attacks and developing defense strategies for deep learning and machine learning systems against backdoor poisoning attacks. They proposed three types of theoretical defense methods, the first one is to simply measure the label distribution of the training data. But it is not very effective. The second one is through an outlier detector, and the third is to evaluate through additional auxiliary pristine data for deep learning models.

In [9], the authors of the paper prescribed that a model's prevention is based on cryptographically authenticating the model. This ensures the correctness of the information used to train a model. In addition, they have proposed a VAMP System, which is used to safeguard the media objects such as audio clips, pictures, and video documents in the machine learning model. Table 2 shows the summarization of research works and a comparative study with our proposed solution. on the last five papers.

As of now, a couple of solutions are theoretically prescribed by various authors in terms of papers. They have suggested the Robust defense method, Optimal Greedy Algorithms, Auto Encoder method, Labeling methods, Proposed VAMP System, generative adversarial networks, etc., These prevention methods are not very effective and optimal in preventing and detecting poisoning attacks.

3   System Implementation

We have proposed an Anomaly detection concept with Cryptographic provenance for preventing and detecting the Machine learning model/web applications from poisoning data. Our idea for implementing this concept practically holds 4 modules. They are as listed below:

1. Building and designing a Machine learning Web Application
2. Hacking and falsely introducing the poisoning data.
3. Developing an Anomaly detector
4. Providing Cryptographic authentication and deployment.

Each of these modules will be developed individually and the prototype will be created by integrating all these modules.

3.1 Conceptual Flow of the Project

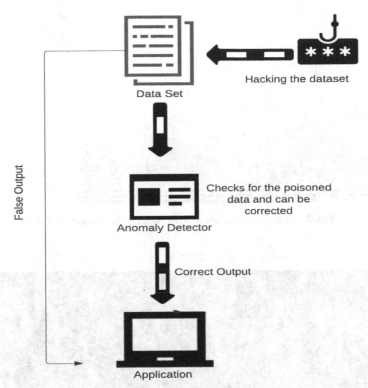

Fig. 1. Conceptual flow of the project

3.2 First Module

Our first module deals with the designing and development of the Machine learning model. As our core concept is related to the field of medicine and its associations, we used a diabetes dataset from the internet.

The Machine Learning model takes some input values such as the number of pregnancies, age, insulin level, blood pressure level, glucose level, BMI, etc., as given in [10]. The output of this model will either be 1 or 0, where 1 refers to the person who suffers from diabetes and 0 refers to that the person is free from diabetes. This ML web app depicted in Fig. 3 is built in Python with a framework named Streamlit and by the packages such as NumPy, Pandas, Pillow, and SciKitLearn.

We have trained the model by the diabetes analysis and prediction dataset by Random Forest Classifier Algorithm. This algorithm is a supervised machine learning algorithm, which executes all the steps of ML such as classification, regression, etc., with the help of decision trees. So, the accuracy of this model is approximately 85%–90% (Fig. 4).

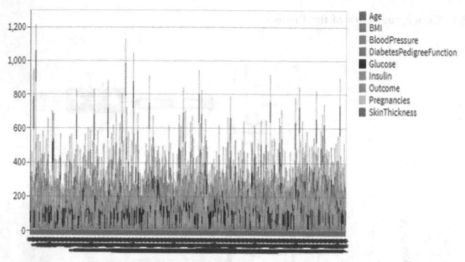

Fig. 2. Graphical representation of the diabetes dataset [10]

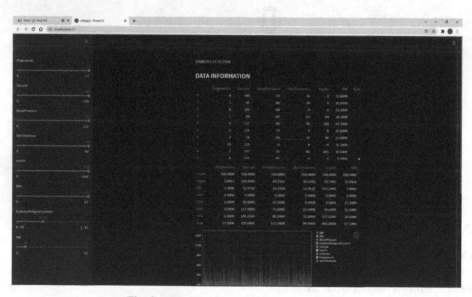

Fig. 3. Web Application of Diabetes Predictor

The graphical representation of the data in the dataset is depicted in Fig. 2. This graph is designed with all the attributes mentioned in the dataset. By this, our simple and efficient machine learning web app is built successfully and will be used for further processes.

USER INPUT

Model Test Accuracy Score

78.125%

Classification

	0
0	1

Fig. 4. Accuracy of the model and the output (Whether the person has diabetes or not)

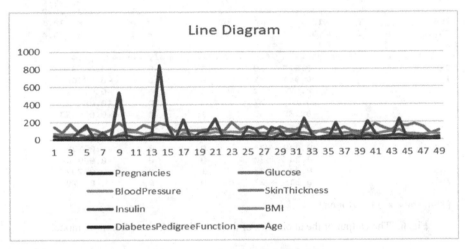

Fig. 5. Line Diagram of the model.

3.3 Second Module

The project's second module deals with injecting poisoning attacks into the model. In general, the hacker injects the poisoned data i.e., false data into the dataset of the model which leads to the corruption of the model. The model's output will not be correct. They inject those attacks into the machine learning model during the training phase of the model or after the development of the model. As it is a trained model with the pre-built dataset, the model could not recognize the injected data. Hacking a model and inserting the poisoning data into its dataset is quite a complex process. Here, we need a model with injected poisoned data. So, we are injecting the false data into the dataset manually.

3.4   Third Module

The development of an Anomaly detector deals with the third module. This utilizes the concept of Anomaly detection, which is nothing but identifying the anomalies in the system or model. An anomaly is such that unidentified data or something which is exceptional to the normal data.

```
       Pregnancies  Glucose  BloodPressure  SkinThickness  Insulin   BMI   \
0                6      148             72             35        0  33.6
1                1       85             66             29        0  26.6
2                8      183             64              0        0  23.3
3                1       89             66             23       94  28.1
4                0      137             40             35      168  43.1
..             ...      ...            ...            ...      ...   ...
763             10      101             76             48      180  32.9
764              2      122             70             27        0  36.8
765              5      121             72             23      112  26.2
766              1      126             60              0        0  30.1
767              1       93             70             31        0  30.4

     DiabetesPedigreeFunction  Age  Outcome  Anomaly  Anomaly_Score
0                       0.627   50        1        0      -0.055846
1                       0.351   31        0        0      -0.085665
2                       0.672   32        1        0      -0.025020
3                       0.167   21        0        0      -0.086189
4                       0.288   33        1        0      -0.037253
..                        ...  ...      ...      ...            ...
763                     0.171   63        0        0      -0.001134
764                     0.340   27        0        0      -0.091359
765                     0.245   30        0        0      -0.069346
766                     0.349   47        1        0      -0.037027
767                     0.315   23        0        0      -0.091795

[768 rows x 11 columns]
```

Fig. 6. The Output of the anomalies of the unhacked Machine Learning model.

We have designed this Anomaly detector tool in Python with the help of Pycaret Library in Jupyter notebook. First, the dataset is to be uploaded, then an environment is set up by creating and analyzing the model. We have used the I Forest - Isolation Forest Algorithm model to detect the misplaced data in the dataset. This algorithm does not require any testing or training, as it deals with unsupervised data. The concept of this model is as follows. If we upload the trained dataset of the model, it will convey that it has no anomalies. Uploading a dataset with injected data will lead to the detection of poisoning data, and it can be removed from the dataset. Our idea is to integrate with the website and launch it as an open-source product for everyone. As it will be very useful for those who use or run their systems in machine learning models.

Figure 5 clearly shows the output values of the anomalies of the unhacked model. As there no changes occur in the model, the values of the anomalies remain 0. After the injection of the poisoned data into the dataset and testing the anomaly detector with the poisoned dataset, the value of the anomalies turns 1 in those columns where the false data are inserted. It indicates to the administrators of the model that there occurred a hack through the injection of the poisoned data in those columns. It also indicates that the records stored in those columns are false data and are to be corrected (Fig. 7).

	Pregnancies	Glucose	BloodPressure	SkinThickness	Insulin	BMI
0	6	148	72	35	0	36.0
1	1	85	66	29	0	26.6
2	8	183	64	0	0	23.3
3	1	89	66	23	94	28.1
4	0	137	40	35	168	43.1
..	...	...	...	...	...	...
763	10	101	76	48	180	32.9
764	2	122	70	27	0	36.8
765	5	121	72	23	112	26.2
766	1	126	60	0	0	30.1
767	1	93	70	31	0	30.4

	DiabetesPedigreeFunction	Age	Outcome	Anomaly
0	0.627	50	12	1
1	0.351	31	0	0
2	0.672	32	14	1
3	0.167	21	124	1
4	0.288	33	1	0
..	...	...	...	...
763	0.171	63	0	0
764	0.340	27	0	0
765	0.245	30	0	0
766	0.349	47	1	0
767	0.315	23	0	0

[768 rows x 10 columns]

Fig. 7. Output of the anomalies of the hacked Machine Learning model.

The anomalies column in the dataset depicts the value which indicates whether the data is being poisoned or not. Figure 6 shows the anomaly values of the hacked model, where the poisoned data is being injected into it and those values in the rows where the values of the anomaly are 1, needed to be checked and changed.

3.5 Fourth Module

Our final module is related to the cryptographic authentication and provenance of the machine learning web application. This is an advanced concept because an anomaly detection tool detects anomalies, but this concept will prevent the injection of mismatched data in the dataset. For implementing this concept practically, the conversion of the ML model/web app into a website is done first. We have proposed two solutions for this concept.

One is authenticating cryptographically by using Themis Software. This is provided by MYSYS2 MSYS, a library that provides cryptographic services. It is open source and is used for storage authentication, and messaging of data. The other concept is authentication by SSL certificates. Secure Socket Layer converts HTTP into HTTPS, where it provides security, encryption, and authentication. It uses the concept of cryptography as the host will hold the private key to access the server, and the clients are given the public key to access the website. These concepts are to be implemented in our project to prevent the injection of poisonous data into the dataset of the web application.

Integrating all the modules and deploying the prototype is the final step of the project. Testing is to be carried out at this stage. We may notice some issues and problems during the testing phase, and they are to be rectified in the corresponding modules. After the testing process and the arrival of the final optimal output, we conclude that this project is completed successfully.

4   Comparative Study of Existing Works with Our Proposed System

Table 1. Classification of research works and comparative study with our proposed solution of first four papers.

S NO.	Title of the paper	Published Year	Comparative study with our proposed system	Publication
01	*Manipulating Machine learning: Poisoning attacks and countermeasures for regression learning*	2018	Against Poisoning attacks, they Designed a principled robust defense method. We designed an anomaly detector for the same	Security and privacy Symposium of IEEE
02	*Mitigating poisoning attacks on machine learning models: A data provenance-based approach*	2017	To identify poisonous attacks, they Used Information about the origin and transformation of data points in the training set	Journal on Artificial Intelligence and Security
03	*Preventing Data poisoning attacks by using generative models*	2020	Used MNIST Dataset against poisoning data and built Auto Encoder, a generative model. We have designed a model for health care with a diabetes dataset and built an Anomaly detector	IEEE Journal
04	*Detection of adversarial training examples in poisoning attacks through Anomaly Detection*	2018	Defense mechanism based on the outlier detection-based scheme to detect attacks. Our system is based on deviation and novelty-based schemes to detect and prevent,	Journal on Machine Learning

Table 2. Classification of research works and comparative study with our proposed solution for the next 5 papers.

S NO.	Title of the paper	Published Year	Comparative study with our proposed system	Publication
05	*A Poisoning attack against online Anomaly Detection*	2017	The authors used the Optimal Greedy Attack Algorithm. We have used the Isolation Forest algorithm for outlier detection which is more efficient than others	ResearchGate Online library
06	*Data Poisoning attacks against Online Learning*	2018	Preventing Poisoning attacks in Learning platforms by developing Attackers' algorithms with optimization problems. Our solution is to prevent those in healthcare platforms by developing an anomaly detector	ResearchGate Online Library
07	*De-Pois: An attack agnostic defense against Data poisoning attacks*	2021	De-Pois model imitates the target model's behavior using General Adversarial Behavior and distinguishing the poisoned samples from the original ones. Here, the anomaly detector distinguishes the poisoned data from the original data through outlier detection	IEEE Access
08	*Targeted BackDoor attacks on Deep Learning Systems using Data Poisoning*	2018	They proposed two types of defense methodologies namely, label distribution, and evaluation through new auxiliary data. We proposed one solution for detection and another for the prevention of poisoning attacks	Online Journal from the University of California
09	*Preventing Machine Learning Poisoning Attacks Using Authentication and Provenance*	2021	They proposed a VAMP system to protect media files that rely on Cryptographically based authentication. Our solution has been carried out with MYSYS2 MSYS software for authentication	Online journals in Research Gate

5 Architectural Model

5.1 System Requirements

The hardware requirements are the basic ones, such as A Laptop or a Personal Computer with a RAM of at least 4 GB with a minimum of an i3 processor and limited storage space.

On the other hand, the software requirements are Jupyter Notebook with the above-mentioned python libraries or Google Collaborator, PyCharm, Themis, MYSYS2 MSYS, Visual Studio Code, and Flask for converting the model into a website

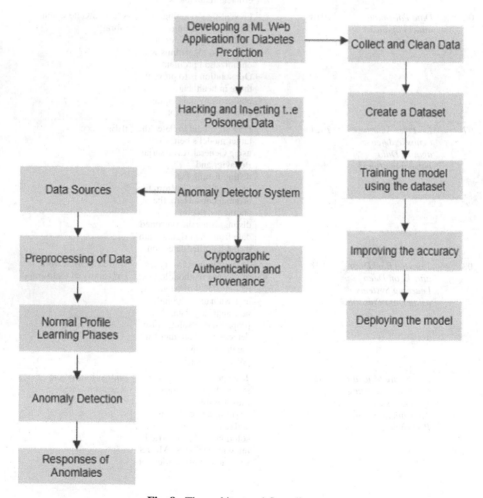

Fig. 8. The architectural flow diagram.

Figure 8 depicts the overall flow model for the project. It explains each module and the sub-modules of project.

6   Results and Discussion

We have taken medical-based web applications for the demonstration of our project idea. The same preventive methods can be implemented in any type of model. Thus, the anomaly detector is built using python, which accurately detects the anomalies i.e. mismatched data row by row of the dataset. Through this Anomaly detection system and Cryptographic authentication of the website, the machine learning web application is secured from the hands of attacks.

7   Conclusion and Future Scope

In this modern world, everything is being hacked and modified. To avoid those situations, this paper describes the complete prevention of machine learning web apps using cyber security tools. The proposed framework or project model will be so valuable and helpful for the medical database holders of the organization or hospitals. Therefore, the private information of the employees and the patients of the hospital will be secured and there will be no chances of hacking and modifying the information stored in the database. Further, this can be implemented in all the fields to secure their database /datasets in the machine learning models. People also will trust that all their valuable info will be stored safely and is never used for illegal actions.

References

1. Jagielski, M., Oprea, A., Biggio, B., Liu, C., Nita-Rotaru, C., Li, B.: Manipulating machine learning: poisoning attacks and countermeasures for regression learning. arXiv:1804.00308v3 [cs.CR] (2021)
2. Baracaldo, N., Chen, B., Ludwig, H., Safavi, J.A.: Mitigating poisoning attacks on machine learning models: a data provenance based approach. In: AISec 2017, November 3, 2017, Dallas, TX, USA 13
3. Aladag, M., Catak, F.O., Gul, E.: Preventing Data Poisoning Attacks By Using Generative Models
4. Paudice, A., Muñoz-González, L., Gyorgy, A., Lupu, E.C.: Detection of Adversarial Training Examples in Poisoning Attacks through Anomaly Detection. arXiv:1802.03041v1 [stat.ML] (2018)
5. Kloft, M., Laskov, P.: A "Poisoning" Attack Against Online Anomaly Detection
6. Wang, Y., Chaudhuri, K.: Data Poisoning Attacks against Online Learning. arXiv:1808.08994v1 [cs.LG] (2018)
7. Chen, J., Zhang, X., Zhang, R., Wang, C., Liu, L.: De-Pois: an attack-agnostic defense attacks data poisoning attacks
8. Chen, X., Liu, C., Li, B., Lu, K., Song, D.: Targeted backdoor attacks on deep learning systems using data poisoning
9. Kane, K, England, P, Stokes, J.W: Preventing Machine Learning Poisoning Attacks using Authentication and Provenance. arXiv:2105.10051v1 (2021) [cs.CR]
10. https://www.kaggle.com/datasets/mathchi/diabetes-data-set - Dataset for Diabetes Detection from Kaggle

Machine Learning-Based Solutions for Securing IoT Systems Against Multilayer Attacks

Badeea Al Sukhni[1]($\boxtimes$), Soumya K. Manna[1], Jugal Manoj Dave[2], and Leishi Zhang[1]

[1] School of Engineering, Technology and Design, Canterbury Christ Church University, Canterbury, Kent CT1 1QU, UK
{b.alsukhni331,soumyakanti.manna,leishi.zhang}@canterbury.ac.uk
[2] Directorate of Research and Publications, Rashtriya Raksha University, Lavad, India
jugal.dave@rru.ac.in

Abstract. IoT systems are prone to security attacks from several IoT layers as most of them possess limited resources and are unable to implement standard security protocols. This paper distinguishes multilayer IoT attacks from single-layer attacks and investigates their functioning. For developing a robust and efficient IDS (intrusion detection system), we have trained a few machine learning (ML) approaches such as NB, DT, and SVM using three standard sets of IoT datasets (Bot-IoT, ToN-IoT, Edge-IIoTset). Instead of using all features, the ML models are trained with similar features of multilayer IoT attacks to use optimal computational power and minimum number of features in the training dataset. The NB model achieves an accuracy of 57%–75%, while the DT model achieves an accuracy of 93%–100%. The outcome of the two ML models reveals that training with similar features possesses a higher accuracy level.

Keywords: IoT device · Multilayer attacks · Machine learning · Similar features

1 Introduction

It is estimated that by 2027, 41 billion Internet-of-Things (IoT) devices are to be used in a variety of life aspects, including transportation, healthcare, smart homes and cities, and many more [1]. This is due to the ubiquitous connectivity and decision-making capabilities of IoT devices [2]. As a result, there will be an increase in the number of security attacks on IoT networks and causing serious problems such as stealing personal information, high compensation, reputational damage and financial losses. For instance, researchers from Kaspersky claim that in the first six months of 2021, there were 1.5 billion attacks on IoT devices that were vulnerable, compared to the 639 million in the previous six months. [3].

As per our investigation, researchers have categorized IoT architecture into several layers for example three-layer [4–6], four-layer [7, 8] and five-layer [9] architectures. However, this article is focused on the most cited one, which is the three-layer architecture consisting of the physical layer, the network layer, and the application layer. Due to the layer-based architecture in IoT systems, signals from physical sensors can

R. S. Tomar et al. (Eds.): CNC 2022, CCIS 1893, pp. 140–153, 2023.
https://doi.org/10.1007/978-3-031-43140-1_13

be transported to cloud-based user applications via the network layer. However, each of these layers employs various technologies and services. Due to its multilayer heterogeneous architecture and limitation of computational resources, there are no such standard security frameworks incorporated in IoT devices. Therefore, IoT devices are vulnerable to a variety of security attacks due to unsecured cross-linking and access points at several layers. In the occasions of multilayer attacks, IoT devices can be affected from the sensor level to the cloud level sometimes simultaneously making it difficult to monitor and track. As mentioned, multilayer attacks can be harmful to IoT devices as they aim to exploit more than one layer of IoT architecture. For example, Denial of Service/Distributed Denial of Service (DoS/DDoS), Man-In-The-Middle (MITM), cryptanalysis, eavesdropping and side channel attacks target the M2M, network and cloud layers of the IoT system. According to the IBM Security X-Force report for 2022 [10] 74% of IoT attacks are caused by Mozi botnets to launch MITM attacks. Hence it is required to distinguish multilayer attacks from single-layer attacks. There is still a lack of research for finding the behavioural patterns and similarities of multilayer IoT attacks. As a preliminary part of our research, we have identified the multilayer attacks and distinguished them from single-layer attacks, and described the behaviours of those attacks through their similarity of features.

In order to secure IoT devices from a wide range of security attacks, researchers have tried to develop robust intrusion detection technologies using several novel techniques such as standard multi-bit encryption techniques, secured network protocols such as Point-to-Point Tunneling Protocol (PPTP), Secure File Transfer Protocol (SFTP) and multiple firewalls etc. In the meantime, it is also necessary to detect IoT attacks at different layers. There are various Machine learning (ML) models proposed for developing the Intrusion Detection Systems (IDS) of IoT systems. Usually, the significant features are extracted from the standard datasets of IoT attacks and used to train different ML models for detecting those attacks. We have investigated several articles which have utilized several ML techniques on standard or self-made datasets to evaluate the effectiveness of the models. For instance, Ur Rehman et al. [11] proposed a novel model for detecting and identifying DDoS attacks called DIDDoS that shows its ability to detect new attacks that have not been trained on. The authors used several learning algorithms such as Naïve Bayes (NB), Gated Recurrent Unit (GRU) which is a type of Recurrent Neural Network (RNN), and Sequential Minimal Optimization (SMO). Also, they used the CICDDoS2019 dataset to evaluate their model, and the achieved accuracy of the model is 99.94%. Shanmuga Priya et al. [12] applied three ML classification algorithms: K-Nearest Neighbors (KNN), Random Forest (RF), and NB for the detection of DDoS attacks that are targeting IoT networks. Also, they created their own dataset using the hping3 tool to generate DDoS attacks with the use of packet size and delta time features to distinguish DDoS packets. The proposed model results in detecting all types of DDoS attacks with a detection accuracy of 98.5%. However, their model is only able to detect DDoS attacks produced by hping3 and may not be able to detect attacks produced by other tools.

Similarly, Doshi and Apthorpe et al. [13] proposed a binary classification model that classifies the IoT network traffic into normal and abnormal DDoS attacks. In order to detect DDoS attacks including TCP SYN flood, HTTP GET flood, and UDP flood the authors created their own dataset and deployed different ML algorithms such as KNN, RF, Support Vector Machine (SVM), Decision Tree (DT), and Deep Neural Networks (DNN). The models achieved detection accuracy higher than 99%. Mukhtar et al. [14] used ML algorithms to safeguard systems from side-channel attacks such as NB, SVM, RF, and multilayer Perception (MLP) with the ECC datasets, and the model achieved an accuracy of 90%. In [15], the authors employed various machine learning (ML) models, including Naive Bayes (NB), Decision Trees (DT), Support Vector Machines (SVM), k-Nearest Neighbors (KNN), Random Forest (RF), AdaBoost, Logistic Regression (LR), and Extreme Gradient Boosting (XGBoost), to identify multiple types of attacks, such as Man-in-the-Middle (MITM), Denial of Service (DoS) and Distributed DoS (DDoS), Cross-Site Scripting (XSS), ransomware, scanning, backdoor, password attacks, and data injection. This analysis was conducted using the ToN-IoT dataset. The results demonstrated that the XGBoost classifier outperformed the other algorithms, achieving an impressive accuracy rate of 98%. Additionally, Zolanvari et al. [16] introduced a machine learning model aimed at detecting diverse Internet of Things (IoT) attacks, including backdoor, command, and SQL injection attacks. The authors curated their own dataset and applied seven algorithms: DT, SVM, NB, LR, RF, KNN, and Artificial Neural Networks (ANN). The outcomes indicated that the RF classifier outperformed the alternatives, achieving an F-measure value of 96.81%. Moreover, Anthi et al. [2] proposed a three-layer anomaly-based IDS for detecting several IoT attacks including7replay, DoS/DDoS, MITM attack, spoofing and reconnaissance. Their approach consists of nine supervised classification algorithms (NB, SVM, MLP, LR, J48, Zero R, Bayesian Network (BN), One R and RF) that have been applied to their own dataset. The system's results showed that the J48 classifier outperformed the others in terms of F-measure, with values ranging from 90% and 98%.

Table 1. Existing studies on IoT multilayer attacks

References	Multi-layer Attacks	Datasets	Datasets Features
[11]	DDoS	Not IoT dataset	All features
[12]	DDoS	Own dataset	All features
[13]	DDoS	Own dataset	All features
[14]	Side-channel	Not IoT dataset	All features
[15]	MITM, DoS/DDoS, XSS	IoT Dataset	All features
[16]	SQL injection	Own dataset	All features
[2]	Replay, DoS/DDoS, MITM	Own dataset	All features
Our Paper	Encryption attacks (Side-channel, Eavesdropping, MITM, and Cryptanalysis), DDOS, Replay, and Malicious code injection	IoT Datasets	Similar features and patterns

To our knowledge, only the aforementioned studies touched on the topic of multilayer attacks as most of the existing studies focused on security attacks that target a single IoT layer. This highlights the necessity for a new area of research that focuses on identifying attacks that target multiple layers of IoT architecture since the existing ones are limited to one or a subset of multilayer attacks. After evaluating the accuracy and F-measures of those ML models, they seem to be effective at detecting multilayer attacks. However, it is still not conclusive to find the appropriate one. In most of the studies, those ML models have been trained on all types of significant features from several types of attacks shown in the dataset. It is also worth investigating the similarity of patterns and features of these attacks. Table 1 provides a comparison between the existing studies and our paper. In this article, we propose to train ML models on the common features of multilayer attacks instead of all features set to improve the efficiency of the models. The organization of this paper is structured as follows: in Sect. 2, we present the research's methodology, our novel framework, the taxonomy of multilayer IoT attacks and their similar patterns and features, pre-processing and feature extraction, as well as training ML algorithms on similar and all features of multilayer attacks. Section 3 concludes the paper and highlights the future scope.

2 Methodology

For detecting multilayer IoT attacks, we have proposed and analysed an ML-based approach by training with similar features of multilayer IoT attacks. First of all, multilayer attacks which usually target more than one layer of an IoT system, have been identified and separated from single-layer attacks. Alongside, the behavioural patterns of those multilayer IoT systems have been analysed to find any commonalities of those attacks as it will help us to optimise the development of IoT security framework. We have planned to use several ML (supervised and unsupervised) for developing an intelligent intrusion detection system (IDS) to detect multilayer attacks. In order to train those models, several datasets (consisting of the features associated with security attacks) have been utilised for cybernetic and physical systems. However, we have only considered those datasets which only consist of features associated with IoT multilayer attacks. We have found three such standard datasets such as Bot-IoT, ToN-IoT and Edge-IIoTset.

To find the similarity of behaviours of IoT attacks, the similar features of mainly four well-known multilayer IoT attacks (Encryption, DoS/DDoS, Code Injection and Replay) have been identified. The process will probably optimize the whole process by reducing the number of training features for example, instead of training the ML models with all features of the dataset, we would like to train with only similar features of multilayer IoT attacks. It may save computational resources and can be a great benefit for real-time training. In the end, the following models SVM, NB and DT have been utilized for training with those similar features as well as training the models on all features to compare the results. To evaluate the effectiveness of our approach, the accuracy of those models has been analysed. The overall methodology is shown in Fig. 1.

2.1 Identification of Multilayer Attacks and Their Similarities

Several studies addressed IoT attacks on the three-layer IoT system and discussed the possible security solutions to handle these attacks. In Ahmad and Alsmadi [17] IoT taxonomy, the physical layer consists of several attacks including side-channel attack, physical damage, node jamming, eavesdropping, etc. The network layer attacks are divided into **encryption attacks** (MITM, caching, spoofing, session hijacking, packet

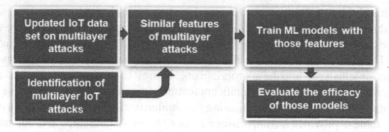

Fig. 1. Methodology of the proposed framework

manipulation, cryptanalysis and RFID cloning), **DoS/DDoS attacks** (packet flooding, battery draining, SYN flood, botnet, ping of death, slowloris, etc.), **routing attacks** (sybil, wormhole/sinkhole, forwarding and nmap/port attack), and **middleware attacks** (brute-force, dictionary attack, message replay, etc.). The application layer attacks are divided into **malware attacks** (virus, ransomware, spyware, etc.), **privacy attacks** (spear phishing, phishing, social engineering, etc.), and **code attacks** (SQL injection, Cross Site Scripting (XSS), malicious script, session hijacking, etc.). Also, the authors have provided information about IoT large-scale attacks (Botnet, ping of death, TCP SYN flooding, etc.). In another instance, the authors in [18] added to their three-layer taxonomy a new attack category called encryption attacks that consists of (cryptanalysis, side channel, and MITM attacks).

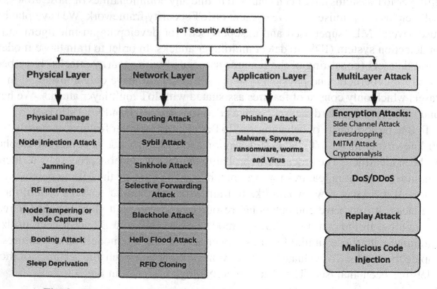

Fig. 2. The three-layer IoT Security attacks including multilayer attacks

Moreover, Khanam et al. [4] added a category called multilayer/ dimensional attacks alongside the three-layer IoT attacks which consist of the side channel, DoS, MITM, and cryptanalysis attacks. Furthermore, in [19] the authors addressed RFID security attacks on three-layer IoT systems and added two new categories. The first category is called strategic layer attacks which consist of attacks that target commercial secrets and critical production information such as social engineering, competitive espionage, etc. The second category is multilayer attacks that consist of covert channels, crypto, traffic analysis, side channel, replay, and DoS attacks. Based on the above investigation, the multilayer attacks are identified and discussed in this section with their common patterns and similarities. The three-layer IoT attacks have been summarized in several pieces of literature [4, 17–19] as well as identify multilayer attacks, which target multiple layers of the IoT system (Fig. 2).

The first category shows the IoT physical layer which is vulnerable to node injection attack which is a type of MITM attack, sleep deprivation which is a type of DoS attack, booting attacks, jamming, RF interference, node tampering and physical damage. The second category in the Figure is the IoT network layer which is vulnerable to routing, sinkhole attacks which is one of the routing attacks, hello flood attacks, RFID cloning attacks, selective forwarding attacks, sybil attacks and blackhole attacks. The third category is the IoT application layer, which is a target for several attacks such as malware, worms, virus, spyware, ransomware and phishing attacks. And lastly, the multilayer attacks include Encryption attacks (side channel, eavesdropping, MITM, and cryptanalysis), DDOS, replay, and malicious code injection attacks.

1) **Encryption Attack:** The intruder used this attack to compromise the three layers of the IoT system to break the encryption algorithms that are used to safeguard the communication channels between IoT devices. Side channel, eavesdropping, cryptanalysis, and MITM attacks are examples of this attack [4, 17, 18, 20].

a) Side Channel Attack: The attackers target the encryption devices in order to obtain the encryption keys and steal sensitive information. Power consumption attacks, timing attacks, and electromagnetic attacks are examples of these attacks.

b) Eavesdropping attack: There are two ways to implement eavesdropping attacks whether in active or passive mode. In the passive mode, the attacker eavesdrops on the data exchanged between two legitimate devices and gains the encryption key needed to decrypt confidential data which results in users' privacy invasion without users' awareness. MITM is an example of an active eavesdropping attack, which will be discussed in the next point.

c) MITM Attack: It is an active attack, where the attacker acts as a router between two nodes that are exchanging sensitive information and leads the attacker to capture the encryption key to decrypt and modify the data. As shown in Fig. 3, a node injection attack is a type of MITM that compromises the IoT physical layer. ARP poisoning, ICMP redirection, port stealing, DHCP spoofing are examples of MITM attacks that target the network layer. DNS spoofing and session hijacking target the IoT application layer.

d) Cryptanalysis Attack: This attack is different from the other encryption attacks as the attacker attempts to decrypt sensitive data without acquiring the encryption key. As shown in Fig. 3, Ciphertext-only attacks, Known-plaintext attacks, Chosen-plaintext attacks and Brute-force attacks (including FTP and SSH-patator) are examples of cryptanalysis Attacks.

2) **DoS/DDoS Attack:** Basically, this attack is about overwhelming the target IoT device or network with a high amount of flood traffic by initiating a 3-way TCP handshake

but without completing the last stage (ACK) to make the service unavailable for future requests even for legitimate users. A botnet attack is a group of infected IoT devices with malware that can be used to launch DoS/DDoS attacks. [4, 21]. As shown in Fig. 3, sleep deprivation and sensor data flooding are examples of DoS/DDoS attacks at the physical layer. ICMP, SYN, UDP and hello floods are compromising the network layer. Lastly, heartbleed, goldenEye, slowloris, slowhttptest, zero-day, HTTP and DNS floods are exploiting the application layer [22].

3) **Replay Attack:** An adversary compromises both IoT physical and network layers using this attack to get sensitive information and mislead the receiver device by storing the transmitted data and broadcasting them later to one or more parties, resulting in exhausting system resources such as processors, batteries and memories [4, 21].

4) **Code Injection Attack:** the cybercriminal targets both IoT physical and application layers using this attack. In the physical layer, the attacker injects malicious code such as malware into the IoT nodes, forcing them to execute specific actions or even gain access to the IoT system [18]. As seen in Fig. 3, SQL injection, Cross site Script (XSS) and Malicious script are code injection attacks that can be used to target the IoT application layer.

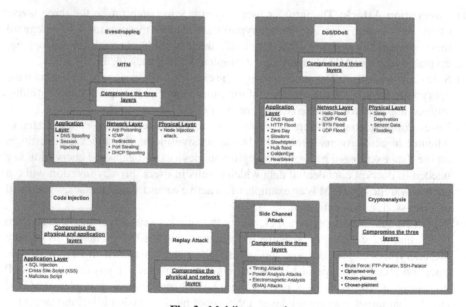

Fig. 3. Multilayer attacks

We observed that there are common patterns in these multilayer attacks, for instance, eavesdropping, MITM and replay attacks are interception attacks against data confidentiality, where an unauthorized user gains access to sensitive data, IoT devices and applications. Besides, DoS/DDoS attacks can be considered as interruption attacks that are against the availability of services by flooding the network with a massive amount of traffic to cause chaos in the IoT network operations. Moreover, code injection attacks can be considered as fabrication attacks that are against data integrity by creating illegitimate information within the IoT system. Cryptanalysis and side channel attacks are against data confidentiality, these attacks are compromising cryptographic algorithms to gain sensitive information. We also investigated the publicly available datasets that have been proposed and used by several researchers to tackle multilayer attacks. Table 2 presents a brief analysis of these datasets [15, 23–25]. As shown in Table 2, KDD CUP 1999, NSL-KDD, NSW-NB15, CICIDS2017 and CICDDoS2019 datasets are not specific to IoT systems. However, Bot-IoT, ToN-IoT, Edge-IIoTset and N-BaIoT datasets are specific to IoT systems. This paper will focus on utilizing Bot-IoT, ToN-IoT, Edge-IIoTset as they are the recent datasets and include most of the multilayer attacks.

Table 2. Datasets Analysis

Dataset	Year	IoT Specific	Total Features	Total Attacks	Multilayer Attacks
KDDCUP 99	1999	No	41	4	DoS
NSL-KDD	2009	No	43	4	DoS
UNSW-NB15	2015	No	49	9	DoS
CICIDS2017	2017	No	80	14	DoS, XSS, SQL Injection
BoT-IoT	2018	Yes	45	10	DoS/DDoS
N-BaIoT	2018	Yes	115	2	Botnet attacks (Mirai and Gafgyt)
ToN-IoT	2020	Yes	44	9	DoS/DDoS, SQL Injection, XSS, MITM
Edge-IIoTset	2022	Yes	61	14	DoS/DDoS, SQL Injection, XSS, MITM

2.2 Pre-processing and Feature Extraction

In order to find the similar features between the multilayer attacks in the Bot-IoT, ToN-IoT, Edge-IIoTset datasets, we have investigated thoroughly these datasets to find the common features in the datasets, as shown in Table 3, and then performed data preprocessing to remove the unnecessary features from the raw data, as shown in Table 3.

After investigating Bot-IoT, ToN-IoT, Edge-IIoTset datasets, we found common features between multilayer attacks as shown in Table 3. In Edge-IIoTset dataset, we found 31 common features between DDoS_HTTP, DDoS_ICMP, DDoS_TCP, DDoS_UDP, MITM, SQL injection and XSS attacks. In the ToN-IoT dataset, we found 32 common features between DoS, DDoS, MITM, SQL injection and XSS attacks. Besides, in the BoT-IoT dataset particularly (UNSW_2018_IoT_Botnet_Final_10_best_Training.csv) we found that all the 16 features are significant and common between DDoS_HTTP, DDoS_TCP, DDoS_UDP, DoS_HTTP, DoS_TCP, DoS_UDP attacks.

Table 3. List of common features of multilayer attacks (pre-processing)

Datasets	Multilayer Attacks	Total Number of Common Features	Common features
BoT-IoT	DDoS_HTTP, DDoS_TCP, DDoS_UDP, DoS_HTTP, DoS_TCP, and DoS_UDP	16	pkSeqID, proto, saddr, sport, daddr, dport, seq, stddev, N_IN_Conn_P_SrcIP, state_number, mean, N_IN_Conn_P_DstIP, drate, srate, max, min
Edge-IIoTset	DDoS_HTTP, DDoS_ICMP, DDoS_TCP, DDoS_UDP, MITM, SQL injection and XSS	31	frame.time, ip.src_host, ip.dst_host, arp.dst.proto_ipv4, arp.src.proto_ipv4, arp.hw.size,arp.code, icmp.seq_le, http.request.version, http.file_data, http.content_ length, http.request.method, http.request.full_uri, http.response, tcp.dstport, tcp.srcport, tcp.options, tcp.connection.fin, tcp.connection.rst, tcp.flags, tcp.connection.syn, tcp.connection.synack, tcp.flags.ack, tcp.payload, tcp.len, tcp.ack, tcp.ack_raw, tcp.seq, tcp.checksum, udp.stream, dns.qry.name
ToN-IoT	DoS, DDoS, MITM, SQL injection and XSS	32	ts, src_ip, src_port, dst_ip, dst_port, proto, service, duration, src_bytes, dst_bytes, conn_state, missed_bytes, src_pkts, src_ip_bytes, dst_pkts, dst_ip_bytes, dns_query, dns_qclass, dns_qtype, dns_rcode, dns_AA, dns_RD, dns_RA, dns_rejected, http_version, http_resp_mime_types, http_trans_depth, http_method, http_uri, http_response_body_len, http_status_code, http_user_agent

Furthermore, we performed data pre-processing on the three datasets before training the ML algorithms to remove the unnecessary features. As shown in Table 4, The Edge-IIoTset dataset, has 21 significant features to identify multilayer attacks such as ip.src_host, ip.dst_host, arp.hw.size, arp.opcode, etc. The ToN-IoT dataset has 13 significant features and these features are ts, src_ip, src_port, dst_ip, dst_port, proto, etc. For the BoT-IoT dataset, all 16 features are significant including pkSeqID, proto, saddr, sport, etc. We also converted the IP addresses (src_ip, dst_ip, ip.src_host, ip.dst_host, saddr and daddr) in the three datasets into numbers, and the string data (proto and attack_label) into numbers too.

2.3 Training ML Algorithms on the Similar Features

There are various ML models have been proposed for IDS on IoT systems because of their ability to fast processing and high accuracy in detecting and identifying unsolicited traffic in IoT networks at early stages [7]. Furthermore, ML models show promise in detecting new attacks that have not been trained on, using their self-learning capabilities

Table 4. List of common features of multilayer attacks (post-processing)

Datasets	Multilayer Attacks	Total Number of Common Features	Common features
BoT-IoT	DDoS_HTTP, DDoS_TCP, DDoS_UDP, DoS_HTTP, DoS_TCP, and DoS_UDP	16	pkSeqID, proto, saddr, sport, daddr, dport, seq, stddev, N_IN_Conn_P_SrcIP, state_number, mean, N_IN_Conn_P_DstIP, drate, srate, max, min
Edge-IIoTset	DDoS_HTTP, DDoS_ICMP, DDoS_TCP, DDoS_UDP, MITM, SQL injection and XSS	21	ip.src_host, ip.dst_host, arp.hw.size, arp.opcode, icmp.seq_le, http.content_length, http.response, tcp.dstport, tcp.connection.fin, tcp.connection.rst, tcp.len, tcp.flags, tcp.connection.syn, tcp.connection.synack, tcp.flags.ack, tcp.ack, tcp.ack_raw, tcp.seq, tcp.checksum, udp.stream, dns.qry.name
ToN-IoT	DoS, DDoS, MITM, SQL injection and XSS	13	ts, src_ip, src_port, dst_ip, dst_port, proto, duration, src_bytes, dst_bytes, src_pkts, dst_pkts, dns_qclass, dns_qtype

[11]. This section is focused on training and evaluating ML models, NB, SVM and DT on three datasets Bot-IoT, ToN-IoT, Edge-IIoTset using similar features of multilayer attacks. We used python libraries such as the scikit-learn to implement these models on our proposed system and divided the datasets into 70% as training and 30% as a testing set, as well as evaluated the performance using the accuracy metric. We show the results in Fig. 4 and Table 5.

From the following table, it can be concluded that DT achieved higher detection than the other ML models with an accuracy of 99.9%, 100% (because of overfitting) and 93.9% in BoT-IoT, ToN-IoT and Edge-IIoTset datasets, respectively.

Table 5. Comparative results (training with all features and similar features)

BoT-IoT Dataset		
ML Model	Accuracy % of similar features	Accuracy % of all features
NB	75.3	75.3
DT	99.9	99.9
SVM	100	100
ToN-IoT Dataset		
ML Model	Accuracy % of similar features	Accuracy % of all features
NB	57.3	56.9
DT	100	100
SVM	39.9	39.9
Edge-IIoTset Dataset		
ML Model	Accuracy % of similar features	Accuracy % of all features
NB	59	29.9
DT	93.5	73.35
SVM	65	53.23

Besides, SVM showed good results after the DT with an accuracy of 100% (because of overfitting), 39.9%, and 65% and the NB algorithm achieved an accuracy of 75.3%, 57.3%, 59% in BoT-IoT, ToN-IoT and Edge-IIoTset datasets, respectively. These results indicate that DT has outperformed other ML algorithms and is effective in identifying multilayer attacks on IoT systems with high accuracy. Also, the DT algorithm achieved gains for confidentiality, integrity and availability when applied to the IoT systems. We have also trained the three algorithms with all features of ToN-IoT and Edge-IIoTset datasets to compare the results with similar features of the multilayer, we have not trained the BoT-IoT at this stage as the common and all features are the same. As shown in the above table, the accuracy of DT and SVM are the same in the ToN-IoT dataset, however, the accuracy of NB is decreased to 56.9%. Also, in the Edge-IIoTset dataset, the accuracy of the three algorithms decreased too, with 29.9% in NB, 73.355% in DT and 53.23% in SVM. This indicates that training ML models with similar features are more effective to detect multilayer attacks than training the models on all features.

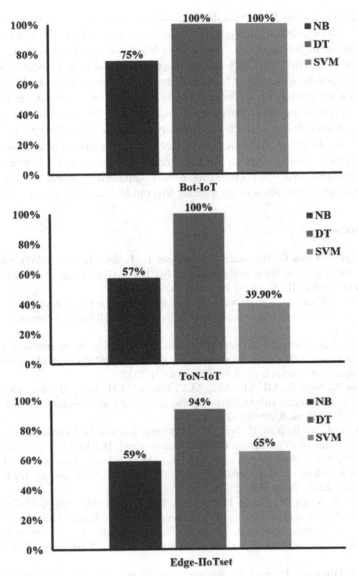

Fig. 4. Accuracy results of three datasets after training with similar features

3 Conclusion

In this paper, the property and behaviours of multilayer attacks and their distinguishable patterns from single-layer attacks have been discussed. It has appeared that these types of security attacks can target more than one layer of IoT systems and hence possess severe damage to IoT devices. We have evaluated the similarity of patterns of these attacks through their similar features in three IoT datasets (Bot-IoT, ToN-IoT, Edge-IIoTset datasets). Three ML algorithms SVM, DT, and NB models have been trained with all similar features to classify the multilayer attacks to preserve users' privacy, IoT device security, and the availability, integrity, and confidentiality of data. The results show that the DT achieved higher detection than the other ML models, with an accuracy of 99.9%, 100% and 93.9% in BoT-IoT, ToN-IoT and Edge-IIoTset datasets, respectively. Besides, training ML models with similar features is more effective to detect multilayer attacks than training the models on all features as the results show a decrease in the model's accuracy while training the models with all features. The limitation of this approach is that few significant features which are explicitly relevant to specific types of multilayer attacks may be discarded. Also, the significance of features should be evaluated for each IoT attack before finding the similarity between multilayer attacks. Hence, our future scope of research is to develop a smart and novel computational framework by optimally selecting the number of features for training ML models in multilayer attacks.

References

1. Ferrag, M.A., Friha, O., Hamouda, D., Maglaras, L., Janicke, H.: Edge-IIoTset: a new comprehensive realistic cyber security dataset of IoT and IIoT applications for centralized and federated learning. IEEE Access **10**, 40281–40306 (2022)
2. Anthi, E., Williams, L., Słowińska, M., Theodorakopoulos, G., Burnap, P.: A supervised intrusion detection system for smart home IoT devices. IEEE Internet Things J. **6**(5), 9042–9053 (2019)
3. Daws, R.: Kaspersky: Attacks on IoT devices double in a year, Internet of Things News. IoT Tech News (2021). https://www.iottechnews.com/news/2021/sep/07/kaspersky-attacks-on-iot-devices-double-in-a-year/. Accessed Oct 31 2022
4. Khanam, S., Ahmedy, I.B., Idna Idris, M.Y., Jaward, M.H., Bin Md Sabri, A.Q.: A survey of security challenges, attacks taxonomy and advanced countermeasures in the internet of things. IEEE Access, **8**, 219709–219743 2020
5. Tahsien, S.M., Karimipour, H., Spachos, P.: Machine learning based solutions for security of internet of things (IoT): a survey. J. Netw. Comput. Appl. **161**(102630), 102630 (2020)
6. Al-Garadi, M.A., Mohamed, A., Al-Ali, A.K., Du, X., Ali, I., Guizani, M.: A survey of machine and deep learning methods for internet of things (IoT) security. IEEE Commun. Surv. Tutor. **22**(3), 1646–1685 (2020)
7. Malhotra, P., Singh, Y., Anand, P., Bangotra, D.K., Singh, P.K., Hong, W.-C.: Internet of things: evolution, concerns and security challenges. Sensors (Basel) **21**(5), 1809 (2021)
8. Hassija, V., Chamola, V., Saxena, V., Jain, D., Goyal, P., Sikdar, B.: A survey on IoT security: application areas, security threats, and solution architectures. IEEE Access **7**, 82721–82743 (2019)
9. Butun, I., Osterberg, P., Song, H.: Security of the internet of things: vulnerabilities, attacks, and countermeasures. IEEE Commun. Surv. Tutor. **22**(1), 616–644 (2020)
10. IBM. IBM Security X-Force Threat Intelligence Index, Ibm.com. Available at: https://www.ibm.com/reports/threat-intelligence/ (Accessed: November 1, 2022)
11. ur Rehman, S., et al.: DIDDOS: an approach for detection and identification of distributed denial of Service (DDoS) cyberattacks using Gated Recurrent Units (GRU). Future Gener. Comput. Syst.118, 453–466 (2021). https://doi.org/10.1016/j.future.2021.01.022
12. Priya, S.S., Sivaram, M., Yuvaraj, D., Jayanthiladevi, A.: Machine learning based DDOS detection. In: 2020 International Conference on Emerging Smart Computing and Informatics (ESCI) (2020)
13. Doshi, R., Apthorpe, N., Feamster, N.: Machine learning DDoS detection for consumer Internet of Things devices, arXiv [cs.CR] (2018)

14. Mukhtar, N., et al.: Improved hybrid approach for side-channel analysis using efficient convolutional neural network and dimensionality reduction. IEEE Access: Pract. Innovations, Open Solutions **8**, 184298–184311 (2020). https://doi.org/10.1109/access.2020.3029206
15. Gad, A.R., Nashat, A.A., Barkat, T.M.: Intrusion detection system using machine learning for vehicular ad hoc networks based on ToN-IoT dataset. IEEE Access **9**, 142206–142217 (2021)
16. Zolanvari, M., Teixeira, M.A., Gupta, L., Khan, K.M., Jain, R.: Machine learning-based network vulnerability analysis of industrial internet of things. IEEE Internet Things J. **6**(4), 6822–6834 (2019)
17. Ahmad, R., Alsmadi, I.: Machine learning approaches to IoT security: a systematic literature review. Internet of Things **14**(100365), 100365 (2021)
18. Atlam, H.F., Wills, G.B.: IoT Security, Privacy, Safety and Ethics, pp. 123–149. Springer, Cham (2020)
19. Mitrokotsa, A., Rieback, M.R., Tanenbaum, A.S.: Classifying RFID attacks and defenses. Inf. Syst. Front. **12**, 491–505 (2010)
20. Ahmad, Z., Shahid Khan, A., Wai Shiang, C., Abdullah, J., Ahmad, F.: Network intrusion detection system: a systematic study of machine learning and deep learning approaches. Trans. Emerg. Telecommun. Technol. **32**(1), e4150 (2021)
21. Kumar, R., Sharma, R.: Leveraging blockchain for ensuring trust in iot: a survey. J. King Saud Univ. Comput. Inf. Sci. **34**(10), 8599–8622 (2022)
22. Ferrag, M.A., et al.: RDTIDS: rules and decision tree-based intrusion detection system for Internet-of-Things networks. Future internet **12**(3), 44 (2020)
23. Manesh, M.R., Kaabouch, N.: Cyber-attacks on unmanned aerial system networks: detection, countermeasure, and future research directions. Comput. Secur. **85**, 386–401 (2019)
24. Nawir, M., Amir, A., Yaakob, N. Lynn, O.B.: Internet of Things (IoT): taxonomy of security attacks. In: 2016 3rd International Conference on Electronic Design (ICED), pp. 321–326. IEEE 2016
25. Alhowaide, A., Alsmadi, I., Tang, J.: Ensemble detection model for IoT IDS. Internet of Things (Netherlands) **16**, 100435 (2021). https://doi.org/10.1016/j.iot.2021.100435

Securing Internet of Things Using Machine Learning Techniques: A Systematic Review

Barkha Kumari[1(✉)], Vinay Singh[1(✉)], and Mohit Kumar[2(✉)]

[1] Usha Martin University, Ranchi, Jharkhand 835103, India
singhvarsha35@gmail.com, vinaysinghumu@gmail.com
[2] MIT-ADT University, Pune 412201, India
mohitsmailbox13@gmail.com

Abstract. Our current period is the era of the Internet of Things (IoT). The latest evolution in information technology, software and paraphernalia have hastened the stationing of huge number associated smart and familiar appliances in evaluative system like industries, Agriculture, Healthcare, Transportation, Home automation and environment control. The data transmission over the network without necessitating of any human to human (H2H) or human to machine (H2M) role, increases the trustworthiness and customers satisfaction, but it also unlatched a gateway for attackers or intruders for executing various types of attacks for unauthorized access information manipulation or information disclosure which increases the security risk. Machine learning technology is one of the optimum solutions to mitigate various security threats. In This paper a literature survey on a different security threat in a IoT technology and solution of security issues using machine learning approach and a brief explanation of different attacks in IoT applications has been presented. This work covers issues related to securing data generated in different application area of IoT system such as IIoT (Internet of Things for industries) and IoSHT (Internet of Things for smart healthcare system). The future scope of machine learning techniques to ensure safety and challenges are discussed.

Keywords: Internet of Things (IoT) · IIoT (Internet of Things for industries) · IoSHT (Internet of Things for smart healthcare system) · human to human (H2H) · human to machine (H2M)

1 Introduction

A web of intelligent devices which can exchange information through the network is called Internet of Thongs. It is a foremost expeditiously technology used in past tenner in numerous applications. The smart devices are placed in a different territory to catch the information and some occurrences. In the Internet of Things technology, users can access and control their smart devices remotely from anywhere and anytime. This ubiquitous feature of IoT technology makes it endangered from several threats and risks [1, 28].

Intruders takes benefits from the lack of security and make these Internet connected devices zombies and botnet. When large number of devices are endangered, they become

© The Author(s), under exclusive license to Springer Nature Switzerland AG 2023
R. S. Tomar et al. (Eds.): CNC 2022, CCIS 1893, pp. 154–165, 2023.
https://doi.org/10.1007/978-3-031-43140-1_14

part of the various types of attacks. These devices are controlled by the intruders to launch various attacks [2].

This several applications of the Internet of Things, covers range from enterprise IoT and consumer IoT to industrial IoT and manufacturing IoT. Internet of Things covers a broad radius of applications like agriculture, smart cities, smart homes, smart grids, health care and traffic monitoring etc. For the sake of securing Internet of Things (IoT) devices and system, the various approaches based on machine learning are proved to be propitious alternative. Machine Learning algorithms are used to develop a model based on past data and training data to performs prediction or make decisions without requiring any explicit programming. Various Machine Learning (ML) algorithms are used to train the model. These models are used to detect different types of attacks and come up with the solution of risk minimization. Machine Learning technology has been proved to be one of the best solutions to detect several types of attacks and vulnerabilities by using trained model and tackle them efficiently [1]. Various literature review articles have been presented there since 2017, most of them covered different types of IoT attacks and their possible solutions.

The list of major contribution of this work are as follows:

a) This paper providing a literature survey on a different security threat in a IoT technology and solution of security issues using machine learning approach.
b) A brief explanation of different attacks in IoT applications and its type.
c) This work covers the issues related to the securing data generated in different application area of IoT systems such as IIoT (Industrial Internet of Things) and IoSHT (Internet of smart healthcare Things).
d) Finally, we have highlighted the future scope of machine learning to ensure security in IoT infrastructure and challenges in IoT application.

Rest of the content of this paper is organised as follows:

In this paper Sect. 2 shows the Literature Review of related work. Section 3 describes various attacks in IoT and its types. In Sect. 4 we have discussed security in Internet of things using machine learning techniques. Section 5 describes a review on use of machine learning in IIoT (Industrial Internet of Things). Section 6 discusses a review on use of machine learning in smart healthcare system. Section 7 discusses Future scope of machine learning in security of IoT. Section 8 describes Challenges in IoT Security. Section 9 concludes the paper.

2 Literature Review

A Literature review intimates the knowledge and understanding of recent research performed in a specific area before carry out a novel investigation. The main aim of a literature review is enabled us to discover what findings has been done already and determine what is unacquainted inside our research area. The security in Internet of Things (IoT) is an emerging research area which gains an attention from different research association. In this literature review, the authors explained about the perceptivity of the IoT technology and the solution to mitigate security risks in IoT using ML.

In Table 1 we presented here a summary of some already done research work related to various security issues in IoT technology and their mitigation using machine learning approaches.

Table 1. Related work on various security issues and their mitigation in IoT using Machine Learning techniques.

Reference paper	Year	Contribution
M. Bagga et al. [3]	2020	This paper presents a machine learning (ML) security framework to addresses the growing security concerns in the IoT space. Software Defined Networking (SDN) providers and Network Functions Virtualization (NFV) are utilized by security framework to minimize various threats and also examines the most common threats. This paper strongly believes that a comprehensive security system is enabled by combined use of SDN, NFV and machine learning solutions
L. Xiao et al. [4]	2018	In This article, an attack model of IoT systems has been explored, and also performed review on IoT security solutions using various machine learning techniques. It also focuses on various machine learning techniques for IoT authorization, data access control, secured upload and download and malware detection techniques to protect the privacy of data
D.J. Atul et al. [5]	2021	The purpose of this work is to provide superior developments in the communication paradigm of CPS-based Internet of Things systems in the area of EASH (Energy-Aware Smart Home System). It also analyses the issues of security, irregularities, and service failures and provides a paradigm based on an improved communication paradigm, specifically, it proposes the Energy Aware Smart Home (EASH) framework. Using this feature, EASH analyses the problem of communication failure and types of network attacks. Using the machine learning method, non-standard resources of the communication paradigm are categorized. The performance results presented the use of algorithms in machine-readable learning is a good path to differentiate between the damaged and strong segment with a critical degree of high accuracy
K. Mandal et al. [6]	2020	This paper focuses on the security challenges of access to the IoT system. Analyze the various attacks of the access system, the effects and location attacks on the IoT network. Also, the main focus on the algorithm of the machine learning class used in the IoT system network to improve the effectiveness of attack detection

(continued)

Table 1. (*continued*)

Reference paper	Year	Contribution
M. Shafiq et al. [7]	2020	In this paper, a new efficient feature selection approach is proposed for the active element selection problem for different types of cyber-attacks detection on IoT network traffic by using Botnet-IoT databases and also enhances the strategic Machine learning performance. To this end, a new framework model has been proposed. First, a novel feature selection method called the CorrAUC, then based on CorrAUC, a new feature selection feature CorrAuc has been developed and designed, based on a precision wrap to select the feature accurately and efficiently and also select the functional features of the chased ML algorithm by using the AUC metric. It also used TOPSIS integrated with Shannon Entropy based on a soft bijective set to verify selected features for detecting malicious traffic on IoT networks
N. Ravi et al. [8]	2020	This paper has proposed a way to find and reduce access to the IoT network. The approach is based on a novel modified reading model called SDRK. SDRK leverages target deep neural networks and unregulated integration methods
S. Rathore et al. [9]	2018	In this paper a fog-based threat detection framework based on fog computing paradigm and a new ELM-based approach on Semi-supervised Fuzzy C-Means (ESFCM) has been proposed. The method ESFCM uses a semi-supervised fuzzy algorithm to handle the different issues of labelled data and the Extreme Learning Machine (ELM) algorithm to provide efficient performance with quick acquisition rate
M. Hasan et al. [10]	2019	In this paper, the performance of several machine learning models has been compared for the prediction of different types of attacks. This paper used different types of machine learning algorithms like Logistic Regression (LR), Support Vector Machine (SVM), Decision Tree (DT), Random Forest (RF), and Sensory Neural Network (ANN). The proposed method has identified 99.4% accuracy of Decision Tree, Informal Forest, and ANN. The proposed method has also proved that Random Forest method works relatively well

(*continued*)

3   Attacks in IoT and Its Type

In recent years, the IoT technology has been suffering many kinds of attacks which leads the consciousness for using IoT things more delicately, this portion outlines many different types of attacks and their impacts.

Table 1. (*continued*)

Reference paper	Year	Contribution
E. Anthi et al. [11]	2019	In This paper a three-layer intrusion detection system (IDS) has been proposed. Proposed method uses a very secure technique to identify a popular cyber-attack on IoT networks. This system includes of three major functions. First one is separation of the type and profile of normal behaviour of each IoT devices linked to the network, second one is detection of malicious packets in the network during an attack and third one is separation of the types of attacks which has been used
V. Neerugatti et al. [12]	2019	In this paper a standardized attack detection method MLTKNN, based on a KNN algorithm has been proposed. The proposed method has been simulated in imitation of Cooja by 30 motes and calculated with a very well rating and a false standard for the proposed acquisition method. In this paper the performance of the given method was effective in terms of retardation, delivery rate of packets and pointer detection

3.1 Types of Attacks

Attacks in IoT can be classified into two categories-cyber-attacks and physical attacks. Further cyber-attacks can be classified into passive and active attacks.

An attempt to cripple computer system (Steal, delete, alter, destroy data or use a breached computer system) to execute attacks is called a cyber-attack. Different methods are used to execute a cyber-attack that includes man-in-the-middle attack, phishing, malware, ransomware or other methods. Attacks that physically damage IoT things is refer to as physical attacks.

In physical attacks, the attacker harms components of IoT system to stops the services [13].

3.1.1 Active Attacks

In an active attack, an intruder or attacker continuously tries to access, steal, and modify the data and information in an unauthorized way to halt the system configuration and services [1]. Different kinds of active attacks are DoS, DDoS, Spoofing, man-in-the-middle, session replay and message alteration etc.

a) **Denial-of-Service (DoS) Attack-**Denial of service (DoS) attacks are largely accountable for interrupt the system services by sending huge number of fake requests with the intention of real users to make unable to access and communicate with the server. Additionally, DoS attacks keep IoT devices always active, reducing battery life due to fake heavy traffic in the server.

b) **Spoofing-**Spoofing attacks will reveal the identity of the user to a great extent to gain illegal access to the system in the IoT system. Spoofing attacks can be launched very easily on an IoT access network. By using a fake identity, such as a Media

Access Control (MAC) or Internet Protocol (IP) address of a legitimate user's identity, spoofing attackers can claim to be another legitimate user of an IoT device.

c) **Jamming Attack-**Jamming attacks can be a very destructive attack in any network. This attack generates the fake traffic jams over the network by interrupting the transmission medium between nodes. Moreover, this attack degrades the performance of IoT devices by using more memory, bandwidth, and power etc.

d) **Man-in-the-middle (MIM) Attack-**Man in the middle attacks exploit the IoT system devices by spying, harming, or disrupting their activities. In which intruders acted as a part of the system of communication when the intruders are connected directly to another node. So that it may be interfere message transmission by establishing forgery and deceiving original data in order to modify real data and information.

3.1.2 Passive Attacks

In passive attacks an intruder or attacker try to access the data and information illegally from the system only but does not perform any manipulation in the system configuration. Different kinds of passive attacks are Traffic analysis, Spying, Eavesdropping and release of message content etc.

a) **Traffic analysis-**In a traffic analysis attacks, an attacker tries to observe or access the network traffic. From the traffic analysis attacks, the attackers try to learn or hear something important about the person or organization illegally.

b) **Monitoring-**Monitoring attacks in the network enables attackers to see or observe what is happening in their network in order to gain important information unlawfully.

c) **Eavesdropping-**This attack is also known as snooping or sniffing attack. This attack is a stolen of information as it is travelled over the network through several connected smart devices in IoT applications.

3.1.3 Physical Attacks

Attacks that physically damage IoT things is refer to as physical attacks. In physical attacks, the attacker harms components of IoT system to stops the services [13] (Fig. 1).

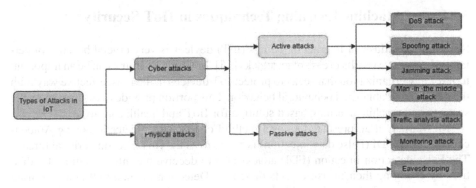

Fig. 1. Classification of IoT attacks

4 Use of Machine Learning Techniques for IoT Securing IoT

Over the current years, the area of machine learning has stimulated remarkable interest. Numerous domains are making use of machine learning (ML) for their evolution and for security of IoT as well [14, 24].

As contrast to other conventional methods, different approaches of machine learning (ML) are used to protect and provides solution to IoT devices against cyber-attacks [14]. For the sake of securing IoT system, approaches based on machine learning are a propitious alternative. By using ML algorithms, we can develop a model, based on past data, which is also known as learning data to perform prediction to make decision, without requiring any explicit programming to do so.

Types of Machine Learning algorithms are Supervised learning, Unsupervised learning and Reinforcement learning. Supervised learning is basically, teach or train the system based on pre recorded data that is clearly labeled. In which some of the past data is previously marked with the accurate answer. Supervised learning helps in IoT security to make intelligent prediction and responses based on the experience or behavior. When vulnerabilities and threats occur, such as DoS or DDoS attacks, machine learning approaches compares current IoT system behavior with previous behavior patterns from threats and takes defensive action. Unsupervised learning techniques doesn't any output data for given input, this algorithm tries to identify the pattern among the datasets by classify these data into different cluster. Many unsupervised machine learning approaches are used to securing IoT devices from DoS, DDoS and privacy protection.

In a reinforcement learning approach, the system learns from reciprocity with its surroundings by taking actions to maximize overall feedback.

Feedback can be a reward from the output of a given execution. While the system uses trial and error methods, there are no prior actions and no specific execution. Using trial and error methods, the system recognizes and executes the praised approach from its experience to get maximum rewards [1].

So, reinforcement learning is used to reconfigure the IoT devices arrangements in pursuance of the surroundings.

5 Use of Machine Learning Techniques in IIoT Security

Securing the industrial Internet of Things (IoT) devices is very crucial because of certainly destructive results in case of an attacks [15]. Machine Learning can be an important tool for any organization that seeks to protect IoT devices in the most effective way with the detection of abnormal behavioral behavior. This portion provides a discussion on the security and machine learning based solution for IIoT and health care IoT.

M. Mariam et al. presented a novel method of FDI attack detection using Autoencoders [AEs]. FDI (False data injection) is refers to as the IIoT affecting critical threats. The False detection injection (FDI) attacks aim to deceive the infrastructure of industries by changing their measurements of sensor. Detection method FDI attack of used Autoencoders (AEs) to help in identifying the manipulated or comprised data. This method cleaned the alter data using the denoising AEs. In this work the author also used SVM based approach for identifying false data. This approach proposed Autoencoders classification approach to detect false data injection attacks. The proposed detection method offers better detection performance compared to the SVM based method. The limitation of this method is that the presented algorithm is capable to detecting an attack that destroys the correlation between values of sensors. If the attacks are capable of maintaining this correlation, AE may not be able to detect it [15].

H. Vargas et al. presented an integrated application for the identification and restrictions of the intruders on the edge. KNN technique a supervised machine learning approach was selected to identifying and minimizing the risk of attacks in real time manners in IIoT. This proposed approach proved to be best in same aspects to the traditional approaches such as Intrusion detection system (IDS) in the identification of more sophisticated attacks [16].

M.E. Khoda et al. proposed two new methods for selecting classified enemy samples. The first approach is based on the distance from the center point of the malware clusters and the another one is based on an extracted probability measure from kernel-based learning (KBL). Both approaches performed very well in random sampling method and the KBL sampling technique by improving detection by 6% [17]. M. Ozay et al. presented the false data injection threat detection approach in the physical layer of smart grid. In this approach, machine learning algorithms (supervised and semi-supervised) has been used to classify the measurements as secured or compromised. The following threat detection framework has been used to exploit all available prior knowledge about the system and overcomes the limitations arising from the sparse structure of the problems [18].

P. Arachchige et al. proposed a framework called PriModchain that imposes trust and privacy on IoT data and information by combining differential privacy, federated ML, Ethereum blockchain and smart contracts [19].

6 Use of Machine Learning in Health Care IoT Security

Health care industry is adopting revolutionary technologies very fast. Increasingly healthcare system challenging through the chronic disease to the elderly population, limit the capabilities of health care systems, specialist, and service providers to quality health care service in order to improve patient outcomes.

These challenges have led them to the path of advanced technologies such as the Internet of Things (IoT), artificial intelligence, machine learning and data analytics, among which IoT has received the most attention from healthcare providers. Healthcare system has clasp ML and IoT technology in order to automated systems makes medical reports, prediction of disease and most importantly, conducting monitoring of patients in real time manner. The unification of Internet of Things (IoT) and ubiquitous system in healthcare system have built the current medical system "Smart". Medical health care system is not restricted to treat the patients only. By using wearables and embedded healthcare things or devices, smart medical healthcare system can constantly keep an eye on crucial symptoms of a patient and immediately identify and take precautionary action on critical medical conditions [26, 27]. However, this growing serviceability of smart medical healthcare system uplift various security bother and there is various way to exploit the smart health care system by the intruders [20].

A. Newaz et al. proposed HealthGuard, a novel machine learning security framework for detecting malicious activities in an intelligent healthcare system. In this paper, Health-Guard uses four different detection techniques based on machine learning (Artificial Neural Network, Decision Tree, Random Forest, K-Nearest Neighbor) to detect malicious activities in SHS. HealthGuard is an effective security framework for an intelligent healthcare system with 91% accuracy in detecting various attacks [21].

O. Sangpetch et al. presented an adoptive security content framework for exchange health information in IoT ecosystem. The proposed framework can help alleviate privacy and security concerns and increase adoption of IoT systems in healthcare [22].

S. Singh et al. presented blockchain and federated learning capacitate protected structure for preservation of the privacy in smart health care system, where blockchain established an IoT cloud computing environment for privacy and security. In this work, users can get a well-trained machine learning model without sending personal data to the cloud [23].

Mohit et al. proposed a novel framework for IoMT. They utilized Rooted Elliptic Curve Cryptography with Vigenere Cipher (RECC-VC) for securing IoMT. For privacy preservation Exponential K-Anonymity algorithm (EKA) was used in this work and for analyzing sensitivity level of data they proposed Improved Elman Neural Network (IENN) [25].

7 Future Scope of Machine Learning in Security of IoT

There have paramount research scopes in the area of security solution in IoT platform using machine learning. To solving the security issues of IoT platform using machine learning approach, there is a need of Incremental learning because in real world scenario, data is changing endlessly. Integrating the features of incremental learning and deep learning, can be a powerful technique to identify existing and newer attacks faster. A robust machine learning algorithm is needed because existing algorithms are good for theory but all are not accepted in real world scenario because data are changing rapidly. Since there are complexities in routing procedure of IoT network which leads the security risks. To mitigate the risk of cyber-attacks and physical attacks, simplification of routing process in IoT network is important. A lightweight security solution is needed.

8 Challenges in IoT Security

The major challenges about infusion of securing the IoT technology are:

a. The huge quantity of data is obtained through the IoT smart devices. It's a challenging to generate relevant information from the collected data. so, there is a need to develop an algorithm that could identify and sense irrelevancy or abnormalities in collected data.
b. Securing the IoT devices from cyber-attacks and physical attacks.
c. Accuracy of identifying newer attacks is lesser.
d. The capacity of storage and calculation capabilities are limited. These limitations headed to security issues and risk of attacks.

e. The major risk of The IoT platform is theft of data and information, main reason of data stolen is predominate nature of sensing capability of IoT devices.
f. Insufficiency of reliable authentication and access control.
g. Routing procedure is complicated in IoT Network, which lead to security risks.
h. Interoperability is a major challenge because there are diversity and heterogeneity associated with IoT devices.
i. Overlong handling time due to computational complexities.

9 Conclusion

This surveyed some of the most important security risks and its solution by using different algorithms of machine learning, challenges in IoT applications like what is in progress to mitigate the security risks and future scope of machine learning based solution in IoT applications. We have covered the issues related to security of data generated in different application area of IoT system like IIoT (Industrial Internet of Things) and IoSHT (Internet of smart healthcare Things). This study from the existing research work is look forward to set out as an useful resource for the security improvement of upcoming Internet of Things applications using ML.

References

1. Tahsien, S.M., Karimipour, H., Spachos, P.: Machine learning based solutions for security of Internet of Things (IoT): a survey. J. Netw. Comput. Appl. **161**, 102630 (2020)
2. Ahmad, R., Alsmadi, I.: Machine learning approaches to IoT security: a systematic literature review. Internet Things **14**, 100365 (2021)
3. Bagaa, M., Taleb, T., Bernabe, J.B., Skarmeta, A.: A machine learning security framework for IoT systems. IEEE Access **8**, 114066–114077 (2020)
4. Xiao, L., Wan, X., Lu, X., Zhang, Y., Wu, D.: IoT security techniques based on machine learning: how do IoT devices use AI to enhance security? IEEE Signal Process. Mag. **35**(5), 41–49 (2018)
5. Atul, D.J., Kamalraj, R., Ramesh, G., Sankaran, K.S., Sharma, S., Khasim, S.: A machine learning based IoT for providing an intrusion detection system for security. Microprocess. Microsyst. **82**, 103741 (2021)
6. Mandal, K., Rajkumar, M., Ezhumalai, P., Jayakumar, D., Yuvarani, R.: Improved security using machine learning for IoT intrusion detection system. In: Materials Today: Proceedings (2020)
7. Shafiq, M., Tian, Z., Bashir, A.K., Du, X., Guizani, M.: CorrAUC: a malicious bot-IoT traffic detection method in IoT network using machine-learning techniques. IEEE Internet Things J. **8**(5), 3242–3254 (2020)
8. Ravi, N., Shalinie, S.M.: Semisupervised-learning-based security to detect and mitigate intrusions in IoT network. IEEE Internet Things J. **7**(11), 11041–11052 (2020)
9. Rathore, S., Park, J.H.: Semi-supervised learning based distributed attack detection framework for IoT. Appl. Soft Comput. **72**, 79–89 (2018)
10. Hasan, M., Islam, M.M., Zarif, M.I.I., Hashem, M.M.A.: Attack and anomaly detection in IoT sensors in IoT sites using machine learning approaches. Internet Things **7**, 100059 (2019)
11. Anthi, E., Williams, L., Słowińska, M., Theodorakopoulos, G., Burnap, P.: A supervised intrusion detection system for smart home IoT devices. IEEE Internet Things J. **6**(5), 9042–9053 (2019)

12. Neerugatti, V., Mohan Reddy, A.R.: Machine learning based technique for detection of rank attack in RPL based Internet of Things networks. Int. J. Innov. Technol. Explor. Eng. (IJITEE) **8**, 5 (2019). ISSN 2278–3075. Machine Learning Based Technique for Detection of Rank Attack in RPL based Internet of Things Networks (July 10, 2019)

13. Deogirikar, J., Vidhate, A.: Security attacks in IoT: a survey. In: 2017 International Conference on I-SMAC (IoT in Social, Mobile, Analytics and Cloud) (I-SMAC), pp. 32–37. IEEE (2017)

14. Hassija, V., Chamola, V., Saxena, V., Jain, D., Goyal, P., Sikdar, B.: A survey on IoT security: application areas, security threats, and solution architectures. IEEE Access **7**, 82721–82743 (2019)

15. Aboelwafa, M.M., Seddik, K.G., Eldefrawy, M.H., Gadallah, Y., Gidlund, M.: A machine-learning-based technique for false data injection attacks detection in industrial IoT. IEEE Internet Things J. **7**(9), 8462–8471 (2020)

16. Vargas, H., Lozano-Garzon, C., Montoya, G.A., Donoso, Y.: Detection of security attacks in industrial IoT networks: a blockchain and machine learning approach. Electronics **10**(21), 2662 (2021)

17. Khoda, M.E., Imam, T., Kamruzzaman, J., Gondal, I., Rahman, A.: Robust malware defense in industrial IoT applications using machine learning with selective adversarial samples. IEEE Trans. Ind. Appl. **56**(4), 4415–4424 (2019)

18. Ozay, M., Esnaola, I., Vural, F.T.Y., Kulkarni, S.R., Poor, H.V.: Machine learning methods for attack detection in the smart grid. IEEE Trans. Neural Netw. Learn. Syst. **27**(8), 1773–1786 (2015)

19. Arachchige, P.C.M., Bertok, P., Khalil, I., Liu, D., Camtepe, S., Atiquzzaman, M.: A trust-worthy privacy preserving framework for machine learning in industrial IoT systems. IEEE Trans. Ind. Inform. **16**(9), 6092–6102 (2020)

20. Aldahiri, A., Alrashed, B., Hussain, W.: Trends in using IoT with machine learning in health prediction system. Forecasting **3**(1), 181–206 (2021)

21. Newaz, A.I., Sikder, A.K., Rahman, M.A., Uluagac, A.S.: HealthGuard: a machine learning-based security framework for smart healthcare systems. In: 2019 Sixth International Conference on Social Networks Analysis, Management and Security (SNAMS), pp. 389–396. IEEE (2019)

22. Sangpetch, O., Sangpetch, A.: Security context framework for distributed healthcare IoT platform. In: Ahmed, M., Begum, S., Raad, W. (eds.) HealthyIoT 2016. LNICST, vol. 187, pp. 71–76. Springer, Cham (2016). https://doi.org/10.1007/978-3-319-51234-1_11

23. Singh, S., Rathore, S., Alfarraj, O., Tolba, A., Yoon, B.: A framework for privacy-preservation of IoT healthcare data using Federated Learning and blockchain technology. Future Gener. Comput. Syst. **129**, 380–388 (2022)

24. Kumar, M., Mukherjee, P., Verma, K., Verma, S., Rawat, D.B.: Improved deep convolutional neural network based malicious node detection and energy-efficient data transmission in wireless sensor networks. IEEE Trans. Netw. Sci. Eng. **9**, 3272–3281 (2021). https://doi.org/10.1109/TNSE.2021.3098011

25. Kumar, M., Kavita, Verma, S., Kumar, A., Ijaz, M.F., Rawat, D.B.: ANAF-IoMT: a novel architectural framework for IoMT enabled smart healthcare system by enhancing security based on RECC-VC. IEEE Trans. Ind. Inform. **18**, 8936–8943 (2022). https://doi.org/10.1109/TII.2022.3181614

26. Upadhyay, S., et al.: SmHeSol (IoT-BC): smart healthcare solution for future development using speech feature extraction integration approach with IoT and blockchain. J. Sens. **2022**, 1–13 (2022)

27. Upadhyay, S., et al.: Feature extraction approach for speaker verification to support healthcare system using blockchain security for data privacy. Comput. Math. Methods Med. **2022**, 1–12 (2022)

28. Pratap, A., Kumar, A., Kumar, M.: Analyzing the need of edge computing for Internet of Things (IoT). In: Singh, P.K., Wierzchoń, S.T., Tanwar, S., Ganzha, M., Rodrigues, J.J.P.C. (eds.) Proceedings of Second International Conference on Computing, Communications, and Cyber-Security. LNNS, vol. 203, pp. 203–212. Springer, Singapore (2021). https://doi.org/10.1007/978-981-16-0733-2_14

Predicting Students' Performance Employing Educational Data Mining Techniques, Machine Learning, and Learning Analytics

Ashraf Alam[(✉)] [iD] and Atasi Mohanty [iD]

Rekhi Centre of Excellence for the Science of Happiness, Indian Institute of Technology Kharagpur, Kharagpur, West Bengal, India
ashraf_alam@kgpian.iitkgp.ac.in

Abstract. Student success is important in colleges and universities since it is often used as a measure of the institution's effectiveness. Identifying at-risk students early on and implementing preventative measures might have a major impact on their academic performance. In recent years, predictions made using machine learning techniques have become more common. Although there are many examples of successful utilization of data mining techniques in academic literature, these methods are frequently restricted to educators with expertise in computer science or, more specifically, artificial intelligence. Before implementing an effective data mining strategy, there are several decisions that must be made, such as defining student achievement, identifying important student characteristics, and selecting the most suitable machine learning approach for the particular issue. The objective of this investigation is to offer a complete set of instructions for educators interested in utilizing data mining techniques to predict student performance. To achieve this goal, we have analyzed the relevant literature and compiled the current state of the art into a methodical approach in which all the options and parameters are discussed at length and rationales have been given for their selection. By lowering the barrier to entry for data mining tools, this initiative will unleash their full potential for usage in the classroom.

Keywords: Predictive Analytics · Data Mining · Machine Learning · Higher Education · Teaching · Learning · Artificial Intelligence · Pedagogy · Curriculum

1 Introduction

The prevalence and importance of computers have risen substantially during the last several decades [1]. Massive volumes of diverse data have been collected as a consequence, which may be mined using data mining techniques to reveal previously unknown associations and trends [2]. Data mining analysis methods may be roughly classified as follows: First, there are the tried and tested methods of statistics (regression analysis, discriminant analysis, cluster analysis); second, there are AI methods (fuzzy logic, neural computing, genetic algorithms); and third, there is machine learning (e.g., swarm optimization,

R. S. Tomar et al. (Eds.): CNC 2022, CCIS 1893, pp. 166–177, 2023.
https://doi.org/10.1007/978-3-031-43140-1_15

symbolic learning, and neural networks) [3]. The latter makes use of cutting-edge statistical methods together with heuristics from artificial intelligence [4]. Different fields may benefit from these techniques for different reasons; for example, they may help in spotting patterns, predicting behavior, or summarizing trends [5]. Raw data, or data from several sources that have not been cleaned to remove noise, duplicates, or inconsistencies, is integrated as the first step in most data mining processes [6]. Next, the data that has been filtered and summarized is converted into a compact structure that can be comprehended by data mining software. After gathering data, an analyst conducts an analysis to unearth fascinating patterns that may be highlighted in the final display [7].

Recently, data mining has found applications in many fields, such as medicine, business, and academia [8]. Because of the development of educational database management systems, there are currently several educational databases from which useful information may be mined through data mining techniques. Therefore, the field of Education Data Mining (EDM) was born. Knowledge patterns relating to educational phenomena, the instructional process, and student performance have become more important to uncover, making EDM a vital tool in the present day [9]. Predicting performance, retention, success, contentment, achievement, and dropout rate are just a few of the many crucial educational outcomes that data mining has shown adept at predicting [10].

To uncover new information, EDM uses an iterative process of hypothesis creation, testing, and refinement. Numerous literary works, comprising books and articles, have been produced on educational data mining, along with case studies. However, it still presents a difficult undertaking for teachers, especially those who are not acquainted with data mining, to effectively apply these methods to tackle their distinct educational dilemmas [11]. The execution of each data mining process entails configuring several variables and options that collectively influence the output's quality.

The present investigation seeks to fill the previously mentioned gap by furnishing a comprehensive manual, facilitating greater accessibility to data mining technologies, and unlocking their full potential for application in the realm of education. Predicting how well college students will do is a major focus of this investigation. As such, a methodical process has been developed based on the state of the art, in which all important considerations and limitations are exhaustively discussed and described. The subsequent section outlines the meaning of academic achievement and elucidates its definition and evaluation in diverse research studies, emphasizing the attributes that can be employed to anticipate academic advancement. In Sect. 3, we detail the methodology that was used in the literature review. In Sect. 4, we compare the performance of several data mining methods for making predictions about students' academic progress. In Sect. 5 we summarise the whole assessment process and draw our final conclusions. Finally, this article concludes with Sect. 6 where we outline potential avenues of research.

2 Academic Success

Student performance is an integral part of universities since it serves as a crucial gauge of the quality of the education provided there [12]. The research literature presents various interpretations of academic success. Based on these explanations, students may be considered successful if they demonstrate the following characteristics: academic excellence, participation in education-oriented activities, satisfaction, attainment of desired knowledge, skills, and abilities, perseverance, accomplishment of academic objectives, and the post-graduation performance of alumni [13]. There are numerous facets to this notion, but the six most important are: achievement in school, satisfaction, growth in abilities and competencies, tenacity, realization of educational objectives, and professional advancement [14].

There have been requests for a more complex definition of academic success, but the vast bulk of the literature defines it as nothing more than academic accomplishment. The most important criteria in determining academic success are a student's grade point average (GPA) and cumulative grade point average (CGPA), both of which are grade systems used by institutions to offer an assessment scale for students' academic achievement or grades [15]. Perseverance in the classroom, also known as academic resilience, is mostly measured by students' grades and GPAs, the two most often used measures of academic performance [16].

3   Performance Prediction

With the help of early performance prediction of their learners, decision-makers may boost their students' success rate by organizing the proper training and taking the essential actions at the appropriate moment [17]. Many studies have used data mining techniques to foretell students' academic performance. Multiple strata are being pursued:

1. Predicting how well a student will do in their last year in college [18].
2. Making a year-end prediction on students' growth [19].
3. Estimating how well a student will do in a certain class [20].
4. Estimating how well a student will do in an examination in each subject [21].

Since poor performance on a single exam does not always portend a negative outcome, that level of literature is left out of this discussion. The terms educational data mining, data mining approaches, academic achievement, predicting students' academic performance, and academic success were the keywords that were used to search for relevant publications in Google Scholar, JSTOR, Science Direct, EBSCO, Springer Link, IEEE Xplore, and ProQuest.

4   Contributing Factors to Academic Achievement

The initial and vital phase in predicting students' academic achievement in tertiary education is to accurately define academic success [22]. This definition would aid in identifying the necessary information that must be collected and analyzed [23]. The current research concentrates on academic accomplishment, student demographics, e-learning activities, psychological characteristics, and environments, while numerous other factors have been explored in existing literature concerning their impact on predicting students' academic success. Academic achievement and student demographics were the two most significant criteria and were featured in 71% of the research papers. Both students' personal assessment scores and cumulative grade point averages are recognized as major predictors of EDM performance. Successful academic performance in the past is the most important factor, accounting for almost 38% of the total. To put it simply, they are the relics of the pupils' past that continue to weigh them down emotionally. In many cases, this is evidenced by students' grades or other measurable academic achievements, such as pre-college and college data. Pre-college data, which includes high school records, can be used to assess students' ability to maintain a consistent level of performance [24]. They openly discuss a wide range of topics that interest them (i.e., courses grade). Information such as test scores taken before applying to a university might also be provided. Previous semester GPAs or CGPAs, course marks, and grades from course assessments (such as assignments, quizzes, lab work, and attendance) are all included in the university data [25].

There is a lack of consensus in the literature on how students should be categorized. Numerous studies have shown its impact on students' success, highlighting the significance of variables such as students' genders, ages, races, socioeconomic backgrounds, and parental occupations. A number of aspects of the student's context were identified as influential, including the kind of programme, the format of classes, and the duration of the semester. Many researchers included somewhat influential statistics from students' e-learning activities such as the number of logins, the number of contributions to discussion boards, and the total number of times the information was seen. How the student acts and thinks outside of the classroom shapes their personality. Multiple studies show that they affect students' performance in the classroom. Student interest, study habits, stress and anxiety, self-control, preoccupation time, and motivation were shown to be significant predictors of academic achievement.

5 Predictive Data Mining Methods for Students' Academic Performance

In the creation of a prediction model using data mining methods, several elements must be considered, such as the kind of model to develop or the methodology and techniques to apply. The examined papers classify the degree level, year level, and course level as the variable in student success prediction, providing examples of each characteristic and data on their frequency.

Numerous case studies have been published in an effort to predict degree-level academic success. The creation of a model for predicting Cumulative Grade Point Average (CGPA) can be accomplished through two widely used techniques: Classification, where the CGPA goal is categorized as a multi-class issue such as letter grades or an overall rating, and binary class problem such as pass/fail. The alternate method, known as regression, involves making predictions about the CGPA's actual numerical value. Students come from a broad variety of academic disciplines, including but not limited to engineering, computer science, mathematics, and the arts and design. It is worth highlighting that research that employed predictors, comprising university data - particularly grades obtained in the initial two years of the program, outperformed those that solely relied on demographics or pre-university data. Information about the software platform, algorithm, sample size, highest accuracy, and accompanying methodology is discussed in the following sections.

In recent years, there has been a decline in the number of published case studies that seek to forecast yearly academic performance. Studies that incorporated university data in addition to socioeconomic characteristics and pre-university data showed more reliable results. Finally, studies that attempt to predict course-level academic performance may be made public. Foreseeing success at the course level is perceived to be less challenging than predicting success at the degree or year level, and can result in precision levels exceeding 90%. Similar to what was discussed in the undergraduate and graduate parts, the comparison work provides accuracy levels ranging from 59% to 91%. 93% accuracy is reached at the course level.

6 Predicting Students' Performance Using Data Mining Model

Here, we compile a set of steps that are suggested for doing when predicting a student's performance with the use of educational data mining techniques. All options to be considered at various points are explained, along with an overview of best practices gleaned from the literature. Methods of long standing were used to develop the proposed framework. This procedure comprises six primary components: data collection, preliminary data preparation, statistical analysis, data preprocessing, data mining execution, and outcome evaluation. In the following sections, we will talk in further detail about each of these stages.

6.1 Inquiring

There are several places to look for the information needed for educational data mining. The evidence suggests that prior academic success is the most important factor. Data relevant to either the time before or during university study may be easily retrieved from the ubiquity of the Student Information System (SIS). While the SIS can give information on students' ages, genders, and ethnicities, it may not necessarily reveal students' socioeconomic backgrounds. If so, we may deduce this from existing data or ask the students themselves via surveys. Student information systems (SIS) may be used to collect information on a student's physical and social environments, but psychological information will most likely need the student to fill out a survey. Lastly, the records of students' online learning activities shall be analyzed.

6.2 Preliminary Information Gathering

Raw data is information in its original format that has not been altered or cleansed in any way to make it more suitable for use in statistical analysis or modelling. Redundant, inconsistent, incorrect, and erroneous information may be included in data sets that are mostly gathered by integrating tables from other systems. This necessitates preliminary processing of the raw data, including 1) selection, 2) cleaning, and 3) the introduction of additional variables. It is at this point that the process becomes both lengthy and important.

6.3   Selection of Data

When past academic achievements are taken into account, such as including all high school and college courses taken, the gathered data might have a very large size. Complexity in computing may suffer as a result. As an added caution, it is possible that poor predictions may be made if all the data is included in the analysis. This is especially true in cases of data dependency or redundancy. The importance of determining which features are important or warrant inclusion in the research cannot be overstated. This cannot be done without a thorough familiarity with both the data and the goals of the data mining process. Data selection, also known as 'Dimensionality Reduction' consists of both vertical (attributes/variables) and horizontal (instances/records) choices. It is also worth noting that models built with fewer features might be easier to understand.

6.4   The Process of Cleaning Data

Inconsistent or inaccurate data, as well as background noise, are common problems with data sources. Missing data refers to instances in which a value for a certain variable just isn't there in the data set. One definition of an outlier is a data point that is extremely out of line with the rest of the information in the dataset. Discrepancies and gaps in EDM are common, according to the research. It is crucial to acquire the knowledge to manage these factors without jeopardizing the accuracy of the forecast. Overall, there is no silver bullet for dealing with missing data or outliers; rather, a combination of techniques should be explored. In this article, however, we strive to summarize and synthesize the most important research-based techniques.

Unresolved missing values might be problematic for certain classifiers. Logistic regression, naive bayes, neural networks (NN), and support vector machines (SVMs), for example, need full observation, whereas random forests and decision trees may handle the missing data. There are two methods that may be used to fill in the blanks when data is absent. The first is called a listwise deletion and it involves getting rid of either the attribute or the variable, i.e., getting rid of the row when there aren't many missing values and getting rid of the column when there are. Imputation offers a different method for handling missing data, involving the replacement of absent values with available ones. This can involve using statistical measures like the median or mean, a pre-determined value for numerical data, or selecting a value at random from the distribution of missing data. Detecting outliers, or anomalies, can be achieved through visual methods such as constructing histograms, box plots, or stem and leaf plots, and observing data that deviates significantly from the norm. After identifying these outliers, the data used for modeling can be refined by either removing them altogether or categorizing the numeric variable, either by dividing the data into groups or retaining the outliers.

6.5   Generation of a New Variable

It is possible to generate new variables by combining pre-existing ones. When carried out with expertise in the subject matter, this could enhance the efficacy of the data mining system. A popular variable, such as grade point average, is just one instance of what could be retrieved from the SIS system. A student's GPA for the semester, taken at face value, is the same as the student's average grade for that semester. Not much can be inferred about this student's long-term trend from just one semester. A student's academic performance might remain static (with a steady GPA), increase gradually, or drastically deteriorate. Therefore, it would be helpful to calculate the change in GPA between semesters. In the ensuing sections, we have summarized the situations we discovered in the EDM literature that dealt with accurate prediction despite the absence of a systematic process for creating new variables.

6.6 Examination by Means of Statistics

Performing preliminary statistical analysis, especially through visual means, enables a more thorough understanding of the data prior to embarking on more complex data mining techniques and algorithms. Data-mining software has a descriptive statistics module. Additionally, professional tools like STATISTICA and SPSS may give a plethora of insight. This epiphany can be immensely helpful in shaping the subsequent phases of the Data Mining procedure, such as detecting anomalies while preparing the data, revealing patterns in incomplete data, scrutinizing the distribution of every variable, and establishing the correlation between the independent variables and the target variable. At the interpretation stage, statistical analysis is used to provide more context for the DM model's results.

6.7 Preparation of Data

The penultimate step before data analysis and modelling is preprocessing, which involves data transformation, handling of uneven data sets, and feature selection. The data must be transformed so that any inconsistencies are removed, making the dataset more amenable to data mining. There are certain methods that may be found in EDM for future outcome forecasting. Data normalization is a method of scaling data that is implemented when there is a diverse range of scales present within the dataset and the data mining algorithm is unable to make any explicit assumptions regarding the distribution of the data. Artificial neural networks and K-nearest neighbors are two notable examples of such algorithms. The normalization of data can potentially enhance the precision and efficiency of mining algorithms, thereby leading to superior outcomes. Some common normalizing techniques include bi-weight (Bi-weight), tanh (Tanh), double sigmoid (DSand), median (MD), z-score (ZS), decimal scaling (DS), and min-max (MM).

The simplest method of discretization, called "binning," entails transforming a continuous numerical variable into a finite number of distinct categories by splitting it into a fixed number of "bins" and assigning a particular range of values to each attribute within each bin. Discretization is essential when using DM methods that solely operate with categorical data, like Naive Bayes, Apriori, and C4.5. Noise in the data is reduced and outliers are identified thanks to discretization, which also boosts model accuracy. Discrete features are also less complicated to clarify, interpret, and organize. Switch needs to be done using numeric variables, since they work better with DM techniques. It is thus necessary to use one of the following methods to convert data into numeric variables. When assigning labels, choose a value ranging from 0 to N(class-1)34, where N is the total count of the labels. A dummy variable is used to represent a single category level, which is a binary variable with possible values of 0 or 1. The value 1 indicates the presence of the level, and 0 indicates its absence. For each active level, a separate dummy variable is created. Combining levels can help to reduce the number of levels in our categorical variables, and thus enhance the efficiency of our models. We can achieve this by grouping together all similar-looking level sets in a domain. However, it's crucial to bear in mind that not all of these techniques lead to better outcomes. Therefore, we need to repeatedly model and experiment with various preprocessing scenarios, evaluate the model's performance, and choose the best outputs.

6.8 Lack of Consistency in the Data

In the realm of EDM (Educational Data Mining) applications, it is customary for the dataset to exhibit unevenness, indicating that one class may have a smaller number of samples compared to other classes. This imbalance could manifest as, for instance, a disproportionate ratio of students who failed to those who passed. This disparity has the potential to reduce the effectiveness of data mining techniques. The optimal method is re-sampling, often known as under- or over-sampling. Under-sampling is the practice of reducing the size of the primary class by deleting instances at random or by using some other form of class balancing. The expression "oversampling" refers to the approach of increasing the number of instances in a minority class by randomly replicating specific samples or by intentionally producing new samples.

6.9 Functional Optimization

Once the dataset is prepared for modeling, the essential variables can be selected and entered into the modeling approach. Feature selection is a crucial step in achieving optimal outcomes in data mining. Its objective is to identify a subset of input data attributes that effectively represent the input data, diminishes the impact of irrelevant factors, and produces dependable predictions. Feature selection allows for faster computations, more accurate predictions, and a deeper understanding of the underlying data. Feature selection strategies may be categorized as either filters or wrapper approaches. Filter approaches are a preprocessing phase that ranks features to find the highest-ranking ones, which are then applied to the predictor. Wrapper approaches involve encapsulating the predictor within a search algorithm that seeks to identify a subset that results in the most favorable predictor performance, which serves as the basis for feature selection. Embedded strategies provide another choice for model training that does not necessitate dividing the data into training and testing sets initially and incorporates variable selection as a component of the training procedure. Meanwhile, many data mining tools are already equipped with a range of feature selection techniques, thereby simplifying the process of experimenting with them and determining the most suitable one.

7 Data Mining Models

Foretelling outcomes in EDM applications often require the use of both predictive and descriptive data mining algorithms. Predictive models use supervised learning techniques to estimate the expected values of dependent variables by taking into account the characteristics of pertinent independent variables. On the other hand, descriptive models employ unsupervised learning functions to extract patterns that illustrate the fundamental structure, relationships, and interdependencies of the data. Models that make predictions, like classification and regression, are called predictive models, whereas models that provide descriptions, like those that make groups and associations, are called descriptive models. The three most common methods are regression, clustering, and classification. In the realm of classification, the most favored methods include Bayesian networks, neural networks, and decision trees. Although logistic regression analysis is a common regression technique, linear regression is also frequently employed. Clustering techniques encompass discriminant analysis, neural networks, K-means algorithms, and Fuzzy clustering. In the initial stage, predictive or descriptive models may be selected, followed by the selection of model-building algorithms from the top 10 data mining methods ranked by their performance. If a model is to be used, it should be easily understandable and explainable, such as a decision tree or a linear model. Once the algorithms have been selected, they need to be configured before they can be used effectively. To obtain valuable output from the models, good parameter values must be inputted in advance by the user. Several tuning techniques are utilized to identify the most appropriate parameters for the data mining algorithms, with the trial-and-error method being one of the easiest and simplest approaches for non-specialist users. To find the optimal settings for a given parameter, many tests must be run with varying values for that setting.

8 Technology for Extracting Useful Information from Large Datasets

The researcher can analyze the information in a number of ways because of the availability of a variety of open-source tools for data mining, such as ML tools. Statistical modelling, visualization, and predictive analysis all benefit greatly from the availability of such programmes. WEKA is the most popular software for predictive modelling. Because it comes equipped with several pre-made tools for visualization, regression, association rules, categorization, and data preparation, it has attracted a large user base. Because of how simple and straightforward it is to use, even for individuals with no prior knowledge of programming or data mining, it has attracted a large audience.

9 Analyzing the Outcomes

In practice, however, numerous models are often built, making it imperative to evaluate them all and choose the most promising one. Classification algorithms are often evaluated using the confusion matrix. For a given model of success prediction, there are four key metrics. TP stands for the number of students who were correctly classified as 'successful', and it is a measure of how well schools do at classifying their students. FP (False Positive) is the number of smart pupils that were wrongly labelled as 'not smart'. True Negative (TN) is the percentage of students that were correctly classified as failures. There are a variety of performance indicators used to evaluate the models of different classifiers. Almost all performance measures may be traced back to the confusion matrix and the information included inside it. It is recommended to evaluate these parameters jointly for more reliable results. Metrics for classifying problems are the focus of this research.

10 Conclusion

Through early student performance prediction, universities are able to make well-informed choices, such as providing students with the right kind of training at the right time, to boost their success rates. Investigation of instructional material may be helpful in reaching one's learning goals. Using EDM methods, we may develop success-prediction models for our students, leading to greater achievement overall. However, data mining techniques may seem daunting and complex to those who lack technological expertise. There are a lot of options to consider, and even with the specialized equipment, the operation is complex. This investigation offers well-defined directives for employing EDM to anticipate future events. Although the sample population was limited to undergraduates, the outcomes can be smoothly applied to graduate-level coursework. It is tailored for individuals who possess no previous familiarity with AI, ML, or data mining. Much inquiry has been devoted to identifying indicators that can anticipate students' academic accomplishments, which were gauged by their level of scholastic attainment. Our inquiry demonstrated that the most prevalent indicators are students' past academic performances, demographics, e-learning involvement, and psychological characteristics. In terms of prediction methodologies, the categorization approach has been used by a plethora of algorithms to forecast student performance. Also proposed is a six-step process, with comprehensive explanations of each step. While this research avoids going into much technical detail, it does explore all possible designs and implementations and compiles best practices from the existing literature.

The primary conclusion of this analysis is that EDM should be used with undergraduate students in any field, including the humanities, the social sciences, and so on. Any additional data that may aid in the discovery of new determinants can be easily incorporated into the analysis, including data on faculty such as competence, recruitment criteria, academic qualifications, etc. The presented outcomes are based on prior investigations concerning subjects such as the feasible delineation of academic achievement, qualities required to evaluate it, fundamental components, and so forth.

References

1. Romero, C., Ventura, S.: Educational data mining and learning analytics: an updated survey. Wiley Interdisc. Rev.: Data Min. Knowl. Discov. **10**(3), e1355 (2020)
2. Alam, A.: Challenges and possibilities in teaching and learning of calculus: a case study of India. J. Educ. Gifted Young Sci. **8**(1), 407–433 (2020)
3. Ang, K.L.M., Ge, F.L., Seng, K.P.: Big educational data & analytics: survey, architecture and challenges. IEEE Access **8**, 116392–116414 (2020)
4. Alam, A.: Pedagogy of calculus in India: an empirical investigation. Periódico Tchê Química **17**(34), 164–180 (2020)
5. Baek, C., Doleck, T.: Educational data mining versus learning analytics: a review of publications from 2015 to 2019. Interact. Learn. Environ. **31**, 1–23 (2021)
6. Alam, A.: Possibilities and challenges of compounding artificial intelligence in India's educational landscape. Int. J. Adv. Sci. Technol. **29**(5), 5077–5094 (2020)
7. Lemay, D.J., Baek, C., Doleck, T.: Comparison of learning analytics and educational data mining: a topic modeling approach. Comput. Educ.: Artif. Intell. **2**, 100016 (2021)

8. Alam, A.: Test of knowledge of elementary vectors concepts (TKEVC) among first-semester bachelor of engineering and technology students. Periódico Tchê Química **17**(35), 477–494 (2020)
9. Chen, G., Rolim, V., Mello, R.F., Gašević, D.: Let's shine together! A comparative study between learning analytics and educational data mining. In: Proceedings of the Tenth International Conference on Learning Analytics & Knowledge, pp. 544–553 (2020)
10. Alam, A.: Should robots replace teachers? Mobilisation of AI and learning analytics in education. In: 2021 International Conference on Advances in Computing, Communication, and Control (ICAC3), pp. 1–12. IEEE (2021)
11. Şahİn, M., Yurdugül, H.: Educational data mining and learning analytics: past, present and future. Bartın Univ. J. Fac. Educ. **9**(1), 121–131 (2020)
12. Alam, A.: Possibilities and apprehensions in the landscape of artificial intelligence in education. In: 2021 International Conference on Computational Intelligence and Computing Applications (ICCICA), pp. 1–8. IEEE (2021)
13. Rienties, B., Køhler Simonsen, H., Herodotou, C.: Defining the boundaries between artificial intelligence in education, computer-supported collaborative learning, educational data mining, and learning analytics: a need for coherence. In: Frontiers in Education, vol. 5, p. 128. Frontiers Media SA (2020)
14. Alam, A.: Educational robotics and computer programming in early childhood education: a conceptual framework for assessing elementary school students' computational thinking for designing powerful educational scenarios. In: 2022 International Conference on Smart Technologies and Systems for Next Generation Computing (ICSTSN), pp. 1–7. IEEE (2022)
15. Alam, A.: A digital game based learning approach for effective curriculum transaction for teaching-learning of artificial intelligence and machine learning. In: 2022 International Conference on Sustainable Computing and Data Communication Systems (ICSCDS), pp. 69–74. IEEE (2022)
16. Dhankhar, A., Solanki, K., Dalal, S.: Predicting students performance using educational data mining and learning analytics: a systematic literature review. In: Raj, J.S., Iliyasu, A.M., Bestak, R., Baig, Z.A. (eds.) Innovative Data Communication Technologies and Application. LNDECT, vol. 59, pp. 127–140. Springer, Singapore (2021). https://doi.org/10.1007/978-981-15-9651-3_11
17. Alam, A.: Investigating sustainable education and positive psychology interventions in schools towards achievement of sustainable happiness and wellbeing for 21st century pedagogy and curriculum. ECS Trans. **107**(1), 19481 (2022)
18. Salihoun, M.: State of art of data mining and learning analytics tools in higher education. Int. J. Emerg. Technol. Learn. (iJET) **15**(21), 58–76 (2020)
19. Alam, A.: Social robots in education for long-term human-robot interaction: socially supportive behaviour of robotic tutor for creating robo-tangible learning environment in a guided discovery learning interaction. ECS Trans. **107**(1), 12389 (2022)
20. Wibawa, B., Siregar, J.S., Asrorie, D.A., Syakdiyah, H.: Learning analytic and educational data mining for learning science and technology. In: AIP Conference Proceedings, vol. 2331, no. 1, p. 060001. AIP Publishing LLC (2021)
21. Alam, A.: Positive psychology goes to school: conceptualizing students' happiness in 21st century schools while 'Minding the Mind!' Are we there yet? Evidence-backed, school-based positive psychology interventions. ECS Trans. **107**(1), 11199 (2022)
22. Alam, A.: Mapping a sustainable future through conceptualization of transformative learning framework, education for sustainable development, critical reflection, and responsible citizenship: an exploration of pedagogies for twenty-first century learning. ECS Trans. **107**(1), 9827 (2022)

23. Alam, A.: Employing adaptive learning and intelligent tutoring robots for virtual classrooms and smart campuses: reforming education in the age of artificial intelligence. In: Shaw, R.N., Das, S., Piuri, V., Bianchini, M. (eds.) Advanced Computing and Intelligent Technologies. LNEE, vol. 914, pp. 395–406. Springer, Singapore (2022). https://doi.org/10.1007/978-981-19-2980-9_32

24. da Silva, L.M., et al.: Learning analytics and collaborative groups of learners in distance education: a systematic mapping study. Inform. Educ. **21**(1), 113–146 (2022)

25. Alam, A.: Cloud-based e-learning: scaffolding the environment for adaptive e-learning ecosystem based on cloud computing infrastructure. In: Satapathy, S.C., Lin, J.CW., Wee, L.K., Bhateja, V., Rajesh, T.M. (eds.) ICICC 2021. LNNS, vol. 459, pp. 1–9. Springer, Singapore (2022). https://doi.org/10.1007/978-981-19-1976-3_1

COVID-19 Detection Using State-of-the-Art Deep Learning Models on X-Ray and CT Images

Sitaram Patel[1] and Nikhat Raza Khan[2(✉)]

[1] IES University Bhopal, Bhopal, India
[2] IES College of Technology Bhopal, Bhopal, India
research@iesbpl.ac.in

Abstract. COVID-19, was first detected in Wuhan coronavirus has widespread consequences since it effectively stopped all human activity. The current gold standard for detecting COVID-19 illness relies on nasopharyngeal swabs, which can lead to mistakes due to human error. These tests are not sensitive enough to be used for early diagnosis. These disadvantages highlight the requirement for a completely automated system that can detect COVID-19 disorders utilizing deep learning (DL) algorithms and a massive dataset of X-ray images available to the public. We have offered various state-of-the-art DL approaches in this post. These approaches include DenseNet201-based transfer learning (TL), GDCNN (Genetic Deep Learning Convolutional Neural Network), ResNet50, CNN integrated with SVM classifier, DarkCovidNet, etc. These models assist medical professionals in determining whether or not a CXR taken of a patient reveals the existence of COVID-19. The performance measures used to evaluate these models are compared in this research. This research suggests that when compared to other models, the GDCNN model performs better. These findings suggest that the DarkCovidNet and DenseNet201-based TL models work well, with the former achieving 98% accuracy and the latter 96% accuracy. Also, it can be employed when conventional diagnostic methods, such as RT-PCR, come up short.

Keywords: Chest X-Ray (CXR) · COVID-19 · Artificial Intelligence · Computed Tomography (CT) · Deep Learning · Transfer Learning

1 Introduction

Since January 2020, the novel coronavirus "SARS-CoV-2", dubbed COVID-19 by WHO, has swiftly feast over the world, triggering a pandemic that has had far-reaching effects and triggered a health and economic catastrophe on a scale never before seen during periods of relative calm [1, 2]. In response to the growing concern about the newly discovered coronavirus and the pressing have to collect data on the virus's epidemiology, diagnosis, and therapy, the number of COVID-19-related publications has skyrocketed [3]. This has created an inundation of information that is challenging to organize and utilize for health professionals and public health authorities [4].

It's possible that the quality of the research articles produced during the COVID-19 epidemic was compromised by the urgent requirement to provide proof and the race

R. S. Tomar et al. (Eds.): CNC 2022, CCIS 1893, pp. 178–191, 2023.
https://doi.org/10.1007/978-3-031-43140-1_16

amongst scientific publications to be the first to publish what may turn out to be the most significant findings. In addition, peer review and other editorial filters could be less stringent for COVID-19 manuscripts than usual because of time constraints [5]. The number of errors found in COVID-19 articles indicates a shift in the editing section [6]. Based on the Retraction Watch database, 108 works about COVID-19 were withdrawn by May 2021. Considering how long it often takes to delete a publication, this is likely only the beginning of the problem. Furthermore, the lack of available space for publishing research addressing other pertinent scientific issues may hinder the publication of such studies.

AI has made numerous advancements in recent years. Automatic FE from complex data is made possible by ML and DL in particular. Medical professionals and scientists utilize this equipment, so it must be doing something right [8]. Specifically, DL technology has made strides in many other disciplines, including chemistry, computer vision, medical imaging, robotics, medical imaging, and biology [9]. For this reason, alternative ML techniques can benefit from DL-driven approaches that eliminate the need for feature engineering.

ML and DL continue to improve, which has greatly helped medical professionals. This year's COVID-19 has been getting much attention from scientists, epidemiologists, and city officials [10, 11]. X-ray imaging has been used in no. of research to identify and find COVID-19 disorders [12].

This study aims to analyze several DL methods for transmission prediction in the wake of COVID-19. This work is notable because it compares the effectiveness of standard prediction approaches to the DL technique for predicting retrieved and verified COVID-19 based on CXR and CT data. The GDCNN, ResNet50, DenseNet201-based TL, CNN paired with SVM classifier, and DarkCovidNet are presented and compared to five DL-based algorithms.

The key contributions are considered as follows for this work:

1) To solve the scarcity and insufficiency of a dataset that leads to overfitting and achieving less accuracy.
2) Utilizing a diversity of DL algorithms for early identification of COVID-19.
3) Comparison among different deep learning-based techniques in terms of performance metrics.

The following description provides a structure for the remaining part of the task. In Sect. 2, we examine relevant research and provide a comparison table. Section 3 presents the research gaps of this research that remain to solve. The next Sect. 3, provides a brief overview of deep learning and its techniques. Then, a summary of the pre-trained and sequential models is given in Sect. 3. In Sect. 4, we report the results of comparing the various DL-based models for some useful performance indicators. Section 5 concludes the analysis by discussing the implications for the future.

1.1 Aim and Impact

A key objective of this work is to generate a robust detection application that uses DL technology to identify COVID-19 characteristics in CXR. Clinical results might be enhanced by using this instrument to speed up patient identification and referral.

By making the DL model publicly available, it could be utilized to combat current outbreaks and future ones that employ similar algorithms.

This program can be expanded for use in other, more widespread, high-impact areas of biomedical imaging.

1.2 Objectives

- To learn about and grasp the most significant DL approaches for COVID-19 detection.
- To compare the different DL-based techniques to know the best model by achieving the highest results.

2 Related Work

Numerous research studies have attempted to model, estimate, and predict the viral of COVID-19 using data from CXR and computed tomography (CTG) scans taken of people infected with the virus [13]. In this work, Pandey and Pandey [14] Added a Feature Pyramid Network (FPN) to ResNet101V2 to identify CT scan pictures as normal or COVID-19 positive. ResNet101V2 with Feature Pyramid Network has achieved statistically insignificant accuracy. By employing DL, the suggested FPN guarantees a high level of performance in identifying COVID-19 in CT scans, with a 97.79% success rate in tests. The purpose of Li [15] is to employ computer vision technology, which is fast, cheap, and easy to use, to identify outbreaks. On a public Kaggle dataset, the authors tested DenseNet, VGG, and ResNet, finding that DenseNet produced the findings with an efficiency of 95%; this gives them a reason to be optimistic about future development.

In this work, Mohammad Ayyaz Azeem et al. [16] have employed ResNet50, VGG16, InceptionV3, and DenseNet121, four TL models, for the classification tasks. The accuracy, sensitivity, and specificity of classifications made using VGG16 superior to other approaches. VGG19 approach has a 94% accuracy rate when identifying and categorizing COVID-19, normal, or pneumonia. It also had a 94.20% specificity and a 94% sensitivity rate.

In this study, Balik and Kaya [17] proposed better precision by colorizing X-ray pictures using DL techniques and producing sharper images using pre-trained networks. This resulted in a diagnosis of Covid-19 Pneumonia, which was considered normal. A 98.78% accuracy was achieved in the research.

Chaudhary et al. [18] recommended a two-phase CNN-based classification framework to identify COVID-19 & CAP in chest CT scan pictures. The proposed framework shows promise as a first-stage screening instrument for COVID-19/CAP differential diagnosis, with validation accuracy of over 89.3% at more nuanced 3-way COVID-19 categorization. They created a two-stage classification model that obtained 90% total accuracy and sensitivity of 0.85, 0.90, and 0.94 in identifying COVID-19, CAP, and normal persons.

In this paper, Irmak et al. [19], Employing existing public datasets, develop a unique, robust, and highly resilient CNN classifier for identifying COVID-19. In CXR, this model can identify COVID-19 with a precision of 99.20%. Validation using clinical data sets shows the model's value.

Anwar and Zakir [20] apply DL to analyze chest CT scans to detect COVID-19. The three learning rate methodologies employed are decreasing the learning rate when modeling performance plateaus, cycling learning rate, & maintaining constant learning rate. F1-score was 0.9 for the reduce-on-plateau approach, 0.86 for the cyclic learning rate, and 0.82 for the constant learning rate. Table 1 summarises the existing work and their limitations.

Table 1. Comparative study of COVID-19 detection research papers

Publication/Year	Title	Technique Used	Limitations
Journal of Healthcare Engineering, 2021	COVID-19 Patient Identification Utilizing X-Ray Chest Pictures To use an ANN-Based DL Prototype	CNN-based DL fusion	Dataset is insufficient
Radiology, 2020	Using AI to Detect COVID-19	CNN model - COVNet	Dataset clarification is not clear
"Computers in Biology & Medicine", 2021	Scat-NET: COVID-19 detection with CNN approach employing scatter gram images	CNN model - ScatNet	Dataset is insufficient Overfitting problem in case of a large number of classes
Journal Pre-proofs, 2021	A New Coronavirus Illness 2019 (COVID 19) Pneumonia Screening DL System	Classification models in CNN and voting classifier	There was only a certain amount of model samples available. There was a limit on the number of people who may participate in the training and testing

Lemmas, Propositions, and Theorems. The numbers accorded to lemmas, propositions, and theorems, etc. should appear in consecutive order, starting with Lemma 1, and not, for example, with Lemma 11.

3   Research Gaps

According to our research survey of previous research, we have concluded that the previous researches have a limited dataset of COVID patients' CXR images. The deep learning model for feature extraction was too dense to train on such a small dataset, so we used the transfer learning approach and created the custom dataset by using two publicly available CXR datasets for COVID-19 detection.

The related work review reveals the following gaps in our understanding of the topic:

- There aren't a lot of models suggested for multiclass categories.
- Ultrasound has only been employed for imaging in a small handful of investigations.
- There are currently no DL-based full end-to-end platforms available in real-time.

A. Modalities of Dl for Covid-19 Diagnosis

Diagnostic pictures for COVID-19 are currently in short supply. Research on DL methods with X-ray & CT scan images to diagnose COVID-19 is ongoing. Like the human body, X-rays may pass through and around many different materials. Therefore, X-rays help image the human body's internal components. A CT scan may create cross-sectional pictures of the body using computers and a spinning X-ray apparatus. CT scans offer greater details than their conventional X-ray counterparts. Ultrasound uses sound waves to create a picture in real time. In addition, several researchers use a combination of imaging modalities to identify COVID-19 patients. Several studies, organized in Table 3 and Table 4, explore DL's potential in various picture contexts. Table 2 summarises the applications of Deep Learning in COVID-19.

Overview of Deep Learning

The recent trend in processing medical pictures is the use of DL. The goal is to facilitate a smoother diagnosis process and help radiologists obtain a more accurate analysis by providing a quantitative analysis of suspicious lesions. Already, DL has outperformed people on several identifications and computer vision applications [24]. DL techniques have a more complicated design than classic ones. The first of DL's three primary steps, pre-processing and improvement for each input, is accomplished using this architecture. The input is then utilized in the second stage, which is FE. In the third phase, several classifiers are used to categorize the inputs. One such method is DL, which aids the system in accurately processing complex visual tasks.

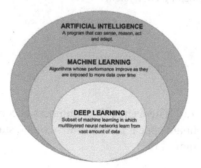

Fig. 1. Family of deep learning

Regarding information processing patterns in the human brain (Fig. 1), the DL subset of ML is influenced by those observed in the human brain. DL may run without any rules being written by humans; instead, it relies on a significant quantity of information to classify objects to input. Some different AI techniques have been applied in the search for the best network for usage in radiography and medical image processing. Well-known examples of DL-based networks include CNNs and Recurrent Neural Networks

(RNNs), both of which have found widespread application in medical research fields such as NLP, computer vision, & speech recognition, with often impressive results. CNN has demonstrated promising outcomes in medical image processing, particularly in image classification, segmentation, and localization.

B. Basic Architectures of Deep Neural Network (DNN)

Examples of DL methods include RNNs, DNNs, and DBNs. DNNs may be constructed using ANNs by adding many hidden layers between the output and input layers, as illustrated in Fig. 2. The DNN may express simple and complicated interactions in models where objects are seen as a layered mixture of primitives. In this configuration, data is sent directly from the input layer to the output layer; no intermediate layers are involved. An abundance of architectural & algorithmic variations facilitates DL's use [25].

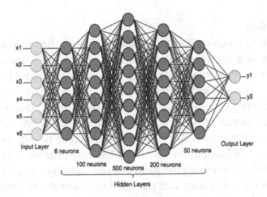

Fig. 2. Architecture of DNNs

Table 2. Applications of Deep Learning in COVID-19.

S. No.	Model	Data Type
1.	CB-STM-RENet based on deep CNN	X-ray pictures totaling 15127
2.	Majority voting of five deep TL framework i.e., Xception, Inception_resnet_v2, EfficientNetB0, EfficientNetB3, and EfficientNetB5	There were 349 positive COVID-19 CT scans from 216 patients, & 397 negative scans, classified as either normal or showing other lung illnesses
3.	GDCNN	X-ray pictures exceeding 5000 CXR images in total Dividing pneumonia into typical and different types of diseases
4.	DL-CRC (GAN, CNN, generic)	The three-class categorization of X-ray pictures includes 5794

(continued)

Table 2. (*continued*)

S. No.	Model	Data Type
5.	DenseNet201 based TL	pneumonia, 209 COVID-19, 27228 normal pictures
6.	ResNet50V2 applies the feature pyramid network designed layers	1262 CT scans out of 2492 are positive for COVID-19, whereas 1230 are negative
7.	ResNet50	A total of 4173 CT pictures and 2168 COVID-19 images
8.	CNN integrates with the SVM classifier	200 X-rays Normal, 2066 Pneumonia
9.	DarkCovidNet	CXR pictures 125 COVID-19,500 Negative Results

C. Transfer Learning

The approach of TL in machine learning is the transfer of the information increased by a CNN from a given & associated data set to tackle a separate but associated issue [27]. TL is predicated on the notion of generating learning by utilizing knowledge received from an associated work and applying it to a novel task via transfer. Researchers favor pre-trained DL networks because they have previously been trained on other datasets and can be improved to achieve high accuracy with a much smaller dataset; as a result, they are favored by researchers [28, 29], who performed an in-depth examination of TL practices. TL is a kind of learning in which the learning procedure is not initiated from the beginning but rather from patterns gained when tackling a previously solved issue. Previous learning is used this way, and the need to restart the learning procedure from the beginning is avoided.

As the name implies, this development style is often used for pretrained frameworks. Deep evolution neural networks serve as the foundation for these pretrained models. This approach is used in deep learning to train a CNN for a categorization issue employing big-scale training datasets. The accessibility of data for firstly training is key to the effectiveness of a training process since CNN models could learn to extract important attributes from a picture in Fig. 3. Based on CNN's ability to detect & pick the most remarkable visual aspects, it is determined whether or not this model is appropriate for TL.

a. Transfer Learning Strategies

DL is one of several techniques that have been successfully used to reap the advantages of TL. There are a few instances in this section:

- **Transfer learning for NLP:** If it comes to ML & DL, textual data poses a wide range of issues. Different strategies are used to convert or vectorize them. Fast-Text & Word2Vec are two examples of embeddings that were created utilizing a variety of training datasets. Transferring the information from the source activities allows them to be used in various other tasks, including sentiment analysis & document categorization.

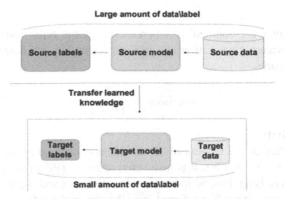

Fig. 3. Conceptual diagram of TL technique.

- **Transfer learning for Audio/Speech:** NLP & Computer Vision are examples of fields where DL has been effectively utilized to challenges using audio data. It has been shown that ASR models built for English may be utilized to boost the effectiveness of speech recognition systems for other languages, including German. Transfer learning has also had a significant impact on automatic speaker recognition.
- **Transfer learning for Computer Vision:** Many computer vision activities, including object detection and identification, have been effectively implemented utilizing multiple CNN architectures for deep learning. In this study, they discuss the transferability of deep neural network properties

4 Comparative Results and Discussion

In this part, the specifics regarding the performance evaluation metrics, CT images, x-ray images, and state-of-the-art deep networks are discussed, along with the dataset that was utilized, information regarding the development, a standard testing and training process, and the findings.

4.1 Performance Evaluation Metrics

The COVID-19 identification using the DL model's comparative analysis is carried out, and the findings are given individually. Overall classification precision, accuracy, recall, specificity, and f1-score have been accepted as measures to evaluate the efficiency of the models. Below is a breakdown of the metrics:

a. **Accuracy**

It is the most often used & easiest indicator for determining how many right predictions were made over the data. The ratio of appropriately predicted illness symptoms to the total no. of input images supplied.

$$Accuracy = \frac{TN + TP}{TP + FN + TN + FP} \tag{1}$$

b. **Precision**

True positives are counted as a percentage of the total positives (TP + FP) obtained. An accurate prediction is a ratio of accurately predicted pictures to the total no. of pictures.

$$\text{Precision} = \frac{TP}{TP + FP} \tag{2}$$

c. **Recall(Sensitivity)**

It is described as the amount of TP instances calculated by an average number of true positives (TP + FN). It is also referred to as TPR (True Positive Rate) or sensitivity. There is a relationship between the positives and the number of pictures in the leaf category. It is often referred to as the sensitivity rate or TPR.

$$\text{Recall} = \frac{TP}{TP + FP} \tag{3}$$

d. **F1-Score**

It is a weighted harmonic mean of accuracy and recall; also, it has been extensively employed in numerous ML methods over the last several years. It is described as the harmonic mean of the model's recall & accuracy across a whole time. It is a metric utilized as a statistical measure to evaluate a model's performance in a certain situation.

$$F_\beta = \frac{(1 + \beta^2)(\text{Precision} - \text{Recall})}{\beta^2 * (\text{Precision} + \text{Recall})} \tag{4}$$

e. **Specificity**

The specificity of a diagnostic test is defined as its capacity to identify disease-free individuals. FP, TP, TN, & FN represent true, false, positive, and negative results. Those cases where the COVID-19 picture was correctly categorized as pneumonia TP and those where it was misclassified as something else FN were analyzed. If a pneumonia picture is correctly categorized as pneumonia TN and wrongly classified as COVID-19 FP, then TN is the accurate classification, and FP is the incorrect classification.

$$\text{Specificity} = \frac{TN}{TN + FP} \tag{5}$$

4.2 Comparative Analysis with X-Ray and CT Images

The performance of the considered models is summarized in Table 3. There is a concise summary of the benefits, drawbacks, and computing complexity of the various X-ray image analysis algorithms that were compared and discussed.

Table 3. Models Accuracy Using X-Ray Images.

S. No.	Author's Name & Year	Model Name	Used Dataset	Accuracy (in %)
1.	M. C. Arellano & O. E. Ramos (2020) [30]	DenseNet-121	COVID-19 Database of Radiographic Images and Chest X-Ray 14	Obtain 94.7
2.	M. M. Ahsan et al. (2021) [31]	VGG 16 MobileNetV2	Open-source Kaggle Repository CXR dataset COVID-19	Achieve 100
3.	K. Foysal Haque et al. (2020) [32]	CNN	GitHub repository, in addition to the Kaggle repository	Up to 97.56
4.	M. Z. Islam et al. (2020) [33]	LSTM-CNN Network	repository on GitHub, SIRM, Radiopaedia, TCIM, Mendeley, and Kaggle	Up to 99

Table 4 provides an accurate summary of the models under discussion. A summary of the various CT image analysis techniques' benefits, drawbacks, and computing complexity are provided.

Table 4. Models Accuracy Using CT Images.

S. No.	Author's Name/Year	Model	Dataset	Accuracy
1.	C. Wu et al. (2020) [36]	COVID-AL	Consortium for ChestCT Image Research in China	Get 95%
2.	H. Gunraj et al. (2020) [37]	COVIDNet-CT	COVIDx-CT	Get 99%
3.	T. Mahmud et al. (2021) [38]	CovTANet	MosMed dataset	Get 95.8%
4.	F. Shi et al. (2020) [39]	Two 3D-ResNets	CTScans from several cooperative	93.3%
5.	X. Wang et al. (2020) [40]	DeCoVNet	Radiology Department Picture Archiving and Communication System (PACS) CT images of COVID-19 patients	90%
6.	A. A. Ardakani et al. (2020) [41]	ResNet101	PACS HRCT pictures of patients	Obtain 99.5%

4.3 Comparison with State-of-the-Art Techniques

Due to a lack of data and images, there are a lot of studies about how DL can be used to find COVID-19 diseases. Below Table 5 represents the comparative outcomes in terms of evaluation parameters: accuracy, f1-score, specificity and sensitivity, etc. According to this table, Babukarthik et al. [44] utilized a DL model based on a GDCNN to distinguish between X-ray pictures of COVID-19 and healthy subjects. They managed to achieve a 99% success rate overall (Fig. 4).

Table 5. Comparative Results Analysis of State-of-the-Art DL-based Approaches.

Model	Accuracy	F1-Score	Sensitivity	Specificity
GDCNN [45]	0.99	0.96	1	0.97
DenseNet201-based transfer learning [46]	0.96	0.96	0.96	0.96
ResNet50 [47]	0.94	0.96	0.94	0.98
CNN combined with the SVM classifier [48]	0.94	0.94	0.91	0.99

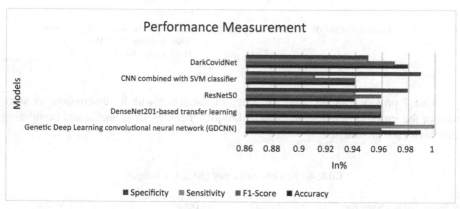

Fig. 4. Comparison Graph of the Deep Learning techniques in terms of Performance Parameters

ResNet50, CNN combined with SVM classifier, and DarkCovidNet. The evaluation of these models was carried out with a focus on the following four performance parameters, i.e., accuracy, sensitivity, f1-score, specificity etc. The GDCNN model obtained the highest values: 99% of accuracy, 96% of f1-score, 100% of Sensitivity, and 97% of Specificity. In addition, the CNN combined with the SVM classifier obtains 94% accuracy, f1-score, 91% sensitivity, and 99% specificity. This model found the highest value for the specificity parameter among other models. And the DarkCovidNet model found 98% accuracy, 97% f1-score, and 95% sensitivity and specificity, respectively. This comparative graph clearly shows that the GDCNN model gives the highest accuracy value than other methods.

5   Conclusion and Future Work

The patient's health and the disease's progress are both improved by prompt diagnosis. This research used medical imaging data from both Covid-19 and nonCovid-19 subjects. This research aimed to examine whether deep TL is applicable to the MRI diagnosis of COVID-19. The primary impetus was the difficulty of building DNNs from the start without ready access to enormous collections of pictures. In this study, we will look at some of the DL methods currently in use and address TL in some depth. We have offered a few DL-based models to facilitate a comparison of several performance indicators, including accuracy, f1-score, specificity, sensitivity, etc. ResNet50,

GDCNN, DenseNet201-based TL, CNN paired with SVM classifier, and DarkCovid-Net models are employed for DL. The GDCNN model had the greatest reliability value in the comparisons. In addition, DenseNet201-based transfer learning and DarkCovid-Net also perform well. And the remaining ResNet50 and CNN combined with SVM classifier models obtained the same accuracy values, i.e., 94%, which is also good. But the GDCNN model outperforms well in comparison to the other models.

In the future, you can put your efforts toward developing more effective multiclass categorization models. The time and workforce required for manual labeling can be reduced using weakly supervised DL systems. However, ultrasonography has only been employed as an imaging technique for COVID-19 identification in a small number of investigations. In this way, future ultrasound data may be utilized by researchers. As viral infection in lung areas are severe infection phase, authors may look into other organs impacted by the virus in the future. To better detect COVID-19 instances in major hotspots, scientists can construct an end-to-end system employing DL techniques.

References

1. Wang, L., Wang, Y., Ye, D., Liu, Q.: Review of the 2019 novel coronavirus (SARS-CoV-2) based on current evidence. Int. J. Antimicrob. Agents (2020). https://doi.org/10.1016/j.ijantimicag.2020.105948
2. Sohrabi, et al.: World Health Organization declares global emergency: a review of the 2019 novel coronavirus (COVID-19). Int. J. Surg. (2020). https://doi.org/10.1016/j.ijsu.2020.02.034
3. Dehghanbanadaki, H., et al.: Bibliometric analysis of global scientific research on Coronavirus (COVID-19). Med. J. Islam. Repub. Iran (2020). https://doi.org/10.34171/mjiri.34.51
4. Jones, R.C., et al.: Evaluating trends in COVID-19 research activity in early 2020: the creation and utilization of a novel open-access database. Cureus (2020). https://doi.org/10.7759/cureus.9943
5. Kagan, Moran-Gilad, J., Fire, M.: Scientometric trends for coronaviruses and other emerging viral infections. Gigascience (2020). https://doi.org/10.1093/gigascience/giaa085
6. Homolak, J., Kodvanj, I., Virag, D.: Preliminary analysis of COVID-19 academic information patterns: a call for open science in the times of closed borders. Scientometrics (2020). https://doi.org/10.1007/s11192-020-03587-2
7. Davenport, T., Kalakota, R.: The potential for artificial intelligence in healthcare. Futur. Healthc. J. (2019). https://doi.org/10.7861/futurehosp.6-2-94
8. Xue, W., Li, Q., Xue, Q.: Text detection and recognition for images of medical laboratory reports with a deep learning approach. IEEE Access (2020). https://doi.org/10.1109/ACCESS.2019.2961964
9. Butt, Gill, J., Chun, D., Babu, B.A.: Deep learning system to screen coronavirus disease 2019 pneumonia. Appl. Intell. (2020). https://doi.org/10.1007/s10489-020-01714-3
10. Mohamadou, Y., Halidou, A., Kapen, P.T.: A review of mathematical modeling, artificial intelligence and datasets used in the study, prediction and management of COVID-19. Appl. Intell. (2020). https://doi.org/10.1007/s10489-020-01770-9
11. Goel, T., Murugan, R., Mirjalili, S., Chakrabartty, D.K.: OptCoNet: an optimized convolutional neural network for an automatic diagnosis of COVID-19. Appl. Intell. (2021). https://doi.org/10.1007/s10489-020-01904-z
12. Zeroual, Harrou, F., Dairi, A., Sun, Y.: Deep learning methods for forecasting COVID-19 time-series data: a comparative study. Chaos Solitons Fractals (2020). https://doi.org/10.1016/j.chaos.2020.110121

13. Pandey, Pandey, K.: An extended deep learning based solution for screening COVID-19 CT-scans. In: 2022 9th International Conference on Computing for Sustainable Global Development (INDIACom), pp. 173–176 (2022). https://doi.org/10.23919/INDIACom54597.2022.9763194

14. Li, Z.: COVID-19 classification with CT scan and advanced deep learning technologies. In: 2022 3rd International Conference on Computer Vision, Image and Deep Learning & International Conference on Computer Engineering and Applications (CVIDL & ICCEA), pp. 458–462 (2022). https://doi.org/10.1109/CVIDLICCEA56201.2022.9824858

15. Azeem, M.A., Khan, M.I., Khan, S.A.: COVID-19 detection via image classification using deep learning on chest X-ray (2021). https://doi.org/10.1109/EE-RDS53766.2021.9708588

16. Balik, Kaya, M.: Detection of Covid-19 and pneumonia from colorized X-ray images by deep learning (2021). https://doi.org/10.1109/DASA53625.2021.9682404

17. Chaudhary, S., Sadbhawna, Jakhetiya, V., Subudhi, B.N., Baid, U., Guntuku, S.C.: Detecting COVID-19 and community acquired pneumonia using chest CT scan images with deep learning (2021). https://doi.org/10.1109/ICASSP39728.2021.9414007

18. Irmak, E.: A novel deep convolutional neural network model for COVID-19 disease detection (2020). https://doi.org/10.1109/TIPTEKNO50054.2020.9299286

19. Anwar, T., Zakir, S.: Deep learning based diagnosis of COVID-19 using chest CT-scan images (2020). https://doi.org/10.1109/INMIC50486.2020.9318212

20. Russakovsky, O., et al.: ImageNet large scale visual recognition challenge. Int. J. Comput. Vis. (2015). https://doi.org/10.1007/s11263-015-0816-y

21. Nguyen, K., Fookes, C., Ross, A., Sridharan, S.: Iris recognition with off-the-shelf CNN features: a deep learning perspective. IEEE Access (2017). https://doi.org/10.1109/ACCESS.2017.2784352

22. Pathak, Y., Shukla, P.K., Arya, K.V.: Deep bidirectional classification model for COVID-19 disease infected patients. IEEE/ACM Trans. Comput. Biol. Bioinform. (2021). https://doi.org/10.1109/TCBB.2020.3009859

23. Fan, D.P., et al.: Inf-Net: automatic COVID-19 lung infection segmentation from CT images. IEEE Trans. Med. Imaging (2020). https://doi.org/10.1109/TMI.2020.2996645

24. Mondal, M.R.H., Bharati, S., Podder, P.: Diagnosis of COVID-19 using machine learning and deep learning: a review. Curr. Med. Imaging Former. (2021). https://doi.org/10.2174/1573405617666210713113439

25. Dargan, S., Kumar, M., Ayyagari, M.R., Kumar, G.: A survey of deep learning and its applications: a new paradigm to machine learning. Arch. Comput. Methods Eng. **27**(4), 1071–1092 (2020). https://doi.org/10.1007/s11831-019-09344-w

26. LeCun, G., Bengio, Y.: Deep learning, pp. 1–10 (2015)

27. Arellano, M.C., Ramos, O.E.: Deep learning model to identify COVID-19 cases from chest radiographs (2020). https://doi.org/10.1109/INTERCON50315.2020.9220237

28. Ahsan, M.M., Alam, T.E., Trafalis, T., Huebner, P.: Deep MLP-CNN model using mixed-data to distinguish between COVID-19 and Non-COVID-19 patients. Symmetry (Basel) (2020). https://doi.org/10.3390/sym12091526

29. Foysal Haque, K., Farhan Haque, F., Gandy, L., Abdelgawad, A.: Automatic detection of COVID-19 from chest X-ray images with convolutional neural networks (2020). https://doi.org/10.1109/iCCECE49321.2020.9231235

30. Islam, M.Z., Islam, M.M., Asraf, A.: A combined deep CNN-LSTM network for the detection of novel coronavirus (COVID-19) using X-ray images. Informatics Med. Unlocked (2020). https://doi.org/10.1016/j.imu.2020.100412

31. Mohammed, M.A., et al.: Benchmarking methodology for selection of optimal COVID-19 diagnostic model based on entropy and TOPSIS methods. IEEE Access (2020). https://doi.org/10.1109/ACCESS.2020.2995597

32. Wang, L., Lin, Z.Q., Wong, A.: COVID-Net: a tailored deep convolutional neural network design for detection of COVID-19 cases from chest X-ray images. Sci. Rep. (2020). https://doi.org/10.1038/s41598-020-76550-z
33. Wu, C., et al.: Risk factors associated with acute respiratory distress syndrome and death in patients with coronavirus disease 2019 pneumonia in Wuhan, China. JAMA Int. Med. **180**(7), 934–943 (2020). https://doi.org/10.1001/jamainternmed.2020.0994
34. Gunraj, H., Wang, L., Wong, A.: COVIDNet-CT: a tailored deep convolutional neural network design for detection of COVID-19 cases from chest CT images. Front. Med. (2020). https://doi.org/10.3389/fmed.2020.608525
35. Mahmud, T., Rahman, M.A., Fattah, S.A.: CovXNet: a multi-dilation convolutional neural network for automatic COVID-19 and other pneumonia detection from chest X-ray images with transferable multi-receptive feature optimization. Comput. Biol. Med. (2020). https://doi.org/10.1016/j.compbiomed.2020.103869
36. Shi, F., et al.: Review of artificial intelligence techniques in imaging data acquisition, segmentation, and diagnosis for COVID-19. IEEE Rev. Biomed. Eng. (2021). https://doi.org/10.1109/RBME.2020.2987975
37. Wang, X., et al.: A weakly-supervised framework for COVID-19 classification and lesion localization from chest CT. IEEE Trans. Med. Imaging (2020). https://doi.org/10.1109/TMI.2020.2995965
38. Ardakani, Kanafi, A.R., Acharya, U.R., Khadem, N., Mohammadi, A.: Application of deep learning technique to manage COVID-19 in routine clinical practice using CT images: results of 10 convolutional neural networks. Comput. Biol. Med. (2020). https://doi.org/10.1016/j.compbiomed.2020.103795
39. Rohila, V.S., Gupta, N., Kaul, A., Sharma, D.K.: Deep learning assisted COVID-19 detection using full CT-scans. Internet of Things (Netherlands) (2021). https://doi.org/10.1016/j.iot.2021.100377
40. Farid, Selim, G.I., Khater, H.A.A.: A novel approach of CT images feature analysis and prediction to screen for Corona virus disease (COVID-19). Int. J. Sci. Eng. Res. (2020). https://doi.org/10.14299/ijser.2020.03.02
41. Babukarthik, R.G., Ananth Krishna Adiga, V., Sambasivam, G., Chandramohan, D., Amudhavel, A.J.: Prediction of Covid-19 using genetic deep learning convolutional neural network (GDCNN). IEEE Access (2020). https://doi.org/10.1109/ACCESS.2020.3025164

Edge Discerning Using Improved PSO and Canny Algorithm

H. Harish[1,2]([✉]) and A. Sreenivasa Murthy[2]

[1] Maharani Lakshmi Ammanni College for Women Autonomous, Bangalore, India
hh.harish@gmail.com
[2] Electronics and Communication Department, UVCE, Bangalore University, Bangalore, India

Abstract. In applications of image processing edge detection plays an important task. In this paper, the identification of edge using improved particle swarm optimization (IPSO) edge segmentation is proposed. Several conventional edge detection algorithms like Canny, Sobel, and Prewitt algorithms have not much intelligence in edge segmentation technique when compared to IPSO. In the process of segmenting edges in an image, intensity likeness of individual cluster of image pixels to be optimized. There exists many research techniques to determine edges of an image using effective optimized segmentation techniques. When IPSO with canny algorithm compared with PSO algorithm, the results are more accurate because of adding Search counter (SC) counter in IPSO and applying canny algorithm further. In this paper, edge segmentation done using improved PSO optimized technique that are present on images. Textural features extracted from IPSO segmented images using Gray Level Co-occurrence Matrix (GLCM). Textural extracted features are classified using Random Forest algorithm and obtains 98% accuracy.

Keywords: IPSO · image edge segmentation · random forest · canny algorithm · GLCM

1 Introduction

Information about Intensity and orientation of edges in images are used as input for processing and detecting the objects in computer vision systems. Accurate and precise information about edges is a fundamental to the success of image vision system. Hence, the detection of precise and exact edges is vital part of image processing algorithm. The partitions between different areas is explained by an edge, which helps in image segmentation and recognition of objects. In computer vision applications edge is a key attribute. Hence, edge detector schemes will solve the degradation of edges. Threshold and edge connecting are commonly used techniques in application of computer vision. The gray tone discontinuity of image improved by thresholding technique using neighborhood operators [1]. Most of the edge detectors detects edge pixels by first order derivate. The intensity of the pixel in first order derivate is larger than some threshold or second order derivative where the intensity of the pixel withstand a zero

R. S. Tomar et al. (Eds.): CNC 2022, CCIS 1893, pp. 192–202, 2023.
https://doi.org/10.1007/978-3-031-43140-1_17

crossing. Operators based on gradient generally produces fragmented and dense edges [2]. Performance of all operators are good on sharp edges. The shortcomings of these operators is effective if images have definite edge types and are extremely receptive to noise, this usually causes splinters/fragmented edges. Edge detection problems can also be solved by optimization, whose main aim is to minimize the cost. Finding the best solution within a given constraint of a problem called optimization. Genetic algorithm (GA), swarm optimization, ant colony optimization (ACO) are few of the computational intelligent techniques. PSO is a universal stochastic global search technique for solving complex and nonlinear optimization problems. Biological populations and social behavior of animals such as schooling of fish and flocking of birds inspire PSO. In this paper, an improvised particle swarm optimization technique with canny algorithm is proposed. To the proposed system BSD500 image dataset is fed as input. The positional best and overall best value of the images are estimated using IPSO algorithm. The IPSO technique deliver edge segmentation for the given image input. The obtained color segmented image used in edge identification. In this paper, to improve performance the sc counter added in the algorithm, which stores the swarm values in previous iterations. The GLCM method extracts energy, homogeneity, correlation and contrast features. 98% accuracy is achieved through Random forest algorithm classifier.

2 Literature Survey

There are different edge detector operators such as Prewitt, Sobel, Robert operators which are classified as first order derivative. These operators searches for the highest and least intensity values to identify edges. The other way of classifying the operator is by second order derivative, which extracts picture maxima nearness by zero crossing [3]. A fitness based PSO algorithm inspired by Artificial Bee Colony (ABC) proposed improves the speed of convergence, updating a new position and provides solution by updating better searching space [4]. Wen-Chang cheng proposed an algorithm for lane line detection and tracking using particle filters for detecting lanes [5]. Edge detection based on swarm intelligence using beetle and butterfly optimization were discussed by choosing the values which are optimal for finding the best solution [6]. Binary PSO detects edges based on minimizing multi objective fitness function, which outperformed various classical edge detectors in terms of F-score average and standard deviation [7]. Deep hybrid architecture proposed by combining convolutional neural network and the recurrent neural network (RNN) in detecting multiple continuous frames of a driving scene, which outperformed the difficulty in handling the lane detection [8]. Segmentation of lane line by watershed technique is performed and an estimated accuracy rate of 98% is obtained using JRip classifier [9]. Similar best accuracy rate obtained using swarm particle optimization technique [10]

A function-addressing image with noise and broken edges proposed in localization of accuracy by using discrete particle swarm technique for edge detection and compared this with traditional Canny and robust rank order method that results in smooth and accurate detecting in edges [11].

Image edge is detected using AdaBoost and decision algorithm tree in extracting deep features of image. This gives better result in edge detection when tested with machine learning algorithms [12]. A convolution based generative adversarial end to end network proposed to discriminate segmentation mapping which could improve the result of segmentation by finding the change in ground value and result obtained. This betters the mapping performance of segmentation [13].

Pixel difference network works on difference convolution that combines the popular traditional operators of edge detectors into convolutional operators for good performance and high accuracy task. BSDS 500 and VOC dataset are used for PiDiNet for recording various parameters [14]. Segmentation and detection of edges were proposed using traditional Canny edge and watershed technique, classifier results accuracy of 98% [15].

3   Methodology

3.1   Overall Structure of Algorithm

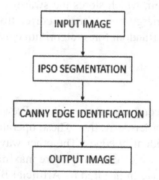

Fig. 1. Overall process flowchart

Figure 1 demonstrates the overall process for edge segmentation. The color input image segmented using IPSO and made smooth at the edges and further canny algorithm identifies the edges more accurately.

3.2   IPSO Algorithm

PSO works on the swarm intelligence and was originally proposed by J. Kennedy and R. Eberhant in 1995 [16] as evolutionary technique. The algorithm inspired by social interaction of animals and birds such as animal herding, ant colonies or bird flocking. PSO is a universal metaheuristic search optimization technique used in various applications of engineering field. In computer vision, PSO technique used in identifying the object, segmentation, edge detection of objects and classification. PSO uses particles to find candidate solution. Particle is a simple object that has properties and group of particles called swarm. These particles traverse complete the search space to discover possible solution in the randomly selected search space. Individual particle discover the search space to find the best solution possible for the search space. The optimal solution of the individual particles within the swarm using the fitness coefficient is made based upon experience of the individual past and adjacent values stored.

The particles best position known is named as personal best (pbest) in search space and best position of entire swarm in the given space is named as global best (gbest). Based on fitness coefficient pbest and gbest values evaluated and updated at the current execution stage in search space. Particle velocity and position will get restructured until the optimum best value is obtained.

The particles in PSO technique initiated arbitrarily with known population, which includes position and velocity of particles. Individual particle fitness examined by pbest and gbest value assigned. The particles iterate at least once in search space to reach a particular target and swarm population is proportional directly to number of iteration. Number of iteration increases as population of swarm increases.

The population of swarm's $\propto$ number of iterations

Each particle velocity and position is upgraded by succeeding equation repeatedly to find most global favorable.

$$\vec{v}_i = w\vec{v}_i + c_1 R_1 (\vec{p}_{i,best} - \vec{p}_i) + c_2 R_2 (\vec{g}_{i,best} - \vec{g}_i) \tag{1}$$

$\vec{v}_i$ and $\vec{p}_i$ are velocity and position of ith particle. $\vec{p}_{i,best}$ and $\vec{g}_{i,best}$ are the particle best discovered position and swarms position in that iteration. The inertia is introduced to avoid convergence of particle in the search plane and represented by w. Acceleration coefficient is represented by c1 and c2 specifying particle movement in single iteration, R_1 and R_2 is the uniformly distributed random variables between 0 and 1 indicating movement of particle in search space. $c_1 R_1 (\vec{p}_{i,best} - \vec{p}_i)$ and $c_2 R_2 (\vec{g}_{i,best} - \vec{g}_i)$ are referred as cognitive and social components particles positions are updated using the (2) equation.

$$\vec{p} = \vec{p}_i + \vec{v}_i \tag{2}$$

3.3 IPSO in Image Edge Segmentation

IPSO is an optimized technique used in image enhancement and image segmentation in the field of image processing. In this work, IPSO technique is used to segment edges of color images for BSD500 image dataset. Manipulation of RGB component is done in this process. SC counter is an internal counter, which keeps track of evolution of swarms. SC counter improves the performance of edge segmentation by tracking the number of times swarm is evolved. A threshold is set to initiate the algorithm, that identifies the image is a color image or not. Value of the threshold is set to three for color image as it have red, green, and blue color components.

A input image to be segmented is loaded initially. If the image inputted is a color image then the RGB intensity values of individual pixels have to be worked. Before processing the image, normalize the image and calculate the RGB intensity values.

Below steps helps in understating IPSO edge segmentation in image:

Step 1: Images to be segmented are read as input.

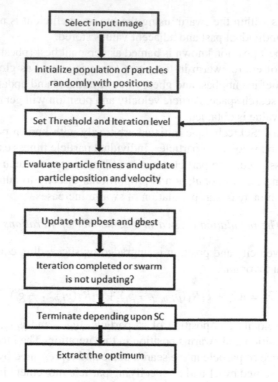

Fig. 2. IPSO Flowchart

Step 2: Swarm population initialized randomly in the range (0–256) for RGB and maintain the values obtained in each column in ascending order (Fig. 2).

Step 3: Set threshold and iteration level. Avoid convergence by setting the inertia factor for individual weight of particles.

Step 4: Evaluate the particle fitness in the given search area and update the best position of the particles. Also, update particle's position and velocity.

Step 5: The particle repetition is limited or removed in the search space till global best value is obtained by updating.

Step 6: SC counter is internal counter which is introduced to identifies the swarm during each iteration. Delete un-updated particles depending upon the swarm SC counter value and reset the threshold. SC_{max} is the maximum threshold which is achieved over each iteration, NK is number of particles vanishes after the swarm with improvement in fitness.

$$sc = SC_{max} + \left(1 - \frac{1}{Nk+1}\right) \tag{3}$$

Step 7: Step 3 to step 6 is repeated till no change in the particle values is observed. The optimum gbest contains the result of edge identified output values is obtained.

The image identified with edge pixels using IPSO for color image by separating the background and foreground pixels. The SC counter avoids iteration levels and helps in providing the optimized solution set quicker. The SC counter stores the iteration levels along with gbest values at each iteration.

Canny edge detection algorithm applied to segment the edges from the images. The multiple features of the edge segmented images is extracted using region of interest (ROI) and classifiers.

3.4 Canny Edge Detection

Canny edge detection algorithm is one of the convention algorithm used in discerning the edges in the images with multi-stage [17].

$$\bullet\, Edge\_Gradient(G) = \sqrt{(G_x^2 + G_y^2)} \qquad (4)$$

where G(x) and G(y) represents horizontal and vertical direction of image. Edged are always perpendicular to gradient values.

3.5 Feature Extraction

The image which has been preprocessed is portrayed with the help of the process called as feature extraction. Feature extraction extracts the important attributes of the image, which generates a vital information of the image for identification. Feature extraction is dimensionality reduction method obtained by manageable groups of data by reducing the initial set of large data. It also reduces redundant data without losing the relevant information from high-level information such as shape, texture, and color. Features classified as low and high level. Extracted features directed from original images classified as low-level features. High-level features constructed on features of low-level. Shape, texture and color are the image features. One of the image vital property is texture. Texture of the image is a regional descriptor helps in process of retrieval. Texture feature used to classify and recognize objects that has similar findings between images. Texture can be classified into structural and statistical methods [18]. Co-occurrence matrices, Markov random fields, Fourier power spectra, fractal model are few of the statistical methods. In this work, mathematical calculation using the Gray level co-occurrence matrix (GLCM) method is used.

3.6 GLCM

GLCM is one of the important texture feature technique using second-order texture statistical features proposed in 1973 by Haralick and others. It is a square matrix that focus the relationship and distribution of gray levels in the images. The values are real numbered and are non-negative. Spatial information in the neighboring pixels are obtained in various direction and distances which extracts patterns of same frequency in various directions. Based on the contents texture features are calculated. The GLCM measures intensity in the image pixel of interest. In proposed work, four features of textural features is extracted from GLCM,

[1] Correlation
[2] Contrast
[3] Homogeneity
[4] Energy

Correlation: The Eq. (5) measure the joint probability occurrences, how the pixels are correlated to their neighbour pixel over the complete image. The value of correlation ranges between 1 or -1 for a negatively or positively correlated image. For a contrast image correlation is infinity.

$$Correlation = \sum\nolimits_{i,j} \frac{I(i,j)(i - \mu i)(i - \mu j)}{\sigma i \sigma j} \qquad (5)$$

Contrast: The local variations in the measure of the intensity between neighboring pixel. It is also named as variance and inertia and is defined by the Eq. (6).

$$contrast = \sum\nolimits_{i,j} I(i,j)(i - j)^2 \qquad (6)$$

Homogeneity: Homogeneity is referred as inverse different movement. It estimates the homogeneity with larger values between pair objects of smaller gray tone. The image homogeneity feature is defined by Eq. (7).

$$Homogeneity = \sum\nolimits_{i,j=0}^{N-1} \frac{P(i,j)}{R} \qquad (7)$$

Energy: Energy is referred as angular second moment. Measure of the homogeneity of the image is energy, which used to detect the disorder and measure the occurrence of the pairs repeated within an image. The Eq. (8) is sum of the squared elements of GLCM within the Range $= [0, 1]$, for contrast image energy is 1, which s maximum.

$$Energy = \sum\nolimits_{i,j} I(j,j)^2 \qquad (8)$$

The correlation, contrast homogeneity and energy extracted from textural features and loaded column-wise in excel sheet, each column representing fields of four features.

The BOSCH dataset consists of 1000 images and BSD-500 has 200 images. These dataset consists of blur-free jpg formatted color images and treated as input. BOSCH R&D dataset are 5-megapixel resolution images and is downscaled version [19]. The manuscripts demonstrate the tested IPSO.

Table 1 illustrates the results obtained from various techniques. Table 3 demonstrates the result comparison with various techniques and image number in the table states in the image number in the database. The complete approach on edge identification on BSD-500 dataset and BOSCH R&D dataset is an important work in computer vision application.

Table 2 shows the comparison with Hoeffding Tree, JRip and Random Forest classifier accuracy results. When compared to the JRip and Hoeffding tree classifier Random Forest classifier gives best results.

Table 1. Results with IPSO and proposed system with BOSCH R&D images

INPUT IMAGE	IPSO SEGMENTATION	IPSO-CANNY

Classifier summary of Random forest:

- Perfectly Classified: 98%
- Imperfectly Classified: 0%
- RMS error: 0.1295
- Kappa statistic: 1

Table 2. Results comparison with proposed method

Sl. No.	Classifiers	Accuracy
1	JRip	97%
2	Random forest	98%
3	HoeffdingTree	96%

Table 5 demonstrates the comparison results for proposed system with other methods. In Table 4 Sl No. 3 is proposed work of this manuscript which has accuracy of 98%, which is far better than other methods.

Table 5 represents precision, recall and F-score of BPSO, ACO, GA and IPSO techniques. When compared other techniques IPSO-Canny achieves F-score of 0.723.

Table 3. Results comparison with canny and propsed system with BSD-500 images

Image number	CANNY	IPSO	IPSO-CANNY
118035			
181018			
163014			

Table 4. Results comparison with other techniques

Sl No.	Technique	Accuracy
1	PSO	90%
2	FO-DPSO	96.21%
3	IPSO-Canny	98%

BPSO, ACO, GA values were used in BSD500, same process is carried on IPSO-Canny technique for our lane line dataset.

Figure 3 represents graphical comparison of various techniques for BSD-500 and BOSCH R&D datasets.

Table 5. Precision, Recall and F-score of other techniques and proposed system

Techniques	Precision	Recall	F-Score
BPSO	0.4235	0.4325	0.4301
ACO	0.3846	0.3751	0.3797
GA	0.2762	0.2814	0.2787
IPSO-Canny	**0.803**	**0.765**	**0.723**

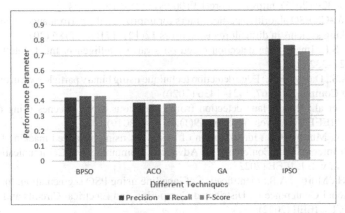

Fig. 3. Graphical comparison of various techniques

4 Conclusion

As we are internally working on edge discerning present on roads from BOSCH R&D dataset and BSD-500 dataset. Canny, Sobel and Prewitt algorithms have not much intelligence in edge identification on standalone when compared to IPSO-canny in the image edge identification or segmentation process. When compared to PSO algorithm the proposed improved algorithm stabiles the swarm optimization using SC counter. The IPSO output fed as input to canny edge discerning algorithm in grayscale mode. Hence accuracy of edge discerning is more appropriate. The values of the gbest and pbest are evaluated from the neighbor pixels. The IPSO algorithm segments the image input. Canny edge discerning algorithm easily identifies the edges with more accuracy after IPSO. Four features such as correlation, homogeneity, contrast and energy are extracted using the GLCM technique and classified using Random Forest, Hoeffding tree and JRip classifier algorithm. Random Forest achieves 98% accuracy, JRip classifier achieves 97% accuracy and HoeffdingTree algorithm achieves 96% of accuracy for GLCM features. If the image quality is bad then the identification of edge may be incorrect from this technique and treated as limitation of the technique. This technique may also be applied for video frames in the identification of edges.

References

1. Chaudhuri, S., Chatterjee, S., Katz, N., Nelson, M., Goldhaum, M.: Decision of blood vessel in retinal images using two dimensional matched filters. IEEE Trans. Med. Imaging **8**, 263–269 (1989)
2. Peli, T., Malah, D.: A study of edge detection algorithms. Comput. Graph. Image Process. **20**, 1–21 (1992)
3. Dagar, N.S., Dahiya, P.K.: Soft computing techniques for edge detection problems: a state-of-the-art review. Int. J. Comput. Appl. **136**(12), 28–34 (2016). ISSN: 0975-8887
4. Sharma, K., et al.: Fitness based particle swarm optimization. Int. J. Syst. Assur. Eng. Manag. **6**(3), 319–329 (2015). https://doi.org/10.1007/s13198-015-0372-4
5. Cheng, W.-C.: PSO algorithm particle filters for improving the performance of lane detection and tracking systems in difficult roads. Sensors **12**(12), 17168–17185 (2012)
6. Khaleel, S.I.: Image edge detection based on swarm intelligence. Int. J. Intell. Eng. Syst. **14**(6), 321–332 (2021)
7. Dagar, N.S., Dahiya, P.K.: Edge detection technique using binary particle swarm optimization. Procedia Comput. Sci. **167**, 1421–1436 (2020)
8. Zou, Q., et al.: Robust lane detection from continuous driving scenes using deep neural networks. IEEE Trans. Veh. Technol. **69**(1), 41–54 (2019)
9. Harish, H., Murthy, A.S.: Identification of lane lines using advanced machine learning. In: 2022 8th International Conference on Advanced Computing and Communication Systems (ICACCS), vol. 1. IEEE (2022)
10. Harish, H., Murthy, A.S.: Identification of lane line using PSO segmentation. In: 2022 IEEE International Conference on Distributed Computing and Electrical Circuits and Electronics (ICDCECE). IEEE (2022)
11. Setayesh, M., Zhang, M., Johnston, M.: Edge detection using constrained discrete particle swarm optimisation in noisy images. In: 2011 IEEE Congress of Evolutionary Computation (CEC). IEEE (2011)
12. Cui, J., Tian, K.: Edge detection algorithm optimization and simulation based on machine learning method and image depth information. IEEE Sens. J. **20**(20), 11770–11777 (2019)
13. Su, Z., et al.: Pixel difference networks for efficient edge detection. In: Proceedings of the IEEE/CVF International Conference on Computer Vision (2021)
14. Shi, Q., Liu, X., Li, X.: Road detection from remote sensing images by generative adversarial networks. IEEE Access **6**, 25486–25494 (2017)
15. Harish, H., Murthy, A.S.: Lane line edge detection using machine learning. IJONS **13**(75), 51039–51046 (2022). ISSN: 0976-0997
16. Kennedy, J., Eberhart, R.: Particle swarm optimization. In: Proceedings of ICNN 1995-International Conference on Neural Networks, vol. 4. IEEE (1995)
17. Haralick, R.M.: Statistical and structural approaches to texture. Proc. IEEE **67**(5), 786–804 (1979)
18. Canny, J.: A computational approach to edge detection. IEEE Trans. Pattern Anal. Mach. Intell. **6**, 679–698 (1986)
19. BOSCH Dataset. https://boxy-dataset.com/boxy/download

Sniffit: A Packet Sniffing Tool Using Wireshark

Sourit Singh Rajawat, Pallavi Khatri[✉], and Geetanjali Surange

ITM University, Gwalior, Gwalior, India
souritsingh12@gmail.com, {Pallavi.khatri.cse,
Geetanjali.surange}@itmuniversity.ac.in

Abstract. Sniffers has highest capacity or capability for monitoring and validating the internet traffic. Sniffers play a crucial role in any organization's ability to manage computer networks effectively and efficiently. Sniffer allows us to control, observe, and record passwords used for telnet, user login, and FTP connections. Without changing them, this inspects and sniffs packets as they move via a network. Network administrators can evaluate, comprehend, and extract relevant information from the content of packets that have been sniffed using the sniffer by utilising the sniffer to decode or convert the captured packets. Any organisation will benefit from this. Hackers also utilise sniffers to carry out their nefarious deeds, such as breaking into other users' computers and accounts to gain access to all the necessary data or information. This research paper's major goal is to build and install a new sniffer tool called sniffit and to introduce the protocols that are used to analyse packets. According to implementation results, the Sniffer tool builds a packet database that is encoded. Moreover, the front end shows the relevant data in response to user requests or needs.

Keywords: Packet Sniffer · Network Monitoring · NIC · WinPcap

1 Introduction

A password-finding programme called a sniffer is used to search for passwords so that they can later be broadcast over a network or on a computer. Sniffer sniffs the incoming and outgoing data packets, or the network traffic, so that packets can be collected and the password discovered. Sniffing can be done in one of the two techniques listed below:

I. Employing network analyzers and tools for packet sniffing.
II. Using tools for network sniffing.

Sniffing is possible in wireless and wired networks alike. Sniffer is the name of the programme that is installed on a host machine and used to traverse all network traffic, regardless of its destination. Sniffer records each packet that is sent across the network. Each packet carries a MAC address, IP addresses of source and destination, and the payload. Intercepting the network and capturing the packets using sniffers or other network packet sniffing tools, an attacker can quickly learn the secret or hidden information. SniffPass, Ace Password Sniffer, and Wireshark are some other sniffers that

R. S. Tomar et al. (Eds.): CNC 2022, CCIS 1893, pp. 203–212, 2023.
https://doi.org/10.1007/978-3-031-43140-1_18

can be used for business purposes. One of the most popular and secure sniffer tools is Wireshark. To begin sniffing, these utilities must be installed on the host computer. These sniffers intercept data transmitted using protocols like POP3, IMAP4, SMTP, FTP, and HTTP used for password-based authentication. Due to security concerns, the majority of websites do not employ these protocols. In this research article, we suggest a brand-new sniffer for wired networks called Sniffer. Although there are many sniffers that are readily available as software packages on the market, in this article we concentrate on the ways and approaches that turn a computer device into a sniffer without the need to install any third-party software on it. This article focuses on the techniques used by sniffer software that turns any legitimate machine in to a data sniffing machine. Various methods have variety of inter-networking devices which are used for keeping an eye on network activity and sniffing packets discussed in this study. Additionally, it covers all possibility for packet sniffer network analysis. This article is divided into the sections below, which are as follows:

The relevant works and research of other writers are included in Sect. 2, often known as the literature survey. The study of methodologies and techniques, or the process by which we might design a sniffing tool utilized for intranet and internet sniffing, is covered in Sect. 3. The approaches for network traffic analysis are explained in Sect. 4. Section 5 talks with Sniffer's implementation specifics and outcomes. The final section includes a conclusion and a list of difficulties to come.

2 Literature Survey

This section discusses about the relevant work in the field of network analysis, detection, creation of network packet sniffer module in brief. Using AntiSniff methods authors in [3] have proposed a sniffer detection technique. According to the authors some packet sniffers are not weak for detection, they are detectable. AntiSniff technique is used to perform the multiple tests to examine whether any host are behaving irresponsibly. Ryan Spangler explained three tests which are Network & machine latency tests, DNS tests, and Operating system specific tests. For operating systems like Windows 9X and NT specific test a like ARP test is used and ping test is used for Linux and NetBSD Kernels. Network and machine latency tests are defined as Echo test, Ping drop test, and ICMP Time Delta test. Kirykos and McEachen, Siang [2] proposed a sniffing tool implemented for TinyOS based sensor networks. Initial explanations of the methods used by the TinyOS system for filtering network data came from Kirykos and McEachen, Siang. TinyOS sniffer uses the fundamental hardware and software elements in lieu of TCP dump and a Java application. In Fig. 1, the TinyOS Sniffer is explained. The developed programme makes it simple to add features and new subsystems without affecting how the primary system functions.

Network packet sniffing is essential for network observation and troubleshooting, as authors in [4] have found in their study of analyzing the traffic captured by packet sniffers. Essential units that are used while the analysis is the hardware used, driver that captures the data, buffer for storing the captured data, unit for decoding the data, unit for modification of data, and data transfer unit. Analyzers are used for traffic monitoring. Furthermore, their study shows that sniffing data in a wireless network is less

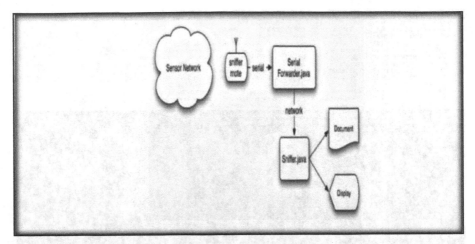

Fig. 1. Block diagram of TinyOS Sniffer [2]

complicated than it is in wired LANS. They employ three methods to evaluate network traffic: forensics analysis, batch analysis, and real-time analysis. Commercially available programmes like Soft Perfect Network Protocol, Tcpdump, and Wireshark.

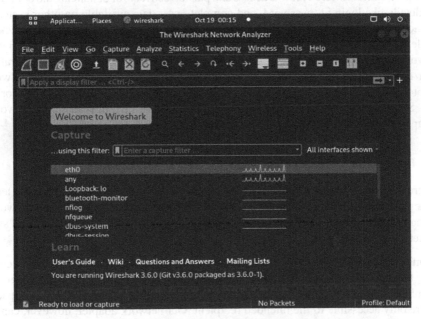

Fig. 2. Wireshark Tool (Analyzing Traffic)

Figure 2 and 3 illustrates the basic functionality of Wireshark.

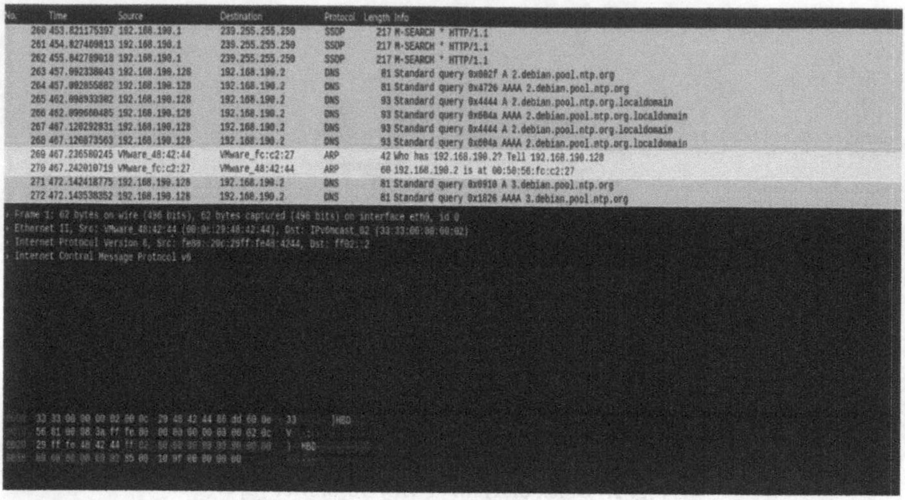

Fig. 3. Wireshark Tool (Packet Analyzing)

3 Proposed System

In the past, sniffers offered remote access and packet recovery for beneficial and confidential details like login id, password, and complete user data available on other systems. To monitor and validate communications, our work here focuses on sniffing packets inside of organisations. Additionally, it aids with password recovery. For both intranetwork and cross-network users, we recover passwords by examining network traffic. Inter-network in this context refers to several network segments, whereas intra-network denotes activity within a single segment, in this case, the segment of our monitoring host. Sniffer uses the same method for sniffing and monitoring intra- and inter-networks to capture traffic.

3.1 Intra and Internetwork Sniffing

Before we begin capturing the data we must analyse the network traffic. Multiple techniques are available for traffic analysis, but the most effective one depends on networking hardware and network architecture. (a hub or switch). To inspect the data and sniff packets, take the following actions:

Promiscuous Mode: Initially, we must set up the sniffer settings on the machine (computer that will monitor and sniff the traffic). This device serves as a network sniffer. By default, no computer can access the network traffic of other computers, so that packets are only accessible to the intended recipient. Our network adapter, however, can be configured specifically to allow a system to accept whole traffic that is travelling inside the segment. Promiscuous mode is what it is called. It is a Network Interface Card's operation mode. Non-promiscuous mode in NIC is activated by default, but when it is switched to promiscuous mode, the computer begins to receive all network packets.

Hub and Switch Based Networks: Internetworking devices like a hub or switch are used to connect various network segments to one another. In order to access all incoming packets from every network segment linked via either hub or hub supported networks, it is required to set the adapter to promiscuous mode. The hub is the main component that transmits each packet that passes through it. The task of packet capturing is crucial in switch-based networks. The majority of organisations now use switches rather than hubs. A switch, as opposed to a hub, only transfers a packet to its destination after receiving it on a port. The Content Addressable Memory (CAM) table, which contains the ports connected to each MAC address for all hosts, is maintained by a switch. When a packet for a port is received, it display the port's MAC address and sends the packet there. This feature limits traffic sniffing and monitoring in switched networks. A network will accept the packets only if they are explicitly sent to it with its address mentioned regardless of the adapter configuration. The Switch will block the entry of unidentified packets into the network section. Switches' main purpose is to reduce network traffic, not to stop network monitoring, hence sniffing packets is also viable in switched networks.

There are two types of switches:

1. Managed switches and
2. Unmanaged switches.

Aunique capability that allows them to be set up to replicate every packet on a particular port that is connected to Sniffer is seen when managed switches are used. Traffic monitoring and sniffing are made simpler to use by this feature, also known as port mirroring. This capability is activated by managed switches, which then connect the host to the designated port and record data in promiscuous mode. Unmanaged switches are still frequently used because they are more affordable even though managed switches are better for a sniffer. There are three ways to enable network traffic on unmanaged switches. First, use a managed Switch to link the network segment. But it is exceedingly improbable that this approach will be used.

The second technique involves flooding a CAM table. Spoofing ARP is the last available technique.

CAM Table Flooding: The MAC address of hosts and the matching port they are connected to are stored in a MAC table maintained by switches and are periodically updated. A switch may experience packet flooding, often known as fraudulent traffic. The fake packets may travel from distinct MAC addresses. A switch broadcasts all incoming packets to all ports rather than route them to the intended target port, this behaves like a hub and while transit all packets are captured.

ARP Spoofing: Weakness in ARP protocol is exploited in this method. A LAN uses the ARP (Address Resolution protocol) to find the MAC addresses for the hosts' associated IP addresses. When a computer tries to transmit a packet to a machine on a different segment through a router on a local network, and vice versa, the routers MAC address must be known. An ARP packet is then sent to every host connected to the network to get the MAC address o each of them. The IP address of the target whose MAC address is being sought is included in the sent ARP packet, also known as the query. The IP address retrieved is then compared with the IP address of each host. MAC address of the adapter is returned back when a match is found. IP/MAC address pairs are cached in ARP database in OS of every host so as to minimize the number of ARP queries. The OS only sends an ARP query if the desired MAC address is not present in the database. After reply for the query is received, other machines may reply, but only the machine with the required MAC address is required to react. Other operating systems could also simply take the answers to ARP queries that they did not start. A host can use all these features to fake its MAC address and appear to be any other device. The Sniffer functions by giving any host the bogus router MAC address and the false host MAC address to the router. The host and router then will communicate by transferring data to the fictitious MAC address provided by the Sniffer. The Sniffer host's MAC address was used to offer a wrong MAC address to both the router and the host. While the switch is delivering packets, our host and the other two will be communicating. In order to make the communication between the original source and the destination untraceable, the sniffing host must also handle it. Therefore, the packets between the router and the server must be sent again. In order to intercept communication by presenting a fake MAC address, the ARP spoofing method places the Sniffer between routers and computer devices. The ARP-Spoofing method is simple and practical.

There are following points for monitoring the traffic:

1. The effectiveness of this approached depends on the network architecture because some computer configurations prevent ARP spoofing.
2. When Sniffer is operating on a network, ARP spoofing might occasionally cause issues for other users with internet access.
3. A sort of network (Man in the Middle) attack is ARP spoofing.

4 Network Traffic Analysis Tool

After the packets have been intercepted and analyzed, the data is then sent in text form. Many tools are present for analyzing the traffic. WinPcap is used for capturing the packets and analyzing them.

WinPcap: Windows Packet Capture is a free and open-source software. For packet capturing packets in transit and analyzing them it offers a wide variety of structures and processes. It is a Windows adaptation of libpcap. It seizes the messages that are being sent over and received over a network, buffers them, and then displays the data in a variety of ways. Because WinPcap only works with a promiscuous NIC, the user must have higher rights. It only displays the raw packet content.

At several network stages, the packet content is encrypted for confidentiality using a variety of different protocols. In order to retrieve user information and make it comprehensible, the information must first be decrypted. This has resulted in the development of a variety of cryptanalysis methods, each of which is reliant on variations in the cryptographic cyphers used for encoding and demands an in depth understanding of symmetric key and asymmetric key methods for cryptography. In this section e discuss more detail about the implementation's particulars and the outcomes. In order to conduct packet sniffing, we use the WinPcap tool.

The sniffing procedure uses three basic parts.

- The first step entails collecting an adapter list, and the
- Second involves choosing a specific interface and then grab them.
- The last component filters and saves the packets after decoding them.

Proposed Work Flow

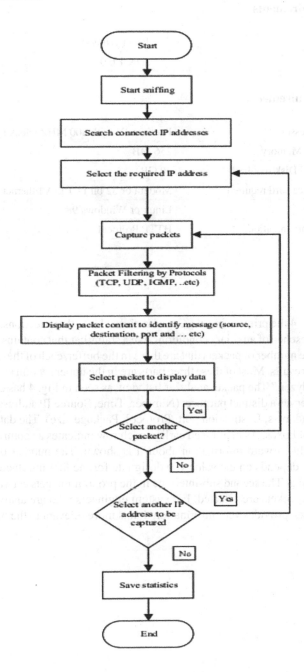

5 Experimental Setup

For implementation purpose, we have used JavaJDK1.6.0 on Microsoft visual studio IDE (2010).

Software Requirements

Language used	Java (Swings)
Version of JDK	JDK 1.6.0

Hardware Requirements

Supporting processor	Pentium IV with 800 MHZ Clock speed
Random Access Memory	256 MB
Capacity of Hard Disk required	40 GB
Network Inter face card required	Modem or 32 bit PCI/ISA Ethernet
Supporting OS	Linux or Windows 98
Protocol for communication	HTTP Protocol

6 Results

As shown in Fig. 4 the primary interface can be divided into three sections. In addition to this there is a presence of auxiliary conditions like a status bar that contains a progress bar that indicates the number of packets that are there in the buffer, each of these sections also reveals specific results. Most of these three parts are in the upper section are referred to as the "packet analyzer." The packet analyzer list view as seen in Fig. 4 has eight columns, each of which serves a distinct purpose: (Number, Time, Source IP address, Source port, Destination IP address, Destination port, Protocol, Package size). The data is displayed as a collection of boxes. As mentioned earlier, each row indicates a captured packet, and basic and straight forward information about it is shown. The number of packets that will be captured depends on the value you designate for the first interface buffer before you start capturing. The second sub-interface in the programme gets activated when any of the collected packets are selected. For system engineers who are analyzing network data, this interface provides very information that is more relevant to the packet selected for analysis.

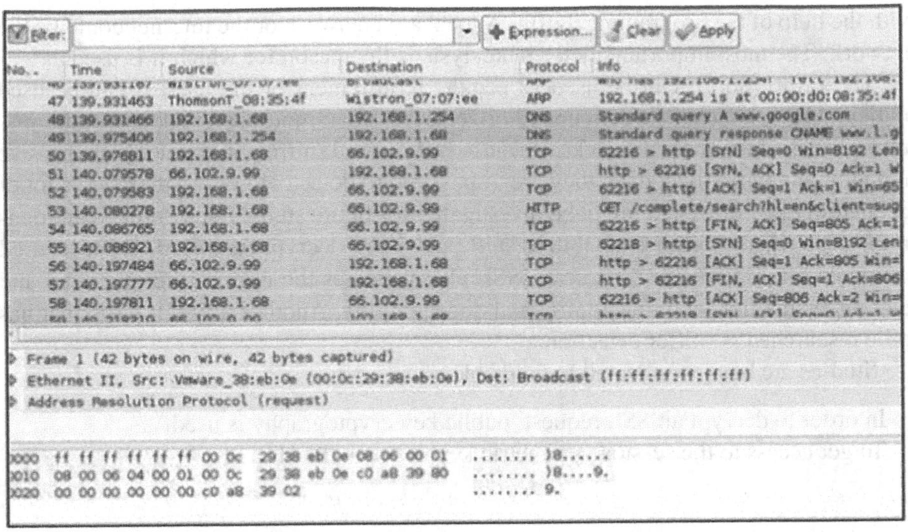

Fig. 4. Analyzing the Network Traffic [1]

Comparison of Proposed approach is done with the existing Packet sniffing tools as tabulated in Table 1.

Table 1. Comparison between Sniffit and other sniffing tools

S. No.	Property	Wireshark	Tcp du mp	Cain &Abel	Sniffit
1	OS supported	Windows,Unix	Unix	Windows	Windows Xp/linux or window 98
2	Disk usage	81 mb (windows),448 mb (unix)	448 kb	10 mb	256mb
4	User interface	GUI and CLI	CLI	GUI	GUI
5	Open source	Yes	Yes	No	Yes
6	No. Of protocols	more than 1000	TCP/IP	No protocols	TCP/IP
7	UDP traffic	Yes	No	Yes	Yes

7   Conclusions and Future Work

A machine in a network can be configured as a sniffer with good technical understanding of networking essentials and cryptography. Skill to implement a protocol and network design always supports the sniffer configuration. Network security can be improved with the help of the programme Sniffit. A local area network or the internet could be the network. The most important factor in analysis is the reason for which it is used.

The utility Sniffit can be used as per the requirement of the user. It can be used maliciously by attackers to gain unauthorized access to remote servers or as an administrative tool to administer networks. Because sniffers and sniffing instruments are passive in nature and just collect data, they are impossible to detect. However, there are a lot of fascinating directions that might be investigated for future study. Future study can focus in the area where Sniffer is unable to sniff packets or decrypt passwords from secured protocols like HTTPS/SSL requests. SSL also validates the user on the other end and guarantees the link's confidentiality and dependability. Another difficult issue that has to be researched is sniffer detection.

Studies are being conducted in fields like:

- In order to decrypt an SSL request, public key cryptography is used.
- To get access to the session symmetric key to break the HTTPS.

References

1. https://www.codewithc.com/wp-content/uploads/2015/03/network-packet-sniffer-java.jpg
2. McEachen, J.C., Siang, T.H., Kirykos, G.: Design and implementation of a modular wireless sensor network sniffer (2006)
3. Spangler, R.: Packet sniffer detection with Antisniff
4. Asrodia, P., Patel, H.: Network traffic analysis using packet sniffer. Int. J. Eng. Res. Appl. **2**(3), 854–856 (2012)
5. Xu, J., Liu, W., Zeng, K.: Monitoring multi-hop multi-channel wireless networks: online sniffer channel assignment, pp. 579–582 (2016). https://doi.org/10.1109/LCN.2016.97
6. Patel, N., Patel, R., Patel, D.: Packet sniffing: network wiretapping. In: IEEE International Advance Computing Conference (IACC 2009), Patiala, India, 6–7 March 2009, pp. 2691–2696 (2009)
7. Oluwabukola, O., Oludele, A., Ogbonna, A.C., Chigozirim, A., Amarachi, A.: A Packet Sniffer (PSniffer) application for network security in Java. In: Issues in Informing Science and Information Technology, vol. 10, pp. 389–400 (2013). https://doi.org/10.28945/1818
8. Tuli, R.: Packet sniffing and sniffing detection. Int. J. Innov. Eng. Technol. **16**, 22 (2020). https://doi.org/10.21172/ijiet.161.04
9. Bukie, P.T., Oyo-Ita, E.U., Ideba, M.E., Oboyi, J.: An enhanced Sniffing Tool for Network Management I. Background (2019)

Electronics Circuits for Communication Systems

Design of a Dielectric Resonator Antenna with Two Drilled Hollow Cylinders for Wide Bandwidth

Gaurav Kumar[1]($\boxtimes$) and Rajveer Singh Yaduvanshi[2]

[1] Department of Electronics and Communications, Guru Gobind Singh Indraprastha University, Delhi, India
gaurav0191@gmail.com
[2] Department of Electronics and Communications, Netaji Subhash University of Technology, Delhi, India

Abstract. This paper depicts the research done for the enhancement of the bandwidth of the antenna. A proposed antenna is designed by combining various studies on a single antenna, such as the use of different permittivity dielectric resonators and the creation of a hollow space between dielectric resonators. The dielectric resonator antenna consists of microstrip line fed, ground-plane elements, and the dielectric resonator material is in the form of stacked dielectric slabs. The antenna is excited by using the aperture couple method on the 50-Ω transmission line. This proposed design enhances 47% of the impedance bandwidth of the antenna. The total dielectric resonator antenna bandwidth is approximately 7 GHz. And the frequency of the operation is lies between 10.10 to 16.90 GHz. The antenna has applications in defense RADARs, weather RADARs, satellite communication, and other communications purposes. The antenna is designed using the simulation tool namely high frequency structure simulator (HFSS) software model.

Keywords: Wide bandwidth · Dielectric Resonator Antenna · Circular Polarisation · Stacked Antenna

1 Introduction

Dielectric resonators are famous for their different applications, which vary according to the permittivity of the material used to design the antenna. In terms of losses, these types of resonators have minimal losses and do not participate in conducting losses as they are made up of dielectric material. Dielectric resonator antennas have three-dimensional geometry, which provides high pliancy and multifaceted, ease in choosing dimensions as compared to planar (2D) geometry, and also permits the use of different electrical and physical dimensions related to applications and use of the antenna [1]. As per requirement, different methods could be used to enhance bandwidth [2–5], gain [6] or any other parameter of the antenna. For bandwidth Some of the methods investigated thus far involve connecting two different permittivity dielectrics with a ground plane

R. S. Tomar et al. (Eds.): CNC 2022, CCIS 1893, pp. 215–225, 2023.
https://doi.org/10.1007/978-3-031-43140-1_19

[7–9]. The cross coupling of the dielectric resonator using a conducting patch [10–12] is one way to enhance the bandwidth of the antennas. Recently, stacking [12], hollow cylinder [13], cylindrical DRA [14], hemi spherical DRA [15] of DRA have been introduced to boost the antenna gain and overall antenna bandwidth. A compact-based dielectric resonator antenna with a cylinder inside is suggested to combine the features of two dielectric shapes in one antenna [16]. Resonating modes TE_{xyz} developed in the dielectric resonator material are the key factors in the transmission and receiving modes of the antenna signal [17]. Circular polarization with low axial ratio values enables antennas to operate in all directions with equal efficiency [18]. A low axial ratio value is always desirable, but there are chances that the magnitude of the energy transmitted in a particular direction may be affected due to circular polarization, as the same magnitude will disperse the energy in all directions with equal strength.

In this paper, methods to improve the antenna bandwidth are shown. Bandwidth is the foremost parameters in antenna designing. To improve the result, two hollow cylinders were drilled on a rectangular DRA. As a result, the dielectric resonator antenna bandwidth is 6.80 GHz (almost 7 GHz). The antenna has an ultra-wide band for transmitting and receiving signals. The antenna is capable of working in the 10.20 GHz to 16.90 GHz i.e., X-band in the frequency spectrum and ku band in the frequency spectrum. As an application view of the antenna, the antenna has vast applications in weather radio detection and ranging, military RADARs, communications purposes, etc.

2 Antenna Design

Antenna design is done on the software tool HFSS, named Ansys High Frequency Structure Simulator, version 13.0. Antenna design depends on the desired applications. Based on the different applications needed, we can alter the design of the antenna as per convenience. The antenna in this paper is designed on a material flame retardant epoxy 4 (FR4) with a dielectric constant of 4.4, dimensions of 48 mm length and breadth, and a height of 1.4 mm. Figure 1 shows the general design of the DRA (dielectric resonator antenna), consisting of a general geometry for the antenna. DRA is made up of a ground plane, a microstrip-fed line, an input port, and a ground plane slot that transmits energy through the strip-fed line to the dielectric resonator material. The resonating frequency is the frequency at which transmission losses are minimal. Based on the resonating frequency, higher modes are generated.

A slot on the ground plane is calculated [19],

$$l_s = S_1 = S_2 = 0.4 \times \lambda o \times \sqrt{\epsilon_{ef}} \tag{1}$$

$$\epsilon_{ef} = (\epsilon_0 + \epsilon_d)/2 \tag{2}$$

where,

l_s represents the slot length
ϵ_{ef} is effective permittivity
ϵ_0 is the permittivity of the substrate of the antenna
ϵ_d is the permittivity of the material of antenna

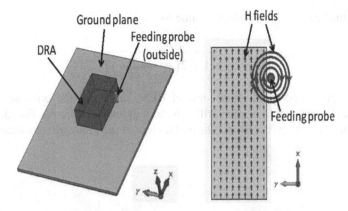

Fig. 1. General schematic diagram for RDRA

s_1, s_2 are dimensions of slot on the ground plane

Theoretically, the resonant frequencies of the microwave antennas and high frequency antennas are computed by the mathematical equation,

$$f_o = \frac{c}{2\pi \sqrt{\epsilon_r}} \sqrt{k_x^2 + k_y^2 + k_z^2}$$

Also,

$$k_x = \frac{\pi}{a}$$

$$k_y = \frac{\pi}{2b}$$

$$d = \frac{2}{k_y} tanh\left(\frac{k_{yo}}{k_y}\right),$$

$$k_{yo} = \frac{2}{k_y} \sqrt{k_x^2 + k_z^2}$$

where,

f_o is the calculated resonating frequency of the antenna
m, n, p are the modes generation in the DR antenna
a, b, d are the dimension of the DR antenna

Further equations can be solved using transcendental equations.

$$k_y tan\left(\frac{k_y d}{2}\right) = \sqrt{(\epsilon_r - 1)k_o^2 - k_y^2}$$

By using Binomial expansion in above equation to find the expression for k_y,

Hence, final expression to find the value for k_y is,

$$k_y = \frac{n\pi}{b\left[1 + 2\left(\frac{1}{bk_o\sqrt{(\epsilon_r - 1)}}\right)\right]}$$

Figure 2 presented the detailed view of HFSS design of the proposed design of the DR antenna, consisting of dual drilled hollow cylinders, whereas Fig. 3 shows the position of the hollow cylinders and the aerial view of the dielectric resonator antenna.

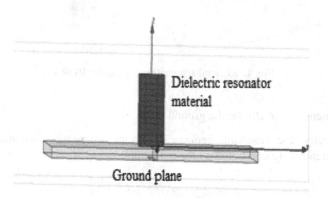

Fig. 2. Schematic design of the DR antenna proposed (side view)

The feeding (input) is done be strip line feeding (micro) on base of substrate and on the above of substrate ground plane, which is conducting surface and an etching is done on it. Dielectric resonators of different permittivity i.e., 4.4 and 12.8 are placed alternatively, such that different permittivity dielectric resonators attach together. For wide band width, two hollow cylinders are drilled such that the cylinders have a separation of 180° on the same plane. Drilled hollow cylinders are of 0.78 mm each and the height of the hollow cylinders is the same as the size of dielectric resonators (Fig. 4).

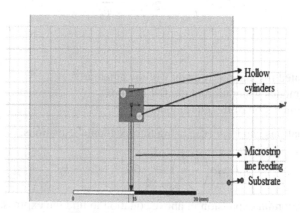

Fig. 3. Top view of the antenna

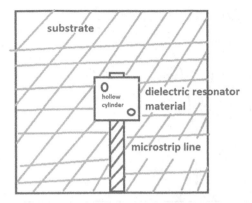

Fig. 4. Schematic Diagram of the posterior view of the proposed antenna design

Dimension of each resonator is of length 5.2 mm, breadth of the resonator is 5.2 mm and the height of each resonator is 0.6 mm. The number of resonators is 12, hence the height of the antenna is 7.2 mm. The range of the operation of the antenna is from 10.10 GHz to 16.90 GHz.

3 Results and Discussions

Using the software tool, various antenna parameters have been studied, which are required to understand how an antenna is working. There are various parameters of the antenna like scattering parameters, antenna gain, voltage standing wave ration, polar plot, radiation pattern etc. have been investigated and are within permissible limits, which indicates that between the frequencies of 10.10 GHz and 16.90 GHz, the antenna is working efficiently. The antenna bandwidth is approximately 7 GHz, and much higher than normal bandwidth. So, the given antenna shows the ultra-wideband nature of the system.

Below, various antenna parameters have been shown with respect to a frequency graph.

In Fig. 1, a scattering parameter graph has been shown, the graph shows the antenna return loss or scattering parameter. From the graph, it can be easily concluded that the range of the DR antenna is 10.10 GHz to 16.70 GHz, and hence the impedance bandwidth is approximately 7 GHz. For return loss, the scattering parameter, i.e., S_{11} (dB) should be less than -10 dB (decibels) so that the antenna can transmit the signal efficiently. S_{11} indicates that output is calculated from 1 when input is given to 1. Foremost parameter used for evaluating the efficiency of DRA. In antenna designing, this the foremost parameter to investigate the capability of the dielectric resonator antenna (Fig. 5).

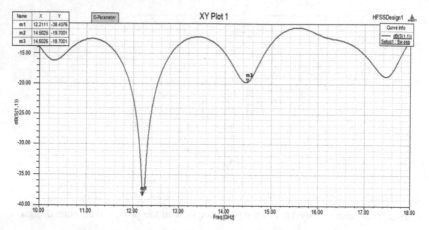

Fig. 5. Return loss (S11) (dB) vs. frequency [GHz] graph

From above graph it is clearly seen, the simulated return loss is −39 dB (<−10dB) at 12.10 GHz frequency, also for further whole range of frequency is <−10 dB. Which shows that antenna is working in the whole range of frequency making it wide bandwidth antenna.

Figure 6 shows the simulated value of the VSWR (voltage standing wave ratio) with respect to the corresponding frequency.

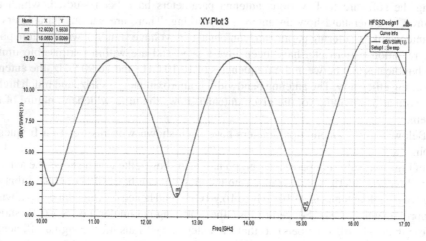

Fig. 6. VSWR vs. Frequency Plot

The voltage standing wave ratio is denoted by VSWR. It is defined as the measurement of radio frequency power transferred to the load from the source through transmission line.

Mathematically,

$$V = 1 + |\Gamma_1|/1 - |\Gamma_1|$$

Also,

'Γ_1' denotes the coefficient of the reflection of the radio waves
'V' denotes the VSWR

Figure 7 depicts the gain of DR antenna vs frequency on the whole range of frequency spectrum.

Gain of radio antenna is the propensity of the antenna to radiate in to the free space. From the graph the gain of DR antenna is 6.57 dB at 14.10 GHz.

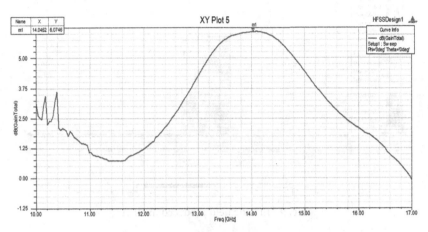

Fig. 7. DR antenna Gain Vs. Frequency plot

In Fig. 8, the magnetic field generated from the transmission line via microstrip line is shown. Magnetic field and electric field components are responsible for radiating the

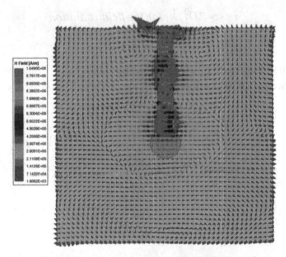

Fig. 8. Magnetic field at microstrip fed on the substrate and ground plane

radio waves. The intensity of the magnetic waves produced in the antenna through the feed line is clearly visible in the figure.

Figure 9 shows representation of electric field production in dielectric resonator antenna. These are also called modes generation in the DRA. TE_{xyz}, TE_{111}, TE_{113}, etc.

These are the regenerating modes in the antenna which are responsible for dual band, triple band antenna.

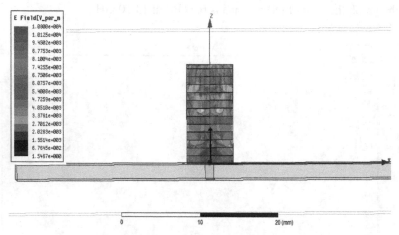

Fig. 9. Electric field produced in DRA

Figure 10, is the radiation pattern of the graph. It is the energy dispersed in the environment w.r.t. the direction of antenna.

Mathematically,

The radiating pattern of the DR antenna is given by

$$r \gg 2D_1^2/\lambda_1 \text{ for far field radiation}$$

where,

D_1 is the uttermost measurement of the DR antenna and
λ_1, is length the waves of the radio waves

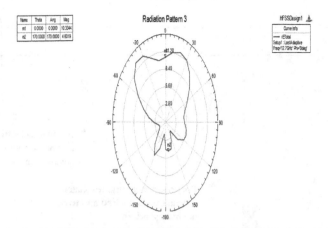

Fig. 10. Radiation pattern of the antenna

Figure 11, is the polar plot graph of the proposed DR antenna. It is three dimensional pictorial view of the energy radiated through transmission of the signal.

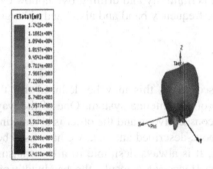

Fig. 11. Polar plot of the DRA.

Differentiation of the return loss of the proposed design of the DRA and antenna with same size and stack of same material but no drilled hollow cylinders in it is shown in Fig. 12.

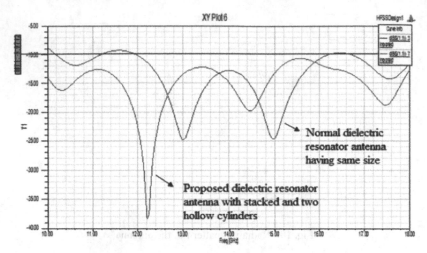

Fig. 12. Comparison of results

In the above comparison, it can be seen that when we use stack form of dielectric resonator with different permittivity and drilling two hollow cylinders in it, return loss get reduced for the same frequency band and also bandwidth got increase.

4   Conclusions

With the above discussed result, this may be deduced that there are many ways to enhance the bandwidth of the antenna system. One of the ways is by using different permittivity resonators consecutively, and the other is by creating some hollow space in the resonators. In the above-described antenna, we have used both methods to increase the bandwidth of DRA. It is always desirable to allow transmission of the signal on numbers of frequencies. Hence, as a result, the bandwidth of antenna is 6.80 GHz, which is approximately 7 GHz. Ultimately, antenna is showing ultra-wide band nature of the transmission of the signals. Which means antenna is capable to work between 10.20 GHz to 16.90 GHz. Further, more investigation can be done to enhance gain and obtain circular polarization in the same antenna.

Acknowledgement.   We acknowledge Mr. Chandra prakash, Lab attendant of AIACT&R to allow liberal access to the microwave lab to perform various software access.

Conflict of Statement.   The biographers of this paper proclaim that there is not any conflict of interest in doing and completion of this paper work.

References

1. Petosa, A.: Dielectric Resonator Antenna Handbook. Artech House Inc., Norwood (2007)

2. Lapierre, M., Antar, Y.M.M., Ittipiboon, A., Petosa, A.: Ultra wideband monopole/dielectric resonator antenna. IEEE Microw. Wireless Compon. Lett. **15**(1), 7–9 (2005)
3. Ge, Y., Esselle, K.P.: A dielectric resonator antenna for UWB applications. Presented at the IEEE International Antennas and Propagation Society International Symposium, North Charleston, SC (2009)
4. Pan, Y.M., Zheng, S.Y.: A low-profile stacked dielectric resonator antenna with high-gain and wide bandwidth. IEEE Antennas Wirel. Propag. Lett. **15**, 68–71 (2016)
5. Ge, Y., Esselle, K.P., Bird, T.S.: A wideband probe-fed stacked dielectric resonator antenna. Microw. Opt. Technol. Lett. **48**(8), 1630–1633 (2006)
6. Nasimuddin, Esselle, K.P.: A low profile compact microwave antenna with high gain and wide bandwidth. IEEE Trans. Antennas Propag. **55**(6), 1880–1883 (2007)
7. Petosa, A., Ittipiboon, A., Antar, Y.M.M., Roscoe, D., Cuhaci, M.: Recent advances in dielectric-resonator antenna technology. IEEE Antennas Propag. Mag. **40**(3), 35–47 (1998)
8. Petosa, A., Simons, N., Siushansiana, R., Ittipiboon, A., Cuhaci, M.: Design and analysis of multisegment dielectric resonator antennas. IEEE Trans. Antennas Propag. **48**, 738–742 (2000)
9. Walsh, G., Young, S.D., Long, S.A.: An investigation of stacked and embedded cylindrical dielectric resonator antennas. IEEE Antennas Wireless Propag. Lett. **5**, 130–133 (2006)
10. Esselle, K.P., Bird, T.S.: A hybrid-resonator antenna: Experimental results. IEEE Trans. Antennas Propag. **53**, 870–871 (2005)
11. Janapsatya, J., Esselle, K.P., Bird, T.S.: Compact wideband dielectric-resonatoron-patch antenna. Electron. Lett. **42**(19), 1071–1072 (2006)
12. Kumar, G., Singh, M., Ahlawat, S., Yaduvanshi, R.S.: Design of stacked rectangular dielectric resonator antenna for wideband applications. Wireless Pers. Commun. **109**(3), 1661–1672 (2019)
13. Kumar, G., Yaduvanshi, R.S.: Dielectric resonator antenna with hollow cylinder for wide bandwidth. In: Sivakumar Reddy, V., Kamakshi Prasad, V., Jiacun Wang, K.T.V., Reddy, (eds.) ICSCSP 2021, vol. 1413, pp. 441–446. Springer, Singapore (2022). https://doi.org/10.1007/978-981-16-7088-6_40
14. Kumar, G., Yaduvanshi, R.S.: Design of a cylindrical dielectric resonator antenna for 5G communications. In: 2022 IEEE Delhi Section Conference (DELCON), pp. 1–3. IEEE (2022)
15. Kumar, G., Yaduvanshi, R.S.: Circularly polarised hemi-spherical dielectric resonator antenna for dual band applications. In: 2022 IEEE Delhi Section Conference (DELCON), pp. 1–4. IEEE (2022)
16. Walsh, A.G., DeYoung, C.S., Long, S.A.: An investigation of stacked and embedded cylindrical dielectric resonator antennas. IEEE Antennas Wirel. Propag. Lett. **5**(1), 130–133 (2006)
17. Singh, M., Gautam, A.K., Yaduvanshi, R.S., Vaish, A.: An investigation of resonant modes in rectangular dielectric resonator antenna using transcendental equation. Wireless Pers. Commun. **95**(3), 2549–2559 (2017). https://doi.org/10.1007/s11277-016-3932-2
18. Nalanagula, R., Darimireddy, N.K., Kumari, R., Park, C.W., Reddy, R.R.: Circularly polarized hybrid dielectric resonator antennas: a brief review and perspective analysis. Sensors **21**(12), 4100 (2021)
19. Sehrawat, N., Kanaujia, B.K., Agarwal, A.: Calculation of the resonant frequency of a rectangular dielectric resonator antenna using perturbation theory. J. Comput. Electron. **18**(1), 211–221 (2019)

Triple-Wideband Antenna for RF Energy Harvesting

Shailendra Singh Ojha[✉], P. K. Singhal, and Vandana Vikas Thakare

Department of Electronics, Madhav Institute of Technology and Science, Gwalior, (M.P.) 474005, India

ssojha20@gmail.com, pks_65@yahoo.com2, vandana@mitsgwalior.in

Abstract. The article presents a triple-wideband antenna for microwave energy harvesting (EH) applications. The antenna works from 1.1 GHz to 1.4 GHz with 300 MHz of bandwidth, 1.5 GHz to 2.2 GHz with 700 MHz of frequency, and 2.4 GHz to 2.67 GHz with 270 MHz of bandwidth. The proposed antenna is capable of receiving microwave energy from the 1.2 GHz band, the GSM 1800 MHz band, the UTMS 2100 MHz band, and the ISM 2450 MHz band. The intended antenna is analysed for various parameters in these frequency bands. Radiation efficiency at 1.25 GHz is 99%, at 1.8 GHz is 98% at 2.1 GHz is 96%, and at 2.45 GHz is 73%. The antenna gain achieved at these frequencies is 2.5 dBi, 3.6 dBi, 4.4 dBi, and 2 dBi, respectively. The VSWR is less than 2 in the entire band of operation. The impedance of the antenna is 49 Ω at 1.25 GHz, 47 Ω at 1.8 GHz, 51 Ω at 2.1 GHz, and 58 Ω at 2.45 GHz. Due to these characteristics, the intended antenna is suitable for microwave energy harvesting applications.

Keywords: Ultra-Wideband · High gain Antenna · Efficient antenna · RF EH

1 Introduction

Utilizing wireless energy collection and transmission, rectennas have fascinated a lot of consideration recently because of the rise in demand for various applications, including the IoT, wireless chargers, low-power devices, and medical equipment [1]. Numerous studies have shown that low-power devices can be powered by a variety of microwave transmitters, together with TV, Bluetooth, cellular, FM, cellular, and Wi-Fi organizations [2, 3]. But convoluted propagation circumstances, spreading schedules, and varying standards for these communications lead to fluctuating ambient RF power that changes over time and space. To assure the requisite power for varied real-world applications, RF energy must therefore be harvested from a wide frequency spectrum [4].

Rectennas are used to capture RF energy and are primarily composed of an antenna and a rectifier. According to Fig. 1. The antenna's task is to gather microwave signals from the surrounding area and transfer them to a rectifier. The antenna is a deciding factor in capturing energy, depending upon the power available in the environment due to various microwave sources. An antenna can be chosen that can capture microwave power efficiently from various frequency bands. After determining whether the antenna

R. S. Tomar et al. (Eds.): CNC 2022, CCIS 1893, pp. 226–237, 2023.
https://doi.org/10.1007/978-3-031-43140-1_20

will be single band, multiband, wideband, or an antenna array, the rest of the rectenna's circuitry can be designed.

The next task is to design an appropriate matching network [4], as matching circuits are key to achieving higher conversion efficiency. Several varieties of Schottky diodes can be employed for rectification.

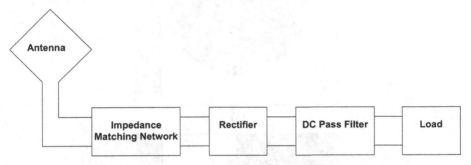

Fig. 1. Rectenna for RF energy harvesting (RFEH) system

For an efficient RFEH system, various types of rectennas can be designed that can work at various frequency bands, i.e. multiband rectennas [4–9]. An alternate option to cover more frequency bands is ultra-wideband rectennas [10–14]. In designing these rectennas, a very important function is played by the antenna. The main part of a multi-band rectenna is an antenna; therefore, ultra-wideband rectenna require ultra-wideband antennas. Various types of wideband antennas are presented in [9, 15–21].

This article is organized as follows: The design process as well as the antenna's simulation and fabrication outcomes are presented in Sect. 2. On an FR-4 substrate having, a 4.4 dielectric constant and a 1.6 mm substrate height, the antenna is constructed and it is modelled in CST MW Studio 2018. Finally, Sect. 3 presents the conclusion.

2 Designing of Antenna

A triple wideband antenna is planned that can work in three frequency bands, from 1.1 GHz to 1.4 GHz, 1.5 GHz to 2.2 GHz, and 2.4 GHz to 2.67 GHz with a bandwidth of 300 MHz 700 MHz, and 270 MHz respectively. The proposed antenna covers GSM 1800 MHz, UTMS 2100 MHz, and ISM 2450 MHz. Figure 2 portrays the circular patch antenna with a slot; the antenna's front perspective is portrayed in Fig. 2 (a). The radius of the patch is 28 mm, and the dimensions of the two parasitic patches are 10 mm × 30 mm. Two slots are introduced into the patch so that a multiband response is received. Two rectangular slots have dimensions of 3 mm by 40 mm and 2 mm by 40 mm, respectively. The suggested antenna's backside is shown in Fig. 2(b); the ground planes' measurements are 10 mm by 80 mm and 40 mm by 80 mm, respectively.

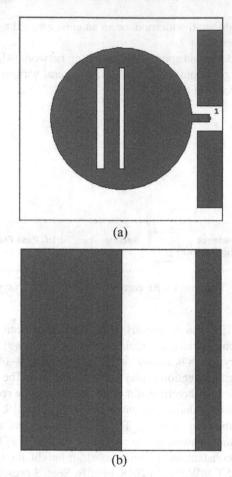

(a)

(b)

Fig. 2. (a) Front sight of the antenna. (b): Back sight of the antenna

Figure 3 depicts the simulated returnloss. The simulated returnloss shows that the proposed antenna works in three bands, i.e., from 1.1 GHz to 1.4 GHz with 300 MHz of bandwidth, 1.5 GHz to 2.2 GHz with 700 MHz of frequency, and 2.4 GHz to 2.67 GHz with 270 MHz of bandwidth. Minimum returnlosses obtained in the first, second, and third bands are −27.8 dB at 1.26 GHz, −33.7 dB at 1.62 GHz, and −18 dB at 2.45 GHz.

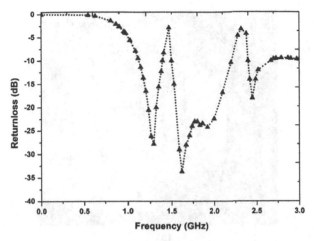

Fig. 3. Simulated returnloss

The fabricated antenna's front and back views are revealed in Figs. 4 (a) and 4 (b), respectively. Fabricated antenna testing equipment is revealed in Fig. 5. Figure 6 compares the return loss that was simulated and measured, simulated and measured returnloss shows that the proposed antenna works in three bands with 300 MHz of bandwidth, 700 MHz of frequency, and 270 MHz of bandwidth. The minimum simulated returnloss obtained in the first, second, and third bands are −27.8 dB at 1.26 GHz, −33.7 dB at 1.62 GHz, and −18 dB at 2.45 GHz. The minimum simulated returnloss obtained in the first, second, and third bands is −25 dB at 1.29 GHz, −21 dB at 1.67 GHz, and −17 dB at 2.49 GHz.

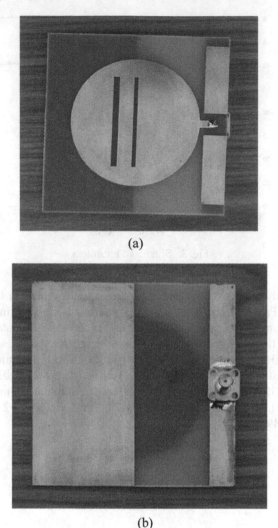

(a)

(b)

Fig. 4. (a): Front sight of designed antenna. (b): Back sight of designed antenna

Figure 7 depicts the 1.25 GHz radiation pattern at 1.25 GHz, having 2.5 dBi gain and a 99.9% radiation efficiency. Figure 8 depicts the radiation pattern at 1.8 GHz, having of 3.6 dBi gain and 98% radiation efficiency. Figure 9 depicts the radiation pattern at 2.1 GHz, having 4.4 dBi gain and 96% radiation efficiency. Figure 10 depicts the radiation results at 2.45 GHz, having 2 dBi gain and 73% radiation efficiency.

Figures 11, 12, 13, and 14 illustrate the relative current density distributions for antennas operating at frequencies of 1.25 GHz, 1.8 GHz, 2.1 GHz, and 2.45 GHz.

The VSWR of the antenna is also one of the key parameters. Figure 15 depicts the VSWR's frequency-dependent variations. The VSWR obtained in all the intended bands

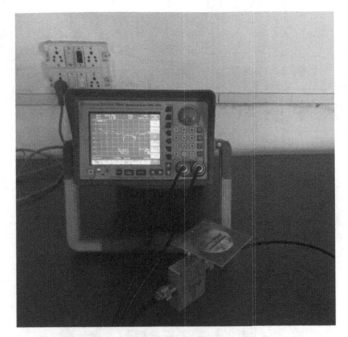

Fig. 5. Testing of fabricated antenna

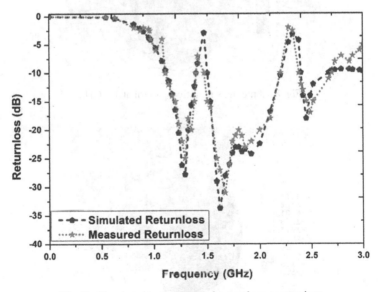

Fig. 6. Simulated and measured returnloss comparison

is less than 2. VSWR obtained at 1.25 GHz is 1.09, 1.8 GHz is 1.13, 2.1 GHz is 1.2, and 2.45 GHz is 1.34.

232   S. S. Ojha et al.

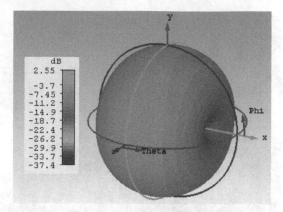

Fig. 7. Antenna's radiation pattern at 1.25 GHz

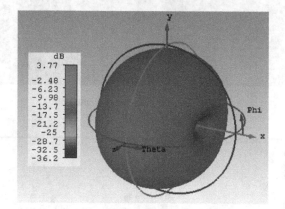

Fig. 8. Antenna's radiation pattern at 1.8 GHz

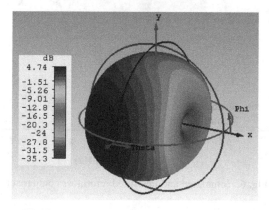

Fig. 9. Antenna's radiation pattern at 2.1 GHz

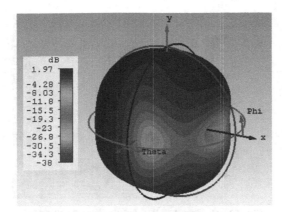

Fig. 10. Antenna's radiation pattern at 2.45 GHz

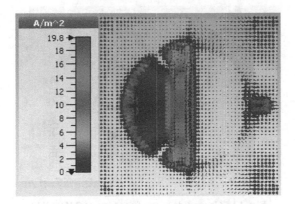

Fig. 11. Current density of antenna at 1.25 GHz

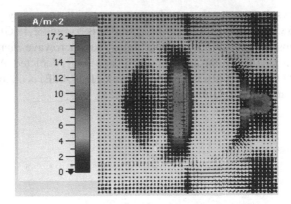

Fig. 12. Current density of antenna at 1800 GHz

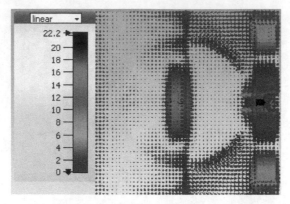

Fig. 13. Current density of antenna at 2100 GHz

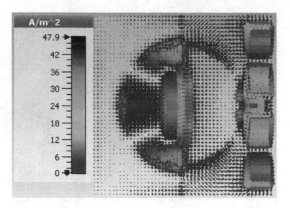

Fig. 14. Current density of antenna at 2450 GHz

Table 1 shows how antenna impedance varies with frequency; the impedance measured at 1.25 GHz is 49, 1.8 GHz is 47, 2.1 GHz is 51, and 2.45 GHz is 58.

One of the most crucial factors for applications like microwave energy harvesting is the antenna's gain. In Table 2, the antenna's gain variation is depicted. A gain of 2.4 dBi is obtained at 1.25 GHz, 3.55 dBi is obtained at 1.8 GHz, 4.4 dBi is obtained at 2.1 GHz, and 2 dBi is obtained at 2.45 GHz.

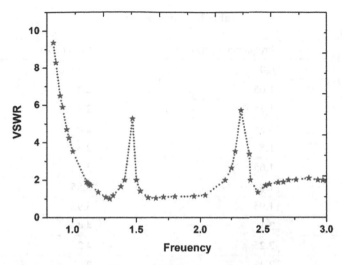

Fig. 15. VSWR of antenna

Table 1. Variation of impedance of the antenna with respect to frequencies

S. No	Frequency (GHz)	Impedance (Ω)
01	0.5	90
02	0.9	22
03	1.05	20
04	1.25	49
05	1.35	60
06	1.5	34
07	1.65	51
08	1.8	47
09	1.95	44
10	2.1	51
11	2.25	100
12	2.45	58
13	2.55	75
14	2.7	55
15	3	38

Table 2. Gain of antenna

S. No	Frequency (GHz)	Gain (dBi)
01	0.9	2
02	1.05	2.2
03	1.25	2.4
04	1.35	2.6
05	1.5	2.3
06	1.65	3.1
07	1.8	3.55
08	1.95	3.95
09	2.1	4.4
10	2.25	4.2
11	2.45	2
12	2.55	3.2
13	2.7	4
14	3	4.5

3 Conclusion

A triple-wideband antenna is designed for RFEH. The projected antenna works from 1.1 GHz to 1.4 GHz with 300 MHz of bandwidth, 1.5 GHz to 2.2 GHz with 700 MHz of frequency, and 2.4 GHz to 2.67 GHz with 270 MHz of frequency. The proposed antenna is capable of receiving microwave energy from the 1.2 GHz band, GSM1800 MHz band, UTMS2100 MHz band, and ISM2450 MHz band. The intended antenna is analysed for various parameters in these frequency bands. Radiation efficiency at 1.25 GHz, 1.8 GHz, 2.1 GHz, and 2.45 GHz is 99%, 98%, 96%, and 73% respectively. The antenna gain achieved at these frequencies is 2.5 dBi, 3.6 dBi, 4.4 dBi, and 2 dBi, respectively. The VSWR is less than 2 in the entire band of operation. The antenna's impedances vary from 47 Ω to 58 Ω at the intended frequency bands. These qualities make the intended antenna appropriate for RFEH applications.

References

1. Ojha, S.S., Singhal, P.K., Thakare, V.V.: Dual-band rectenna system for biomedical wireless applications. Measur.: Sens. **24**, 100532 (2022)
2. Joseph, S.D., Huang, Yi., Hsu, S.S.. H.: Transmission lines-based impedance matching technique for broadband rectifier. IEEE Access **9**, 4665–4672 (2021)
3. Vyas, R.J., et al.: E-WEHP: a batteryless embedded sensor-platform wirelessly powered from ambient digital-TV signals. IEEE Trans. Microw. Theory Tech. **61**(6), 2491–2505 (2013)
4. Song, C., et al.: A high-efficiency broadband rectenna for ambient wireless energy harvesting. IEEE Trans. Antennas Propag. **63**(8), 3486–3495 (2015)

5. Ho, D.-K., et al.: Dual-band rectenna for ambient RF energy harvesting at GSM 900 MHz and 1800 MHz. In: 2016 IEEE International Conference on Sustainable Energy Technologies (ICSET). IEEE (2016)
6. Gajanan, P., et al.: A dual-band microwave energy harvesting rectenna system for WiFi sources. In: 2019 IEEE Indian Conference on Antennas and Propogation (InCAP). IEEE (2019)
7. Chiluveru, A., Akashe, S., Ojha, S.S.: Design of RF energy harvesting circuit at 900 MHz for low-powered DC applications. In: Zhang, Y.-D., Senjyu, T., So–In, C., Joshi, A. (eds.) Smart Trends in Computing and Communications: Proceedings of SmartCom 2020, pp. 401–410. Springer Singapore, Singapore (2021). https://doi.org/10.1007/978-981-15-5224-3_39
8. Chandravanshi, S., Sarma, S.S., Akhtar, M.J.: Design of triple band differential rectenna for RF energy harvesting. IEEE Trans. Antennas Propagat. 66(6), 2716–2726 (2018)
9. Shen, S., Chiu, C.-Y., Murch, R.D.: A dual-port triple-band L-probe microstrip patch rectenna for ambient RF energy harvesting. IEEE Antennas Wirel. Propag. Lett. 16, 3071–3074 (2017)
10. Song, C., Huang, Y., Zhou, J., Carter, P.: Improved ultrawideband rectennas using hybrid resistance compression technique. IEEE Trans. Antennas Propagat. 65(4), 2057–2062 (2017)
11. Zhi-Xia, D., Bo, S.F., Cao, Y.F., Jun-Hui, O., Zhang, X.Y.: Broadband circularly polarized rectenna with wide dynamic-power-range for efficient wireless power transfer. IEEE Access 8, 80561–80571 (2020)
12. He, Z., Liu, C.: A compact high-efficiency broadband rectifier with a wide dynamic range of input power for energy harvesting. IEEE Microwave Wirel. Compon. Lett. 30(4), 433–436 (2020)
13. Ojha, S.S., et al.: 2-GHz dual diode dipole rectenna for wireless power transmission. Int. J. Microw. Opt. Technol. 8(2), 86–92 (2013)
14. Ping, L., Song, C., Huang, K.M.: Ultra-wideband rectenna using complementary resonant structure for microwave power transmission and energy harvesting. IEEE Trans. Microwave Theory Techn. 69(7), 3452–3462 (2021)
15. Agarwal, A., et al.: Design of CPW-fed printed rectangular monopole antenna for wideband dual-frequency applications. Int. J. Innov. Appl. Stud. 3(3), 758–764 (2013)
16. Agarwal, A., Singhal, P.K.: Design and analysis of printed circular disc monopole antenna for L-band frequency applications. Int. J. Microw. Opt. Technol. 8, 138–144 (2013)
17. Agarwal, A., et al.: Analyse the performance of planar rectangular monopole antenna on modify ground Plane for L-band applications. J. Global Res. Electron. Commun. 1(1) (2012)
18. Arrawatia, M., Baghini, M., Kumar, G.: Broadband bent triangular omnidirectional antenna for RF energy harvesting. IEEE Antennas Wirel. Propag. Lett. 15, 1–1 (2015)
19. Gao, S., et al.: A broad-band dual-polarized microstrip patch antenna with aperture coupling. IEEE Trans. Antennas Propag. 51(4), 898–900 (2003)
20. Bais, A., Ojha, S.S.: Design and development of UWB antenna using CNT composite for RFID applications. In: 2016 Symposium on Colossal Data Analysis and Networking (CDAN). IEEE (2016)
21. Deng, C., Li, Y., Zhang, Z., Feng, Z.: A wideband isotropic radiated planar antenna using sequential rotated L-shaped monopoles. IEEE Trans. Antennas Propagat. 62(3), 1461–1464 (2014)

Dual-Band Antenna and Low Pass Filter Design for Wireless Energy Harvesting

Shailendra Singh Ojha[✉], Ranjeet Singh Tomar, Shyam Akashe, Bhupendra Dhakad, Sadhana Mishra, and Mayank Sharma

Department of ECE, ITM University, Gwalior, (M.P.) 474005, India
{shailendraojha.ec,RanjeetSingh,shyam.akashe,
bhupendradhakad.ec,sadhanamishra.ec,
mayanksharma.ec}@itmuniversity.ac.in

Abstract. This communication presents the dual-band antenna and a low-pass filter for RF energy harvesting (EH). An RFEH structure mainly comprises four parts: an antenna, a low-pass filter, a matching circuit, and a rectifier. The proposed antenna is designed for 1.24 GHz and 2 GHz. A 5-element low-pass filter is designed that is capable of suppressing higher-order harmonics. These components are crucial for high radio frequency power to DC conversion. The antenna and low pass filter are simulated using CST MW Studio 2018. These parts are simulated on an FR-4 substrate with a 4.4 dielectric constant and a 1.6 mm dielectric height.

Keywords: Dual-band · Returnloss · Rectenna · Power Conversion · energy harvesting · Low Pass Filter (LPF)

1 Introduction

Nowadays, technology has advanced, necessitating sensors that propose dealings with real-world quantities. This leads to an increase in the number of devices that truly require new energy transfer technology [1, 2]. The wireless energy transfer idea [3] is an especially interesting way to give energy to numerous devices altogether, sidestepping the need for batteries or even connected connections. The power radiated in RF is intercepted by an antenna and then transformed to DC by a rectifier. The energy obtained can be utilised to operate low-powered devices.

The arrangement of the antenna and rectifier is frequently mentioned as a rectenna. The produced power of a structure depends on the rectifier and antenna, which should have higher efficiencies for overall good performance. Microstrip patch antennas can be a good choice because these antennas have high efficiency and gain and are also easy to fabricate. Rectenna was first introduced by W.C. Brown [4].

Many antennas, for example, dipole antennas [5, 6], patch antennas [7–12], and rectennas [13–16], are used for signal reception. Signals can be received in both bands using a dual-band rectenna. The diode in the rectifier is put into the series, which tends to provide higher efficiencies [17, 18]. Due to the radiation of required harmonics brought on by the overall decline in efficiency, rectenna have a harmonic problem. When microwave power is intercepted by a rectenna, output harmonics of the original frequency are also created by the Schottky diode when it produces direct current (dc) of the incoming energy [19]. To suppress higher-order harmonics. The low-pass filter is used, and the matching circuit is used to provide better efficiency. [20–22] anticipate the use of various Schottky diode topologies with rectifiers in parallel. Though the antennas used in [22] and [23] are not able to reject higher-order harmonics, these methods can provide great RF-DC conversion efficiency if optimized.

The conventional rectifier system is exposed in Fig. 1 [24]. Every individual component must be optimised for better performance of the rectenna.

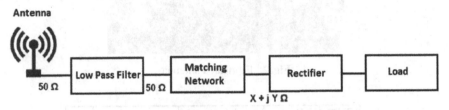

Fig. 1. Rectenna system

In this communication, a dual-band rectenna is projected that consists of a patch antenna that works at 1.24 GHz and 2 GHz. A low-pass filter is considered to have a cut-off frequency of 2 GHz, which rejects higher-order harmonics. Hence, the Schottky diode provides better results. The L-section matching network is also designed for better performance as it matches the impedance of the diode to the 50 Ω input resistance. The antenna and low pass filter (LPF) are designed and simulated in CST MW Studio 2018.

2   Receiving Antenna Design

Antenna plays a crucial role in RFEH arrangements. The antenna decides the frequency band from where it will receive the energy. The multiband antenna can receive power from various frequency bands and hence can provide more output. These types of antennas are suitable for RFEH applications. A Dual-band antenna is designed that can intercept power from 1.24 GHz and 2 GHz. Figure 2 demonstrates the design and fabrication of the dual-band antenna on FR-4 lossy. A patch measures 57 mm in length, 71.5 mm in breadth, and a feed length of 32 mm. Its simulated return loss curve is revealed in Fig. 3. It provides a return loss of −28 dB at 1.24 GHz and −19 dB at 2 GHz.

Figure 3 displays a comparison of simulated and real return losses. The findings of the simulation and the measurements show good agreement.

Figure 4 depicts an antenna's 2D radiation pattern at 1.24 GHz, having a 4.2 dBi as major lobe magnitude. The 3-dB angular width is 97.23 degrees, and the primary lobe's orientation is 0 degrees. Figure 5 depicts the 2 GHz 2D radiation results, having 5.8 dBi as a main lobe magnitude. 47 degrees is both the primary lobe's direction and its 3-dB angular breadth. The side lobe level is −2.7 dB.

240   S. S. Ojha et al.

Fig. 2. Fabricated antenna

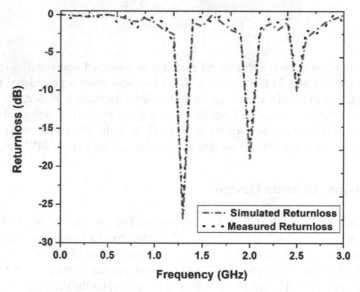

Fig. 3. Simulated and measured return loss comparison antenna

Figure 6 displays the 3D radiation results of at 1.24 GHz, having maximum directivity of 6.29 dBi. Figure 7 depicts the 3D radiation results at 2 GHz having, maximum directivity of 5.55 dBi. Figures 8 and 9 demonstrates the current density 1.24 GHz and 2 GHz for planned antenna.

Another important parameter for antenna is its gain. Gain of proposed antenna also evaluated. Figure 10 shows the variation of the gain of the antenna with frequency. Gain obtained at 1.24 GHz is 3.3 dBi and at 2 GHz is 2.3 dBi.

Directivity Abs (Phi=90)

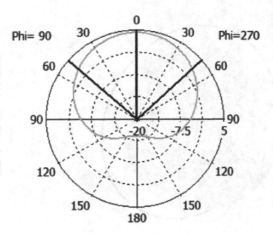

Theta / Degree vs. dBi

Fig. 4. Radiation pattern at 1.24 GHz

Directivity Abs (Phi=90)

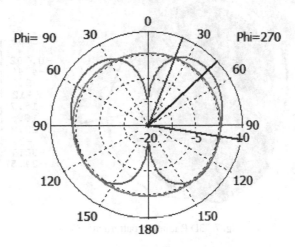

Theta / Degree vs. dBi

Fig. 5. Radiation pattern at 2 GHz

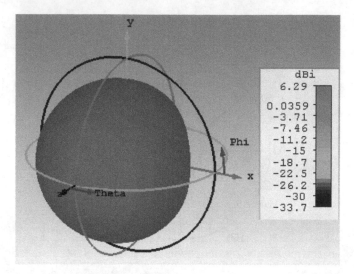

Fig. 6. 3D Radiation pattern at 1.24 GHz

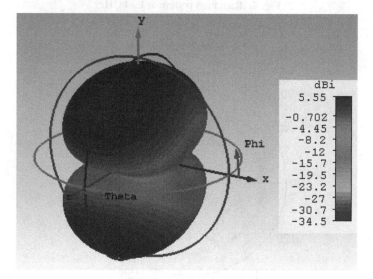

Fig. 7. 3D Radiation pattern at 2 GHz

3   Five-Element Filter Design

Higher-order harmonics are generated by Schottky diodes, which are used for RF-DC conversion [25]. These higher-order harmonics affect the conversion efficiency and output voltage (dc) [26, 27]. For this concern, the use of a microstrip filter is essential to call off the effect of these harmonics and get better circuit performance.

A 5-element stepped impedance low pass filter is designed at 2-GHz which is capable of removing higher-order harmonics. The 5th-order Chebyshev ladder filter is shown in

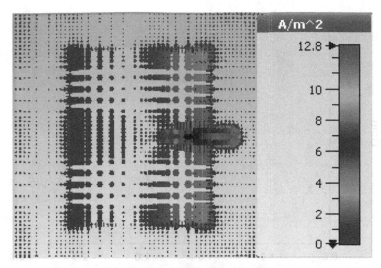

Fig. 8. Current density at 1.24 GHz

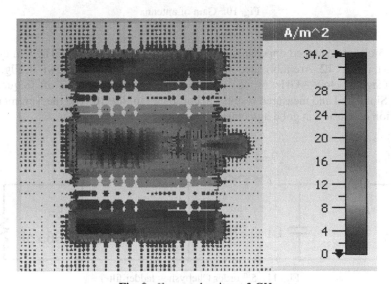

Fig. 9. Current density at 2 GHz

Fig. 11, having five elements: $C_1 = 0.963$ pF, $L_2 = 4.154$ nH, $C_3 = 2$ pF, $L_4 = 4.154$ nH, $C_5 = 0.963$ pF, R_{in} and R_L are 50 Ω. These parameters are converted into the microstrip lines for fabrication on FR-4 lossy substrate dimensions of microstrip lines for the filter are shown in Fig. 12. C_1 is equivalent to 3.1 mm × 9 mm, L_2 is equivalent to 8.5 mm × 0.88 mm, C_3 is equivalent to 7.1 mm × 9 mm, L_4 is equivalent to 7.5 mm × 0.88 mm, C_5 is equivalent to 3.1 mm × 9 mm and 50 Ω resistors are equivalent to 16.3 mm × 3 mm microstrip line as shown in Fig. 8.

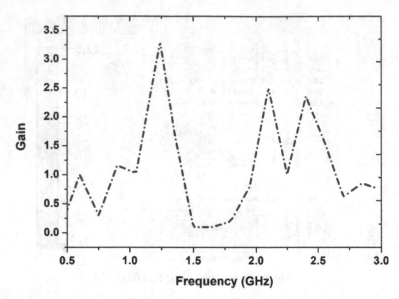

Fig. 10. Gain of antenna

The 5-element stepped impedance low pass filter is designed at 2 GHz. Dimensions are shown in Fig. 12. Are fabricated on an FR-4 lossy substrate as shown in Fig. 13. It passes a signal below 2 GHz, as we can see in Fig. 14, where the cut off frequency is 2 GHz. Simulated and measured results are compared in Fig. 10. The measurement and simulation results are in good agreement.

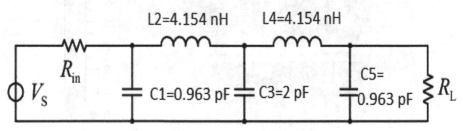

Fig. 11. 5th order Chebyshev ladder filter

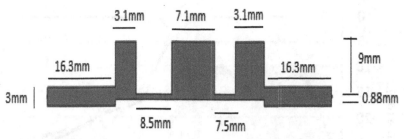

Fig. 12. Dimensions of 5th order Chebyshev ladder filter

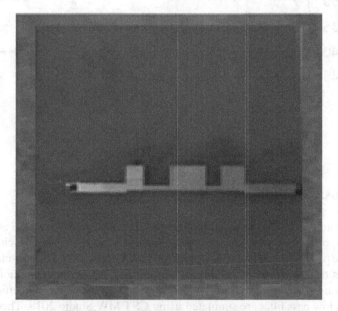

Fig. 13. 5-element stepped impedance LPF

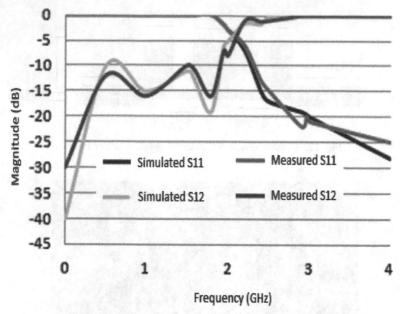

Fig. 14. Simulated and measured result comparison

4 Conclusion

A dual-band antenna and a low-pass filter for RFEH is designed. An RFEH arrangement mainly comprises four parts: an antenna, a low-pass filter, a matching circuit, and a rectifier. The proposed antenna is designed for 1.24 GHz and 2 GHz. A 5-element low-pass filter is designed that is capable of suppressing higher-order harmonics. These components are crucial for high radio frequency power to DC conversion efficiency. The antenna and low pass filter are simulated using CST MW Studio 2018. These parts are simulated on an FR-4 substrate with a 4.4 dielectric constant and a 1.6 mm dielectric height.

References

1. Wagih, M., et al.: RF-powered wearable energy harvesting and storage module based on E-textile coplanar waveguide rectenna and supercapacitor. IEEE Open J. Antennas Propag. **2**, 302–314 (2021)
2. Ping, L., Song, C., Huang, K.M.: Ultra-wideband rectenna using complementary resonant structure for microwave power transmission and energy harvesting. IEEE Trans. Microwave Theor. Techn. **69**(7), 3452–3462 (2021)
3. Mattsson, M., Kolitsidas, C.I., Jonsson, B.L.G.: Dual-band dual-polarized full-wave rectenna based on differential field sampling. IEEE Antennas Wirel. Propag. Lett. **17**(6), 956–959 (2018)
4. Ojha, S.S., Singhal, P.K., Thakare, V.V.: Dual-band rectenna system for biomedical wireless applications. Measurement: Sens. **24**, 100532 (2022)

5. Ojha, S.S., et al.: 2-GHz dual diode dipole rectenna for wireless power transmission. Int. J. Microw. Opt. Technol. **8**(2), 86–92 (2013)
6. Ye, H., Chu, Q.-X.: A broadband rectenna for harvesting low-power RF energy. In: 2016 International Symposium on Antennas and Propagation (ISAP). IEEE, (2016)
7. Suh, Y.-H., Chang, K.: A high-efficiency dual-frequency rectenna for 2.45-and 5.8-GHz wireless power transmission. IEEE Trans. Microw. Theory Tech. **50**(7), 1784–1789 (2002)
8. Agarwal, A., et al.: Design of CPW-fed printed rectangular monopole antenna for wideband dual-frequency applications. Int. J. Innovation Appl. Stud. **3**(3), 758–764 (2013)
9. Agarwal, A., Singhal, P.K.: Design and analysis of printed circular disc monopole antenna for l-band frequency applications. Int. J. Microwave Opt. Technol. **8**, 138–144 (2013)
10. Agarwal, A., et al.: Analyse the performance of planar rectangular monopole antenna on modify ground plane for L-band applications. J. Global Res. Electron. Commun. **1**(1) (2012)
11. Yang, Y., et al.: A 5.8 GHz circularly polarized rectenna with harmonic suppression and rectenna array for wireless power transfer. IEEE Antennas Wirel. Propag. Lett. **17**(7), 1276–1280 (2018)
12. Lou, X., Yang, G.-M.: A dual linearly polarized rectenna using defected ground structure for wireless power transmission. IEEE Microw. Wirel. Compon. Lett. **28**(9), 828–830 (2018)
13. Mansour, M.M., Kanaya, H.: High-efficient broadband CPW RF rectifier for wireless energy harvesting. IEEE Microw. Wirel. Compon. Lett. **29**(4), 288–290 (2019)
14. Liu, Y., et al.: A low-profile lightweight circularly polarized rectenna array based on coplanar waveguide. IEEE Antennas Wirel. Propag. Lett. **17**(9), 1659–1663 (2018)
15. Sakamoto, T., et al.: 5.8-GHz series/parallel connected rectenna array using expandable differential rectenna units. IEEE Trans. Antennas Propagat. **61**(9), 4872–4875 (2013)
16. Song, C., et al.: A high-efficiency broadband rectenna for ambient wireless energy harvesting. IEEE Trans. Antennas Propagat. **63**(8), 3486–3495 (2015)
17. Li, X., Yang, L., Huang, L.: Novel design of 2.45-GHz rectenna element and array for wireless power transmission. IEEE Access **7**, 28356–28362 (2019)
18. Marian, V., et al.: Potentials of an adaptive rectenna circuit. IEEE Antennas Wirel. Propagat. Lett. **10**, 1393–1396 (2011)
19. Matsunaga, T., Nishiyama, E., Toyoda, I.: 5.8-GHz stacked differential rectenna suitable for large-scale rectenna arrays with DC connection. IEEE Trans. Antennas Propag. **63**(12), 5944–5949 (2015)
20. Shen, S., Chiu, C.-Y., Murch, R.D.: A broadband L-probe microstrip patch rectenna for ambient RF energy harvesting. In: 2017 IEEE International Symposium on Antennas and Propagation & USNC/URSI National Radio Science Meeting. IEEE (2017)
21. Yang, S.Y., Kim, J.: Wireless power transmission using dipole rectennas made on flexible cellulose membrane. IET Microw. Antennas Propag. **6**(7), 756–760 (2012)
22. Song, C., et al.: Matching network elimination in broadband rectennas for high-efficiency wireless power transfer and energy harvesting. IEEE Trans. Ind. Electron. **64**(5), 3950–3961 (2016)
23. Haboubi, W., et al.: An efficient dual-circularly polarized rectenna for RF energy harvesting in the 2.45 GHz ISM band. Prog. Electromagnetics Res. **148**, 31–39 (2014)
24. Sun, H., Geyi, W.: A new rectenna with all-polarization-receiving capability for wireless power transmission. IEEE Antennas Wirel. Propag. Lett. **15**, 814–817 (2015)
25. Guler, U., Sendi, M.S.E., Ghovanloo, M.: A dual-mode passive rectifier for wide-range input power flow. In: 2017 IEEE 60th International Midwest Symposium on Circuits and Systems (MWSCAS). IEEE (2017)

26. Chuma, E.L., et al.: A compact fractal structure based rectenna with the rectifier circuit integrated. In: 2017 IEEE International Symposium on Antennas and Propagation & USNC/URSI National Radio Science Meeting. IEEE (2017)
27. Shen, S., Chiu, C.-Y., Murch, R.D.: A dual-port triple-band L-probe microstrip patch rectenna for ambient RF energy harvesting. IEEE Antennas Wirel. Propag. Lett. **16**, 3071–3074 (2017)

Performance Analysis of Various Digital Adders

Jay Sutradhar$^{(\boxtimes)}$, Sadhana Mishra, and Shyam Akashe

ITM University, Gwalior, India
joy.dhar0161@yahoo.com, {sadhanamishra.ec,
shyam.akashe}@itmuniversity.ac.in

Abstract. Adders are the focal point of complicated arithmetic tasks such as expansion, duplication, division, and exponentiation, among others. The majority of these frameworks use adder in a fundamental manner that affects the overall pace of the framework. To achieve these demands, control use and proliferation deferral must be reduced in the primary building area, the adder cell. This paper reviews various adder work for low-power performance and a simulated analysis of key parameters based on a 1-bit hybrid full adder circuit using 32 nm process technology.

Keywords: Adders · VLSI · CMOS · MOSFET

1 Introduction

Since the inception of the IC industry, there has been a need to accomplish an improved plan metric of execution, control, zone, and cost to time ratio. In reality, these parameters are interlinked with Moore's Law. However, when the scaling of transistor size moved towards 20 nm, certain fundamental parameters could no longer be scaled down, notably the operating supply voltage which is pivotal for dynamic behavior of the system. Furthermore, similar to control, upgrading for one aspect, such as execution, naturally turned into significant discounts in different zones. Another restriction as processes approached 20 nm was that lithography was trapped at an ArF brightening source with a wavelength of 193 nm while the procedure fundamental component was pushing submicron of 20 nm. Submersion lithography and two-fold designing, are few of the various techniques that made this possible. This further increased the inconstancy of the design process. There were also other innovations on the way, for example, high-K metal entryways, which reduced-to a limited extent - door leakage difficulties. Regardless, the truth was that the marginal window for simplification among the previously identified plan variables was closing.

Large Scale Integration allowed a single chip with several transistors fabricated together for creating integrated circuits. Modern concepts of VLSI refer the chip of micron sized transistors. Thus, a global concept of VLSI architecture was adopted to manufacture these chips. Recent innovations have progressed to size down the transistor size to nanoscale such that at a relatively smaller size, the number of transistor count increased massively. As a result of this upsetting notion, it finds use in the realms

R. S. Tomar et al. (Eds.): CNC 2022, CCIS 1893, pp. 249–259, 2023.
https://doi.org/10.1007/978-3-031-43140-1_22

of superior processing and communication frameworks, nonpartisan systems, wafer-scale reconciliation, microelectronic frameworks, and inventive work. In the present and near future, there will be a growing need for these chip-driven devices. To achieve these demands, we must reduce our size, power, and productivity. Control dispersion has become a crucial aim in the design of both basic and complex circuits. Previous approaches presented to increase the region of a fan-out tree may result in intemperate power use owing to discarding short-out present.

High power consumption in small devices is a serious problem. High power use is associated with decreased battery life as well as additional packaging and cooling requirements. Static power dispersion due to standby spilling streams is an important component of aggregate power distribution. Omnipresent devices feature several types of segments, many of which remain out of gear while performing a particular purpose. Static power dispersion in these out-of-gear segments and spillage control dispersal in the dynamic section comprises a massive amount of aggregate power distribution in the framework. The reduction of this leakage component becomes critical for effective power administration [1]. Because of the further scaling of MOS devices, an emotional improvement in MOS device execution has been achieved. Because of spilled streams, this has increased control dispersion. Until now, the primary leakage section has been the depletion of the source sub-limit current [2].

The in-demand computing electronics revolutionized the global market. Smart work stations, video and media frameworks, communications, image processing are among a few industrial advancements that were achieved using the nano-scaled VLSI computing devices. These devices and frameworks need quick, high-throughput computations, complicated functions, and consistently continuous handling capabilities. The size, weight, and longevity of batteries limit the functionality of these devices. These quality issues led the researchers to expand the plan of new methodologies to create more efficient and productive ways to save battery life in addition to the optimized functionality of the device. This decreases the control utilization compared to the level of execution significantly [3].

Signal integrity is a critical problem in VLSI circuits and is becoming more important as the basic component size of gadgets shrinks to 180 nm or less. The inductive coupling is a notable component of the circuit commotion. As described by Moore's law, the coupling tends to increase for increased clock speed, I/O drivers and increased number of in-board transistors. Thus, resulting in an increased inductive coupling between supply to ground rails. It is a fundamental and testing configuration assignment to manage the amount of inductive clamor incorporated in the power rails.

2   Literature Review

Alongside the other people who worked with Partha [1]. Existing designs such as static CMOS, complementary pass-transistor logic, pass gate adders, transmission function adders, hybrid logic with static CMOS, and so on were used by researchers to evaluate performance criteria of PDA. Power, delay and area are the key attributes of a functional adder that were compared between the existing designs. The comparisons were carried out using these designs as their point of departure.

Colleagues who were assigned to operate under Pygasti Juveria's direction [2] Due to the availability of one-of-a-kind xNOR and xOR circuits, it is now viable to utilize whole adders in high-speed applications such as video processing. Other examples include image processing and signal processing. AND and OR are both examples of logical operations that may be carried out using these circuits. In particular, full adders are in great demand, and customers are searching for models that have a high driving capacity as well as a low output capacitance. Other desirable characteristics for full adders are low output capacitance and low output resistance. The outcomes of the simulation reveal that the full adders that are recommended utilize a great deal less energy and have a considerably shorter latency in comparison to the designs that are considered as being the most cutting-edge that are now available. To put the icing on the cake, they also give the most efficient power delay device that can now be bought, particularly when compared with circuits that are already in operation. This is the cherry on top of everything else. In addition, the full adders that were recommended had a high degree of dependability over a wide variety of output loads. This was a significant benefit. One of the reasons why they were suggested was because of this factor.

T. Subhashini as well as the other staff members [3, 4] that collaborated with him. The authors constructed an additional set of six FA cells by combining the xOR gates that were recommended with the xOR–xNOR gates that were used in their development. The FA cells have a larger range of applications than the other cells. It has been brought to our notice that the newly developed circuits give considerable gains in the areas of speed, accuracy, and convergence. Both in terms of the amount of power it consumes and the amount of time it takes to carry out an operation, a ripple carries adder is unequivocally better than a hybrid full adder. When we look at the two distinct kinds of adders' side by side, we see that this is the case. After conducting exhaustive tests on a variety of hybrid full adder circuits designed to simulate the ripple carry adder, it was determined that the recommended circuits performed admirably across the board. This was one of the conclusions that were reached. This was one of the discoveries that were made as a consequence of the testing that was done. It has been proved that when the supply voltage is changed to 1.8 V, this adder circuit design offers faster response times and reduced power usage. This is in contrast to older designs of adder circuits, which both required a greater amount of power to function properly. This finding holds regardless of the voltage that was decided to be used for the supply (1.8 V).

Kota Santhosh and the other researchers that worked with him were the ones who carried out the study [4]. As soon as the study was completed, it became abundantly evident that placing inverter doors on the primary channel of a circuit has several concerns that need quick attention from the personnel responsible for doing so. These problems include but are not limited to the following: These drawbacks may be summarised as follows: In addition to this, there is an error in the system that has to be repaired, and that error is a complaint that might be considered constructive. There is a need for the system to be enhanced. Both the delay time and the yield capacitance will increase as a result of this input, which implies that the circuit will have an improved capacity to make use of the more energy that is now accessible to it. To put it another way, the circuit will be in a position to make more efficient use of the energy. Following the completion of this phase, the Author delivered brand new xOR/xNOR doors as well as xOR–xNOR doors, both of which solved all of the issues that were raised in the review that was mentioned earlier. The researchers found that the suggested circuits consistently delivered a high degree of performance across the board after deploying FA cells in a broad variety of environments. This was discovered after they found that the recommended circuits consistently gave the highest level of performance.

The group that P. Rajesh was in charge of, also included several other individuals [5]. It is common knowledge that this type of feedback has a detrimental effect on the performance of a circuit because it causes an increase in the amount of power that is required, the length of delay, and the output capacitance. This is because it causes a positive feedback loop, which in turn causes a positive feedback loop. A rise in the output capacitance is another effect that this kind of feedback has on the circuit. As a direct result of this, the author gave novel perspectives on the xOR/xNOR and xOR–xNOR gates, both of which had been found to have problems in previous research. xOR/xNOR and xOR–xNOR gates had both been demonstrated to have its demerits.

Researchers M. Loga Lakshmi and her colleagues have devised a method that enables full-swing functioning while concurrently maintaining both characteristics. More can be read about this strategy in [6]. In the arrangement that the corporation advises its clients to use, there are ten transistors as well as a power supply that only has one phase and one voltage. These are only two of the numerous elements that come together to form this configuration as a whole. At this very moment, the work on the Tanner platform that was being done to create it has come to an end and is finished. The ideas were not investigated in isolation, but rather in conjunction to the antecedent study and the results of the examination. Neither idea is studied in a vacuum. Neither idea is considered in a vacuum at any point (base work). When weighed against the efforts that were made in the past, the consequences are manifesting in a manner that is enormously more favorable. The fundamental work architecture must be carried out in its totality to achieve the effects that will follow if this paragraph is to remain accurate. The design has been examined in terms of how much space it occupies, how quickly it can move, and how efficiently it uses electricity, and all of these aspects have been compared to earlier incarnations of the product that is now under discussion.

In collaboration with several other academics, Rahul Jadia and his colleagues [7] are working toward the common objective of lowering the amount of power that is used by digital circuits. Creating efficacious circuit topologies that would not limit the power degradation of hybrid adder cells will be the objective that has to be achieved. We reached this conclusion after reading a large number of papers regarding 65 nm. We saw that the recommended design draws extremely little power from the power source, which led us to believe that this is the case. Because of this, we concluded that the 65-nm technology would be the most suitable one to implement. The adder is the most significant part of an ALU, and there is a direct and strong link between the efficiency of the adder and the total efficiency of the processing. The author plans to provide the basis for the later construction of a multiplication cell by employing the recently produced low-power adder cell as the principal component of the structure. This will allow the author to give the groundwork for the later fabrication of a multiplication cell.

Those involved in research are lending a hand to R. Deebigai's efforts [8]. During our examination of the 45-nm CMOS manufacturing process, several encouraging facts came to light. In recent years, it has become abundantly clear that the method of design known as hybrid-CMOS is advantageous in terms of reducing both the amount of power that is used and the footprint that is required. This has become the case because hybrid-CMOS can reduce both power consumption and space requirements. The method that is used to evaluate the circuit indicates that there is a significant flaw in the circuit as a result of the presence of two NOT gates that have a high-power consumption on the route that is necessary. This flaw is caused by the fact that the route has two NOT gates. The fact that the problem still exists demonstrates this point. The fact that the difficulties that were outlined earlier may be circumvented by taking the path that was advised makes it abundantly evident that this is the alternative that needs to be chosen as the one that ought to be employed. The circuit that has been presented makes use of hybrid full adders, which, because of the versatility of these components, may be beneficial in a range of settings and scenarios.

The study has been conducted by M. L. Tejaswini and other scientists [9]. After modeling the proposed xOR–xNOR circuit as well as the FA cells in the cadence virtuoso environment tool, we then evaluated the efficiency of both by parallel analysis of the results generated by the two models while using 90 nm GPDK CMOS technology. This allowed us to determine whether or not both models were effective. Because of this, we were able to assess whether or not the planned circuit would work. It was necessary to carry out this technique to decide whether the strategy had a higher rate of success. The researchers were able to produce an extra four FA cells by integrating into a single structure both the xOR gate and the xOR–xNOR gate. This allowed them to combine the functionality of both gates. It has been hypothesized that FA cells might be put to service in a diverse array of various contexts. [citation needed] This research also provides a more accurate way of calculating the size of transistors in digital circuits. As a result of the flexibility of this technology, it may be used in a variety of settings to meet a variety of needs. To make the procedure more precise, this study was carried out to improve its accuracy. The development of the XOR-XNOR circuit led to a reduction in latency as well as peak-to-average power consumption (PDP) which was much greater than that of other competing systems. Both of these advantages were realized at the same time. On the other hand, hybrid design logic circuits are often exclusively used in very specialized settings, such as medical imaging. Although the primary objective of this circuit was to hasten the process of producing the sum and carry, additional objectives included reducing the amount of power that was wasted and shrinking the size of the circuit by utilizing a smaller number of transistors. Both of these objectives were accomplished by the circuit. These goals were considered secondary in comparison to the main purpose, which was to speed up the process of creating the sum and carry. To complete this process, it is necessary to construct circuits that have a high level of efficiency, a low level of latency, and a low level of power consumption. All three of these characteristics should be kept to a minimum.

Following the findings of the modeling of the Ripple Carry Adder, M. Venkayya and colleagues [10] found that the proposed circuits had a performance that was astounding in every one of the scenarios that were evaluated. This was found to be the case with all of the proposed circuits. This fact came to light as a direct consequence of the findings made as a direct result of the modeling of the Ripple Carry Adder. In addition to being an essential component of the overall strategy, the accuracy and coherence of this one-of-a-kind method are also essential aspects of the overall plan.

During the process of creating the circuit for the required 1-bit hybrid full adder cells, Md. Shahbaz and his colleagues [11] adopt a TG logic. Because it operates at a fast speed while using a relatively low amount of power, the circuit that was proposed is more power-efficient than other similar circuits that are already in use. This is one of the reasons why the idea was proposed in the first place (about 23.3W). With the assistance of the HSPICE software, the simulation was carried out, and the following parameters served as inputs for the program: Along with the 90 nm CMOS technology, the input parameters of 1.2V and 1GHz are accounted for in this computation as well. This particular circuit can operate at frequencies up to one gigahertz, which is the highest frequency that it is possibly capable of achieving (1,000 GHz).

R.K.Uma Maheswari and her colleagues have published an article [12] in which they talk about some of the discoveries that they have uncovered. A single document that contains tabulated data on all key parameters of study, including the observations from PDA. Simulation based data and graphs were created to simplify the process of making comparisons. This document has been created to help simplify the process of making comparisons. The comparisons presented in this article were designed to make them more intuitive to readers. Before the proposed full adder circuit design can be constructed, the xNOR/xNOR circuit, which is based on a variety of viable alternative designs, has to be designed. xNOR stands for cross-over and xNOR stands for cross-over. This is because there are many feasible alternatives to the current architecture. This work has to be accomplished before the adder circuit design that has been supplied in its entirety may be constructed.

[13] Those investigators who collaborated with Madabhushi Sai Meghana throughout their time working together Not only has it been demonstrated, through the use of simulations, that the presence of positive feedback in the circuit adds an extra barrier, but it has also been shown, through the use of simulations, that there are NOT any doors in the circuit. Both of these points have been demonstrated through the use of simulations. The feedback causes a rise not just in the output capacitance but also in the total amount of power that is consumed and the overall delay of the system. This is because the output capacitance is proportional to the total amount of power utilized. The performance of this design is exceptional across the board regardless of how the components are set out because the data that was collected from numerous implementations of FA circuits in a wide variety of different configurations demonstrates this. The data was collected from numerous implementations of FA circuits in numerous different configurations. This was shown by the fact that the functionality of the design was not dependent on the order in which the components were placed.

A broad range of xOR/xNOR and xOR-xNOR circuits will be analyzed and compared to one another in the paper [14] that was authored by B. Dharani and his colleagues. The article may be found here. This research is an extension of the work that B. Dharani and his colleagues [14] have already accomplished. When there is a higher requirement for anything, whether it be more power, more delay, or more dereliction, there is a greater need for a larger number of transistors. This is because transistors are analog components. This led to the development of a more efficient xOR/xNOR gate that makes use of a smaller number of transistors as a direct result. As a direct result of this, the latency as well as the amount of power used has been significantly reduced (PDP).

M. Naga Gowtham and his colleagues have done a significant amount of research in this area, and the findings of that research have been published [15]. After the adder circuit was built from scratch using 10 transistors, its power consumption, as well as the length of time it took for it to react, were both measured and analyzed after they had been put through the construction process. These data were gathered throughout the process of developing and testing the circuit during that step of the process. In the second version of this project, the whole Subtractor circuit was built using just 8 transistors. This reduced the number of components needed by half. In addition, the circuits that were recommended were built using 15, 20, and 40 transistors, respectively. Because there was very little variance in the data, the author first took sure to analyze each one carefully, and then they utilized timing diagrams to calculate the power levels and delay durations for each component. This was done because there was very little fluctuation in the data. This was done since there was very little fluctuation in the results, therefore it was deemed necessary to do so. It was anticipated that by the time the project came to a close, an integrator that would bridge the gap between the DSCH2 software suite and the Micro wind software suite would have been created and put into production. This was to have been accomplished according to plans. A comparison was made between the power dissipation, the latency, and the layout area of the hybrid circuit that was suggested with those of already-existing circuits. When determining the value for the layout area variable, the size of the transistors was taken into consideration.

In this regard, the efforts that have been put in by Simhadri Mohan Krishna and his other colleagues [16] have shown to be highly beneficial. In addition to the energy-delay product being a primary issue in the VLSI industry, it has been hypothesized that Adder would be advantageous in power-efficient applications. This idea has been put forth. In addition, the deployment of ground-breaking circuits and creative design techniques is on the agenda for today. In addition, the configuration that was proposed reduces the overall amount of power consumption by around 9.5% while concurrently increasing the power density by 1.5%. Given that the design scenario has already been determined, it is preferable to arrive at a delay of around 8 percent. This is because the design scenario has already been set.

[17] Researchers who are collaborating with Professor M.C. Parameshwara and working under his direction. In light of this, it constitutes a significant advancement in comparison to the prior theory. The proposed FA also outperforms previous adders that have been reported in the past when applied to an interconnected multi-cell scenario, while simultaneously maintaining or improving upon its performance when applied to a scenario involving a single cell. The proposed field application circuit might provide the answer that's been looking for applications that need very large-scale integration (VLSI).

[18] Together with the other members of her team, Chella Santhosh has made significant contributions to the planned plan put into action, and the results are analyzed in conjunction with those obtained via the use of processes that are more traditionally understood. An extra internal logic structure has been built to imitate complete adder cells; the following paragraphs will provide a more in-depth explanation of this structure. This structure's purpose is to emulate full adder cells. Following a significant amount of consideration and examination, it was determined that this would be a venture that would be well worth pursuing. According to the author's calculations, it seems that in the not-too-distant future, the technology operating at 130 nm will have a higher energy efficiency compared to the technology operating at 90 nm.

3   1-Bit Full Adder

Adders are the integral to any computational devices available in the world. From recent advancement in AI to the basic blocks such as DSPs make use of adders for their functional achievements. Considering the complexity in deep sub-micron manufacturing of transistors, area and performance has hit hard on the industry. Therefore, encouraging more researchers into developing new advanced and improved design of this computational unit. As most of the designing structure in the industry has switch to automated and reliable tools to design and fabricate the chips, therefore techniques to improve the design has reached its peak. At the core of all functional chip lies the heart of computational block, adder. Therefore, no compromise on the designing on the adder block is observed at level of manufacturing and use. The project is progressed from a scratch with the available study material on the HSPICE tool, in integration with the waveform generator tool. The models are built in correspondence with the HSPICE syntax and different parameters regarding the performance is studied in detail in the sections mentioned latter.

This section shows the implementation of a full adder cell. The simulation software used for this work is hspice. Figure 1 shows the implementation of the circuit in the block diagram. A split of three sections can be observed. First, the building block of XNOR uses the pass transistors.

Table 1 shows the truth table of a single bit full adder block. This enables the functionality check of any cell that imitates the design of a full adder unit or cell.

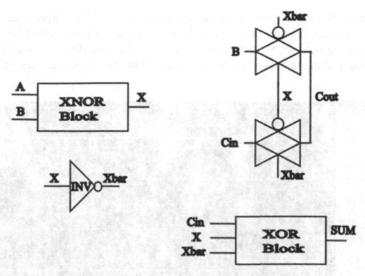

Fig. 1. Block diagram of 1-bit full adder cell.

Table. 1. Truth table of 1-bit full adder.

X	Y	Cin	Cout	S
0	0	0	0	0
0	0	1	0	1
0	1	0	0	1
0	1	1	1	0
1	0	0	0	1
1	0	1	1	0
1	1	0	1	0
1	1	1	1	1

4 Result and Simulation

The full adder block is implemented using a total of 16 transistors. An inverted XNOR output is obtained using a CMOS inverter. Following the first, the second comprises 2 transmission gates to compute the output carry of the cell. Lastly, the sum is evaluated using the pass transistors from the combination of XNOR output, inverted XNOR(XOR) output, and carry-in signals. Four pass transistors were used for this block. Thus, a total of 16 transistors were used to build a 1-bit hybrid full adder cell [1]. 32 nm process technology file was used in the generation of a comparatively better result. Figure 2 and Table 2 show the waveform and parameter values for the 32 nm process that was performed in this paper.

As can be observed from Fig. 2, the voltage swing in 32 nm hybrid architecture suffers poorly because of the short channel effect. This leads to cascading issues and a high short circuit power flowing through the circuit. The cascading may lead to flawed circuit output and the high short circuit power may burn out the system design.

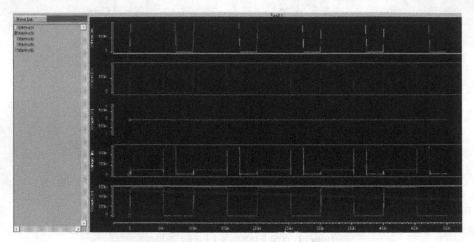

Fig. 2. Simulated waveform of 1-bit full adder cell.

Table 2. The simulation value of various parameters.

	1 BIT FULL ADDER MOS
AVERAGE POWER	1.53E-05
DELAY	9.41E-11
POWER DISSIPATION	3.65E-05
PDP	1.44E-15

5   Conclusion

Adders are a standout amongst the most often used sophisticated segments in the computerized coordinated circuit plan and are a critical component of signal processing analytic applications. With technological advancements, scientists have sought and continue to strive to design adders that enable either speedy or low-power use. In this study, several adder circuits are created and evaluated, such as a half adder, a full adder, a Carry Look Ahead Adder (CLAA), a Carry Select Adder (CSlA), and a Carry Save Adder (CSA), all of which use MOSFETs and are investigated efficiently. A detailed analysis of the 1-bit hybrid full adder and its drawbacks are performed. This shortcoming can be overcome by the use of GNRFET with the same process parameters. The future scope of the paper is to detail various ways to overcome the above-mentioned drawbacks.

References

1. Bhattacharyya, P., Kundu, B., Ghosh, S., Kumar, V., Dandapat, A.: Performance analysis of a low-power high-speed hybrid 1-bit full adder circuit. IEEE Trans. Very Large Scale Integr. (VLSI) Syst. **23**(10), 2001-2008 (2014). https://doi.org/10.1109/TVLSI.2014.2357057
2. Juveria, P., Ragini, K.: Low power and high speed full adder utilising new XOR and XNOR Gates. (IJITEE), **8**(8), 1516–1519 (2019)
3. Subhashini, T., Kamaraju, M., Babulu, K.: Low-Power and rapid adders using new XOR and XNOR gates. IEEE Trans. VLSI Des. Int. J. Eng. Res. Technol. **12**(12), 2072–2076 (2019). ISSN 0974–3154
4. SubbaRao, D., Kota Santhosh, M., Latha, P., Pushpa Latha, M.: Low-power and fast full adder by exploring new XOR and XNOR gates J. Eng. Sci. **11**(1) (2020). ISSN: 0377–9254
5. Rajesh, P., Srikanth, P.N., Vijaya Prasad, K.: Low-power and rapid full adder through exploration of new XOR and XNOR gates. (IJVDCS), 7 (2019). ISSN 2322–0929
6. Loga Lakshmi, M., Jeya Anusuya, S.,.Sathyah, S.V.: Performance Improvement of Low power and fast full adder by exploring new XOR and XNOR gates. Performance improvement of low power and fast full adder by exploring new XOR and XNOR gates, vol. 8(2) (2019). ISSN(Online): 2319–8753 ISSN(Print): 2347–6710
7. Jadia, R, Josh, S.: Design of low power adder cell using XOR and XNOR gate (IJRTE), 9(1) (2020). ISSN: 2277–3878
8. Deebigai, R., Krishnakumar, P.: Low Power Design for Fast Full Adder (IRJET), 7(3) (2020)
9. Tejaswini, M.L., Aishwarya, H., Akhila, M., Manasa, B.G.: High-Speed Hybrid-Logic Full Adder Utilizing High-Performance 10-T XOR–XNOR Cell (IJARSCT), 8(1) (2021). ISSN (Online) 2581–9467
10. Venkayya Naidu, M., Sravana Kumar, Y., Ramakrishna, A.: A 45 nm CMOS technology exploring a low-power and rapid 4-bit full adder with XOR and XNOR gates, IJSDR, vol. 4(11) (2019). ISSN: 2455–2631
11. Shahbaz, M., Patle, D: High-speed hybrid-logic full adder low power16-T XOR– XNOR cell. IEEE Trans. Comput. **4**(5) Int. J. Innovative Res. Technol. Manage. (2020). ISSN: 2581–3404
12. Uma Maheswari, R.K., Marimuthu, C.N.: Implementation of a low-power, fast full adder using novel XOR and XNOR gates. Int. J. Intellect. Advancements Res. Eng. Comput. 7(1). ISSN: 2348–2079
13. Low Power and Fast Full Adder by Exploring New XOR and XNOR Gates
14. Design of XOR/XNOR circuits for Hybrid Full Adder (IJERECE) Volume 7, Issue 5, May 2020, ISSN (Online) 2394–2320. Dharani B., Naresh Kumar K., and Vineela M
15. Naga Gowtham, M., Hari Krishna Reddy, P.S., Jeevitha, K., Hari Kishore, K., Raghuveera, E., Razia, S.: Performance analysis of a low power high speed hybrid full adder and full subtractor circuit. Turkish J. Comput. Math. Educ. **12**(3), 3037–3045 (2021)
16. Krishna, S.M, Lakshmi, M.S, Kumari, K.A., Sampath, P.V.S., Doddi, B.R.: Design and Implementation of a Low Power Delay 1-bit Xnor/Xor Adder ISSN: 0886–9367
17. Parameshwara, M.C.: ICTACT JOURNAL ON MICROELECTRONICS, JULY 2021, VOLUME: 07, ISSUE: 02, ISSN: 2395–1680, "ROBUST AND SCALEABLE HYBRID 1-BIT FULL ADDER CIRCUIT FOR VLSI APPLICATION" (ONLINE)
18. Santhosh, C., Phanikishore, D.S., Kumar, M.R., Priyanka, D., Shanmukha, N., Arthik, S.S.: Energy efficient arithmetic full adders using diverse technology nodes (IJETER), 8(7) (2020). ISSN 2347–3983

Implementation of Low-Power Full Adder Using GNRFET Technology

Jay Sutradhar$^{(\boxtimes)}$, Shyam Akashe, and Sadhana Mishra

ITM University, Gwalior, India
joy.dhar0161@yahoo.com, {shyam.akashe,
sadhanamishra.ec}@itmuniversity.ac.in

Abstract. Adders are fundamental components of more complex arithmetic operations, including addition, multiplication, and division, as well as mathematical procedures. The vast majority of these types of systems, adder components is the most critical path that influences the speed of the system. To satisfy these requirements, the adder cell, which is the fundamental structural component, should have its power consumption and propagation delay reduced. Researchers have tried, and continue to try, to create adders that deliver either rapid speed, low power consumption, decreased space, or a combination of these properties. These technical breakthroughs have allowed them to design adders that give one of these benefits. During this research, a variety of digital adders that are functionally identical to Full Adders and GNRFETs manufactured using 32 nm technology were used to construct this area unit. The adder's equivalent to average power performance parameters and delay is established after being simulated using HSPICE.

Keywords: Adder · 32 nm · GNRFET · MOSFET

1 Introduction

Scaled integration is a conceptual framework that outlines the creation of consolidated circuits through the incorporation of a significant number of circuits based on transistors onto a single chip. It is also known as very large-scale integration (VLSI), which is an acronym that stands for very large-scale integration. Integration at a scaled level is often referred to as integration at a very big scale (VLSI). There is a good chance that the chip in issue is a component of an extraordinarily large-scale integration device. The utilization of very large-scale integration (VLSI) design techniques is obligatory for every chip in a contemporary workplace. The most recent innovation has resulted in a shift away from the production of larger transistors on a chip and toward the production of chips with an infinite number of passageways and tens of billions of small individual transistors. This shift has been brought about as a result of the production of chips with an infinite number of passageways. This change came about as a consequence of a shift in attention from the manufacturing of bigger transistors on a chip to the creation of smaller individual transistors. This allowed for the shift in focus to take place. Wafer-scale joining, normal reasonability systems, unrivaled enrollment and communication

R. S. Tomar et al. (Eds.): CNC 2022, CCIS 1893, pp. 260–272, 2023.
https://doi.org/10.1007/978-3-031-43140-1_23

structures, impartial frameworks, and examination and transformation are some of the sectors that take advantage of it because of its switching configuration. As a direct result of this, there is a growing interest in investing in chip-driven stocks both in the here and now and in the not-too-distant future. This is true for both the here and now and the not-too-distant future. It is quite likely that we will need to reduce the size, power, and force for us to be able to fulfill these requirements; if we are going to be successful in doing so. As a direct consequence of this fact, power dispersion has developed into an essential emphasis at the basis of the construction of simple as well as automated circuits. Prior frameworks that claimed to update the area of a fan-out tree may have resulted in excessive power consumption as a consequence of disregarding the short-out present. This may have caused excessive power consumption. There is no way to rule out the existence of this possibility. The general unique mode control use, the clock control, and consequently the essential overflowing vitality of the combinatory circuits are reduced by up to fifty-five percent, twenty-nine percent, and fifty-three per cent, respectively, when compared to the circuits that have been maintained in CMOS development. This is performed without any reduction in either the speed or the data strength of the connection.

As a consequence of developments at the nanoscale level, both the thickness of the chip and the number of times it is worked have grown. As a direct result of this, the quantity of power that is needed to be used by battery-operated adaptive devices has grown dramatically. Because of the increased expenses associated with shipping and cooling, as well as the risk of quality concerns that cannot be remedied, the usage of control is required for larger contraptions. [3] As a consequence of this, the primary objective of the blueprint for VLSI (wide-scale) planners is to satisfy execution needs while maintaining a power budget that has been predetermined. When seen from this perspective, one starts with the expectation that the control viability will have a more substantial influence. [1] Ever since the birth of the integrated circuit business, there has been a need to boost execution, control, area, cost, and time to promote (opportunity cost) calculations. This is because such improvements are necessary to promote (opportunity cost) calculations. This is because such enhancements are required to facilitate assessments of opportunity cost. This is the reason why this is the case. The impetus for instituting this criterion was the intention of advancing (opportunity cost) estimates as a standard practice. If I'm being straightforward with you, Moore's Law is a significant factor in the whole process of making those criteria more straightforward. [6] Regardless, when the scaling of accumulating centers became closer and closer to 20 nm, a portion of the device characteristics could not be scaled anymore. This was because 20 nm is the smallest size that can be achieved. This occurred as a result of the fact that a 20 nm increase was the smallest one that could be accomplished. This was especially true concerning the voltage of the power supply, which is the single most important component of dynamic power that has to be taken into mind. In addition, the improvements that were made to a single aspect, such as the execution, led to significant improvements that were made in several other domains, such as control. These improvements were made possible by the improvements that were made to the execution. [4] Lithography was stuck at ArF lighting up sources with a wavelength of 193 nm, even though the important component of the plan was pushing sub-20 nm, which led to an additional problem that occurred as the approaches drew closer and closer to 20 nm. This was a difficulty since it stopped the lithography process from progressing ahead, which caused a challenge. The advancement of optical technology, for instance, made it conceivable to conduct procedures like submersion lithography and twofold outlining. Nevertheless, the advancements came with the negative of an increase in irregularity, which was a price that had to be paid for the breakthroughs.

The need to reevaluate the estimates about the arrangement's control, performance, and geographical location, in addition to the cost and the amount of time needed to show anything, also known as the opportunity cost, has stayed the same since the industry of integrated circuits was first established. This time has been referred to as the opportunity cost [7–12]. To tell you the truth, Moore's Law is related to the acceleration of several different processes and activities. This is the most honest answer I can give you. When the scaling of collecting center points came closer and closer to 20 nm, some features of the device's properties, most notably the power supply voltage, could not be scaled any further. This was the case regardless of how small the collecting center points were scaled. This was particularly true when the scale of collecting center points came nearer and nearer to 20 nm. This was the aspect of choosing dynamic power that led to the greatest uncertainty, thus it needed to be taken into consideration. In addition, redesigning for one component, such as performance, sometimes led to major alterations being made in other areas, such as control. This was because of the interconnected nature of these two aspects. The most important part of the process was getting below 20 nm, which presented an additional challenge as the technology advanced near 20 nm. As a consequence of this, lithography was forced to continue making use of ArF lighting up sources with a wavelength of 193 nm, although the technology was moving closer to 20 nm. For instance, as a result of advancements in optical technology, submersion lithography and twofold outlining became feasible [13]. These two techniques are used in the manufacturing of semiconductors. Both of these processes are instances of what are today thought of as being technically doable, even though this improvement came at the cost of an increase in capriciousness. In addition, many innovations were in the process of being adopted, such as high-K metal routes [14, 15], which aided with entrance overflow leakage difficulties to a certain degree. This was one of the many developments that were in the process. Additionally, there were breakthroughs in the following areas: Despite this, the window of opportunity to simplify the many different aspects of the approach, which had been emphasized in the past, was quickly closing [15–20].

The microchip is a device that enables the integration of very extensive amounts of information. Every single chip that is manufactured in today's world makes use of very large-scale integration (VLSI) designs in some aspect of the manufacturing process. The goal of the most recent research is not to increase the total number of transistors that can be found on a chip; rather, the emphasis has changed to the design of a microchip that has a large number of gates in addition to billions of individual transistors that are of a smaller size [21, 22]. This change in focus has come about as a direct consequence of a paradigm shift that has taken place inside the industry. In light of this furious notion, it finds application in the sectors of significant handling and communication structures, neutral frameworks, wafer-scale compromise, microelectronic systems, as well as a creative activity. People will have a stronger interest in chip-driven things both now and in the future, particularly those that are the best in their class in the future.

This attraction will be especially strong in the future. It is anticipated that this pattern will go on [23, 24]. If we are going to be able to fulfill their expectations, it is going to be necessary for us to scale down our operations, both in terms of the electricity they use and the profits they generate. Because of this, properly regulating the distribution of energy has emerged as an essential component in the design of electronic circuits of all levels, from the most fundamental to the most complex. This is due to the repercussions that this has brought about as a result of this. Rejecting the use of short-circuit current, older strategies that were offered to update the area of a fan-out tree may result in the use of unneeded amounts of power, as this research has shown.

2 16T Full Adder Architecture

This section shows the implemented circuit and its waveform using HSPICE software. In Fig. 5 below, an adder block diagram is shown. The implementation of the total sum output of the full adder falls within the purview of the XNOR modules. Utilizing the transistor pair Mp2 and Mn2, which is produced by the inverter that is composed of the transistors Mp1 and Mn1, allows for the controlled inverter to be created in a way that is both efficient and effective. The output of this controlled inverter is effectively the XNOR of A and B, so you may think of it as the combination of both. It does, however, suffer from some voltage degradation, which has been rectified by the use of two pass transistors, designated Mp3 and Mn3, respectively. The pMOS transistors (Mp4, Mp5, and Mp6) and nMOS transistors (Mn4, Mn5, and Mn6) are used to realize the second stage of the XNOR module, which is needed to realize the entire SUM function. This module is utilized to realize the full SUM function. The XNOR modules, which create the sum signal (SUM), are modules 1 and 2, and module 3, which generates the output carry signal, are the modules in question (Cout). The specific design of each module ensures that the overall adder circuit is as efficient as possible in terms of power consumption and delay. This section will go into depth on these modules (Fig. 1).

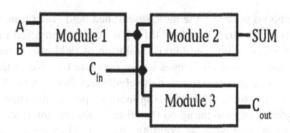

Fig. 1. Block Diagram

The XNOR module is included in the proposed complete adder circuit. Responsible for the majority of the power use during the whole adder circuit. As a result, this module was developed to ensure the least amount of maximizing the power to the greatest extent feasible while avoiding the voltage deterioration possible.

The full adder using Mos Like GNRFET is shown in Fig. 2. XNOR circuit in which the amount of power that is used is decreased to a great degree with the intentional use

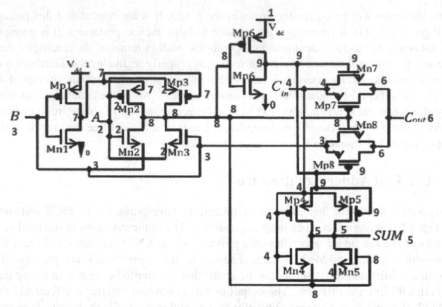

Fig. 2. Full Adder using GNRFET proposed

of a weak inverter (channel) (due to the narrow width of the transistors) structure created by transistors Mp1 and Mn1. Complete operation at the maximum levels of output the integrity of the signals is ensured by level-restoring transistors Mp3 and Mn3.

3   SPICE Model of MOS Type GNRFET

3.1   GNRFET Fundamentals

Graphene nano-ribbons is one of the most researched field effect transistors. This provides an alternative to the traditional MOSFET design that are used for fabrication of most electronic devices. With continuous evolution of field effect transistors, silicon MOS transistors show lots of challenges as we decrease the size of the device. Thus, GNRFETs provide an alternative to solve the challenges faced by the MOSFET.

Unlike carbon nano-tube, GNR is hexagonal two planar allotrope of carbon. This reduces the complexity of fabricating on the silicon substrate interface. GNR can be of two types based on the line edge c-c bonding structure. They are zigzag and armchair. While zigzag shows more metallic characteristics, the armchair structure shows both metallic and semi-conducting property depending on the width of the nano-ribbons [25].

Figure 3 shows the structure of a GNRFET on a silicon substrate with gate and gate dielectric. The width of the nano-ribbons plays a crucial role in controlling the current flowing through the device. Unlive the traditional CMOS devices, the channel voltage is a direct function of the dimer lines, which controls the width of the ribbons. Multiple nano-ribbons can be used for increasing the channel conduction.

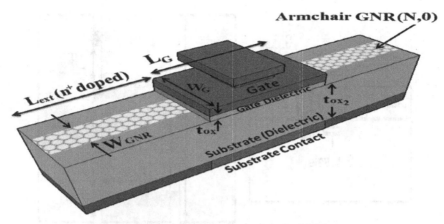

Fig. 3. Structure of an Armchair GNRFET.

The drain current equation of GNRf is shown in Eq. 4.1.

$$I_{ds} = \frac{2qkT}{h} \sum_{\alpha} [\ln\left(1 + e^{\frac{q(V_{ch}-V_S)-\varepsilon_\alpha}{kT}}\right) - \ln(1 + e^{\frac{q(V_{ch}-V_D)-\varepsilon_\alpha}{kT}})] \tag{1}$$

where, k is Boltzmann constant,

h is Planks constant,

V_{ch} is channel voltage,

ε_α is c-c sub band edge and

α is sub band index.

The advantages of GNRFET over MOSFET are:

1. It is highly compatible for fabrication process with silicon interface.
2. Outstanding electrical properties, i.e., excellent conductor of heat and electricity.
3. Can be operated at extreme speed of around 400 GHz.
4. The mobility is twice compared to CNTFET and almost 150 times of MOS field effect transistors
5. Strong, light and high density compared to MOSFET.

3.2 GNRFET Model File

The GNRFET spice model is based schematic design shown in Fig. 4.

This is a MOS structured GNRFET spice model where the nano-ribbons act as the physical channel for conduction. The channel width W_{ch} is defined by using dimer lines N. The dimer lines play a vital role in the sub band charge conduction [26].

The equation for W_{ch}. is,

$$W_{ch} = \frac{\sqrt{3}}{2} \times d_{cc} \times (N + 1) \tag{2}$$

where, d_{cc} is the distance between carbon-to-carbon bond in the lattice.

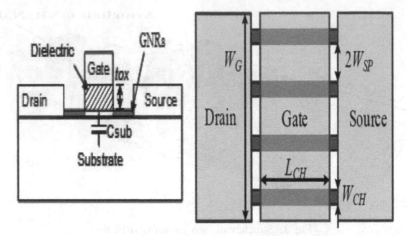

Fig. 4. GNRFET Structure spice model.

To increase the width of the nano-ribbon, the number of dimer lines can be increased. But as a consequence, the band gap reduces. Therefore, the effective on to off current reduces. To avoid a very low on to off current, the maximum dimer lines in a GNR is set to 50. Thus, unlike traditional MOSFET where increasing the channel width the drain current increased, in GNRFET the drain current decreases with the increase in width of nano-ribbons.

Therefore, to increase the conduction of channel the number of nano-ribbons can be increased. According to the spice model, there are no limitations to the number of nano-ribbon in the GNRFET device.

The values of various parameters constraint by this spice model are shown in Table 1 below:

Table 1. Parameter constraints spice model.

Device Parameters	Dimensions
L_{ch}, Channel Length (min/max)	10 nm/100 nm
W_{ch}, Channel Width per GNR (min/max)	0.873 nm(N = 6)/6.36 nm(N = 50)
n_{rib}, Number of GNR per device	1 to many
t_{OX}, , Oxide Thickness (min/max)	0.5 nm/2.5 nm
dop, Doping Fraction	0.001 to 0.015
gates_tied	'0' or '1'

Some keys points are jotted below for this working spice model:

1. The gate width is calculated with respect to W_{ch},

$$W_G = (2W_{SP} + W_{ch}) \times n_{rib}$$

where, $2W_{SP}$ is the spacing between the GNRs and n_{rib} is the number of GNRs.

2. The syntax for nmos GNRFET:

   Xname D G S B GNRFETnmos $nRib = 6$ $N = 12$ $L = 15$n $Tox = 1$n $sp = 2$n dop $= 5$e-3 $p = 0$ $Tox2 = 20$n $gates_tied = $ '0'

3. The syntax for pmos GNRFET:

   Xname D G S B GNRFETpmos $nRib = 6$ $N = 12$ $L = 15$n $Tox = 1$n $sp = 2$n dop $= 5$e-3 $p = 0$ $Tox2 = 20$n $gates\_tied=$'0'

4. Ere, p is the line edge roughness of the device in percent.
5. And $gates_tied = $ '1' indicates that the bottom gate is same as top gate voltage; used in case of double gate device.
6. By default, Tox2 $= 20$n and $gates_tied = $ '0'.
7. For this research, GNRFET based full adder circuit, we used:

   XMPnum D G S B gnrfetpmos nRib $= 1$ n $= 6$ L $= 32$n Tox $= 0.95$n sp $= 2$n dop $= 0.001$ p $= 0$
   XMNnum D G S B gnrfetnmos nRib $= 1$ n $= 6$ L $= 32$n Tox $= 0.95$n sp $= 2$n dop $= 0.001$ p $= 0$

8. Unlike the MOSFET spice model, the MOS-GNRFET spice model does not support the interchangeability of Source(S) and Drain(D).
9. Also, an assumption that the drain voltage is always greater than or equal to the source voltage for this spice model.

4   Results

This section shows the result. The parameters of comparison are-

Average Power,
Delay,
Power Dissipation,
And PDP.

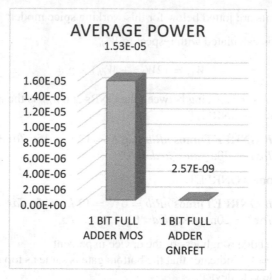

Fig. 5. Power Output

In Fig. 5, power output is shown which shows up to 99% Improvement by using MOS like GNRFET.

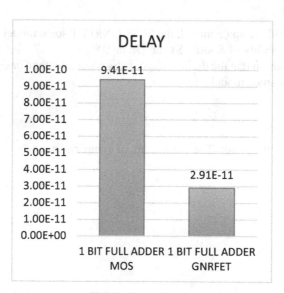

Fig. 6. Delay Output

In Fig. 6, delay output is shown which shows up to 65% improvement by using MOS like GNRFET.

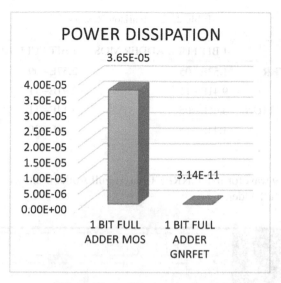

Fig. 7. Power Dissipation Output

In Fig. 7, power dissipation output is shown which shows up to 99% improvement by using MOS like GNRFET.

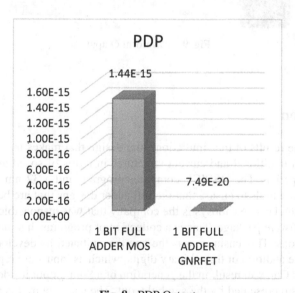

Fig. 8. PDP Output

In Fig. 8, PDP output is shown which shows up to 99% improvement by using MOS like GNRFET.

The tabular comparison results are shown in Table 2 below.

Table 2. Comparison Results

	1 BIT FULL ADDER MOS	1 BIT FULL ADDER GNRFET
AVERAGE POWER	1.53E−05	2.57E−09
DELAY	9.41E−11	2.91E−11
POWER DISSIPATION	3.65E−05	3.14E−11
PDP	1.44E−15	7.49E−20

In below Fig. 9 waveform of GNRFET-based Full Adder is shown which follows the correct results of full adder.

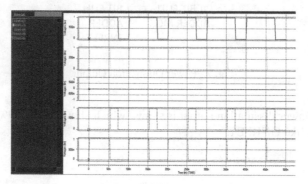

Fig. 9. Waveform Output

5 Conclusion

According to the results of the simulations, the design that makes use of GNRFETs is superior to both traditional and current structures in terms of speed and the potential for power dissipation. The HSPICE computer program and a 32 nm model are both used as simulation tools to ensure that the full adder designs that are being offered can be accurately simulated. Synopsys is the company that was responsible for developing the HSPICE software package. This is a collection of programs that may be used to do SPICE simulations. This business was the one that initiated its development. In a full adder circuit, the addition of three binary digits, which as inputs are represented by the letters A, B, and Cin, will result in the generation of a Sum output in addition to a Carry output, which is represented by the symbol Cout. The Carry output is a representation of the amount that was carried over from the previous calculation. The addition of these three binary digits will result in the generation of these outputs as a consequence of the operation. Within a completely operational adder circuit, these two outputs may be found in very close proximity to one another. If it is feasible to determine that there is another point on the ship that is more important for the Cout signal, then it will be delivered there, provided that there is another location on the ship that is just as important. Full adders are necessary to carry out an accurate examination of the performance characteristics of a comprehensive digital system, and this analysis cannot be carried out without them.

References

1. Bhattacharyya, P., Kundu, B., Ghosh, S., Kumar, V., Dandapat, A.: Performance analysis of a low-power high-speed hybrid 1-bit full adder circuit. IEEE Trans. VLSI Syst. **23**(10), 2001–2008 (2015). https://doi.org/10.1109/TVLSI.2014.2357057
2. Juveria, P., Ragini, K.: Low power and high speed full adder utilising new XOR and XNOR gates. Int. J. Innov. Technol. Exploring Eng. **8**(8), 1516–1519 (2019)
3. Subhashini, T., Kamaraju, M., Babulu, K.: Low-power and rapid adders using new XOR and XNOR gates. Int. J. Eng. Res. Technol. **12**(12), 2072–2076 (2019)
4. SubbaRao, D., Santhosh, K., Pushpa Latha, M.: low-power and fast full adder by exploring new XOR and XNOR gates. J. Eng. Sci. **11**(1), 364–370 (2020)
5. Rajesh, P., Srikanth, P.N., Vijaya Prasad, K.: Low-power and rapid full adder through exploration of new XOR and XNOR gates. Int. J. VLSI Des. Commun. Syst. **07** (2019)
6. loga Lakshmi, M., Jeya Anusuya, S., Sathyah, S.V.: Performance improvement of low power and fast full adder by exploring new XOR and XNOR gates. Int. J. Innov. Res. Sci. Eng. Technol. **8**(2), 133–146 (2019)
7. Jadia, R., Josh, S.: Design of low power adder cell using XOR and XNOR gate. Int. J. Recent Technol. Eng. **9**(1), 2560–2564 (2020)
8. Deebigai, R., Krishnakumar, P.: Low power design for fast full adder. Int. Res. J. Eng. Technol. **07**(03), 2567–2572 (2020)
9. Tejaswini, M.L., Aishwarya, H., Akhila, M., Manasa, B.G.: High-speed hybrid-logic full adder utilizing high-performance 10-T XOR–XNOR cell. Int. J. Adv. Res. Sci. Commun. Technol. **8**(1), 264–269 (2021)
10. Venkayya Naidu, M., Sravana Kumar, Y., Ramakrishna, A.: A 45 nm CMOS technology exploring a low-power and rapid 4-bit full adder with XOR and XNOR gates. Int. J. Sci. Eng. Dev. Res. **4**(11), 156–165 (2019)
11. Shahbaz, M., Patle, D.: High-speed hybrid-logic full adder low power16-T XOR–XNOR cell. Int. J. Innov. Res. Technol. Manag. **4**(5), 29–34 (2020)
12. Uma Maheswari, R.K., Marimuthu, C.N.: Implementation of a low-power, fast full adder using novel XOR and XNOR gates. Int. J. Intell. Adv. Res. Eng. Comput. **7**(1) (2019)
13. Low Power and Fast Full Adder by Exploring New XOR and XNOR Gates
14. Dharani, B., Naresh Kumar, K., Vineela, M.: Design of XOR/XNOR circuits for Hybrid Full Adder. Int. J. Eng. Res. Electron. Comput. Eng. **7**(5), 1–7 (2020)
15. Naga Gowtham, M., et al.: Performance analysis of a low power high speed hybrid full adder circuit and full subtractor circuit. Turkish J. Compu. Math. Educ. **12**(3), 3037–3045 (2021). https://doi.org/10.17762/turcomat.v12i3.1338
16. Mohan Krishna, S., Sai Lakshmi, M., Kumari, K.A., Sampath, P.V.S., Doddi, B.R.: Design and Implementation of a Low Power Delay 1-bit Xnor/Xor Adder
17. Parameshwara, M.C.: Robust and scaleable hybrid 1-bit full adder circuit for vlsi application. Int. Confederation Thermal Anal. Calorimetry **7**(2), 1109–1114 (2021)
18. Santhosh, C.: Energy efficient arithmetic full adders using various technology nodes. Int. J. Emerg. Trends Eng. Res. **8**(7), 3071–3075 (2020)
19. Devnath, B.C., Biswas, S.N.: low power full adder design using PTM transistor model. Carpathian J. Electron. Comput. Eng. **12**(2), 15–20 (2019). https://doi.org/10.2478/cjece-2019-0011

20. Arun Kumar, M., Yadhav, D.: Performance analysis of XOR and XNOR gates employing different logic styles. J. Emeg. Technol. Inov. Res. **8**(8), 60–64 (2021)
21. Yadav, A., Jain, M.: Novel low power and high-speed CMOS-based XOR/XNORs utilising systematic cell design methodology. IEEE Trans. Electron. Dev. **5**(3), 1018–1024 (2017)
22. Padma, S.I., Archana Devi, S., Jennifer, R., Pramma Sathya, V.: Reduction techniques for power and delay on full adder by XOR gate logics using microwind EDA tool. Int. J. Innov. Sci. Res. Technol. **6**, 1094–1099 (2021)
23. Aladale, P.: Design of low power and high-speed full adder cell utilizing new 3TXNOR gate. Int. J. Comput. Sci. Mobile Computing **7**(6), 31–36 (2018)
24. Krishnan, A., Balamurugan, V., Krishnakumar, A., Aparna, A., Ashna, A., Athira, M.: Design of low power high speed full adder circuits using XORXNOR topology. Int. Res. J. Eng. Technol. **7**(5), 7662–7667 (2020)
25. Murugesan, A.: A theoretical description of graphene based transistors. Int. J. Innov. Sci. Eng. Technol. **1**(3), 264–270 (2014)
26. Chen, Y.-Y., et al.: A SPICE-compatible model of graphene nano-ribbon field-effect transistors enabling circuit-level delay and power analysis under process variation. In: 2013 Design, Automation & Test in Europe Conference & Exhibition (DATE). IEEE (2013)

Design of Dual-Polarized Square Microstrip Patch Antenna in KU Band for Weather Applications

R. Harikrishnan$^{(\boxtimes)}$ and Veekshita Sai Choudhary

Symbiosis Institute of Technology (SIT), Pune Campus, Symbiosis International Deemed
University (SIDU), Pune, Maharashtra, India
dr.rhareish@gmail.com

Abstract. The paper discusses about the design of a dual-polarized micro strip patch antenna operating in Ku band working in a bandwidth of 12.8 to 13.8 GHz for weather applications. A square shaped design of patch antenna resonates at a frequency of 13.3 GHz. Coaxial probe is the type of feeding technique used in the antenna. The visible return loss after simulations is −20.564 dB. The feeds have been placed in orthogonal position that is they are placed perpendicular to each other. The desired transmission coefficient is also achieved which is −29 dB. The directivity achieved with this design is 7.138 dBi. This paper shows and aims for the result of designing a square shaped micro-strip patch antenna with coaxial probe feeding aiming for suppression of the cross-polarization, proper isolation among the vertical and horizontal polarization and also to get the ideal reflection coefficient.

Keywords: Dual-polarization · Cross-polarization · Suppression · Isolation · Reflection Coefficient · Square

1 Introduction

Radio waves, Microwaves, Infrared, Ultraviolet, X-rays and Gamma rays make a spectrum of electromagnetic waves. The microwaves are further divided into different frequencies among which Ku band is the one. Ku band has a frequency range of 12 GHz–18 GHz. This band is used for weather applications and also satellite communication. KU-band is far better than the C-band as it can interfere with the terrestrial systems and also has the ability to increase the power of uplinks and downlinks [1]. Among all the bands, Ku band makes it easy for small antennas to work in its range as it has high frequency and has a proper directional main beam [1]. Widely used antenna type in this world is Microstrip patch antennas (MPA). MPA have an upper hand with their light weight, low volume, thin profile configuration, low fabrication cost, effortlessness in the generation of linear polarization, circular polarization, dual-polarization and dual frequency, no need of having cavity back antenna; easy integration with the microwave integrated circuits. Having mentioned all the advantages, there are certain limitations of

R. S. Tomar et al. (Eds.): CNC 2022, CCIS 1893, pp. 273–284, 2023.
https://doi.org/10.1007/978-3-031-43140-1_24

MSA like low bandwidth and gain (less than −6 dB) which have been surmounted with the phase of time with new techniques and experiments. Patch antennas in general provide a gain between 5 to 6 dB and also generate a beamwidth of 3dB which is typically produced in between the angle 70 and degrees [2].

The feeding technique selection can be differentiated depending on the way it transfers the power from feedline to the patch. One of the feeding mechanisms used in antennas is Coaxial probe Fed Microstrip patch Antenna where a coaxial probe is used as a feed and its outer conductor connects with the ground plane (GP) and the inner conductor is connected to the substrate of the radiating patch. While choosing the feeding technique, one should consider how to minimize the spurious radiations generated and the effect of it on the radiation pattern of the antenna [2]. Spurious radiations and surface wave loss are possible due to no proper isolation and impedance mismatch between the feed and the patch, but such type of problem is resolved in antennas having coaxial probe feeding as this feeding technique provides an excellent isolation among the feed and the patch. The electric filed source and the magnetic field source in the radiation mechanism are the two main sources for a dual polarized antenna whose placement is orthogonal [3]. A dual-polarized antenna should always be cautious with the port isolation and cross-polarization. In order to suppress the cross-polarization, the feeds need to be orthogonally placed. The dielectric constant (DC) of antenna is of much importance while designing an antenna. The thickness of a substrate (h) $0.003\lambda \leq h \leq 0.05\lambda$ is typically preferred. λ is wavelength in free space. Ideally, substrates with less DC are considered as they provide higher efficiency, broader bandwidth. They also increase the fringing field at the edges of the radiating patch, and hence increase in the radiation power too. The height of the substrate determines the output produced by antenna. Radiation in MPA occurs due to the fringing fields [4].

The scattering parameters, the radiation of an antenna are the important attributes to be considered for analysing the output of any antenna. S11 refers to the signal reflected at port1 for the signal incident at port1 [5] hence known as reflection coefficient. The S parameters are important as they depend on the frequency, source impedance, load impedance and network and hence a crucial parameter to judge the working of the antenna.

The EM field distribution helps in the determination of radiation of an antenna [2]. In this paper [6], they have demonstrated how dual polarization results in the increase of isolation between the input and output signal, that is, transmitting and receiving signals and orthogonal positioning being the best way of design for the generation of dual orthogonal linearly polarised waves. Comparison between the dual-polarised antenna and circularly polarised antenna led to a conclusion that the polarity purity, efficiency and return loss are much better in the dual-polarised antenna which was 99.89%, whereas the circularly polarised being 98.86%; thus, the paper [7] concluded the dual-polarised antenna to be the best design. In [8], they have implemented a dual-polarised microstrip patch antenna with coaxial probe feeding along with along with capacitive blind via fence which resulted in high isolation, wide beamwidth, less cross-polarization, symmetrical radiation patterns, high port isolation. In this paper [6], microstrip square patch antenna is designed. Coaxial probe feeding and orthogonal positioning of the feeds results in the dual polarization operating in a bandwidth of 12 GHz to 14 GHz. The selection of the substrate, thickness, and positioning has been done accordingly. The following sections will be talking about the proposed work and then the result analysis respectively.

2 Proposed Work

ADS System software has been used to design the proposed antenna. A substrate material being thick and having a low DC should be chosen to have goof efficiency, wider bandwidth and much better radiation on the patch which eventually determine the results of an antenna [4]. The DC and the height of it are inversely proportional. The dielectric loss which is basically the conversion of energy in the dielectric medium to heat, is increased due to increase in the high loss tangent [2]. The length and width of the antenna are same as it is a square shaped patch antenna. In general, the patch length is crucial as it determines the bandwidth of the patch.

Following are the formulas used to calculate the dimensions and values required for the design of the antenna from [2] and [9].

Formula of Width:

$$W = \frac{C}{2f_0\sqrt{\frac{(\varepsilon_r+1)}{2}}}$$

Formula of effective DC:

$$\varepsilon_{reff} = \frac{\varepsilon_r + 1}{2} + \frac{\varepsilon_r - 1}{2}\sqrt{\left[1 + 12\frac{h}{w}\right]}$$

ε_r: DC.
h: Dielectric substrate height.
w: Patch width.

The most important parameters while designing an antenna are: The resonating frequency: The antenna designed here has a resonating frequency of 13.32 GHz and operating range is 12 GHz to 14 GHz. DC, material and its height: the importance of the parameter has been discussed above. 2.2 is the DC for the designed antenna and the substrate chosen is RT Duroid 5880 having a thickness/height of 1.85 mm.

After considering the above parameters and formulas, below are the calculated values as shown in Table 1:

Table 1. Measurement of various dimensions

Dimensions	mm
Height	1.8
Patch Length	6.9
Patch Width	6.9
GP Length	8.4
GP Width	8.4
Radius of the hole	0.1
Radius of dielectric	0.2
Radius of the outer layer of probe	0.3

Flow chart for the procedure of design is shown in the Fig. 1.

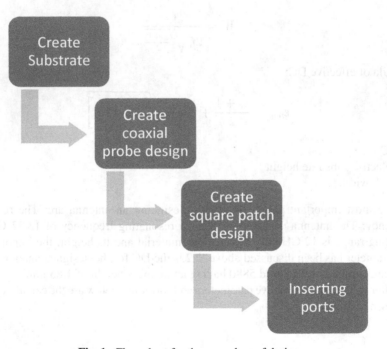

Fig. 1. Flow chart for the procedure of design

Create substrate – In ADS System, Substrate editor is used to create the substrate and here we have made a stack up of air layers with a dielectric material. We are considering RT Duroid 5880 which will be placed right below the "air" layer. Conductor layer PC1 is placed on the dielectric material and is the conducting patch of the antenna, and PC2 layer is placed below the dielectric material which is the GP of the antenna. Add two "air" layers below the dielectric material which are helpful to insert the coaxial probe. The PC4 layer placed on "air" layer is the face of the coax attached to the port. We add three materials for coax probe feeding in the substrate editor itself. These are the metal vias in which one being the hole that is the inner conductor and also the center pin of the coax which is of radius 0.1 mm, other being the dielectric via around it, which is the dielectric core of the coax having radius of 0.2 mm and third being the outer conductor of the coax, that is the outer metal shell of the coax which is having radius of 0.3 mm. Figure 2 shows the substrate created for the antenna.

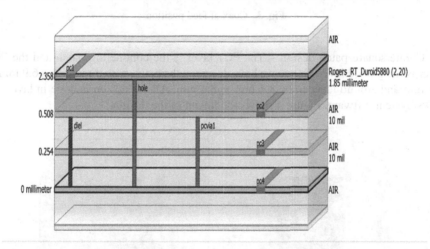

Fig. 2. Creation of substrate

Create coaxial probe design – After initially adding the materials in the substrate, here we draw the hole, dielectric and the outer layer with the measurements mentioned above. In this process of designing the coax, PC4 coax face plate is create by simple Boolean operations done on the coax. Both the feeds are positioned in such a way that they have a phase difference of 90 degrees which is essential for suppressing the cross polarization and also provide proper isolation required for the horizontal and the vertical polarization. Hence, we can clearly say that this step of design determines the cross-polarization suppression and isolation. The distance between the feeds is 2.618 mm. Figure 3 shows the orthogonal positioning of the two feeds. The figure clearly shows that the feed is positioned in such a way that it has 90 degree phase difference.

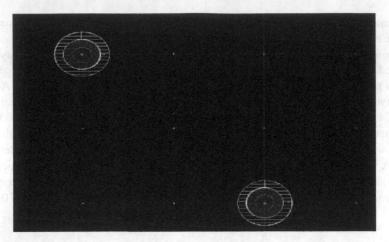

Fig. 3. Coaxial feed position

Create square patch design – The PC1 layer is the conducting patch and the PC2 layer is the ground layer. Hence we have designed the patch with dimensions 6.9 mm × 6.9 mm and ground layer to be 8.4 mm × 8.4 mm. All the design is done in layout of ADS System software. Figure 4 shows the layout of the design.

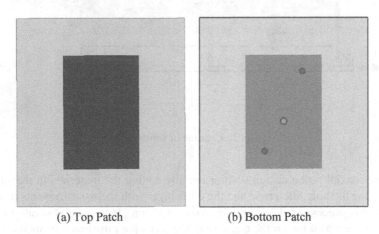

(a) Top Patch   (b) Bottom Patch

Fig. 4. Design Layout of Square shaped Microstrip Patch Antenna

Inserting ports – Input and output ports have been placed at the hole and in between the dielectric and the outer layer. Reference impedance is 50 ohms and the calibration is transmission line. This is an essential step as we provide patch for the power to be transmitted through the coaxial probe. Figure 5 shows the port placing in the coax.

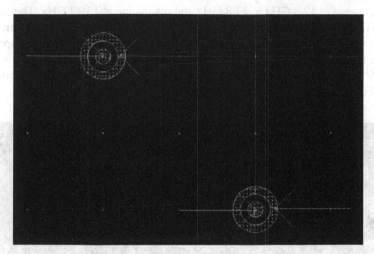

Fig. 5. Placement of ports in the square shaped microstrip patch antenna

3   Result and Analysis

Figure 6 represents the complete design of the antenna. S-parameters are the important consideration to analyse the output of our design, as they have both magnitude and phase information [9]. We can clearly see in Fig. 7 and 8 that the antenna is operating in the frequency range of 12.8 GHz to 13.8 GHz and resonating at 13.32 GHz. The simulated results give the value of S11 as −20.564 dB which is desirable. Ideally, an antenna should have S11 value −10 dB or better and thus the proposed antenna is having proper return loss. The transmission coefficient for the proposed antenna was theoretically supposed to be −28.8 dB or better; and the simulated results provide the transmission coefficient to be -29 dB.

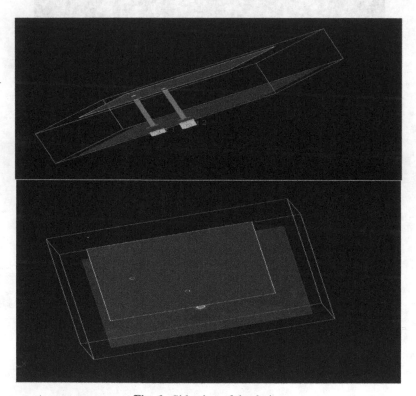

Fig. 6. Side view of the design

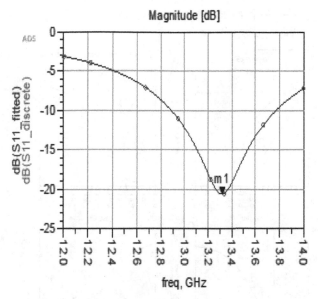

Fig. 7. Reflection coefficient of square shaped MPA

The radiation pattern of the proposed antenna is shown in Fig. 9 and the directivity of the antenna id 7.138 dBi.

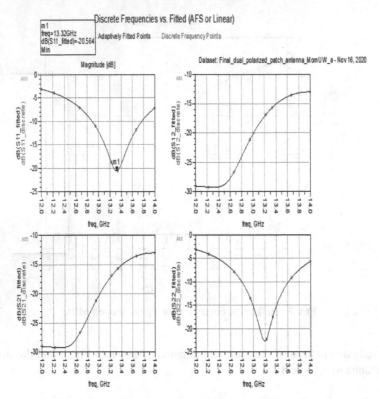

Fig. 8. S- parameters of square shaped microstrip patch antenna

Through the smith chart in Fig. 10, we can clearly see that the curve is approximately near 1.0 of the resistive line, that is, it is having a value of 0.84. This means that the source impedance closely matches the load impedance and thus having minimal reflected power and maximum power transfer from the source to load. Hence, we can conclude that the proposed antenna has good impedance match and resonating properly in KU band.

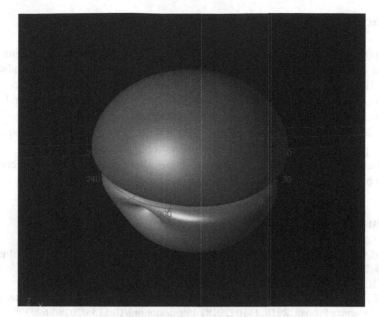

Fig. 9. Radiation Pattern

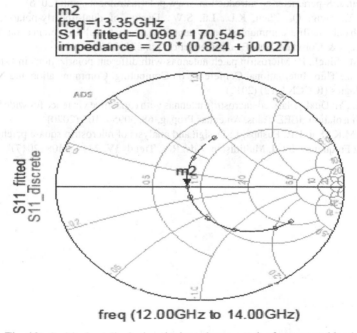

m2
freq=13.35GHz
S11_fitted=0.098 / 170.545
impedance = Z0 * (0.824 + j0.027)

freq (12.00GHz to 14.00GHz)

Fig. 10. Smith chart displaying the impedance match of source and load

4   Conclusion

A dual polarised square patch antenna with coaxial probe feeding operating in KU band that can be used in weather application purposes operating in the bandwidth of 12–14 GHz is designed in this paper. Orthogonal positioning of the feeds resulted in better cross-polarization suppression and isolation between the horizontal and vertical polarizations. Close impedance matching has been achieved, along with good return loss, transmission coefficient and directivity of −20.564 dB, −29 dB, 7.138 dBi respectively. Thus, the proposed antenna can be used for weather applications.

Further improvements can be done by using alternative methods to increase the isolation between the vertical and horizontal polarization.

References

1. Hamad Ameen, J.J.: Rain effect on KU-band satellite system. Electr. Electron. Eng.:Int. J. **4**(2), 13–23 (2015)
2. Garg, R., Bhartia, P., Bahl, I.: Microstrip Antenna Design Handbook (2001)
3. Gao, Z., Fang, Q., Jiang, S.: Research on a novel kind of dual polarized stacked printed antenna. Int. J. Antennas Propag. **2018**, 1–10 (2018). https://doi.org/10.1155/2018/8690308
4. Tripathi, K., Sharma, P., Sharma, S.: Design of coaxial feed microstrip patch antenna for S band application. Int. J. Sci. Res. Dev. **3**, 263–266 (2015)
5. Burnikell, J.:S-parameter an introduction. www.polarinstruments.com (2016)
6. Zhang, Y., Ding, Q., Zhen, K.L., Lü, S.W.: Design of dual-linearly-polarized antenna for Ku-band satellite communication system. In: International Conference on Microwave Technology & Computational Electromagnetics, pp. 221–224 (2011)
7. Singh, M., Singh, P.: Microstrip patch antennas with different polarizations in L-band applications. In: Third International Conference on Computing, Communication and Networking Technologies (ICCCNT'12) (2012)
8. He, Y., Li, Y.: Dual-polarized microstrip antennas with capacitive via fence for wide beamwidth and high isolation. IEEE Trans. Antennas Propag. **68**, 5095–5103 (2020)
9. Kumar, M.K., Sai, P.P., Pushpa, J.: Design and analysis of microstrip square patch antenna at 2.4 GHz Frequency. Int. J. Multidiscip. Adv. Res. Trends **IV**, 2349–7408 (2017)

Tumor Detection Using DWT and SVM in MRI Image

Rajat Rusia[1]([✉]) and Umashankar Kurmi[1,2]

[1] Electronics and Communication, LNCT University, Bhopal, India
rajatrusia@gmail.com
[2] Lakshmi Narayan College of Technology, Bhopal, India

Abstract. The brain is an essential part of the human body, which controls all the activities of the body. It is a very complex part of the human body which is a group of many cells, its work is sent and collected information from the body. A tumor is a mass of tissue formed by a group of abnormal cells that keep accumulating. When a tumor is formed and grows and goes deep into the brain, it is called a brain tumor. The reason for the formation and growth of Bain Tumor is still a subject of research, the reason for which no one knows exactly. A brain tumor is a relatively rare disease. Percent people have it, but its death rate is very high because the brain is the largest organ of the body, everything is controlled from here. It is necessary to identify brain tumor in the early stages so that the death rate can be reduced. For early detection of this problem, a model of a fast and accurate detection technique is being proposed by a computer, in which the data obtained from MRI scan will be processed with Image Segmentation and Detection Algorithm. It employs the Canny algorithm, Otsu algorithm, watershed and PSO algorithms for image segmentation, DWT methods for decomposition and feature extraction, and highly accurate SVM algorithms for tumor classification.

Keywords: MRI IMAGE Algorithm · Image Segmentation · Deep Learning · Brain Tumor · CAD

1 Introduction

One of the most prevalent brain illnesses, tumour, has impacted and taken many lives. According to the International Agency for Research on Cancer, about 97000 individuals die each year and an additional 126000 people are evaluated for neurological illnesses worldwide (IARC). Statistics demonstrate that individuals with brain tumours have a dismal survival rate, despite continued efforts to address the issue. To fight this, professionals have recently started to apply multidisciplinary methodologies to better understand the illness and develop more efficient treatment procedures, such as prescription learning, arithmetic, and software engineering.

Magnetic resonance imaging (MR) and computer tomography (CT) scanning of the brain are the two most common procedures used to identify the presence of a brain tumour and determine its location for the purpose of determining the most appropriate treatment options. Brain tumours can currently be treated in a number of ways. The methodologies and procedures utilised to identify brain tumours using MRI image segmentation are summarized in this publication. The discussion of upcoming developments in cutting-edge brain segmentation research concludes this paper.

2 Brain Tumor

A group of aberrant brain cells make up a brain tumour. Your skull, which is incredibly rigid, guards your brain. Any growth within such a constrained area can provide challenges. There are two types of brain tumours: benign (not cancerous) and malignant (cancerous) (benign). As benign or malignant tumours progress, the pressure inside your skull may increase. Brain injury from this has the potential to be lethal.

Brain tumours can be divided into primary and secondary types. Your brain itself is the site of a primary brain tumour. First-stage brain tumours are frequently totally benign. When cancer cells move from another organ to the brain, such as the lung or breast, this condition is referred to as metastatic brain tumour or secondary brain tumour.

3 MRI Image

MRI employs a strong magnetic field and radio waves to generate precise images of organs and tissues within the human body. Since its invention, MRI techniques have been refined by physicians and researchers to aid in treatment and research. The evolution of MRI has brought a revolution in medicine.

3.1 Fast Facts on MRI Scanning

- MRI scanning is a painless and non-invasive process.
- The first full-body MRI scanner, called the Indomitable, was invented by Raymond Damadian.
- A basic MRI scanner is priced at $150,000 and can cost several million dollars.
- Japan has the highest number of MRI scanners per capita, with 48 machines for every 100,000 people.

4 Literature Survey

The most challenging and promising area is the analysis and processing of MRI brain tumour images. The proper treatment for a tumour patient at the right time can be determined with the help of magnetic resonance imaging (MRI), a modern medical imaging technique that produces superb images of the body's internal organs.

Bahadure et al. [1] For the detection and classification of MRI-based brain tumours, proposed BWT and SVM algorithms are used in image processing. This approach had a 95% accuracy rate. Joseph et al. [2] suggested segmentation of MRI brain images for tumour image detection using the Kmeans clustering algorithm and morphological filtering Image processing is an ongoing study subject in the highly hard field of medical image processing. Alfonse and Salem [3] suggested segmentation of MRI brain images for tumour diagnosis utilising the morphological filtering and Kmeans clustering method Medical image processing is a particularly challenging area of image processing, which is an active study topic. For medical diagnosis, the interior of the human body is imaged using medical imaging techniques.

5 Proposed Method

5.1 Segmentation

In the proposed segmentation process the various algorithms and testing approaches are used are as follows:

Canny Algorithm
Canny edge detection is a technique that reduces the amount of data that needs to be processed while still extracting relevant structural information from various visual objects. It is commonly used in various computer vision systems. Canny discovered that the requirements for using edge detection in all vision systems are similar. As a result, an edge detection method that meets these requirements can be applied in a variety of situations.

Otsu Algorithm
In Otsu's algorithm is a popular thresholding method used for image segmentation. It is used to separate the foreground (object of interest) and background of an image by finding an optimal threshold value that maximizes the variance between the two classes.

    The Otsu algorithm works by considering all possible threshold values and calculating the variance between the foreground and background pixels for each threshold value. The threshold value that maximizes the variance is selected as the optimal threshold. This threshold is used to segment the image into foreground and background regions.

    The steps of Otsu's algorithm for image segmentation are as follows:

Compute a histogram of the image intensities.
Calculate the total number of pixels in the image.
Calculate the cumulative sum of the histogram and the cumulative sum of the histogram multiplied by the intensity values.
Calculate the mean intensity values of the foreground and background pixels for each threshold value.
Calculate the between-class variance for each threshold value.
Select the threshold value that maximizes the between-class variance.
The resulting threshold value is then used to binarize the image, with pixels above the threshold considered part of the foreground and pixels below the threshold considered part of the background.

Using Otsu's algorithm for image segmentation can provide an automatic and objective way to segment images, which can be useful in various applications such as medical image analysis, object recognition, and computer vision.

Watershed Algorithm

Any grayscale image can be regarded as a topographic map, with valleys and peaks represented by low intensity and peaks and hills by high intensity. We start by pouring varied coloured water into each isolated valley (local minimum) (labels). Depending on the peaks (gradients) nearby, water from various valleys will start to converge as it climbs, obviously with varied colours. Where water joins land, we build barriers to stop this. When all of the peaks are submerged, we will stop adding water and start building barriers. The result of segmentation is then produced by the constructed barriers.

However, this method results in over segmented findings because of noise or other anomalies in the image. Therefore, we developed a marker-based watershed method that allows you to select which valley points should be combined and which shouldn't.

Particle Swarm Optimization (PSO)

The initialization region $\Theta' \subseteq \Theta$ of the PSO method is filled with randomly generated particle placements. In order to stop particles from escaping the search space during the initial iterations, velocities are normally initialized within Θ', but they can also be set to zero or small random values. Throughout the algorithm's main loop, the particle's positions and speeds are iteratively updated until a halting requirement is satisfied. There are guidelines for updating:

$$V_I^{\rightarrow+1} = w v_i^{\rightarrow} + \varphi_1 U_1^{\rightarrow} \left(b_i^{\rightarrow} - x_i^{\rightarrow} \right) + \varphi_2 U_2^{\rightarrow} \left(l_i^{\rightarrow} - x_i^{\rightarrow} \right) \qquad (1)$$

$$x_i^{\rightarrow+1} = x_i^{\rightarrow} + v_i^{\rightarrow+1} \qquad (2)$$

5.2 Feature Extraction

For extraction of medical image data we used dyadic scales. Discrete wavelet transform (DWT) can be used to extract features from tumor images. The following steps describe how DWT can be used for feature extraction:

Preprocess the image: Preprocess the tumor image to enhance its features and reduce noise. This can include techniques such as image denoising, contrast enhancement, and edge detection.

Perform DWT: Use DWT to decompose the preprocessed image into its wavelet coefficients. DWT breaks down the image into different frequency bands, allowing us to analyze the image at different scales. The resulting coefficients can be used as features for tumor classification.

Select features: Select a subset of the wavelet coefficients as features for the SVM classifier. This can be done using techniques such as principal component analysis (PCA) or feature selection algorithms.

The equation for DWT can be written as:

$$c(j, k) = 1/\mathrm{sqrt}(2^j) * \mathrm{sum}(h(n)x(n - 2^{jk})) \qquad (3)$$

where:

c(j,k) is the wavelet coefficient at level j and position k, h(n) is the wavelet filter, x(n) is the input image, k is the position index, j is the level index.

The wavelet filter h(n) can be selected based on the desired wavelet family, such as Daubechies, Haar, or Symlet. The DWT algorithm can be applied recursively to obtain multiple levels of wavelet coefficients, which can capture different scales of image features.

5.3 Classification

Support Vector Machine (SVM)

Support vector machines (SVMs) are a type of machine learning algorithm that can be used for classification tasks, such as recognizing tumor images. The discrete wavelet transform (DWT) is a mathematical technique that can be used to analyze signals and images (Fig. 1).

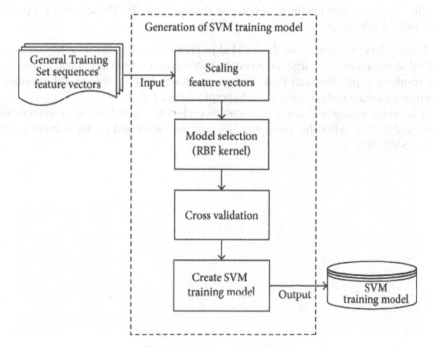

Fig. 1. Training a SVM Model

To train an SVM for tumor recognition using DWT, the following steps can be followed:

Preprocessing: Preprocess the tumor images to enhance their features and reduce noise. This can include techniques such as image denoising, contrast enhancement, and edge detection.
Feature extraction: Use DWT to extract relevant features from the preprocessed images. DWT breaks down the image into different frequency bands, allowing us to analyze the image at different scales. The resulting features can be used to train the SVM.
Training the SVM: it is Split the dataset two part training and testing. Training part used to train the SVM using the extracted features. SVM tries to find a boundary that best separates the two classes of data, in this case, tumor and non-tumor images.
Testing and evaluation: Used testing to check performance of trained system by SVM and calculate performance in term of accuracy, precision, recall and different score measurement.

$$f(x) = \text{sign}(w^T x + b) \tag{4}$$

where:

x is the input image feature vector,
w is the weight vector of the hyper plane.
b is the bias term, sign() is the sign function that returns +1 if the argument is positive or 0, and −1 otherwise.

During the training process, the SVM algorithm tries to find the optimal values of w and b that maximize the margin between the two classes of data (tumor and non-tumor). The resulting hyperplane can then be used to classify new images as either tumor or non-tumor based on which side of the hyperplane they fall.

The model selection is applied to feature vectors to select feature values like size, color, and texture. After this cross-validation of the vector and create a training set of data in SVM (Fig. 2).

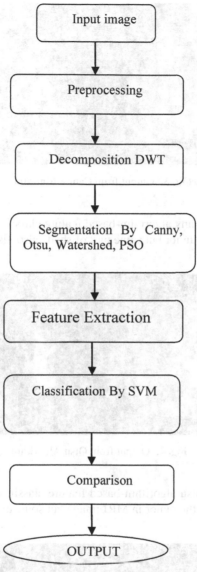

Fig. 2. Flow chart of proposed method

6   Simulation Results

In this section, the implementation results using MATLAB for medical image analysis are displayed, together with their parameters. Here take different MRI images and extract features using cany, otsu, watershed, PSO, and SVM. Here SVM is using the detection of Tumors in MRI Images.

292   R. Rusia and U. Kurmi

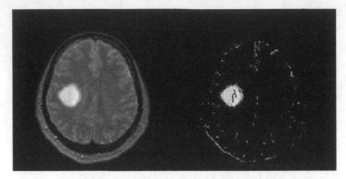

Fig. 3. Output from Canny Algorithm

Figure 3 shows the canny algorthim-based feature classification of MRI images. In this image try to classify tumor but some part of shade also visible.

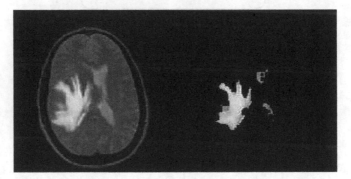

Fig. 4. Output from Otsu Algorithm

Figure 4 shows the otsu algorithm-based feature classification of MRI images. In this image try to classify the tumor in MRI image but some extra sections also extract.

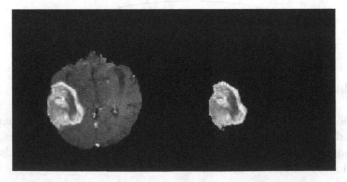

Fig. 5. Output from Watershed Algorithm (Malignant)

Figure 5 shows the Watershed algorithm-based feature classification of MRI images. In this image try to classify the tumor in an MRI image and extract all parts of tumor in image.

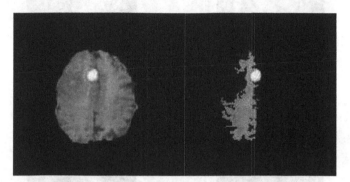

Fig. 6. Output from Canny Algorithm (Benign)

Figure 6 shows the canny algorthim-based feature classification of another MRI images. In this image try to classify tumor but some part of shade also visible (Figs. 7 and 8).

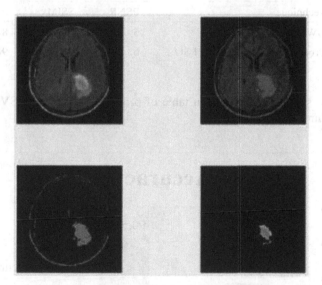

Fig. 7. Output from PSO Algorithm (Malignant)

Figure 4 shows the DWT, PSO, and SVM-based MRI Image Classification and detection of tumors in the image. This is efficient algorithm to get results (Table 1).

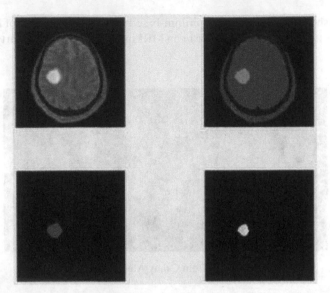

Fig. 8. Output from PSO Algorithm (Benign)

Table 1. Comparison

S.No.	Technique	PSNR	SSIM	Accuracy
1	BWT + SVM	59.63	0.7978	84%
2	Proposed DWT + SVM + PSO	63.24	0.9126	90.54%

This table shows the comparison table of proposed and existing SVM technique accuracy parameter (Fig. 9).

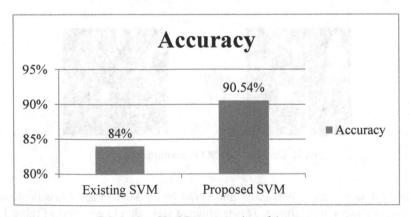

Fig. 9. Graphical Representation of Accuracy

7 Conclusion

The primary aim of this paper is to identify accurate and meaningful information using hybrid DWT and SVM algorithms with minimal errors for medical image processing. In this proposed brain tumor detection algorithm is work based on four section, image preprocessing is first section, after this image segmentation of medical image then extract information using feature extraction and last detect tumor by classification and detection method. The project explores various segmentation methods, and the system utilizes different techniques and parameters to improve efficiency and produce superior results.

The region growing strategy produces better outcomes than the boundary approach and the edge-based approach in segmentation. It is discovered that the tumors are segregated most precisely using the particle swarm optimization approach. Efficiency is improved by the features extracted using the DWT approach since it allows for the extraction of fine tumor details using a variety of characteristics. Support Vector Machine was found experimentally to provide the best classification accuracy of the many classification methods investigated. Due to the fact that a patient's life hinges on the prognoses provided by the system, precision and reliability are vital in tumor diagnosis. By using this hybrid method get higher accuracy of prediction and minimum error.

References

1. Abd Alreda, B.M., Khalif, T.H.K., Saeid, T.: Automated brain tumor detection based on feature extraction from the MRI brain image analysis. Iraqi J. Electr. Electron. Eng. **19**, 1–10 (2020)
2. Alfonse, M., Salem, A.B.M.: An automatic classification of brain tumors through MRI using support vector machine. Egypt. Comput. Sci. J. **40**(3), 11–21 (2016)
3. Bahadure, N.B., Ray, A.K., Thethi, H.P.: Image analysis for MRI based brain tumor detection and feature extraction using biologically inspired BWT and SVM. Int. J. Biomed. Imaging **2017**, 9749108 (2017)
4. Chaddad, A.: Automated feature extraction in brain tumor by magnetic resonance imaging using Gaussian mixture models. Int. J. Biomed. Imaging **2015**, 868031 (2015)
5. Coatrieux, G., Huang, H., Shu, H., Luo, L., Roux, C.: A watermarking-based medical image integrity control system and an image moment signature for tampering characterization. IEEE J. Biomed. Health Inform. **17**(6), 1057–1067 (2013)
6. Cui, W., Wang, Y., Fan, Y., Feng, Y., Lei, T.: Localized FCM clustering with spatial information for medical image segmentation and bias field estimation. Int. J. Biomed. Imaging **2013**, 930301 (2013)
7. Faisal, Z., El Abbadi, N.K.: Detection and recognition of brain tumor based on DWT, PCA and ANN. Indonesia J. Electr. Eng. Comput. Sci. **18**(1), 56–63 (2020)
8. Joseph, R.P., Singh, C.S., Manikandan, M.: Brain tumor MRI image segmentation and detection in image processing. Int. J. Res. Eng. Technol. **3**(1), 1–5 (2014)
9. Kamil, S.Y., Altaei, M.S.M.: Brain tumor diagnosis using MR image processing. Al-Nahrain J. Sci. **23**(2), 67–74 (2020)
10. Kumar, P., Vijayakumar, B.: Brain tumor MR image segmentation and classification using by PCA and RBF kernel based support vector machine. Middle-East J. Sci. Res. **23**(9), 2106–2116 (2015)
11. Kumar, A.: Study and analysis of different segmentation methods for brain tumor MRI application. Multimed. Tools Appl. **82**, 7117–7139 (2022)

12. Qian, Z., Xie, L., Xu, Y.: 3D Automatic segmentation of brain tumor based on deep neural network and multimodal MRI Images. Emergency Med. Int. **2022**, 5356069 (2022)
13. Sharma, N., Ray, A.K., Sharma, S., Shukla, K.K., Pradhan, S., Aggarwal, L.M.: Segmentation and classification of medical images using texture-primitive features: application of BAM-type artificial neural network. J. Med. Phys. **33**(3), 119 (2008)
14. Yao, J., Chen, J., Chow, C.: Breast tumor analysis in dynamic contrast enhanced MRI using texture features and wavelet transform. IEEE J. Sel. Top. Signal Process. **3**(1), 94–100 (2009)
15. Zanaty, E.A.: Determination of gray matter (GM) and white matter (WM) volume in brain magnetic resonance images (MRI). Int. J. Comput. Appl. **45**(3), 16–22 (2012)
16. Chinnam, S.K.R., Sistla, V., Kolli, V.K.K.: SVM-PUK kernel based MRI-brain tumor identification using texture and Gabor. Int. Inform. Eng. Technol. Assoc. **36**(2), 185–191 (2019)
17. Rajan, P.G., Sundar, C.: Brain tumor detection and segmentation by intensity adjustment. J. Med. Syst. **43**(8), 282 (2019). https://doi.org/10.1007/s10916-019-1368-4
18. Choudhury, C.L., Mahanty, C., Kumar, R., Mishra. B.K.: Brain tumor detection and classification using convolutional neural network and deep neural network. In: 2020 International Conference on Computer Science, Engineering and Applications (ICCSEA), pp. 1–4. IEEE (2020)
19. Bhandari, A., Koppen, J., Agzarian, M.: Convolutional neural networks for brain tumour segmentation. Insights Imaging **11**, 77 (2020). https://doi.org/10.1186/s13244-020-00869-4

TiGen – Title Generator Based on Deep NLP Transformer Model for Scholarly Literature

Deepali Bajaj, Urmil Bharti$^{(\boxtimes)}$, Hunar Batra, Eshika Gupta, Arupriya, Shruti Singh, and Tanya Negi

Shaheed Rajguru College of Applied Sciences for Women, University of Delhi, New Delhi, India
{deepali.bajaj,urmil.bharti}@rajguru.du.ac.in, i@hunarbatra.com

Abstract. Finding an appropriate title that comprehends readers clearly about the research is a challenging task. In this paper, we present a tool TiGen to generate suitable titles for their scholarly literature after parsing its abstract as input. We used GPT-2, a deep natural language processing transformer model to generate title suggestions. It is an auto-regressive pre-trained model with masked self-attention. The model has been trained with arXiv dataset which is scraped off selectively to keep the fields of the obtained dataset limited only to "Natural Language Processing". TiGen is fed with a research abstract as input via a transformer architecture of neural networks corresponding to the decoder segment, for generating a list of titles. The results are evaluated using ROUGE-1 and ROUGE-L scores and validated against the state-of-the-art research work in this domain. To prove the usability of our work, the title of this paper is also auto-generated by TiGen.

Keywords: Keyword4 GPT-2 · Natural Language Processing and Generation · Transformer Models · Deep Learning Generative Models · Self-attention style

1 Introduction

Research is growing day by day and so is the number of scholarly articles. Nearly 1.35 lakh scientific scholarly articles are published every year. According to a US government agency, India is the third-largest publisher of science and technology articles all across the world, topped by China [1]. In fact, the number of publications are rising by a million every five years [2] as shown in Fig. 1.

Generally, astute readers search through the database of indexed titles of scholarly literature by typing-in the keywords close to the discipline of their interest. Scholarly articles with the best match to the search criteria pop up first, and many other good papers which do not manage to make it to the top searches get overlooked because of their unremarkable titles. Thus, a suitable title helps readers in finding relevant work across the world of scholarly research. Lousily constructed titles could also increase the chances of immediate desk rejection while peer-reviewing or might mislead potential readers [3]. It is, therefore, important to include the words in the titles that best describe the content of the paper briefly and the readers are likely to use during a searching spree. This is what TiGen is believed to do by facilitating title generation for research papers

© The Author(s), under exclusive license to Springer Nature Switzerland AG 2023
R. S. Tomar et al. (Eds.): CNC 2022, CCIS 1893, pp. 297–309, 2023.
https://doi.org/10.1007/978-3-031-43140-1_26

with all the keywords included just by feeding it with their abstract using advanced artificial intelligence capabilities. Since the abstract of a research article describes the main essence of the author's work and displays crux of the paper, it can be used alone instead of the entire paper to generate congruous titles for the papers.

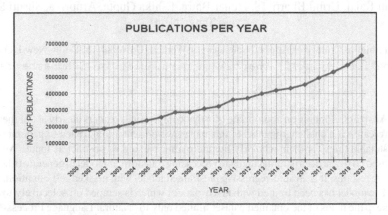

Fig. 1. Number of publications growing per year

With Natural Language Processing (NLP), a subset of Artificial Intelligence (AI), machines have made huge advances in recent years in understanding human language. Transfer learning enabled by pre-trained models is the reason for this surge in its popularity over the time. First addressed for neural networks training in 1976 [4], transfer learning has been on a rise since then. Transfer learning facilitates scientists to train an NLP model on a large dataset and then fine-tune it to create innovative applications. Pre-trained models such as OpenAI GPT [5], GPT-2 [6] (a successor to GPT), and BERT [7] have been the most popular ones among others, with each having its own advantages and disadvantages. Although both BERT and GPT-2 have been satisfactory in text generation, GPT-2 which depends on the decoder-only segment of the transformer, wins the race [8]. The auto-regressive nature of GPT-2 motivated us to use it for our TiGen tool for the title generation task over the auto-encoder based BERT [35] for this work.

We have used transfer learning by adopting the statistical approach toward title generation [9]. The basic idea behind it is to first learn the correlation between the titles and the words in the corresponding abstracts from a given training corpus consisting of 'Abstract-Title' pair, and then apply that learning to generate titles for new abstracts.

For this piece of research work, we scraped 'Abstract-Title' pair of approximately 500 research papers pertaining to the domain of NLP. We have fine-tuned 117M (small) and 345M (medium) GPT-2 models on the scraped corpus for generating titles for research abstracts and further, analyzed the results generated by both the models. Through extensive experimentation and analysis, we observed that the 345M, being a better model, was generating superior results than the 117M. Thus, we restricted ourselves to using 345M as the working model behind TiGen. We have fine-tuned certain parameters like *temperature, top_k, top_p*, etc. to obtain satisfactory results. Most of the results generated by TiGen were coherent and semantically apt. We evaluated the quality of the titles generated by the TiGen for a particular abstract using ROUGE-1 and ROUGE-L scores. To the best of our knowledge, we are the pioneers in using a pre-trained model specifically GPT-2 to carry out the title generation task. Our automatic title generation tool will be useful for researchers engaged in publishing activities by suggesting the most relevant titles for their abstract. In order to demonstrate the usefulness of our research work, the actual title of this paper is also auto-generated by TiGen.

In the following section, we describe what other research work has been undertaken prior to our work in this discipline. Section 3, throws light on the motivation behind our research and establishes the context of this study. Section 4 introduces the dataset, techniques, and software we used to make TiGen a reality. The approach we adopted and the experiments we conducted are described in Sect. 5. Experimental results demonstrating the advantages of this approach are described in Sect. 6. Section 7 concludes the research work along with the future scope of work.

2 Related Work

Many researchers have contributed their efforts towards the field of title generation. Wei Liu et.al. [10] proposed a Quality-Diversity Automatic Summarization (QDAS) model enhanced by *sentence2vec* and applied transfer learning for the Wikipedia Headline Generation task. They primarily worked on summarizing multilingual Wikipedia text and generating titles on low resource corpus. They first focused on extractive summarization of the entire text that contains the key information, then reconstructing the titles based on those summaries.

Similar work using NLP techniques was carried out by Sethi et al. [11]. They proposed title generation by finding the vital theme of the story or a document written in English without the need to the entire text or document. Their proposed system has various steps involved like lexical analysis, part-of-speech tagging, discourse analysis, frequency of tokens, prioritizing frequencies, noun and adjective combination, identifying idiom-based title, etc.

Jin et al. [12] proposed a new probabilistic model for title generation; they divided the process into two steps: finding appropriate words and framing the sequence. Firstly, the words are takeout and stored in an 'information source' which is a kind of interim storage and then on the basis of these extracted words, the title is generated.

Lopez et al. [13] contributed to titling electronic documents using text mining techniques. Their automatic titling method is developed in four steps. Firstly, it determines the characteristics of the texts to be titled, then moving forward it assumes that there are at least a few sentences that might contribute to titling, then it extracts noun phrases for titling as around 85% of the nouns make up relevant titles and at the end, they used ChTITRES approach to rank the noun phrase.

Chen et al. [14] presented a technique for domain adaptation for title generation using artificial titles. The authors used an encoder-decoder RNN model for title generation from a domain marked source to an unlabeled domain target. Sequential training was used to capture the grammatical style of the unlabeled target domain. The source data and unlabeled target domain information were encoded as their definition representations by a bidirectional LSTM.

A. Waheed et al. [15] sampled title tokens from a local distribution of the domain-specific vocabulary to generate a catchy title and closely linking it to its corresponding abstract by exploiting the T5 model. Despite the fact that it's a new technology and it might generate better text, it leaves behind huge carbon footprints because of its big size, hence requiring extensive and prolonged training which is a big concern [16]. Gavrilov et al. [17] used Universal Transformer Architecture with byte-pair encoding that employs self-attention to produce headlines for news articles.

One significant contribution in the field of pre-trained models which motivated us is by Lee et al. [18]. They explored the area of generating patent claims by fine-tuning OpenAI GPT-2. They experimented with the fine-tuning process by considering the first 100 steps and looking at the generated text. On the basis of both conditional and unconditional random sampling, they analyzed the goodness of the generated patent claims.

Nowadays, state-of-the-art (SOTA) models have taken over the world of NLP, making it a model that can be leveraged everywhere for completing any NLP tasks. But most of the existing literature studies mentioned above have adopted primitive approaches like observing the pattern of how titles are structured with POS (part-of-speech) tagging, frequency of tokens, etc. or formulating a summary first after reading the entire text then extracting the main theme to construct the title. Instead of designing algorithms for these primitive techniques manually, SOTA models use attention to extract the text's essence or words of greater importance.

In our work, we've used a pre-trained transformer model (here, GPT-2) instead of using *seq2seq* models (RNN, LSTM) because they handle sequences word-by-word while a transformer achieves parallelization by removing recurrence and convolution and replacing them with self-attention to judge the dependencies between inputs and outputs. Also, *seq2seq* models (RNN, LSTM) can produce fairly relevant titles but they require a large amount of training data, whereas our model can be trained using a smaller dataset. Thus, shortening of the training time as well as improved performance is achieved by our approach.

To ease up the task of writing a research paper, TiGen can generate apt and coherent titles using GPT-2. As of now, we have trained TiGen on only NLP-related scholarly articles' abstracts and their corresponding titles to generate meaningful and innovative titles related to the abstract entered by the user. We use the ROUGE score for evaluating the suggested titles. We assume we are the first ones to carry out research that can generate titles for scholarly articles using the pre-trained language model GPT-2.

3 Background and Motivation

Good, descriptive, and out-of-the-ordinary titles are not only important for scholarly articles but for any other article and even for novels, poems, etc. A certain veteran teacher at a certain meeting said, "I can usually anticipate the mark for a paper by glancing at the title" [19]. These words motivated us in undertaking this research. Even while searching for scholarly articles, articles with striking, descriptive titles tend to draw more attention and hence bring more readers and citations than other papers with monotonous titles which are then usually disregarded no matter their quality. This shows the importance of a good title for a research paper which pushed us a little more towards this purpose.

Going back in time, we can see that many models have served in the field of text generation so far, but with AI progressing every day, new models are debuting every now and then continuously outshining the ones prior to them. Markov Chain [20] was the earliest algorithm mainly used in old versions of smart phone keyboards based on random probability distribution. It models the finite set of states having hooked probability of changing from a given state to another. It predicts the next word on the basis of the current word. As the model has short memory which is an immense concern, the prognosis only involves the active state, it forgets the past states. It does not predict the word based on input sequence i.e. they don't work sequentially rather depend on individual patterns.

Moving forward in time, the context of sequential models is well covered by Recurrent Neural Network (RNN). RNN is a progressive sequence model [21] which processes the data in a sequential form, proceeding word by word. But it is not very virtuous when it comes to handling long sequences as it sometimes mixes up the entire content of adjacent positions, thus greater the steps, greater the challenge for the RNN to make a decision. It also lacks the advantage of fast computing devices such as GPUs. Overcoming the vanishing gradient problem which RNN suffers from, a new neural networks Long Short-Term Memory (LSTM) [22] broadens its features to incorporate the usage of the information i.e. it leverages the process to identify which information needs to be remembered by the cell and which is to be lost. It's good but not good enough to be trained in parallel.

Both RNN and LSTM are used for short-term memory learning, but the invention of the transformer model made every invention listed so far speechless. According to the paper titled 'Attention Is All You Need' [23], transformers are the first transduction models which adopted the mechanism of self-attention for computing representations of its input or output without involving sequence aligned RNNs mostly used in encoder-decoder architecture.

Now transformers have become the model of choice for NLP problems. Their parallelizability allows them to be trained on large datasets. This led to the development of pre-trained systems such as BERT, GPT, etc.

In February 2019, GPT-2 was released by OpenAI as a successor to GPT. It is a pre-trained transformer language model based on deep learning that predicts the next word by looking at the part of the sentence, each token of the word generated has the linkage with the previous word. Its robustness is reasoned with i) Self-attention mechanism which enables the model to focus on only selected sides of the input, and ii) Superiority in quality, also being more parallelizable and requires less time in training. These advantages make GPT-2 a better choice over every other model making it worthy of being the brain behind TiGen.

4 Experimental Set-Up

In this section, we will describe the setup, architecture as shown in Fig. 2 and the approach we adopted to deploy the GPT-2 model for our tool TiGen, in greater depth. Our approach includes scraping of the dataset, fine tuning GPT-2 and its deployment using Google Colab GPU environment.

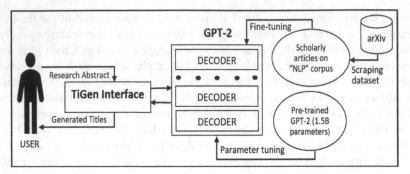

Fig. 2. *TiGen* Architecture

4.1 Dataset

Our training dataset is the corpus of 'Abstract-Title' pairs of approximately five-hundred research papers limited to the keyword 'NLP', which roughly adds up to 140,000 tokens cumulatively. It has been scraped from a public server repository called arXiv which is an open-access repository of e-prints approved for posting after moderation. For the purpose of validation, abstracts of fifty handpicked research papers limited to "NLP" have been used.

4.2 Pre-Trained Models

There are various robust pre-trained models functioning in the real world. But, one of the many reasons why we chose OpenAI's GPT-2 is that it outperforms other language models trained on domains like Wikipedia, news, or books without needing to use these domain-specific training datasets. On language tasks like reading comprehension, summarization, and machine translation, GPT-2 begins to learn these tasks from a dataset of millions of web pages called WebText [6].

Generative Pre-trained Transformer 2 (GPT-2) by OpenAI is a model based on transformers, leveraging the decoder component only. It was trained on an enormous dataset of 40 GB called WebText that the OpenAI researchers derived from the Internet. The GPT-2 model consists of 4 different sizes in terms of architectural hyper parameters including 117M, 345M, 762M, and 1542M. It works on the idea of auto-regression utilizing only the decoder block of the transformer, unlike BERT. The auto-regressive nature of GPT-2 makes the self-attention layer mask future tokens by not attending to tokens that are "in the future" i.e., on the right of the current word, but only to those "in the past". This is called masked self-attention which is absent in BERT. GPT-2 can process up to 1024 tokens and it incorporates a vocabulary of size 50,257.

For TiGen, we experimented with both the 117M model consisting of 12 layers and the 345M model having 24 layers, but not with high-end models like 774M and 1.5B which are incompatible with the Google Colab GPU environment because of limited GPU memory available. We got highly satisfactory results in terms of coherency and relatability with the fed-in abstract by both models. But after rigorous experimentation and analysis, the probability of noteworthy results came out to be greater in the case of the 345M model than the other one. Thus, to get better results every time, we deployed the 345M model for TiGen.

4.3 Deployment

For computing, we leveraged Google Colab for GPU and CPU. Though runtime is limited to only twelve continuous hours per session, it was sufficient for all our experiments because of the low training time required. Such a low-cost solution may make it easier for us to try different experiments. The GPU available on Colab for our experiments was NVIDIA Tesla K80/T4 (randomly allocated) equipped with 15 GB memory when connected with Google Drive.

5 Experiments

This section presents the experiments we conducted to train GPT-2 and parameter tuning for TiGen. Detailed overview of the model and the experiments are also given here.

5.1 Parameters Tuning

GPT-2 is fed with 1.5 billion parameters. *TiGen* uses a combination of some of those parameters to generate apt titles. Few important parameters which *TiGen* used are [24]:

- *length*: It defines the number of tokens to be generated. The default length is 1024 tokens [34]. Greater length corresponds to titles containing large numbers of useless tokens (words) making it lengthy. Smaller length leads to incomplete titles which are not sensible due to incomplete words. TiGen sets the length at 30 characters as this value gives medium-length titles covering the main essence of the abstract.
- *temperature*: It controls the randomness of the text being generated [34]. During experimentation, we observed that a smaller value of temperature was leading to the generation of many duplicate and dull titles. As the temperature increases, the creativity of the text generated increases, so for TiGen we set temperature as 0.80 to produce a combination of interesting, relatable, and sensible words as the title.
- *top_k*: It limits the generated predictions to k predictions. The default value is 0 which completely disables the behaviour. It upgrades the quality by making the probability to deviate from the specified topic low. *Top_k* values can range from 0 to 100. In *top_k* sampling, k most likely next words are selected and probability mass is redistributed among only those words. For sensible titles, we set top_k to 40.
- *top_p*: Nucleus sampling limits the generated predictions to greater than a cumulative probability. *Top_p* ranges from 0 to 1. Despite choosing k most likely words, top_p selects amongst the smallest possible set of words whose cumulative probability exceeds the threshold p. For best results, we set *top_p* to 0.9.
- *prefix*: It enables the model to extract information from it and to generate text beginning with the given character sequence. In TiGen, the research abstract entered by the user is fed as a prefix to the model.
- *nsamples*: It facilitates the user to obtain a desired number of titles at once. For TiGen, *nsamples* has been set to 5, to provide users with up to five title suggestions for their research abstract. Further, we rank the generated samples based on the ROUGE evaluations for each generated title.

5.2   Training Loss in Fine-Tuning

For the language model fine-tuning, causal language modeling (CLM) loss has been used. After 500 epochs of training on the model using NVIDIA Tesla T4/K80 GPU over the corpus, we have attained a training loss of 1.00, with a 1.37 average loss as shown in Fig. 3. It took us approximately an hour to run 500 training epochs. In this experiment, we've set the learning rate to its default value i.e., 1e-4. Learning rate is a hyper-parameter that defines how quickly the neural network is updating the concepts it has learnt.

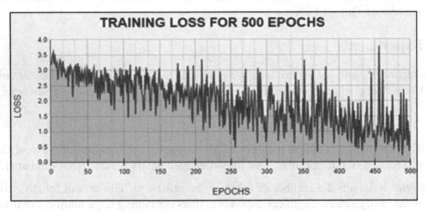

Fig. 3. Training Loss in Fine-Tuning

6   Results

As human judgment on a title quality can be subjective, to give the results generated by TiGen some metrics for evaluation and authenticity, we have used ROUGE scores. Recall-Oriented Understudy for Gisting Evaluation (ROUGE) is a set of metrics used to evaluate the quality of text generated by a model as well as machine translation [25]. According to recent research, it is the most reliable and balanced approach to assess the effectiveness of the text generated by the model. The following ROUGE scoring metrics have been used to gauge the generated titles:

- ROUGE-1: The measure of unigram (one word) overlap of system generated sentences to the reference sentences.
- ROUGE-L: The measure of longest common subsequence (LCS) between our model output and reference sentences.

For TiGen, we calculated F-measures of ROUGE-1 and ROUGE-L for all titles generated for a given abstract using our fine-tuned GPT-2 345M model.

F-measure is the measure of a text's accuracy. It is calculated from precision and recall of text, where precision is the number of true positive results divided by the number of all positive results, including those not identified correctly, and the recall is the number of true positive results divided by the number of all samples that should have been identified as positive.

$$F-measure = \left(1 + \beta^2\right) \cdot \frac{precision.recall}{precision.\beta^2 + recall} \tag{1}$$

where β is the ratio of Precision and Recall.

To evaluate our approach, we have taken one of the previous works titled "Serverless Deployment of a Voice-Bot for Visually Impaired" published in International Conference on Applied Soft Computing and Communication Networks (ACN'20) held in Chennai, India during October 14–17, 2020 [26], and fed its abstract to TiGen to generate titles. For reference, we have presented a list of generated titles ranked according to their F-measure of ROUGE-L evaluations. Table 1 displays the success of TiGen as an automated text generative tool that can be highly helpful to the researchers.

Table 1. Results showing generated titles and ROUGE scores for selected Research Article

Titles generated by *TiGen*	F-Measure	
	ROUGE-1	ROUGE-L
Feed-O-Back: A serverless Teachers Feedback Voice Bot for Visually Impaired Students	0.57	0.57
Serverless conversational AI for visually impaired students: a case study	0.53	0.42
Feed-O-Back bot for visually impaired students for Firebase	0.42	0.42
Feed-O-Back: A serverless conversational machine intelligence tool for visually impaired students	0.46	0.36

We have also compared the generated titles with their actual ones for 50 sample articles pertaining to the domain of "NLP". A comparison of actual and generated titles and their ROUGE scores for eight such research articles is shown in Table 2.

To validate our approach, we have compared our results with that of two other related studies, A. Waheed et al. [15], and Gavrilov et al. [17] as these two studies has presented their results in terms of ROUGE scores. Our results show superiority in terms of average F-measures of ROUGE-1 and ROUGE-L as depicted in Table 3. From the results, it is evident that TiGen is capable of generating highly relevant titles for scholarly literature articles.

Table 2. Comparison of actual titles with generated titles and their ROUGE scores

Actual Title	Titles Generated by *TiGen*	F-Measure	
		ROUGE-1	ROUGE-L
Event-Driven Headline Generation [27]	When headlines land: an event-driven headline generation model	0.63	0.61
Polyglot: Distributed Word Representations for Multilingual NLP [28]	Word embeddings for multilingual nlp	0.8	0.8
Domain Controlled Title Generation with Human Evaluation [15]	Generating domain controlled titles with natural language processing	0.65	0.58
BRAT: a Web-based Tool for NLP-Assisted Text Annotation [29]	Brat: web-based natural language processing tool for structured annotation	0.6	0.6
How Transferable are Neural Networks in NLP Applications? [30]	Transferability of neural networks in nlp	0.62	0.6
Visualizing and Understanding Neural Models in NLP [31]	Visualizing compositionality in neural models for nlp	0.71	0.57
A Primer on Neural Network Models for Natural Language Processing [32]	Neural network models for natural language processing: an overview	0.88	0.77
Attention in Natural Language Processing [33]	Taxonomic hierarchy of attention-based neural networks in natural language processing	0.63	0.63

Table 3. Result comparison with related studies

Approach	F-Measure	
	ROUGE-1	ROUGE-L
A. Waheed et.al (2021)	31.5	21.6
Gavrilov et. al. (2019)	26.86	24.84
TiGen (Our Work)	55.6	51.8

7   Conclusion and Future Work

The growing interest in scientific research leads to several research papers being published every year around the globe. But any scholarly articles get lesser recognition without an apt title. In this paper, we have proposed an approach for title generation for scholarly research papers using an auto-regressive state-of-the-art model to facilitate researchers with a seemingly hectic task of formulating coherent and eye-catching titles for their research papers. We have leveraged a transformer-based pre-trained model i.e. GPT-2 developed by OpenAI. Our tool TiGen manifests the success of GPT-2, which adapts to the natural writing style of the conditioning text to produce a list of relevant titles. Also, different sizes releases of the model make a huge difference in regard to the results. We choose 345M as the larger model produces better results in comparison to the smaller or the default 117M model. Concerning the validation of the obtained results, ROUGE scores are utilized which is a better way to compare automatically generated titles against their respective actual titles. Title of this paper itself is generated using TiGen.

To take this work further in future, other advanced transformer-based models such as GPT-3, an immediate successor to GPT-2, can be used. It is currently under beta-testing and soon its source code will be publicly released. We will polish our work by deploying the 762M and 1.5B size releases of GPT-2 to achieve more progressive and cogent outcomes. The scope of the data on which TiGen is trained can be broadened to other disciplines in future research. Also, we aspire to generate only new and unique titles for the research papers that are free from plagiarism.

References

1. US National Science Foundation: "India is world's third largest producer of scientific articles: Report," The Economic Times. https://economictimes.indiatimes.com/news/science/india-is-worlds-third-largest-producer-of-scientific-articles-report/articleshow/72868640.cms (2019). Accessed: 11 Sep 2022
2. Dimensions, "Publications per year," https://app.dimensions.ai/discover/publication (2021). Accessed: 18 Sep 2022
3. Conn, V.S.: Excellent titles make stellar first impressions. West. J. Nurs. Res. **42**(1), 3–3 (2020). https://doi.org/10.1177/0193945919879036
4. Bozinovski, S.: Reminder of the first paper on transfer learning in neural networks, 1976. Informatica **44**(3), 291–302 (2020)
5. Radford, A., Narasimhan, K., Salimans, T., Sutskever, I.: Improving language understanding by generative pre-training (2018)
6. Radford, A., et al.: Language models are unsupervised multitask learners. OpenAI blog **1**(8), 9 (2019)
7. Devlin, J., Chang, M.-W., Lee, K., Toutanova, K.: Bert: Pre-training of deep bidirectional transformers for language understanding. In: Proceedings of NAACL-HLT, pp. 4171 4186. Association for Computational Linguistics, Minneapolis, Minnesota, 2–7 June 2019
8. Wang, A., Cho, K.: Bert has a Mouth, and it must Speak: Bert as a Markov Random field Language Model, pp. 30–36. Association for Computational Linguistics. Minneapolis, Minnesota (2019)
9. Jin, R., Hauptmann, A.: Learning to select good title words: an new approach based on reverse information retrieval. In: Eighteenth International Conference Machine Learning (ICML-2001) (2001)
10. Liu, W., Li, L., Huang, Z., Liu, Y.: Multi-lingual Wikipedia summarization and title generation on low resource corpus. In: Proceedings of the Workshop MultiLing 2019: Summarization Across Languages, Genres and Sources, pp. 17–25 (2019)
11. Sethi, N., Agrawal, P., Madaan, V., Singh, S.K., Kumar, A.: Automated title generation in English language using NLP. Int. J. Control Theory Appl. **9**(11), 5159–5168 (2016)

12. Jin, R., Hauptmann, A.G.: A new probabilistic model for title generation. In: COLING 2002: The 19th International Conference on Computational Linguistics (2002)
13. Lopez, C., Prince, V., Roche, M.: How to title electronic documents using text mining techniques. Int. J. Comput. Inf. Syst. Ind. Manag. Appl. **4**, 562–569 (2012)
14. Chen, F., Chen, Y.-Y.: Adversarial domain adaptation using artificial titles for abstractive title generation. In: Proceedings of the 57th Annual Meeting of the Association for Computational Linguistics, pp. 2197–2203 (2019)
15. Waheed, A., Goyal, M., Mittal, N., Gupta, D.: Domain-controlled title generation with human evaluation. In: Khanna, A., Gupta, D., Bhattacharyya, S., Hassanien, A.E., Anand, S., Jaiswal, A. (eds.) International Conference on Innovative Computing and Communications: Proceedings of ICICC 2021, vol. 2, pp. 461–474. Springer Singapore, Singapore (2022). https://doi.org/10.1007/978-981-16-2597-8_39
16. Patterson, D., et al.: Carbon emissions and large neural network training. arXiv Prepr. arXiv2104.10350 (2021)
17. Gavrilov, D., Kalaidin, P., Malykh, V.: Self-attentive model for headline generation. In: European Conference on Information Retrieval, pp. 87–93 (2019)
18. Lee, J.-S., Hsiang, J.: Patent claim generation by fine-tuning OpenAI GPT-2. World Pat. Inf. **62**, 101983 (2020)
19. Crosby, H.H.: Titles, a treatise on. Coll. Compos. Commun. **27**(4), 387–391 (1976)
20. Awiszus, M., Rosenhahn, B.: Markov chain neural networks. In: Proceedings of the IEEE Conference on Computer Vision and Pattern Recognition Workshops, pp. 2180–2187 (2018)
21. Graves, A.: Generating sequences with recurrent neural networks. arXiv Prepr. arXiv1308.0850 (2013)
22. Graves, A.: Long short-term memory. In: Graves, A. (ed.) Supervised Sequence Labelling with Recurrent Neural Networks, pp. 37–45. Springer Berlin Heidelberg, Berlin, Heidelberg (2012). https://doi.org/10.1007/978-3-642-24797-2_4
23. Vaswani, A., et al.: Attention is all you need. In: Advances in Neural Information Processing Systems, pp. 5998–6008 (2017)
24. Woolf, M.: How To Make Custom AI-Generated Text With GPT-2. AI Text Generation (2019). https://minimaxir.com/2019/09/howto-gpt2/. Accessed 21 July 2022
25. Lin, C.-Y.: Rouge: a package for automatic evaluation of summaries. In: Text Summarization Branches out, pp. 74–81. Association for Computational Linguistics, Barcelona, Spain (2004)
26. Bajaj, D., Bharti, U., Batra, H., Goel, A., Gupta, S.C.: Serverless deployment of a voice-bot for visually impaired. In: Thampi, S.M., Mauri, J.L., Fernando, X., Boppana, R., Geetha, S., Sikora, A. (eds.) Applied Soft Computing and Communication Networks: Proceedings of ACN 2020, pp. 189–206. Springer Singapore, Singapore (2021). https://doi.org/10.1007/978-981-33-6173-7_13
27. Sun, R., Zhang, Y., Zhang, M., Ji, D.: Event-driven headline generation. In: Proceedings of the 53rd Annual Meeting of the Association for Computational Linguistics and the 7th International Joint Conference on Natural Language Processing (vol. 1: Long Papers), pp. 462–472 (2015)
28. Al-Rfou, R., Perozzi, B., Skiena, S.: Polyglot: Distributed word representations for multilingual nlp. In: Proceedings of the Seventeenth Conference on Computational Natural Language Learning, pp. 183–192. Association for Computational Linguistics, Sofia, Bulgaria
29. Stenetorp, P., Pyysalo, S., Topić, G., Ohta, T., Ananiadou, S., Tsujii, J.: BRAT: a web-based tool for NLP-assisted text annotation. In: Proceedings of the Demonstrations at the 13th Conference of the European Chapter of the Association for Computational Linguistics, pp. 102–107 (2012)
30. Mou, L., et al.: How transferable are neural networks in nlp applications?. In: Proceedings of Conference on Empirical Methods in Natural Language Processing, pp. 479–489. Association for Computational Linguistics, Austin, Texas (2016)

31. Li, J., Chen, X., Hovy, E., Jurafsky, D.: Visualizing and understanding neural models in nlp. In: Proceedings of the 2016 Conference of the North American Chapter of the Association for Computational Linguistics: Human Language Technologies (2016)
32. Goldberg, Y.: A primer on neural network models for natural language processing. J. Artif. Intell. Res. **57**, 345–420 (2016)
33. Galassi, A., Lippi, M., Torroni, P.: Attention in natural language processing. IEEE Trans. Neural Netw. Learn. Syst. **32**(10), 4291–4308 (2021)
34. Bajaj, D., Goel, A., Gupta, S.C., Batra, H.: MUCE: a multilingual use case model extractor using GPT-3. Int. J. Inf. Technol. **14**(3), 1543–1554 (2022)
35. Batra, H., Jain, A., Bisht, G., Srivastava, K., Bharadwaj, M., Bajaj, D., Bharti, U.: CoVShorts: news summarization application based on deep NLP transformers for SARS-CoV-2. In: 2021 9th International Conference on Reliability, Infocom Technologies and Optimization (Trends and Future Directions) (ICRITO), pp. 1–6. IEEE (2021)

Patient Monitoring System for COVID Care Using Biosensor Application

R. Kishore Kanna[1](✉), Sudharani B. Banappagoudar[2](✉), Flosy R. Menezes[3], and P. S. Sona[4]

[1] Department of Biomedical Engineering, Jerusalem College of Engineering, Chennai, India
kishorekanna007@gmail.com
[2] School of Nursing Sciences, ITM University, Gwalior, MP, India
sudharani.sons@itmuniversity.ac.in
[3] Institute of Nursing Education Bambolin, Goa, India
[4] Government College of Nursing, Government Medical College, Trivandrum, Kerala, India

Abstract. This paper focuses on designing a system to provide the patients with supplemental oxygen to prevent hypoxia for and covid patient. The decrease of oxygen in the tissues in patients with heart diseases, lung related diseases and elderly people result in hypoxia. During this covid-pandemic, number of the patient died due to poor monitor system and mainly due to insufficient of the oxygen. The primary objective of this article is to build a method for automatically administering oxygen supplement to patients when necessary. This technology is portable, does not restrict patients' lifestyles, and provides patients with movement flexibility. This device can be used both on hospitals and also in houses for patients with not so critical condition to be monitored. The system is designed to read the heart rate in the body using a heartbeat sensor. As the heart-rate decreases eventually the SpO2 levels in the organs start diminishing thus leading to hypoxia. Here the Arduino Uno operates a solenoid valve using a relay to regulate the required oxygen supply automatically. It also has a temperature sensor to record the body temperature. Portable and lightweight oxygen cylinders are used in this technique to provide intranasal oxygen delivery. A liquid crystal display is used to show the collected data. For similar reasons, this system employs GSM for out-of-the-box calamity-related communication. A buzzer is included into the system to alert the user in the event of an emergency.

Keywords: Hypoxia · Supplement oxygen · Heart rate sensor · GSM

1 Introduction

Till the present day, eminent countries in the world are suffering from different types of diseases. The number of patients struggling illness are increasing day by day. Common diseases, inherited diseases, diseases due to stress, lifestyle etc., affects the person physically and psychologically. Unhealthy lifestyle, irregular food habits and stress due to personal and work-related matters affect the people with chronic illness which my lead to heart disease, lung related disease etc., from young to elderly people irrespective of the age. People living in rural areas or countryside suffering from heart diseases cannot reach the hospital early in case of emergency if the hospital is located farther. Thus, making the continuous monitoring of heart patients not possible. At this pandemic situation, many people died to due to insufficient oxygen and poor monitoring.

Oxygen gas is essential for human survival since it is a fundamental component of innumerable biological processes [1]. The vascular system, namely hemoglobin in red blood cells, is responsible for the transfer of oxygen throughout the body. The heartbeat rate plays a major role in maintaining the saturated oxygen level in the blood. If the heartbeat rate is reduced, the pumping of blood by the circulatory system is slowed thus the oxygenated blood flow is also reduced. As time passes by, the organs and the tissues will be deprived of blood thus causing hypoxia. SpO2 or oxygen saturation is one of the vital parameters that concerns a body's most basic. The SpO2 level measures the saturation of oxygen in the blood. [2] Oxygen saturation (SpO2) is defined as the ratio of oxyhemoglobin to total hemoglobin concentration. It is the proportion of oxygen in the blood. The normal SpO2 level should be about 90–100%. If it is reduced below 90 it leads to hypoxia. If it further decreases below 80% it may lead to organ dysfunction such as heart failure etc.

2   Literature Survey

Hypoxia is a medical condition where a particular organ or the entire body is seized of adequate oxygen source at the tissue level. Hypoxia is mainly sorted into two categories. They are generalized and local. In generalized, the whole body is affected and in local, only a part or an organ of the body is affected. An example of generalized hypoxia is altitude sickness [3]. An example of local hypoxia is ischemia. Hypoxemia and anoxemia is distinctive from hypoxia... Hypoxia is a state of shortage in oxygen source hypoxemia and anoxemia is a state of zero arterial oxygen supply. Anoxia is a state of hypoxia where total oxygen supply is deprived. Hypoxia is of 4 different types.

Ischemic hypoxia refers to insufficient blood flow to a tissue which may occur due to trauma to the tissue. Hypoxemic hypoxia refers to the insufficiency in arterial blood oxygen supply which may occur due to carbon monoxide poisoning, altitude, hypoxic breathing gases etc., Anaemic hypoxia results due to haemoglobin deficiency. Haemoglobin plays an important role of carrying oxygen throughout the body. Histotoxic hypoxia refers to the defect in cells where the cells are unfit to use the oxygen [4].

Another physiological metric widely employed by wireless patient monitoring systems is heart rate (HR). "The definition of heart rate is the number of heart beats per minute," which may also be calculated by the pulse. Pulse and heartbeat are quite similar since the pulse is produced by cardiac contractions that generate an increase in blood pressure. Heart rate or heart beat rate is the direct measurement of pulse [5].

Temperature is expressed in three common scales, Celsius, Fahrenheit and Kelvin. It can express both heat and cold. Temperature is used in all day-to-day activities such as cooking etc., It is used in various departments like natural science, medicine etc., Temperature is more important in the medical field as fever or chillness is the most common symptom of various diseases [6].

Temperature is not an essential function, but it may be used to estimate the organism's burden in conjunction with vital function sensors and information such as heart rate [7]. The typical human body temperature is between 36.5 and 37.5 °C. Temperature below or above the normal range indicates illness. The internal body temperature is regulated or maintained by the circulatory system.

In this system, we are developing a module to monitor the heart rate and temperature of the person and deliver supplement oxygen when necessary. It is designed to be portable and an automatic system. It is also designed to notify the doctor or the person's family through an emergency SMS. It is programmed in such a way that when the heart rate reduces below a certain range it supplies with supplement oxygen. Low oxygen levels may be alleviated by supplemental oxygen. [8].

3 Materials and Methodology

In this system, we are developing a module to monitor the heart rate and temperature of the person and deliver supplement oxygen when necessary. It is designed to be portable and an automatic system. It is also designed to notify the doctor or the person's family through an emergency SMS. It is programmed in such a way that when the heart rate reduces below a certain range it supplies with supplement oxygen. Low oxygen levels may be alleviated by supplemental oxygen [8].

In the proposed system we are designing an automatic delivery of supplement oxygen to patients with heart disease, lung related problems, elderly people and hypoxic patients in case of emergency. It is designed to intimate the person of interest of the patient through the GSM [9].

It encompasses of heart beat sensor and temperature sensor which is the input module section where as the GSM, LCD, buzzer and the solenoid valve is the output module. A power supply board provides the power supply [10]. Connecting the Arduino uno board to the power source. The heart rate sensor is attached to the Arduino uno board's input and the power supply board. The temperature sensor is further connected to the Arduino board's input and the power supply. The relay is linked to the power supply, the Arduino uno's output, and the solenoid valve [11]. The buzzer is connected to the Arduino uno's output pin. The LCD is connected to the Arduino uno's output pins. The Arduino uno and the power supply are linked to the GSM module (Fig. 1).

3.1 Power Supply

The power supply is an electrical device which is used to convert electric current from a source to the right voltage, current or frequency. Power supply circuits are also called as electric power convertors. Based on the power utilized for providing for circuits or devices, power supply circuits are classified into different types. They are unregulated, regulated and switching circuits [12].

The power supply used here is regulated power supply. In order to operate electronic devices most of the electronic devices requires the unregulated AC to be converted into constant DC. The electronic circuits inside the devices should be able to supply a constant DC voltage not beyond the power supply limit. The electronic equipment may break down easily if the supply from the main is fluctuating and not properly limited.

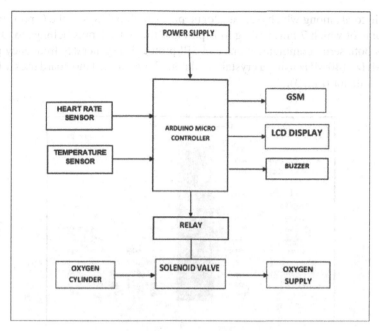

Fig. 1. Block diagram

3.2 Arduino Uno

The Arduino Uno is developed by Arduino.cc. It is based on microchip ATmega328P open-source microcontroller. The latest revised version of Arduino Uno is Arduino Uno R3. The microcontroller board used here is Arduino Uno Rev3. The Board is Equipped with 20 digital input/output pins. Among these 20 pins 6 can be used as Pulse Width Modulation (PWM) output pins and 6 can be used as input analog pins [13]. The board is powered up by connecting it directly to the computer using a USB cable or by connecting it to a power supply through a AC to DC adapter or using a battery (Fig. 2).

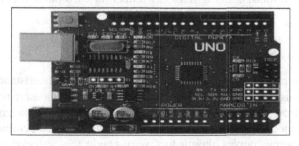

Fig. 2. Arduino Uno R3

ATmega328 belongs to the mega AVR family and is a single chip microcontroller. It was created by Atmel but was later acquired in Microchip Technology in 2016. It has

28 pins in total among which 6 are analogue pins which belongs to the C port. It has 14 digital pins of which 7 pins belong to B port and the other 7 pins belongs to D port. It supports both serial communications and SPI protocol. It generates frequency ranging from 4 MHz to 40 MHz using a crystal oscillator. The Arduino Uno board uses a 16 MHz crystal oscillator (Fig. 3).

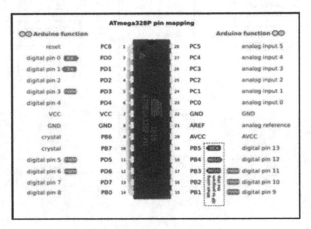

Fig. 3. ATmega 328

3.3 Heart Beat Sensor

An electronic device called the heart beat sensor is used to measure the speed of the heartbeat i.e., heart rate of the human body. The heart beat sensor works by the principle photo-plethysmograph. The principle states that the changes in the intensity of the light passing through an organ is used to measure the changes in the volume of blood in the organ [14]. The heartbeat sensor gives a digital output when the finger is placed on the sensor i.e., between the source and the detector. The source is a LED (IR) and the detector is a photo transistor. The red LED blinks for each pulse when the detector is activated.

3.4 Temperature Sensor

A temperature sensor is typically a thermocouple or a RTD (Resistance Temperature Detector) which uses electrical signal to provide temperature measurement. A temperature sensor is selected depending on the style, stem (sheath), Insertion length, measuring junction and Connection required. There are different types of temperature sensor which include RTDs, thermocouples, thermistors, semi-conductors, infrared etc. The temperature sensor used here is the Semiconductor based temperature sensors. Semiconductor based temperature sensors provide linear output and give fairly accurate output readings if calibrated properly [15]. This type of sensor is highly suitable for embedded applications. They measure temperature ranging from −40 °C to +120 °C and cannot measure high temperatures. The digital output temperature sensors are integrated on a IC chip and is useful for thermal management in microprocessor applications.

3.5 Relay

A relay is an electrically operated switching device and a primary protection for most of the equipment. As a switching device it is used to change one state of the electric circuit to another state. Wherever one signal is necessary to control several circuits or a separate low power signal is required to control a circuit relay can be used.

Relays are classified based on the operating principles. The most common relays use electromagnet to mechanically operate the switch. Based in the operating principles the relays are classified as Electromagnetic relays (AC or DC), Solid state relays, Thermal relays, reed relays, hybrid relays etc.

The relay used here is the Single Pole Double Throw relay. The SPDT relay has one general terminal and two contacts in separate configurations i.e., when the coil is applied with DC voltage, the terminal T is associated to contact 1 allowing the current to flow through fan 1 and fan 2 is closed and when the coil is applied with DC voltage, the terminal T is associated to contact 2 allowing the current to flow through fan 2 and fan 1 is closed (Fig. 4).

Fig. 4. Relay

3.6 Solenoid Valve

"A solenoid valve is an electromechanical device." The solenoid profits electric flow to actuate attractive field and works a system which controls the opening of fluid surge in a valve. There are unmistakable kinds of solenoid valve. In view of the attributes of the electric flow utilized, quality of the attractive field produced, the instrument used to manage the liquid, and the sort and qualities of the liquid they control, the solenoid valve varies

Solenoid valves are generally administered to direct components in fluidics. Solenoids give quick and safe exchanging, high unwavering quality, long administration life, low control power and reduced structure. The solenoid valve utilized here is the one-way or two-way solenoid valve.

3.7 GSM

GSM module stands for Global System for Mobile Communication module. It is a digital mobile network that establish communication between the computer and the GSM module. GSM is an architecture used widely by mobile users in Europe and other parts of the world.

GSM was first utilized in Finland in 1991. It is a standard that was established by the European Telecommunications Standards Institute (ETSI). Since 2014, GSM became the Global Standard for Mobile Communication and is operating in over 193 countries and territories (Fig. 5).

Fig. 5. GSM

3.8 LCD Display

LCD stands for Liquid Crystal Display, and as the name indicates, it is a blend of solid and liquid states of matter. It is an optically balanced electrical device that utilizes the light-regulating characteristics of fluid crystals. These fluid crystals cannot transmit light well and rely on the background lighting to generate images. LCDs are used in a variety of applications, such as laptop computer screens, televisions, instrument panels, mobile phones, cockpit displays in aircrafts, etc.

The working principle behind the LCD is it enables light to go through as the crystals wind and untwist at modifying degrees. If no voltage is passed through the liquid crystal, polarized light is allowed through the 90-degree twisted LC layer. If voltage is passed through the liquid crystals, polarization is altered when the liquid crystals untwist thus blocking the light's path.

The LCD display used here is the 16×2 LCD module. It has 16 rows and 2 columns thus having 32 characters in total Each character is of 5×8-pixel specks. In this manner each character will have 40 pixels and the all-out 32 characters will have 1280 pixels.

3.9 Buzzer

A buzzer may be a mechanical, electromechanical or piezoelectric device used for audio signaling. A buzzer or beeper are used as alarming device, timers or as keystrokes etc.

The buzzer used here is the piezoelectric buzzer also called as piezo buzzer. "The piezo buzzer is based on the principle of reversing of piezoelectric effect." The main component of the buzzer is the piezoelectric element. All piezo elements express phenomenon like piezoelectric effect and reverse piezoelectric effect. When mechanical strain is applied on the piezoelectric element, the material develops an electric field and vice versa.

Therefore, as the name piezoelectric buzzer suggests when the piezoelectric material is exposed to mechanical strain it produces an electric field and vice versa. The buzzer comprises of piezo-crystals put between two conductors. At the point when electric tension is involved, the crystals push one conductor and tug the other. This push and tug create a sound wave.

3.10 Arduino Compiler

The Arduino IDE stands for Arduino Integrated Development Environment. The Arduino IDE is a software that is used as a compiler for the Arduino board. It is a programme that runs on Windows, macOS, and Linux. It is a programming language developed in Java and used to build and upload applications to Arduino adaptable boards. The Arduino IDE supports C and C++ languages.

3.11 Embedded C

The most mainstream programming language in the software field for creating electronic contraptions is Embedded C. In electronic systems each processor used is linked with embedded software. Certain functions performed by the processor is programmed by embedded C.

Electronic devices used in day-to-day life such as mobile phone, washing machine, digital camera etc., work based on microcontrollers that are programmed by embedded C. C code programming is preferred in embedded systems because it is easy to understand with high reliability and it is portable and has high scalability.

4 Working

A block diagram and a flowchart were used to graphically map out the system management process. The cycle stream is intended to direct key moments throughout all stages of a system's lifespan. Circuit diagrams are utilised for everything from original design and manufacture to troubleshooting when dealing with electrical or electronic equipment. For a complicated system, these illustrations were really rather useful. The sensor starts reading data as soon as the power is switched on, as shown in the system's block diagram. In this instance, the system uses two different kinds of sensors to monitor body temperature, heart rate, and arterial oxygen saturation (SpO2). The Arduino receives the analogue values that the sensors have measured and digitises the data. The server refreshes an LCD display while also giving the mobile app access to the measured data. With their mobile app and device, users may monitor their body temperature, oxygen saturation (SpO2), and heart rate. The device starts collecting readings and sending them to the main controller (an Arduino Uno or Node MCU). The Node MCU transmits the measured value to a central server. The system alerts the doctor and the patient and shows the data on the screen when the SpO2 falls below 95% and the HR is below 60 or over 90. The gadget has an LCD display that shows the user the measured value, as does a mobile app. The hardware parts of the system, including the Arduino Uno, node MCU, Bluetooth module, SpO2 sensor, temperature sensor, and power supply, are shown in this diagram. Proteus Design Suite was used to develop this circuit schematic. The completely automated setup is turned on by pressing the on button. The mobile application may access the data once it has been gathered by the sensors and transferred to the processing unit.

IoT was created following a thorough analysis of the techniques and equipment now used in the fields of electronic communication and information processing. That may make a difference for city inhabitants. Since the global population is expanding at an unprecedented pace and chronic illnesses are becoming more prevalent, there is a great need for cost-effective healthcare systems that can manage and offer a broad variety of medical services while reducing total costs. Healthcare monitoring systems may now be improved thanks to the Internet of Things (IoT), which has recently emerged as a major area of research. The objective of the Internet of Things healthcare monitoring system is to accurately track people while connecting different services and objects across the globe through the Internet in order to collect, share, monitor, store, and analyse the data produced by these things. On the other hand, the Internet of Things (IoT) is a new paradigm in which all physical objects that are a part of an intelligent application (such a smart city, smart home, or smart healthcare system) are addressed and managed over the network. The crucial duties of illness detection and patient monitoring will be considerably aided by the use of sensor networks on the human body. Also, you may access the data from anywhere at any time.

5   Result

The heart beat sensor and temperature sensor detect the pulse and the temperature individually. The buzzer provides alarm when sensing the heart rate. The oxygen will be delivered to the patient when the heart rate is less than 65 bpm by the solenoid value. When the heart rate and temperature is sensed, it automatically generates SMS (Short Messaging Service) to representative user phone through GSM (Global System for Mobile Communication).

The input modules and output modules are connected to the Arduino Uno using connecting wires as per the given construction and heart rate will be displayed on the LCD (Liquid Crystal Display) (Fig. 6).

The demand for healthcare increases along with the population in developing nations. The covid-19 virus is very infectious, thus it's important to restrict infected people while also having medical examiners keep an eye on covid-19 sufferers' wellbeing. It is harder to keep an eye on their health when there are more individuals under quarantine. This is an illustration of a suggested machine architecture for a Wi-Fi sensor network for the Internet of Things. Its typical job is to gather and move the many sensors needed in healthcare institutions to monitor patients. In this software, the wireless local area network (Wi-Fi) connects with a number of sensors around the transmitter, such as a thermometer, a blood pressure monitor, and a pulse oximeter. These sensors are physically connected to the client and use sensors to capture information about the client's

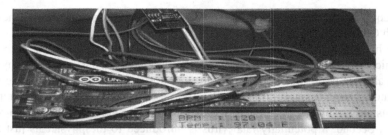

Fig. 6. Patient monitoring system for covid care using biosensor kit

status. The medical agent will surely gather all changes to the medical statuses of their customers from the wireless transmission of a comparable set of data to his receiver location. Moreover, it will really leave voicemails to remind users to take their prescription on time. Each bedside will have a loud bell adjacent to it in case of an emergency. The alert will start when the patient touches the emergency button.

During the pandemic, many isolation centres for Covid-19-infected individuals are created up. Because the illness is so infectious, isolation of patients is essential, but physicians also need to monitor their development. It is difficult for frontline healthcare workers to avoid becoming sick since the symptoms of this rare virus vary greatly from strain to strain. Monitoring the health of several patients who are confined to their homes or isolated in rural areas may be challenging. Both the number of people who are extremely sick and the severity of their illnesses are on the increase. This problem is addressed by an Internet-of-Things-based remote healthcare system that monitors vital signs and would enable the quick monitoring of multiple corona virus patients. Vital sign data is gathered by sensors and sent to a microcontroller-based system, which then uses the Thing Talk platform to broadcast the data to the world. Vital sign data includes heart rate, oxygen saturation, and temperature. An alarm will be delivered if anything doesn't appear right or if the patient presses the emergency button. This arrangement allows physicians to securely see their patients from a distance. A single doctor might manage the care of more than 500 patients at once. Severe health status changes will immediately notify the attending physician. This technology helps in these challenging times by enabling the collection and transmission of data to the server, the storage and use of data in the monitoring system, and the prevention of healthcare personnel from catching any contagious illnesses.

6   Discussion

The research is presented to provide better diagnostic and therapeutic aid for the heart disease patients and Hypoxia patient. Hypoxia is the condition, which occurs due to low concentration of oxygen in blood vessels, which means absence of the blood O2 in the patient's body which leads to fall of heart rate. So, the treatment for hypoxia patient is to provide enough oxygen supplement to the body by sensing the heart rate. The heart beat sensor costs low and it can be used for long time if not damaged. It is of simple construction. It is user – friendly module where everyone can use. It can be used both in hospital and house care for heart disease patients and it prevents the patient from acquiring Hypoxia. This project alerts the concerned person about their heart rate through Global Mobile communication system.

We have designated Covid 19 Quarantine Centers to address the current COVID epidemic. As covid is so infectious, patients should always be isolated, but physicians should also regularly monitor their health. Monitoring the health of everyone who is segregated gets increasingly difficult as there are more verified cases. The most important concerns are as follows: First, medical professionals should routinely check in on their patients. Second, a potentially fatal virus is introduced to the physicians just for the purpose of monitoring. The number of individuals who need medical supervision is steadily increasing. By developing a solution for remote, IoT-based health monitoring of several COVID patients at once, we're here to assist. The system's many sensors monitor the patient's heart rate, body temperature, and blood pressure. Following then, it connects to a wifi internet connection and transmits the data over wifi. The system is under the control of a microcontroller. The IoT Gecko platform (IoT development platform) transmits and receives patient data through IOT so that the covid patient may see it on a distant device. A remote alert is sent through IoT whenever a patient presses the "help" button on an IoT device during a medical emergency. The system is connected to the temperature sensor, the blood pressure sensor, and the heart rate sensor. The blood pressure and heart rate monitors may then be attached by simply wrapping the sensor around the patient's wrist. After being turned on and showing the patient's blood pressure, it is uploaded with a single click to the IoT display. The system-integrated temperature sensor will be used to monitor the situation. By igniting the lighter in front of the sensor, we can see the temperature rise in action. The temperature increases as the camera gets closer to the temperature sensor, and the data is sent to the Internet of Things.

7 Conclusion

This research is useful for heart patient because it performs both therapeutic and diagnostic aid in this device. This system gives heart rate and temperature as input and the output will be given by buzzer (when it sensed), automatic oxygen supply to the patients, SMS to the concern person by displaying heart rate and temperature. The module also displays the output on a LCD to provide assistance to the surrounding person.

References

1. Kiruthika, R., et al.: IOT based patient monitoring system. In: 2022 8th International Conference on Advanced Computing and Communication Systems (ICACCS), vol. 1, pp. 165–168. IEEE (2022)
2. Kasiselvanathan, M., Prasad, J., Sekar, G.: Arduino UNO controller and RTC-based medication reminder and monitoring system. In: Goyal, V., Gupta, M., Mirjalili, S., Trivedi, A. (eds.) Proceedings of International Conference on Communication and Artificial Intelligence: ICCAI 2021, pp. 199–204. Springer Nature Singapore, Singapore (2022). https://doi.org/10.1007/978-981-19-0976-4_17
3. Reena, K.J., Parameswari, R.: IOT based health tracking shoe for elderly people using gait monitoring system. In: 2021 7th International Conference on Advanced Computing and Communication Systems (ICACCS), vol. 1, pp. 1701–1705. IEEE (2021)

4. Shalini, E., Priya, S., Sabitha, S., Shalini, S.R., Shanmugam, C.: Soldiers health monitoring and tracking system. Int. J. Res Eng. Sci. Manage. 4(7), 194–196 (2021)

5. Hryniewicz, O., Kaczmarek-Majer, K.: Monitoring of possibilisticaly aggregated complex time series. In: García-Escudero, L.A., et al. (eds.) Building Bridges between Soft and Statistical Methodologies for Data Science, pp. 208–215. Springer International Publishing, Cham (2023). https://doi.org/10.1007/978-3-031-15509-3_28

6. Kanna, R.K., et al.: Nursing assist module compact patient monitoring system using Iot application. J. Pharm. Negat Results 28, 236–239 (2022)

7. Levonevskiy, D., Motienko, A.: Modeling tasks of patient assistance and emergency management in medical cyber-physical systems. In: Silhavy, R., Silhavy, P., Prokopova, Z. (eds.) Software Engineering Application in Systems Design: Proceedings of 6th Computational Methods in Systems and Software 2022, vol. 1, pp. 299–308. Springer International Publishing, Cham (2023). https://doi.org/10.1007/978-3-031-21435-6_26

8. Varghese, A., Muthukumaraswamy, S.A.: An IoT-based health monitoring system for elderly patients. In: Bhateja, V., Mohanty, J.R., Fuentes, W.F., Maharatna, K. (eds.) Communication, Software and Networks: Proceedings of INDIA 2022, pp. 331–338. Springer Nature Singapore, Singapore (2023). https://doi.org/10.1007/978-981-19-4990-6_29

9. Sai Sreekar, U., Vishnu Vardhan, V., Joseph, L.: Recogn-eye: a smart medical assistant for elderly. In: Shakya, S., Ke-Lin, D., Ntalianis, K. (eds.) Sentiment Analysis and Deep Learning: Proceedings of ICSADL 2022, pp. 105–112. Springer Nature Singapore, Singapore (2023). https://doi.org/10.1007/978-981-19-5443-6_9

10. Chillimuntha, A.K., Harit, K., Sharma, S.: An intensive care unit design of the future. In: Bhatia, D., Chaudhari, P.K., Chaudhary, B., Sharma, S., Dhingra, K. (eds.) A Guide to Hospital Administration and Planning, pp. 125–135. Springer Nature Singapore, Singapore (2023). https://doi.org/10.1007/978-981-19-6692-7_8

11. Balakrishnan, R., Ranganayaki, V.: Sensor based health monitoring system using embedded technology. In: 2022 8th International Conference on Advanced Computing and Communication Systems (ICACCS), vol. 1, pp. 1263–1267. IEEE (2022)

12. Narasimharao, M., Biswaranjan Swain, P.P., Nayak, S.B.: Development of real-time cloud based smart remote healthcare monitoring system. In: Swarnkar, T., Patnaik, S., Mitra, P., Misra, S., Mishra, M. (eds.) Ambient Intelligence in Health Care: Proceedings of ICAIHC 2022, pp. 217–224. Springer Nature Singapore, Singapore (2023). https://doi.org/10.1007/978-981-19-6068-0_21

13. Bhuiyan, M.N., et al.: Design and implementation of a feasible model for the IoT based ubiquitous healthcare monitoring system for rural and urban areas. IEEE Access 29(10), 91984–91997 (2022)

14. Hasan, M.A., Arakeri, M.P.: Remote patient monitoring system using IoT and artificial intelligence: a review. In: 2022 3rd International Conference on Smart Electronics and Communication (ICOSEC), pp. 535–543. IEEE (2022)

15. Sudharsan, S., Arulmozhi, M., Amutha, C., Sathya, R.: IOT-based third eye glove for smart monitoring. In: Fong, S., Dey, N., Joshi, A. (eds.) ICT Analysis and Applications: Proceedings of ICT4SD 2022, pp. 691–701. Springer Nature Singapore, Singapore (2023). https://doi.org/10.1007/978-981-19-5224-1_69

Enhance the Tourism of Unpopular Places by Fuzzy Distance Method

Pharindra Kumar Sharma[1]([✉]), Rajeev Ranjan[3], Sujay Vikram Singh[4], Neha Jain[2], and Mayank Sharma[5]

[1] Sanskriti University, Mathura, UP, India
dr.pharindra@gmail.com
[2] Suresh Gyan Vihar University, Jaipur, India
[3] Jagannath University, Jaipur, India
[4] Banaras Hindu University, Varanasi, India
[5] ITM University, Gwalior, India

Abstract. The importance of a destination image in tourism has the biggest value in marketing when a tourist wants to explore a destination that will help to know all information about that place as well as the nearest place attached with the popular and promoted destinations. Changing pattern of tourist behavior assumed as the driving thrust for emphasizing the relevance of unpopular tourist sites and potential generators of the state's revenue. For reviving the unpopular tourist places, this study aims to identify the potential tourism aspect and development of underrated sites in Jaipur. This research work applies the neural network takes the information from previous experiences of the tourist and some information from the internet and extracted the key objects by fuzzy neural network and then it's recognized by a predefined database. After that, we find out the minimum route between source places to the nearest connecting place through a proposed algorithm.

1 Introduction

Gradually increasing footfalls at a particular destination deplete the physical and cultural resources that emerged as a crowded destination. To control the tourist traffic and maintain the carrying capacity of a destination, it is very necessary to promote the least popular or unpopular sites. Many places with immense tourism potential did not appear on the travel map, bringing financial benefits to the local community. The majority of the cultural, natural, ethnic, and niche tourist destinations are particularly associated with the specific community of the region offering an opportunity to explore both of them. In the high season of tourist movement, hotels and transportation facilities get packed and equally carrying capacity is exceeded. Enhancement of unpopular places has worked with an approach of promoting least known sites but having high tourism potential. Over time, the behaviours of tourists shift from visiting beautiful and spectacular tourist attractions to seeking out off-the-beaten-path destinations and avoiding hotspots packed with visitors seeking the same incredible adventure as them. A state like Rajasthan has immense opportunities where large numbers of popular and unpopular places attract tourists across the globe. Implementing a neural network where indexing popular destinations have to prepare a database will help in identifying the least known sites associated with the mainstream destination. There are clusters of crowded destinations often attached with the least popular higher potential sites, which acts as a driving force of economic booster in developing countries. Social media platforms such as Instagram, Twitter, and Facebook have helped to find exciting tourist locations that are unpopular "untapped sites" and taking shots of them improves the accessibility to the places equally boosts the local economy (Gato et al., 2020). Rajasthan's tourist sites with higher tourism potential need a proper approach of promotion and branding methods, associated with the techniques to search them in the series of already popular sites. For holistic development of the entire region and to maintain an equilibrium of tourist traffic, it is necessary to equally focus on the promotion of unpopular places. When marketing less popular destinations, it is necessary to take a targeted approach that places an emphasis on authenticity, specific niche targeting, partnerships, sustainable tourism, and local engagement. Along with cultural relativism, the engagement and participation of locals is an essential requirement for the evaluation procedures of tourism development (Zhang and Smith, 2019). Other essential requirements include authenticity, integrity, and the upholding of significant universal values.

By highlighting the one-of-a-kind activities and possibilities that can be found in these locations, as well as by collaborating with the communities and companies in the area, it is feasible to attract tourists and encourage the development of sustainable destinations (Piber et al., 2019). The main economic impact is increasing local communities' income and social awareness of the unprivileged local population. In the long vision, it is hoped that poverty and illiteracy can be mitigated and welfare can be increased by tourism activities conducted in the less popular tourism destination. In contemporary times, tourists avoid busy attractions and search for overlooked more nature touched sites. Although the majority of travelers may not be familiar with the unpopular potential destinations and even lack of promotion defined as "Underrated, must-see, and potential destination sites (Pritmoko et al., 2021).

Rajasthan's identity of royal Rajputana forts, palaces, temples and monuments are globally acclaimed, many of them are least popular leads an economical and social impacts on the society. It is prepared to plan a comprehensive strategy for achieve a balance between the unpopular tourist sites with community's income and preservation of these sites. Rajasthan's capital Jaipur is an important segment of India's Golden Triangle, a most preferred tourist Circuit which connects with Delhi and Agra. State has contributed more than 24% of Foreign Tourist Arrivals (2018–19) over 40 million international and domestic tourists visited Rajasthan in 2019. Tourism comprises approximately 15% of the state's economy which supports regional infrastructural development and promotion of unique cultural identity. Tourism accounts almost 3% in Gross State Domestic Product and 5% in overall employment. Tourism and hospitality sector collectively formed the third largest employer after agriculture and textile industry offers an opportunity to equally focus on the untapped potential of least known sites (Singh and Kumar, 2022). According to this study, aims to best possible way to enhance the touristic importance of underrated tourist sites of Rajasthan. In order to achieve this objective, the study used the neural networks which take the information from previous experience of the tourist and some information recognized predefined database.

2   Literature Review

Tourism is an exploration activity that includes identification and optimum utilization in terms of leisure, pleasure, and business purposes (UNWTO, 2013). Most tourist destinations faced situations of high visitor traffic congestion severely affects the physical, social, and environmental impacts on society (Aranburu et al., 2016). Equally, promoting the entire area of a region whether it is popular or unpopular has a holistic approach to inclusive development where the Internet and GPS have played a pivotal role in easily assessing the unapproached tourist sites et al., (Govers et al., 2007). Marketing and promotion of unnoticed sites help to divert the traffic from the hustle-bustle tourist sites. The high season of tourism creates the unavailability of hotel rooms, scarcity of city transport increased pollution and garbage consequently decreasing the sustainability and physical carrying capacity of a destination Pratimoko et al. (2021). Untapping the potential of unexplored tourist sites can connect to the flow of development with the urban infrastructure and civic amenties. A bridge to filled the gap of high demand and supply, and equal distribution of revenue generation to the far sighted region, 5 A's model of Tourism which includes "Attraction, Accommodation, Accessibility, Activity, and Amenity" has suggested for a holistic development of least promoted region (Fatimah, 2015). Most of the offbeat and adventure travellers prefers to explore the fragile destination which are generally not mentioned in the common itinerary of tour operators and travel agents. For making the tourist sites more interesting, amazing, unique, and ecologically sustainable least popular sites have mapped on the famous tourist trails (Han et al., 2016) which coveres tourism products and various stakeholders with similar view. In this regards the cultural & physical landscapes are distinguished as the balance between fragile and explored sites. Their result seems as conservation and preservation of "historically and culturally universal sites" assisting the local communities with capacity building and sense of proud. In continuation with Motivating visitors for the exploration of unpopular higher tourism potential destinations, have multiple benefits socially, economically, politically and most important ecologically. Unexplored tourist sites are the places which have the potential to attract visitors but not promoted strategically. An unpopular potential tourist sites can be defined as "unpolished diamonds of Mines". Tourism has become a leading economic sector, contributing to the GDP of many countries and representing a significant portion of the world's total exports. Visiting unpopular destinations can boost socio-economic development in the region by bringing in revenue and creating jobs in the tourism and hospitality industries. This can lead to an increase in the standard of living for local residents and promote sustainable development (Ferreira et al., 2021). In the process of transforming least popular sites into more constructive and productive one. Although tourism has created an impact over the contribution of achieving local and regional growth in distant geographical areas with socio-politicaland economic vibality (Mathis et al., 2016). It is necessary to conduct research in tourist destinations that are not particularly well known. To begin, it may be helpful to identify the possible benefits of tourism in these places, such as the expansion of the local economy and the creation of new jobs (Parveen, 2018). Second, conducting research can help to discover ways that will maximise the positive effects that tourism has on local communities and the environment while minimising the negative effects that tourism has on those same communities and the environment (Gupta, 2019). Last but not least, research can help to increase awareness about how important it is to preserve local cultures and customs in locations that are not particularly often visited (Rathore et al., 2017).

Hristov and Stoyanova (2020) observed that tourists who travelled to isolated and unexplored locations were looking for an exciting new experience as well as an escape from the crowdedness and commercialism of well-known attractions. In a similar vein, a study that was conducted by Wang et al. (2019) highlighted curiosity, cultural authenticity, and social connections as primary characteristics that prompted tourists to visit less well-known sites.

A variety of other studies have investigated the effects of tourism on the native people and landscapes of less frequented areas. For instance, Yun et al. (2020) conducted research in which they investigated the role that community-based tourism plays in fostering sustainable development in rural and disadvantaged areas. The authors came to the conclusion that participation from the local population, the maintenance of the area's cultural traditions, and the protection of its natural resources were crucial elements in the development of successful tourism in these regions (Rathore and Jodhana, 2012).

Several studies have brought attention to the difficulties and dangers that are associated with tourism in less popular destinations, despite the fact that there is the possibility that it will be beneficial. For example, Chen and Chen (2018) conducted a study in which they discovered that security concerns, such as the presence of crime and terrorism, were a key barrier to the development of tourism in rural and impoverished areas. According to the findings of other research, tourists and local residents face considerable obstacles as a result of restrictions in the infrastructure, such as inadequate transport and a shortage of hotel options (Sharma, 2018).

In general, the research that has been done on less frequented tourist sites reveals that these locations provide chances that are one of a kind and of great value to tourists who are looking for genuine and original experiences. However, in order to guarantee the long-term viability of tourism development in these regions and to guarantee that it will be successful, careful planning and consideration of cultural and safety factors are required.

Table 1. A list of cites of Rajasthan

City_index	City_name	City_index	City_name
1	Ajmer	7	Jodhpur
2	Alwer	8	Kota
3	Bhilwara	9	Hanumangarh
4	Bikaner	10	Sri Ganganagar
5	Bharatpur	11	Sikar
6	Jaipur	12	Udaipur

Table 2. Some unpopular places of jaipur city.

City_index	City_name	Tourism-Place-id	Tourism-Place-name
6	Jaipur	Jaipur_01	Galta Temple
6	Jaipur	Jaipur_02	Chulgiri Jain Temple
6	Jaipur	Jaipur_03	Chandlai Lake
6	Jaipur	Jaipur_04	Amer Sagar
6	Jaipur	Jaipur_05	Kanota Dam
6	Jaipur	Jaipur_06	Sambhar Lake
6	Jaipur	Jaipur_07	Abhaneri
6	Jaipur	Jaipur_08	Nahargarh Biologocal Park
6	Jaipur	Jaipur_09	Bird Park
6	Jaipur	Jaipur_011	Akshardham Temple
6	Jaipur	Jaipur_012	Galta Temple
6	Jaipur	Jaipur_013	Chulgiri Jain Temple
6	Jaipur	Jaipur_014	Chandlai Lake

3 Brief Description of Sites

Galta Temple is an ancient Hindu pilgrimage site located just outside Jaipur in the Indian state of Rajasthan. It is also known as the "Monkey Temple" and was recently featured on National Geographic's multi-award-winning series 'Monkey Thieves. The site consists of a series of temples built into a narrow crevice in the ring of hills that surrounds Jaipur. A natural spring emerges high on the hill and flows downward, filling a series of sacred kunds (water tanks) in which pilgrims bathe [2]. Visitors and pilgrims can ascend the crevasse, continuing past the highest water pool to a hilltop temple from where there are views of Jaipur and its fortifications. Chulgiri Jain Temple is a popular Digambara shrine located on top of the North end of the Jhalana Range in Jaipur, Rajasthan. It was originated in the year 1953 by Jain Acharya Shri Desh Bhushan Ji Maharaj. Chandlai Lake is located on Jaipur Tonk Road, about 30 km from Jaipur 1. It is a haven for nature lovers and photographers who love to capture birds and wildlife. Around 10,000 migratory birds can be spotted hereAmer Sagar is a 17th-century lake that supplied water to Amer and Jaigarh forts. It is situated near Amer Fort between Kheri Gate and the Anokhi Museum. The best time to visit this place is during the monsoon season when the weather is relaxed and you can enjoy amazing views. Kanota Dam is located about 15 km away from Jaipur on National Highway 11 i.e. 'Agra Road'. It has an epic combination of natural beauty and peace.

The dam can astonish its visitors with vibrant scenes. You will find young crowds living their moment there during the Monsoon Season. Sambhar Lake is the largest saline lake in India and is noted for its salt production. Abhaneri is a village in the Dausa district of Rajasthan, famous for its post-Gupta or early medieval monuments, Chand Baori and Harshat Mata Temple. Nahargarh Biological Park is a part of the Nahargarh sanctuary and is located about 12 km from Jaipur on the Jaipur-Delhi highway. It encompasses a large area of 720 hectares and is situated under the Aravalli range. The Park is famous for its vast flora and fauna, and its main aim is to conserve it. At Nahargarh Biological Park, ornithologists can expect to see over 285 species of birds. Akshardham Temple is known for its beautiful architecture, magnificent idols, sculptures, and carvings and is dedicated to the Hindu God, Narayan. Akshardham temple provides a real glimpse of Indian architecture, cultural heritage, and sculptures of Hindu gods to the visitors. It is located in Vaishali Nagar, Jaipur.

4 Data Sampling

India is one of the most beautiful country of the world, too many states of India play a big role in tourism sector, Rajasthan state one of them India. It have most beautiful places, markets, forts, dessert, mountain, beautiful ponds and etc. herein we created a image database of Rajasthan tourism, that images comes from some sources like post experience of tourism and internet through random sampling technique. In this work, we focused on twelve famous cities of Rajasthan tourism as given in Table 1.

5 Proposed Algorithm

In this research paper, we have created a algorithm that employ the image recognition and as well as searching the best safe route for turist, despite above it is also calculated the following important points as optimum distance from source to image destination, best nearest places from destination image. Herein, we adopted the neural network along with fuzzy system, it is best image recognition algorithm for comparing a image objects with database. The block diagram of proposed work is given below.

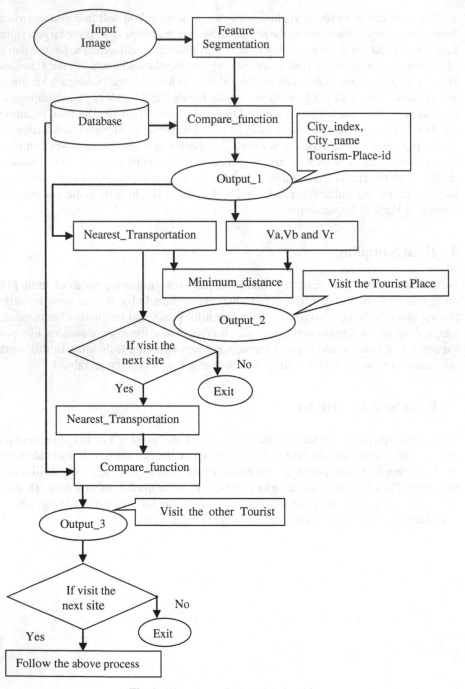

Fig. 1. Flowchart of proposed algorithm.

Algorithm:-

Input- Take an image from tourism destination
Output- Show the best route and best tourist place for tourist

I=Read_function(Image)

[fe1, fe2]=Feature_Extraction(I)

Database={City_index, City_name, Tourism-Place-id, Tourism-Place-name}

For city_index=1 to 12

{

   If (fe1, fe2 belongs to city_index)

   Output (Visit the tourist place)

   Show(City_name)

   Show(City_index)

   Show(Tourism-Place-id)

   [Va,Vb,Vr]=T.point(city_index) // Transportation point

   [md] = Minimum_dist{(Va,Vb,Vr) to Tourism-Place-id }

   [nt1, nt2]=Nearest_transportation.point(I)

   F.destination=Minimum_dist{md, to(nt1, nt2)}

   L.id= list(Tourism-Place-id)

     For i=2 to length(N)

     {

        Nx.destination=minimum_dist(nt1/nt2 to L.id)

        Output (Visit the tourist place)

        i=i+1 }

   end for

6 Result and Simulation

In this research, We are enhanced the many unpopular places of Rajasthan through a feed forward neural network, this network used a database that hold the all information of unpopular places of 12 cities that show in Tables 1 and 2 have to all unpopular places information with their respective city. Here in Table 2, the top 14 beautiful places are showed. The proposed system has taken to an input image according to user; Fig. 1 show the input image (Fig. 2).

Fig. 2. Input image.

In the proposed system, first of all we recognized the input image through own features or objects, note that many objects of the image may appear very uniquely and so easy to compare with database for a process of city searching. Herein, we used neuro-fuzzy algorithm for comparing image objects along with a predefined database for the searching of cities.

After find out the city, this system has played an important role for enhance the tourism. Too many people's are not known the unpopular beautiful places and also not known the best routes, which are big issue for tourism sector.

Now we calculated the best safe routes with minimum distance from three source position as bus stand, railway station and airport of tourist to destination image, it is displayed in Table 3. Despite, the proposed algorithm have to find out best place with respect to distance. The Table 4 are shown all possile tourist place with respect source position, here Fig. 3 have to dipited a rout of source to destination with the help of Google map.

Table 3. Select fist destination tourist place by proposed work

Source_Position	City_name	Address of Destination_image	Tourism-Place-id	Tourism-Place-name	Nearest_Transportation	Distance
Railway Station	Jaipur	Shri Galta Peetham, Galva Ashrama, Jaipur, Rajasthan, 302013, India	Jaipur_01	Galta Temple	Galta park	12.8 km

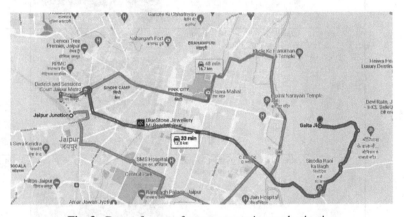

Fig. 3. Best safe route from source to image destination

Table 4. Selected Tourist Place by proposed work

City_name	Tourism-Place-id	Nearest_Tourist Place(Tourism-Place-id)	Nearest_Tourist Place(Tourism-Place-name)	Image	Distance
Jaipur	Jaipur_01	Jaipur_15	Monkey Temple		1 Km
		Jaipur_16	Banana Express Tours Jaipur		2 Km
		Jaipur_17	The Rustic Paths		2.8 Km
		Jaipur_18	Carpet And Textile House		3 Km
		Jaipur_19	Ellora Arts		3 Km
		Jaipur_20	Aryavrit Rajasthan City Day Tour		4 Km

7 Conclusion

The findings of this paper suggests several practical implications to improve the accessibility of least popular and unpopulartourist sites with the help of fuzzy neural system. Marketing unpopular destinations is important for several reasons as it helps in reducing the overcrowding on popular destinations and spread tourism more evenly across different regions. Secondly, it can help to create new opportunities for local businesses and communities. Thirdly, it can help to preserve local culture and heritage by encouraging visitors to explore lesser-known areas (Jun and Mao, 2020). Furthermore, visiting to potential tourism spots can benefit local communities in many ways. When tourists visit an unpopular destination, they can help to support the local economy by spending money on local goods and services. This can help to create jobs and stimulate economic growth in the area. Additionally, tourism can help to preserve local cultures and traditions by providing an incentive for local people to maintain their way of life. Finally, tourism can help to raise awareness about important issues facing local communities, such as environmental degradation or social inequality.

These destinations can map their presence in rajasthan tourist maps by promoting them on various social media and online platforms. It is possible that doing so will assist raise awareness about these areas and attract more tourists. In addition, local governments and tourism organisations can collaborate to improve the infrastructure in these places by undertaking projects such as the construction of new roads and the enhancement of public transport. Last but not least, local communities have the opportunity to collaborate in the creation of fresh tourism attractions and activities that highlight the distinctive history and culture of their region (Rexford et al., 2022). There are many different approaches that can be taken to promote tourism in Rajasthan, particularly in areas of the state that are not particularly well known. For instance, the communities of the surrounding area could band together to create new cultural festivals or events that highlight the distinctive customs of their particular region. In addition, the governments of these locations should consider making investments in new infrastructure projects that would make it simpler for tourists to visit these areas. In conclusion, tourist organisations may endeavour to promote these locations via social media and other internet channels in order to increase visitor traffic.

There are many potential research directions for tourism in unpopular destinations. For an instance, researchers could investigate the factors that influence tourists' decisions to visit unpopular destinations, such as the availability of information about these destinations or the perceived safety of these areas (Priatmoko et al., 2021). Additionally, researchers could explore the impact of tourism on local communities in unpopular destinations and identify strategies for maximizing the benefits of tourism while minimizing its negative impacts. Finally, researchers could examine the role of technology in promoting tourism in unpopular destinations, such as through the use of social media or other online platforms.

References

Aranburu, I., Plaza, B., Esteban, M.: Sustainable cultural tourism in urban destinations: does space matter? Sustainability **8**, 699 (2016)

Fatimah, T.: The impacts of rural tourism initiatives on cultural landscape sustainability in borobudur area. Procedia Environ. Sci. **28**, 567–577 (2015)

Ferreira, F., Castro, C., Gomes, A.: Positive and Negative Social-Cultural, Economic and Environmental Impacts of Tourism on Residents (2021). https://doi.org/10.1007/978-981-33-4256-9_26

Hasan, S., Bhowmik, D., Munne, M.S.: Factors Influencing Tourist Experience: A Case Study of Adinath Temple, Maheshkhali. Int. J. Sci. Bus. **8**(1), 1-11 (2022)

Jun, W., Wu, M.-Y.: How special is special interest tourism – and how special are special interest tourists? A perspective article in a Chinese context. Current Issues in Tourism **23**(16), 1968–1972 (2020). https://doi.org/10.1080/13683500.2020.1750575

Mathis, E.F., Kim, H.L., Uysal, M., Sirgy, J.M., Prebensen, N.K.: The effect of co-creation experience on outcome variable. Ann. Tour. Res. **57**, 62–75 (2016)

Margaryan, L.A.: Review of: heritage, conservation and communities. engagement, participation and capacity building. Edited by Gill Chitty. Tour. Geogr **20**, 573–575 (2018)

Figueroa, E.B., Rotarou, E.S.: Sustainable Development or Eco-Collapse: Lessons for Tourism and Development from Easter IslandSustainability **8**, 93 (2016)

Guiver, J., McGrath, P.: Slow tourism: exploring the discourses. Dos. Algarves A Multidiscip. E-J. **27**, 11–34 (2016)

Gato, M.A., Costa, P., Cruz, A.R., Perestrelo, M.: Creative tourism as boosting tool for placemaking strategies in peripheral areas: insights from portugal. J. Hosp. Tour. Res. **46**(8), 1500–1518 (2020)

Gupta, P.: Development of tourism industry in Rajasthan. Asian J. Multidimen. Res. (AJMR) **8**(3), 114–118 (2019)

Nahargarh Biological Park - Rajasthan Tourism. https://www.tourism.rajasthan.gov.in/nahargarh-biological-park.html

Parveen, W.: Tourism Marketing in Rajasthan: A case Study of Rajasthan Tourism Development Corporation, Doctoral dissertation. University of Kota (2018)

Piber, M., Demartini, P., Biondi, L.: The management of participatory cultural initiatives: learning from the discourse on intellectual capital. J. Manag. Gov. **23**, 435–458 (2019)

Priatmoko, S., Kabil, M., Vasa, L., Pallás, E.I., Dávid, L.D.: Reviving an unpopular tourism destination through the placemaking approach: case study of ngawen temple. Indonesia. Sustainability **13**, 6704 (2021). https://doi.org/10.3390/su13126704

Priatmoko, S., Purwoko, Y.: Does the Context of MSPDM Analysis Relevant in Rural Tourism? Case Study of Pentingsari,Nglanggeran, and Penglipuran. In: Proceedings of the International Conference on Creative Economics, Tourism and Information Management (ICCETIM) 2019, Yogyakarta, Indonesia, 17–18 July, pp. 15–21 (2019)

Paul, J., Kaur, J., Arora, S., Singh, S.V.: Deciphering 'Urge to Buy': A Meta-Analysis of Antecedents. Int. J. Mark. Res. **64**(6), 773–798 (2022). https://doi.org/10.1177/147078532 21106317

Rathore, A.S., Jodhana, L.S.: An empirical analysis of the service operations of rajasthan tourism development corporation hotels. South Asian Journal for Tourism & Heritage **5**, 73–90 (2012)

Rathore, A.K., Joshi, U.C., Ilavarasan, P.V.: Social media usage for tourism: A case of Rajasthan tourism. Procedia computer science **122**, 751–758 (2017)

Rexford, J., Wang, J., Xiao, Z., Zhang, Y.: BGP routing stability of popular destinations. In: Proceedings of the 2nd ACM SIGCOMM Workshop on Internet measurement, pp. 197–202 (2002, November)

Sharma, L.: Emerging trends in marketing innovation: rajasthan tourism. Rajasthan Economic Journal **68** (2018)

Singh, R.B., Kumar, A.: Cultural Tourism-Based Regional Development in Rajasthan, India. In: Practising Cultural Geographies: Essays in Honour of Rana PB Singh, pp. 453–466. Springer Nature Singapore, Singapore (2022)

Sirirak, W., Pitakaso, R.: Marketplace location decision making and tourism route planning. Administrative Sciences **8**(4), 72 (2018)

Zhang, R., Smith, L.: Bonding and dissonance: rethinking the interrelations among stakeholders in heritage tourism. Tour. Manag. **74**, 212–223 (2019)

Author Index

Printed in the United States
by Baker & Taylor Publisher Services